The Islamic Tradition

The Islamic Tradition

An Introduction

Victor Danner

AMITY HOUSE
AMITY, NEW YORK

Published by Amity House, Inc.
16 High Street
Warwick, N.Y. 10990

ISBN: 0-916349-16-0

Library of Congress Catalog Card Number 87-72985

CONTENTS

Preface *ix*
I. The Cycles of Revelation *1*
II. Muḥammad the Messenger *30*
III. The Nature of the Qur'ān *59*
IV. The Spiritual Path of Islam *84*
V. The Sacred Law of Islam *110*
VI. The Islamic Intellectual Tradition *140*
VII. The Arts of Islam *170*
VIII. The Contemporary Muslim World *201*
Notes *226*

Appendix I. Glossary of Islamic Terms *232*
Appendix II. The Ninety-Nine Names *244*
Appendix III. The Names of the Prophet Muḥammad *248*
Appendix IV. The Prophets and Messengers in the Qur'ān *250*
List of References *252*

SYSTEM OF TRANSLITERATION

hamzah	=	’	ḍād	=	ḍ
bā’	=	b	ṭā’	=	ṭ
tā’	=	t	ẓā’	=	ẓ
thā’	=	th	‘ayn	=	‘
jīm	=	j	ghayn	=	gh
ḥā’	=	ḥ	fā’	=	f
khā’	=	kh	qāf	=	q
dāl	=	d	kāf	=	k
dhāl	=	dh	lām	=	l
rā’	=	r	mīm	=	m
zāy	=	z	nūn	=	n
sīn	=	s	hā’	=	h
shīn	=	sh	wāw	=	w
ṣād	=	ṣ	yā’	=	y

Short vowels = a, i, u   Long vowels = ā, ī, ū

Dipthongs = aw, ay

Relative adjective (*nisbah*) = *ī* (masculine), *-iyyah* (feminine)

Tā’ marbūtah = *ah,* but *-at* in construct state

The definite article is written *al-* before words beginning with a lunar letter; but before words beginning with a solar letter the *lām* of the article is changed into that letter to conform more to the rules of pronunciation.

Translations from the Qur'ān into English are based on the Arabic text published in Cairo in 1923.

The word "Sūrah" refers to one of the 114 chapters of the Qur'ān; but rather than indicate the actual name of a particular Sūrah, such as *Sụrat al-Fātiḥah* ("The Chapter of the Opening", the first Sūrah of the Qur'ān), the system employed herein gives instead the number of the Sūrah first and then that of the verse. For example, Sūrah 4:25 means "the fourth Sūrah, verse twenty-five".

''He is the First and the Last,
the Exterior and the Interior.''

(Sūrah 57:3)

PREFACE

Numerous works on Islam have appeared in the West in the past century or so, explaining its ideas and practices, its history, its arts, and a host of other aspects. Most of these books were written by outsiders, a few from the inside. This fact has to be taken into account when questioning both insiders' conclusions and some outsiders' conclusions that might not square with the Islamic tradition. Books written by non-Muslims are not necessarily defective merely because of their perspective, since it is always possible for the author to have a perfectly traditional attitude. Likewise, books written by Muslims are not always to be taken as authentic simply because their authors are of the faith, for many of them are modernists who are merely following in the footsteps of those Western outsiders whom they admire and wish to emulate. As a result, they may contribute little beyond functioning as indices of how the tradition has fared in their own hands. Nor are the conservative Muslims better placed to tell us what their religion is all about, given that they frequently write out of polemical motives. Moreover, they are not always traditional in their conclusions. This is due to the disappearance in recent times of the protective armature of the old Islamic civilization. Conservative Muslims have found themselves in a kind of strange culture that could not but reflect itself in their thoughts and writings.

The great mass of Muslims, however, remain within their traditional culture. But this culture is fast vanishing from the scene as time goes by and as the modern Western world invades the domains of Islam. Within such a state of affairs, it is all the more necessary to see things (such as the arts, the theology, the culture) from the overall perspective of Islamic teachings as found in the tradition. It is precisely from the perspective of the traditional position that we can discern the modernist and the conservative, and distinguish them from traditional thinkers. Islam, like other traditions of mankind, has a world view embodied in a civilization that is rapidly changing. The traditional social supports of the faith — its dress, architecture, literature, political systems, style of life, and the like — have largely vanished. But the religion as such — its simple beliefs, its ritual observances, and its general moral commandments — has survived.

Now, with the demise of the social framework of the faith, a number of modernist interpretations have arisen that have little regard for the traditional teachings and practices and that have provoked reactions from the conservatives. These conservatives tend to be fundamentalists with little use for the deeper aspects of the Islamic intellectual and spiritual tradition. In the midst of this struggle between the conservatives and modernists, the traditional Muslim intellectual has to fend for himself as best he can, for he can no longer count on a homogeneous traditional environment, containing a variety of opinions, sometimes even conflicting teachings, which at least pointed in the same celestial direction. Instead, he must now content himself with standing fast while his fellow Muslims, modernists or conservative fundamentalists, go about changing the tradition from within or reducing it to its most literal interpretations. For the Westerner anxious to fathom the Islamic faith, the extremes of modernism and conservatism which are embroiled in perpetual conflict in the present-day Muslim world seem to indicate the dissolution of the old traditional culture. The modernists and conservatives do not, nor can they, explain to him the miraculous power behind the great civilization of the past. The modernist is opposed to the Islamic tradition; the conservative has a very limited, superficial view of the tradition, rejecting anything that goes beyond his understanding.

Only the tradition can explain its own fruits in the medieval civilization of the Muslim world: the ensemble of doctrines, means of sanctification, morality, and art that went into the makeup of that bygone world. We should remember that the tradition contained both supernatural and human elements, on the one hand, and had numerous levels of application and a multitude of facets, on the other. It had intellectual, spiritual, artistic, political, economic, social and other sides to it. Many of these aspects which were part of the dazzling Islamic culture of the past have now disappeared or been reduced to a shadow of their former selves.

The key to understanding Islam as both a religion and a civilization lies in its traditional doctrines, whether they be gnostic, theological, philosophical, spiritual, cosmological, psychological, or eschatological. Those doctrines were sufficiently varied so that they could embrace the aspirations of the common people and the elite alike, without anyone feeling that his needs had not been provided for or that there was something lacking in the world around him, a world saturated with the beauty of Islam in its architecture, music, literature, clothing, and even the pomp and pageantry of the state.

The traditional doctrines are still intact right down to the present among those who have remained faithful to their heritage, even if the external trappings of the Islamic civilization have for the most part gone by the wayside. These doctrines have stood the test of time and, again and again, after every decline in the history of Islam, they have been reinstated — now more developed, now more complex, now more detailed — to serve as the intellectual spark which awakens the community or the individual into a reaffirmation of the spiritual life.

The spiritual reawakening of any society has always been the function of traditional doctrines. That spiritual function will always be the task of these doctrines, whatever might be the nature of the modern world and its depredations all over the globe. At the same time, because of modern means of communication, the spiritual teachings of all the world religions are now accessible to people of discernment and good faith, in effect to most human beings. We can see that the nature of God, the universe, man, and religion, as understood by Islam, are not too far removed from what other faiths have to say.

The Islamic faith has been explained herein in rather broad terms, and these, hopefully, have preserved its essential contents without too much distortion or loss of objectivity. In recent decades, others have explained the religions of mankind, including Islam, from the same traditional standpoint. The works of René Guénon, A. K. Coomaraswamy, Frithjof Schuon, Seyyed Hossein Nasr, Titus Burckhardt, and Martin Lings, to cite but a few, have all been influenced by the traditional teachings and have been responsible, in turn, for the widespread diffusion of such timeless — and even timely — wisdom in our own days. Their writings prove that there is an ever-living vitality in traditional doctrines and that there will always be individuals interested in their truths, even though the spiritual darkness and turmoil of the times oppose such ageless wisdom, which will have the final say.

I
The Cycles of Revelation

The Historical Background

The Quir'ān is the sacred text of Islam revealed in the Arabic language to the Prophet Muhammad some fifteen centuries ago. It brought the Arab pagans a monotheistic message called Islam, which means "submission to the Divine Will." That message preached that there is but one God and that Muhammad is the Messenger of God.[1]

Belief in the one God called *Allāh*, in His revelations, His angels, His Messengers, in the Day of Judgment, and in the predestination of good and evil were important elements of the new faith. Its essential rituals were the five "pillars of religion", namely, (1) the Testimony of Faith ("There is no divinity but *Allāh*, Muḥammad is the Messenger of *Allāh*"), (2) the five daily prayers, (3) the fast during the month of Ramaḍān, (4) the legal alms, and (5) the pilgrimage to Mecca. In addition to required beliefs and rituals, the faithful were called upon to practice virtues such as charity, humility, patience, contentment, and sincerity, as a means to reforming their moral character. The beliefs, the rites, and the moral reformation were deemed to purify the soul of man and to lead to salvation at the hour of death through entrance into Paradise. The Hells were reserved for those who lived in disbelief, impiety, and immorality.

Traditional Muslim accounts picture the Arab pagans as having been immersed in polytheism and immoral behavior. That is perhaps true for the Arabs in the Arabian Peninsula itself, and had been the case for generations before the coming of Islam. But elsewhere in the Arab lands, especially in Iraq, we find Christian Arab tribes with a rather extensive system of monastic institutions that somewhat mitigate the picture of total darkness which Muslim authorities wish to paint of the age preceding the dawn of the new faith. Perhaps it is out of a desire to contrast more sharply the light of the Qur'ānic revelation with the polytheism of the Arabs that these authorities refer to pre-Islamic days as the "time of ignorance" (the *jāhiliyyah*).

The pre-Islamic Arabs were largely nomadic in culture, but in the Yemen there were settled areas which gave rise to the Sabaean, Minaean, and Himyarite cultures of pre-Christian and early Christian times. We know very little about these urban communities, but their visual arts reveal a strong debt to the prevailing paganism of the Mediterranean lands. In the seventh century A.D., long before the Qur'ān was revealed, the Yemenis had succumbed to the attractive force of the *jāhiliyyah*, as did their fellow Arabs, the Bedouins to the north.[2]

Two great civilizations, the Byzantine and the Persian, maintained fortresses on the desert frontiers to watch over the movements of the Bedouins in Syria and Iraq. They ignored what was happening in the vast stretches of land inside the Arabian Peninsula. The Byzantine civilization was centered in Constantinople, which was the heart of the Greek Orthodox tradition. The Byzantine Greek Emperors considered themselves and their state to be the heirs of the Roman Empire, especially after the demise of the Western Empire in the year 476. On the eve of the Islamic revelation, the Byzantines, under Heraclius I (610-641), were engaged in battling the Persians, resulting in the reconquest of the lands taken by the Persians and in the return of the Holy Cross to its rightful place in Jerusalem. But their provinces in the Near East seethed with controversial Christian teachings whose partisans objected to the heavy yoke of the Greeks. This produced divisiveness in the Eastern Christian world and laid it open for the eventual conquests of the Muslims.

Persia, with its capital at Ctesiphon, was the home of the ancient Zoroastrian tradition which had fallen into decadence. Like the Byzantine civilization, the Zoroastrian culture was sedentary in nature and had also produced marvelous works of art and architecture. The tradition was socially stratified and revolved around a divine monarch; but this millennial Zoroastrian culture was spiritually depleted and on the point of crumbling. Thus, sectarian squabbles in the Christian realms of the East and inner weakness within the Persian Empire helped to pave the way for the Muslim conquests. Considerable portions of the Byzantine Empire and the entire Persian Empire succumbed to the explosive expansion of the Islamic message outside of the Arab homeland.

Muḥammad's mission, as both a Prophet who foretold future events and a Messenger who founded a new religion, was carried out deep inside Arabia, far away from the watchful frontier posts of the Greeks and the Persians. He was a monotheist from his youth — a pure Arab of aristocratic lineage, and an illiterate, like many of his fellow Arabs. His role as the founder of Islam was largely played out in the two towns of Mecca and Medina to the west of the Arabian Peninsula. These were small towns lost in the infinity of the desert surrounding them. To the Persian and Byzantine States, Mecca and Medina were of no account and could be safely ignored, until it was too late. But in the mind of the Prophet, his mission among the pagan Arabs went far beyond the Arabs and reached out to embrace whole regions of the non-Arab world. From his fortieth year, when his mission began, he already knew that the Islamic message would be the last major revelation given to mankind before the Day of Judgment and that he would be the last Prophet to appear in this world.

When the Muslims speak of the Qur'ān as a sacred text, they mean that it is the revealed Word of God to the Islamic community. As we shall see later in greater detail, the Qur'ān was revealed in piecemeal fashion to the Prophet over a long period of time. Its Arabic is said to be sacred in the sense that it is the language used by the Divinity to reveal the saving message of Islam to man. At the same time, Qur'ānic Arabic is the liturgical language of the Islamic tradition.

The contents of the Qur'ān did not catch the Arab pagans by surprise: they knew about the Prophets and Messengers mentioned in it and were aware of the structure of the cosmos which the Book described. What they lacked was the notion of the transcendence of *Allāh* and the message of salvation brought by Islam. While their paganism was unredeeming, they were conscious of their cultural roots in the distant past and of their connections with ancient Prophets and Messengers within Arabia and of the extinct Arab communities of pre-Christian days. Theirs was a nomadic culture which tended to be extremely conservative and strongly entrenched in oral literature: the "word" was everything for them. The Qur'ān was the Word of God: it furnished the Arabs with a complete picture of the Divinity, *Allāh*, an entire cosmology of Semitic nature, including the Heavens and the Hells, and a sacred history of mankind from Adam and Eve in the garden of Eden to the awesome events of the Day of Judgment. In addition, the Prophet left behind his all-important Sunnah (the Prophet's "Norm" in actions and words) which spelled out the commandments and prohibitions which the Muslims must observe to gain salvation at death. The Qur'ān and the Sunnah are the foundations of Islam and have remained unchanged for the past fifteen centuries. At the same time, they are considered to be definitive manifestations of the divine mercifulness which had already expressed itself in previous revelations given to other communities. Since the revelations of *Allāh* to the different peoples of the world contain essentially the same message on the Absolute, we must first see how that message is viewed in Islam then how it interprets the cyclical march of events for mankind as a whole in the light of that doctrine.

Tawḥīd

Islam preaches that monotheism is the basic message of all religions and that, consequently, the Qur'ān merely confirms what was previously taught in other, non-Islamic revelations. Referring to the Torah, the Qur'ān says: "And before it was the Book of Moses, a guide and a mercifulness; and this one is a confirmatory Scripture in their Arabic tongue, that it may warn the unjust and give Good Tidings to the virtuous" (Sūrah 46:12). Likewise, "And when there cometh unto them a Messenger from God, confirming what they have, a party of those who have received Scripture fling the Scripture of God behind their backs, as if they knew not!" (Sūrah 2:101).

Since revelations emanate from the same transcendent Divine Source, it is understandable that they should all affirm, each in its own way, the absolute Oneness of the Divinity, called *Allāh* in Islam. There is, accordingly, no fundamental change in the character of the message embedded within each of the pre-Islamic faiths: "There is no change to the Words of God" (Sūrah 10:64). On the contrary, the same essential message is reiterated whenever revelation establishing a new religion takes place. That being so, revelation is, among other things, a reminder sent to those who have forgotten the true nature of the One: "We have not revealed to thee this Qur'ān," Muḥammad is told, "that thou shouldst be distressed, but only as a Reminder to those who fear, and as a revelation from Him who created the earth and the lofty heavens, the Compassionate, who is established on the Throne" (Sūrah 20:2-5).

The essential teaching of Islam — and, from the Islamic point of view, the essential teaching of all religions — is called *Tawḥīd* ("Divine Unity"). This is the recognition that the Divinity, *Allāh*, is the One who has no second, no associate, no parents, no offspring, no peers. The Divine Unity is both transcendent and immanent in relation to the world, though its immanence does not imply that it undergoes any of the transformations and changes characteristic of the world. The One is above the world and its imperfections; it is within the world but not of it.

The character of the Divinity in the Qur'ān is at once personal and impersonal. Consider the Ninety-Nine Names of *Allāh*, or "the Most-Beautiful Names" of God, as the Qur'ān would put it. "The One," for example, has an impersonal nature in contrast to such names as "the Guide", "the Seeing", and "the Hearing", which have more to do with the personal God, the Lord of the Worlds who creates, sustains, and judges the universe. *Allāh* has an impersonal, infinite Essence when considered as absolute reality, and an ontological nature when considered as Lord of all beings and things, a Lordship that confers upon Him a personal character in relation to His creatures. The former is a nonanthropomorphic principle, the latter is anthropomorphic. The anthropomorphic Divinity is the one familiar to the mass of believers; the nonanthropomorphic Essence of the Divinity is familiar to the contemplative mystics of Islam.

In Islam, *Tawḥīd* is expressed in a famous formula called the *shahādah* ("The Testimony of Faith"), which runs as follows: *Lā ilāha illa 'illāh, Muhammadun rasūlu 'llāh* ("There is no divinity except God, Muḥammad is the Messenger of God"). The *shahādah* has scriptural foundations and is found with great frequency in the recorded statements (*ḥadīths*) of the Messenger, which are an indispensable part of the Islamic faith. The *shahādah* is certainly the most sacred formula of Islam and the very essence of its metaphysical and spiritual foundations. It comprises two parts, a negation and an affirmation: "There is no divinity" is the negation; "except God" is the affirmation. The formula can also be used with numerous other negations and affirmations: "There is no loving one except the Loving One," "There is no guide except the Guide," and "There is no light except the Light," and so on through the Ninety-Nine Names and Qualities or Attributes of the Divinity. When one says, for example, that "There is no guide except the Guide," one is denying that anyone but God could guide, for God alone is the Guide. Or one is affirming that whatever guidance a creature has is really that of the Divine Guide.

In view of the metaphysical and other subtleties contained in the sacred *shahādah*, it is not surprising to find that the great commentators of Islam have given it sufficient attention to fill volumes. It has mystical, theological, meditational, and invocational applications. It has been a mysterious, inexhaustible source of inspiration for those who have reflected on it for long periods of time. It is used as an invocatory and contemplative formula and resembles brief formulas found in other faiths, such as the Hindu *Tat Tvam Asi* ("That art thou", establishing the mystical identity of the believer and the Divinity), or the *Namo Amitabha Buddha* ("Homage to the Buddha of Infinite Light") of Amidist Buddhism. It contains both a profound doctrine and a prayer, and as such is considered to be a source of grace.

The Testimony of Faith actually contains two testimonies: the first one is *Lā ilāha illa 'llāh* and the second one is *Muḥammadun rasūlu 'llāh*. However, the most concise formulation of *Tawḥīd* is to be found in the first testimony, which is the universal content of Islam because it refers to the Divine Unity. The second testimony, by contrast, is less universal than the first because it refers specifically to the Messenger sent to the Islamic community, Muḥammad. Thus, while all religions are ultimately reducible to the doctrine of *Tawḥīd*, their founders are different: within the Abrahamic lineage, we find Abraham, Moses, the Christ, and Muhammad. The perennial message of these founders is of course *Tawīd* as expressed in the first testimony of faith; but the second testimony of faith would change in keeping with their respective names, so that we would have "Abraham is the Messenger of God," "Moses is the Messenger of God," "Jesus is the Messenger of God," and "Muḥammad is the Messenger of God," and so on for other founders outside the world of Abraham.

So Islam, in this respect, recognizes the validity of pre-Islamic revelations and recognizes that other Prophets and Messengers, apart from Muḥammad, also had celestial support for their missions on earth. Hence, Muslins must also show these Prophets reverential respect in different ways. This Islamic attitude contrasts with the more exclusive notions of both Judaism and Christianity, and serves as an exemplary characteristic for the other two faiths to follow.

The gravity of *Tawḥīd* can easily be perceived in the Islamic thesis that consciousness of the Oneness of God is an awareness leading, at the hour of death, to salvation. "Whoever dies," a *ḥadīth* of the Messenger states, "knowing that there is no divinity except God, enters Paradise." The emphasis on knowledge is typically Islamic, for the religion is centered on knowledge, although it has its devotional, even emotional and sentimental features. *Tawḥīd*, in other words, is not simply a theory that stands in need of supplementary elements to be truly effective. On the contrary, it suffices unto itself as a saving Truth.

It is in the idea of *Tawḥīd* that Islam differs profoundly from the Jewish and Christian faiths. In the Jewish faith salvation is contingent upon a certain ethnocentrism revolving around the Chosen People, and this in turn confines the monotheistic concept to them; in Christianity, salvation is bound up with a certain Christocentrism that leads to the worship of the God-Man, who in his turn detracts, by his sublime nature, from the absoluteness of the One.[3]

The confining of *Tawḥīd* to the Chosen People led inevitably to the result that Judaism would never become a world religion, as would Islam, Buddhism, and Christianity, all of which embrace different races and ethnic groups in vast numbers. This is not to say that Judaism did not have its expansive moments in history. Still, there is no gainsaying the limiting influences of the notion of the Chosen People on its expansion. A certain ethnocentric equation of Arab nationalism and Islam took place in the first century of Islam's existence, but this was ultimately negated by the internal opposition of non-Arab Muslims, who soon became the majority. Too, the evidence of the Qur'ān and the *ḥadīths* gave the central role in Islam to the most God-fearing believers, who could be from any ethnic group or race.

In Christianity, the concept of the Trinity implies that the "Word made flesh" (the Christ) will assume a central place, or become the focal point of attention, to the detriment of the transcendent Absolute. Moreover, the

Trinity in itself, however subtle the interpretation, is not, after all, the undifferentiated One. The doctrine of the Incarnation makes Christian monotheistic teachings less influential in the redemption of a soul than they are in Islam for the redemption is effected by the Christ, by the Incarnation of God, not by the Absolute in itself.

It was left, therefore, to Islam to manifest the essentially saving notion that God is One by removing all affiliation with any Chosen People, on the one hand, and by restoring to the One its absoluteness through the abolition of all Incarnationism, on the other. Hence, the unique spiritual contribution of the Islamic revelation lies in its insistence on the dazzling absoluteness of the Divine Unity as being in itself a redemptive notion: *Taḥīd* in itself saves at the hour of death.

Another way to measure the gravity of *Tawḥīd* as a doctrine — and even as a way of life — is to reflect on its opposite, which is *shirk* (''associationism''). While *Tawḥīd* at times is translated as ''monotheism'' and *shirk* as ''polytheism'', these are at best rough approximations of the deeper meanings contained in both words, so crucial for an understanding of Islam and, indeed, of the essence of religion in general. For example, a person who lends to any being or thing in this world an absoluteness belonging only to the Creator is guilty of a hidden *shirk*. ''Hast thou seen him,'' asks the Qur'ān, ''who taketh his own passion for his god?'' (Sūrah 25:43).

Similarly, in the lives of the Messenger and his companions, not to mention the Muslim sages, it is clear that *Tawḥīd* affects the entire being of man, and not just his thinking faculty. It is more than theory, for it involves a concrete way of life that brings into play all that man is. In other words, *Tawḥīd* can be the ordinary oral belief found among the usual believers or it can go beyond this to the pure spirituality of the contemplatives. The latter are exemplified by the Sūfī sages and their followers, who have spiritually extinguished themselves in the Divine Oneness. By rigorous mental discipline, they eliminated within themselves even the subtle *shirk* that is like an interior obstacle, or set of obstacles, blocking their path toward perfect spiritual *Tawḥīd*.

Ṣūfism, or the spiritual Path of Islam, has a great deal to say about the contemplative aspects of *Tawḥīd* which go far beyond the purely verbal expressions of Islamic legal requirements. The spiritual extinction of the ego is a logical consequence of *Tawḥīd* and an aspiration of the Ṣūfīs. Maintaining the ego alongside the Divine Ego (the Divine ''I'') results in spiritual *shirk*, or the conviction that there are two ''I'''s, God's and man's, and that they are irreducible. This is illogical; therefore the illusory ego, the human ''I'', has to go. In some respects, Ṣūfism is the art or science of eliminating the self or the ''I'' in order that the Divine Ego or Self may shine through the purified psychophysical nature of man. In all Islam, Ṣūfism alone perceives the fullness of *Tawḥīd* and of its implications for man.

With this in mind, we can grasp why *shirk* is the cardinal sin in Islam — all others are forgiven. ''Verily,'' the Qur'ān says, ''God forgiveth not that an associate be ascribed to Him. But he forgiveth less than that to whomsoever He will. Whoever ascribes associates to God has committed a tremendous sin'' (Sūrah 4:48). Since the consciousness of the Divine Unity suffices unto itself to obtain salvation in the Hereafter, its opposite, forgetfulness of that Oneness, is not forgiven and is cause for perdition. How could it be otherwise, seeing that in Islam the primary function of man's intelligence is its recognition of the Absolute, its awareness of God, not only in a conceptual manner, but also in a consciousness that discerns things as they really are?

To reject the evidence of the external, revealed Book as well as the evidence of man's inner mind — his heart-mind, as it were — is to veil oneself with ignorance and to plunge into associationism (*shirk*). Eventually, this affects man's existence on earth and has a direct bearing on his posthumous states as well. It is easy to conclude that man's role as representative of God on earth depends on the degree to which his intelligence is aware of *Tawḥīd*. When ignorance veils the spiritual intelligence of man, he is no longer conscious of the One. At that point, *shirk* arises and man's purpose in this world is obscured.

Shirk can be conscious or willful, but it can also be the result of ignorance, and hence falls under this Qur'ānic statement: ''God forgives those who do evil in ignorance and then repent soon afterwards. These are they whom God forgives. God is the Knowing, the Wise! But forgiveness is not for those who commit evil deeds until, when death comes upon one of them, he saith: Verily, I will now repent! Nor is it for those who die while they are disbelievers'' (Sūrah 4:17-18).

In these verses the Qur'ān is not rejecting a sincere repentance at death, but rather a hypocritical or insincere one. A ḥadīth quds (''holy statement'', in which God is said to speak through the Prophet) says: ''O son of Adam, if thou wert to commit sins so as to fill the earth — but not ascribe any associates to Me — I would accord thee the same measure of forgiveness.'' All is forgivable, in other words, except *shirk*.

The correct view of things is restored by revelation (which in Islam is seen as a Scripture) given to a people gone astray, providing their collective blindness is not altogether beyond the influence of divine mercifulness. If it is, then the upheavals and cataclysmic reactions brought on by man's forgetfulness (*ghaflah*) are wrathful celestial interventions that serve to remind man that he cannot with impunity forget his central nature as the representative of God on earth. In the end, both revelation and cataclysm can be considered as divine projections of mercifulness and wrathfulness, respectively, restoring man to his proper state of remembrance.

There is a relationship, of course, between *Tawḥīd* and the remembrance of God (*dhikr*), just as there is between *shirk* and the forgetfulness of God (*ghaflah*). Forgetfulness implies much more than just a lapse of memory. In reality, *dhikr* upholds *Tawḥīd*, while *ghaflah* leads to *shirk* and eventually to disbelief (*kufr*). The remembrance of God can vary from simple ritual prayer to invocatory meditation, but it makes man concentrate on God. To forget God leads to a state of dissipation, spiritually speaking, and cannot but tear man away from his innermost center. As a result, *Tawḥīd* and *dhikr* go together, for one cannot affirm the Divine Oneness of *Allāh* without remembering Him either sporadically or permanently. The ideal, in Islam as in other religions, is the perpetual remembrance of God throughout all of the believer's activities: and hence the Qur'ān speaks of "those who remember God standing, sitting, and reclining" (Sūrah 3:191).

Seen from that perspective, revelation is but a message to man to remember the true nature of *Allāh*, the Universe, and Man. Forgetfulness of the true nature of these realities leads to associationism and disbelief. This forgetfulness gives force to the momentum of man's fallen nature, and that fallen or corrupted character of man, in its turn, is what drives mankind, or the different communities or humanities (*umam*, pl. of *ummah*, "community") step by step to the cosmic cataclysms that in themselves are the prefigurations of the Day of Judgment, the terminal point of the Fall.[4]

The Cycles of Revelation

Islam sees itself as the very last revelation which established a religion on earth. Because of this view, Islam is the last religion to be manifested before the closing of the ages. The Islamic message (*risālah*, which is the same as revelation of *tawḥīd* — condensed, as we saw, in the sacred sentence *Lā ilāha illa 'illāh* — is definitive and represents the final great manifestation of divine mercifulness on a global scale. This message would affect the souls of hundreds of millions of human beings over the past fifteen centuries, holding up for them the posthumous state of salvation (*najāh*) as the fruit of *tawḥīd* and *dhikr*. The vast numbers who have been associated with the Islamic faith since its inception cannot be ignored as proof of the spiritual vitality of its message.

While Islam considers itself the last religion to be revealed to mankind before the coming of the Hour that closes the cycle of mankind on earth, it also sees in the Messenger and Prophet, Muḥammad, the Seal of the Prophets (*khātam an-nabiyyīn*). That phrase is to be found in Sūrah 33:40, and the word "Prophets" refers to all the persons with celestial missions, including the founders of different religions. Muḥammad as the Seal of the Prophets brings to an end, in his own person, the entire line of Prophets stretching back to Adam. Sacred history begins with the Prophethood of Adam and continues through the missions of innumerable Prophets and Messengers, Muḥammad sealing their line. Sacred history ends with the coming of the Day of Judgment. Between Muḥammad and the last Day, Heaven is silent, as it were, and no other major revelation descends into this world.

The principles underlying the Qur'ānic cyclical doctrines are to be found in this famous description of the Divinity: "He is the First and the Last, the Exterior and the Interior, and He is Knower of every thing" (Sūrah 57:3). Metaphysical, cosmological, and spiritual explanations of this verse have come from the pens of numerous Ṣūfīs and others. Two of the Names of God have to do with the beginning and end of all things, namely, the First (*al-awwal*) and the Last (*al-ākhir*), and therefore with the temporal cycles of the created universe. God is "the First" in that He existed before the Creation came into being and is really the Origin of all things; He is "the Last" in that He will continue to exist after the Creation has ceased to be, and thus He is the End of all things.

Between the Origin and End, the different worlds and their cycles of duration come and go. However vast a cosmos might be, it is subject to a beginning and an ending. This is what the Qur'ān calls the *ajal musammā* ("the definite period"), or the fixed duration, of all things. It is a cycle having a beginning and an ending that can be neither hastened nor postponed. The entire universe has its own immense cycle: "God has not created the Heavens and the Earth, nor that which is between them, except with the Truth and for a definite period" (Sūrah 30:8). Within this overall cycle, there are other, lesser ones, such as the period of the earth's existence; within that duration, there are the cycles of the different communities, or religious "humanities", each with its own fixed duration: "And every community has its term, and when their term comes, they cannot postpone it for an hour nor hasten it" (Sūrah 7:34). Finally, even individuals have their particular cycles: "And God will not grant respite to a soul when its term comes" (Sūrah 63:11).

Revelation itself, which is a redemptive message addressed to a particular community, is also subject to the laws of cyclical development affecting mankind. The sacred history of man, as interpreted by the Qur'ān, unfolds between a beginning and an end: the beginning is the Garden of Eden; the end is the day of Judgment. Had there been no Fall, then the Edenic state of Adam and Eve would never have ended, and the perfect *Tawḥīd* that reigned then would have continued. While the Qur'ān speaks of Adam and Eve as falling, the verb used to indicate expulsion from the garden applies to many people: Adam and Eve merely symbolize the primordial mankind which is addressed by the Divinity in these verses: "We Said: Go down, all of you, from it! Now, indeed, there shall come upon you from Me a Guidance: whosoever followeth My Guidance, no fear shall come upon them nor shall they grieve; but as for those who disbelieve and give the lie to Our Signs, they are the companions of the Fire: they shall abide therein!'' Sūrah 2:38-39).

It is the Fall (*al-hubūṭ*) which provokes divine responses, merciful or wrathful. The explulsion from the primordial earthly Paradise did not go unanswered: the Guidance and the Signs mentioned in the verses cited above refer to revelation. Adam had been subjected to the divine wrath, hence his expulsion from the Edenic state. But now he was to be the recipient of divine mercifulness in the form of revelation: ''Then Adam received from his Lord Words, so that He forgave him. Truly, He is Most Forgiving, Merciful'' (Sūrah 2:37).

Before the Fall, the Edenic humanity had lived long in the remembrance of God. Then, at some point toward the end of the Edenic cycle, mankind began to succumb progressively to *ghaflah* (forgetfulness), and that brought on the expulsion. After the expulsion, revelation descended (the Qur'ān also refers to revelation as a ''descent'', *tanzīl*), reminding fallen mankind of what it had forgotten. Once again, there was a state of remembrance (*dhikr*). However, this time, because of the gathering drive of man's fallen substance, the state of remembrance would increasingly be eroded by forgetfulness. This would necessitate yet another revelation, temporarily restoring *Tawḥīd* to its rightful preeminence alongside of *dhikr*.

Nevertheless, no revelation can permanently and universally undo the noxious influences of the Fall. Its momentum and gravitational pull downward, spiritually speaking, are only temporarily arrested by each new revelation brought by a Messenger to a particular community. Only those who are faithful to the message escape the downward pull of fallen human nature. And if they escape, it is precisely because they respond to the attractive force exerted by an invincible Heaven.

The Qur'ān puts man's earthly existence between two extremes: on the one hand is the Garden of Eden, which ended with a fallen humanity; on the other hand is the Day of Judgment, the terminal point for the cumulative effects of the Fall. Without the Fall, there would be no need for revealed messages. Religion, which flows from revelation and seeks to save man from the effects of the Fall, would be unnecessary. That being so, there would no need for a Day of Judgment either. Of course, the Qur'ān is not unique in positing these two extremes to man's terrestrial cycle: other Scriptures have the same notions, more or less. They must be borne in mind when seeking to grasp the necessity for the different messages that descend as time goes by.

The Adams and Eves of the primordial age were almost immortal, and they moved in a world luminous with the Divine Presence. The ''eye of the heart'' (*'ayn al-qalb*) in them was unveiled, illuminating their souls and conferring wisdom and saintliness upon them through its radiance. The Spirit within them, in other words, "saw" the Real in all things, and because its inner eye was uncovered, constantly provided inspiration, so that there was no need for external Scripture. Only when man's inner vision was clouded with *glaflah* was external revelation necessary, as a reminder, a guidance, a healer, restoring man to his former knowledge and equilibrium.

If mankind's history in the Qur'ān, from the Fall to the Day of Judgment, were simply one long downward movement, with no compensatory upward movements, the story would be one of increasing, unrelieved darkness. Instead, there are ups and downs, rebirths and declines, like the peaks and troughs of waves or the alternations of light and darkness.

The Messengers

Governing the peaks of mankind's cyclical existence are the Messengers and Prophets. Their presence at given moments in the flow of human history is decisive for entire populations. They represent projections of celestial mercifulness into the course of man's earthly history: their appearance is determined by the cyclical conditions of decline in a given sector of the world. Then, having accomplished their mission, they also play a role in the future cyclical conditions under which the community (*ummah*) to which they had been sent will operate. They represent the heights in the wave-like cycle of mankind's history on earth. Without them, that history would have been devoid of any spiritual infusions and no doubt would have been ended long ago, if we go by such Qur'ānic verses as: "Were God to punish men for what they deserve, He would not have left a living creature on the earth's surface" (Sūrah 35:45).

A Messenger (*rasūl*) is the founder of a new religion, great or small; the revelation enters this world through him, and its message of salvation is destined to affect the lives of vast or small numbers of human beings. The revelation is addressed to a given group of people who form what the Qur'ān calls a community (*ummah*), and it inaugurates the historical cycle of that group.

The traditional doctrine on Messengers declares that they are impeccable, or sinless, and that this results from their perfectly saintly human nature. Messengership is not a matter of private choice: no one can elect to become a *rasūl*. On the contrary, the Messenger is chosen from all eternity, and it is this celestial choice that guarantees the spiritual integrity of his mission: one of Muḥammad's names is that of "the Chosen" (*al-musṭ afā*). Like the other Messengers, Muḥammad is identified with the universal, impersonal Word (or Logos) intermediate between God and man. His own utterances on this matter point to the cosmic level of his transhistorical reality. In a *ḥadīth*, for example, the Prophet remarks: "I was a Prophet while Adam was still between water and clay." In other words, he was that universal Logos at the center of the Creation. The Logos in Islam is also known by many other expressions, such as "Muḥammadan Light", "the Muḥammadan Reality", "the Universal Intellect", "Muḥammadan Spirit", and so on. As Logos, Muḥammad preexisted the emergence of the earthly line of Prophets beginning with Adam and culminating with himself, fifteen centuries ago. The Logos is construed as both the luminous center of the universe as well as its spherical totality. But here we must remember that the created worlds have different degrees of reality, so that there are spiritual worlds, psychical worlds, and then the material world. The Logos at the center of the universe is identified with the created Holy Spirit (*rūḥ al-quds*), the spiritual sun which radiates out in the celestial paradises. Hence it must not be given an earthly meaning, or a physical one, for it reigns beyond the lower worlds. Nevertheless, the Messenger is a manifestation of the Logos in an exemplary fashion. He is a perfect sage, a perfect saint, by virtue of his having been chosen as a vessel of election.

Messengers are, in themselves, extraordinarily rare manifestations of divine mercifulness (*raḥmah*). Muḥammad is called "a mercifulness" to the creation ("We have not sent thee but as a mercifulness to the universe," Sūrah 21:107). This appellation refers both to his historical role as the founder of the Islamic faith as well as to his transhistorical nature as the Logos at the spiritual center of the universe. The mercifulness of revelation is, of course, in direct contrast to the wrathfulness or rigor of cataclysmic chastisements. The first emanates from the Divine Beauty (*al-jamāl*), the second from the Divine Majesty (*al-jalāl*) — the two complementary aspects of *Allāh* as reflected in His Names, which are the principles operating in the Creation.

While the Logos-Muḥammad is seen as the center of the Creation, the historical Muḥammad is considered to be but a manifestation of that impersonal spiritual reality. Indeed, all other Messengers, Prophets, and saints are like radii issuing from the one, unique, solar Logos-Muhammad at the center of the world. In Ṣūfism where the spiritual reality of Muḥammad plays a very important role in the contemplative life, the Logos-Muḥammad is called "Universal Man" (*al-insān al-kāmil*). Thus, in the sixtieth chapter of his famous work, *al-Insān al-Kāmil*, the fifteenth-century Ṣūfī 'Abd al-Karīm al-Jīlī calls Muḥammad the unique Universal Man of all the ages. All other Messengers and Prophets, and all the sages and saints, are emanations from this one universal reality. To understand this, we must bear in mind that the concept of Universal Man refers to an impersonal spiritual reality connecting Heaven and Earth.

A ḥadīth of the Prophet says: "The first thing God created was the

Intellect'' or, in a variant, ''the Spirit.'' Both Spirit and Intellect in the *ḥadīth* are the Logos-Muḥammad who presides over the unfolding of the Creation. The Logos is intermediate between the particular Spirit in man and the uncreated Spirit of God. The inner Spirit in man is essentially the same as the Universal Spirit (the Logos-Muḥammad), which in turn is identified with the Divine Spirit. From this, it is easy to see why the Logos-Muḥammad plays such an important role in the Ṣūfī contemplative voyage toward union with God: the seeker must first be reabsorbed into his ''Muḥammad Reality'' (synonymous with *al-insān al-kāmil*) before extinguishing himself spiritually in God. The process is similar to the reabsorption of a ray of light into the universal Muḥammadan Light (*nūrmuḥammadī*) first of all and then back into the uncreated Light of *Allāh*. In essence, the individual's own Spirit (or Intellect), the Universal Spirit, and the Divine Spirit are one and the same reality, distinguished only by the different levels of being. As a result, *al-insān al-kāmil* lies within all believers, but is actualized in only a small minority of sages.

Given the uniqueness of Messengers as the founders of religions, they are few in number when compared with the Prophets, whose roles are less universal, as we shall presently see. In the Abrahamic world, we find but four Messengers, Abraham, Moses, Jesus, and Muḥammad, whose missions have governed the lives of hundreds of millions of human beings. While Abrahamism is no longer in existence, the Qur'ān nevertheless states that he was a Messenger who brought a Scripture; the last remnants of his tradition were the *ḥunafā'* (pl. of *ḥanīf*, ''true believer'') of pre-Islamic times, some of whom were known by the Prophet Muḥammad, but they were no longer very strong in their monotheism.

The Messengers are in a class by themselves. While the Qur'ān concerns itself mostly with the Messengers and Prophets within the Abrahamic world of the Near East, it nevertheless leaves room in certain verses for the non-Semitic revelations. ''Of some Messengers,'' it says, addressing the Prophet, ''We have narrated to thee their histories. Of others, We have not'' (Sūrah 4:164). The Qur'ān, rightly understood, has a doctrine on the universality of revelation that allows for the integration of Aryan or Indo-European and Mongoloid or other traditions into the metaphysical and spiritual premises of the teaching on *tawḥīd*. It is a doctrine that has been amplified in the past, as in Mughal India where Dārā Shikōh, the translator of the Upanishads into Persian, spoke of the ''treasures of monotheism'' to be found in these scriptures. Likewise, in the thirteenth century the Persian Ṣūfī, Jalāl ad-Rūmī, affirmed the same ecumenical perspective. This particular Qur'ānic teaching has lain almost dormant over the centuries, but now, when inter-faith understanding is of great importance, its time has come.

The Prophets

After the Messenger comes the Prophet (*nabī*), who is quite different because he does not found a religion. Instead, he plays a twofold role, depending on circumstances: first, within the framework of the religion previously established by the *rasūl*, he renovates its spiritual message, adapting it to changed earthly conditions; second, he prophesies on the unfolding of cyclical events in relation to his community or to the world at large. Like the Messenger, the *nabī* is a perfect sage and saint; he has been chosen from all eternity to be a Prophet; he is unique and incomparable, even sinless. Solomon and David are examples of Prophets sent to rejuvenate their community, which was established by the message (*risālah*) brought from Mount Sinai by Moses. Before Moses, there was Abraham, founder of the now extinct Abrahamic tradition which had been readapted and regenerated by such Prophets as Ishmael, Isaac and, of course, Joseph. In the case of the Prophet Ishmael, his was perhaps a readaptation of Abrahamic monotheism in northern Arabia, which was deployed through his twelve sons, progenitors of the twelve great tribes in that area.

Clearly, the number of Prophets is far greater than that of the Messengers. While the Qur'ān mentions well over two dozen or so Prophets and Messengers, it is evident from the tradition as a whole that the number of Prophets and Messengers is much greater by far than that: in the hundreds for Messengers, and in the thousands for Prophets. Also, it should be remembered that the functions of both Messenger and Prophet can coexist in one person; moreover, all the great Messengers are necessarily Prophets, though the the reverse is not true. The Christ, for instance, was both Messenger and Prophet. As Messenger, he founded the Christian faith; as Prophet, he uttered the predictions touching on the end of the ages, or "the last days". Similarly, Muḥammad was the Messenger who established the Islamic religion, and he was the Prophet who foresaw "the end of time", or the coming of "the Hour".

The Qur'ān teaches that Messengers and Prophets must be equally respected by believers. Addressing the believers, the Qur'ān states: "Say: We believe in God and in that which has been revealed to us and in that which was revealed to Abraham, Ishmael, Isaac, Jacob, and the Tribes and in that which Moses and Jesus were given, and in that which the Prophets were given from their Lord: we make no distinction between any of them" (Sūrah 2:136).

Yet, in an apparently contradictory fashion, the Qur'ān also says: "Of those Messengers, We have caused some of them to excel others" (Sūrah

2:253), which seems to imply that distinctions are being made. In reality there is no contradiction: all Messengers and Prophets possess the same spiritual identity with the Divine Oneness, which is why they must all be equally respected. At the same time, they differ form one another in their outward characters, or in the qualities they manifest, and this is why some "excel" others. Within the Abrahamic tradition, for example, Abraham, Moses, Jesus, and Muḥammad are all identified with God. But they differ, or "excel" one another, given the different cosmic functions they are called upon to exercise.

In this connection, the Christ is known in Islam as the "Seal of Sanctity" (*khātam al-wilāyah*), but this does not mean that Islam sees in him a greater saintliness than in Muḥammad. That could hardly be the case, since both had the same spiritual identity with *Allāh*. Rather, Jesus, during his life and mission, displayed his inner spiritual sublimeness through the performance of miraculous works and the powerful radiance of his presence, which made him inimitable.

By contrast, Muḥammad is called the "Seal of the Prophets" (*khātam an-nabiyyīn*) because he closes the entire cycle of Prophethood which began with Adam, and also because in a sense he synthesizes in his person the whole Prophetic chain and its different qualities. Muḥammad maintained an equilibrium between the inner, contemplative life and the outer, active life. The simplicity of his conduct and the absence of supernatural elements in his daily life meant that he could be easily imitated by all members of his community.

Esoterism and Exoterism: The Path and the Law

Speaking of the contemplative life and of the active life, we should recall here that they refer, respectively, to the esoteric and exoteric dimensions contained in every revealed message. Mention has already been made of the Ninety-Nine Names of *Allāh* in the Scripture: two of those Names are "the Interior" (*al-bāṭin*) and "the Exterior" (*aẓ-ẓāhir*) (Sūrah 57:3). They are rich in metaphysical and spiritual significance. They also represent the principles behind the esoteric (*bāṭinī*) and exoteric (*ẓāhirī*) aspects of the Islamic revelation. Put briefly, esoterism has to do with the Islamic Path (*ṭarīqah*) and exoterism has to do with the Islamic Law (*sharī'ah*). The former deals with the contemplative life, or the inner life of the Spirit in man, while the latter deals with the active life, or with the deeds that lead to salvation.

All major revelations, like the Islamic one, necessarily have these two aspects — contemplative and active — and Messengers and Prophets manifest them in one degree or another during their missions. Since Islam considers itself a remanifestation of the religion of Abraham, and since in Islam the Path and the Law are in perfect equilibrium, it would seem as if that had been the case also for the Abrahamic faith. However, one cannot say the same for either Judaism or Christianity. The Judaic tradition accentuates the exoteric Law and consequently tends to appear historically as a massively formalistic *sharī'ah*. Christianity, by virtue of having no *sharī'ah* at all flowing from the original revelation, accentuates the esoteric message, or at least did so in its early period, and therefore appears as a *ṭarīqah* meant exclusively for a spiritual elect. Islam and its Messenger Muḥammad brought the Abrahamic cycle to a close by manifesting, in the end, the equilibrium between the Path and the Law that characterized Abrahamism in the beginning.

If we consider *Tawḥīd* in the light of the Path, we give it an esoteric interpretation; but if we consider it in the light of the Law, we give it an exoteric one. The former tends to be symbolic and spiritual; the latter, literal and allegorical and moralistic. This twofold interpretation of the doctrine *Tawḥīd* is also true for all which has to do with the remembrance of God (*dhikr*): either an esoteric contemplative prayer or an exoteric ritual practice.

However, the equilibrium between the Path and the Law must not be confused with an equality. Like other great religions, Islam has always recognized the superiority of the contemplative over the active life. The Law must be followed by everyone, contemplative or not, for everyone must engage in action of one sort or another, and the sacred Law of Islam has commandments and prohibitions governing all actions. But, while in principle no one can excuse himself from following the contemplative Path, in practice only a small minority of contemplatives actually do.

There is nothing in the Islamic message, or in any similar revelation, that leads one to conclude that it has to do only with the Law, and not with the Path; it has both facets. While everyone can easily recognize the exoteric meaning of Qur'ānic verses, or of those verses which are obviously literal in meaning, not everyone can grasp the anagogic contents, or the esoteric dimensions, of the Scripture. The esoterist is the one who can discern the deeper layers — the esoteric teachings — of Scripture.

The superiority of the contemplative over the active life is evident in the fact that it is the Path that causes the spiritual regeneration of communities which have fallen into decadence. According to Islamic teachings, the period of lassitude (*fatrah*) between a Messenger and a later Prophet, who readjusts the tradition, is also repeated between one Prophet and another. During these latter periods of weakness, saintly reformers appear on the scene to restore things to spiritual health. Within a given tradition, one would, accordingly, have this succession: a Messenger, then Prophets, then saintly sages who establish, maintain, and regenerate the religion. In Islam, however, there is only one Messenger and Prophet, and that is Muḥammad.

No Prophets will follow him until the Day of Judgment.

If there is no Prophet after Muḥammad, there are, nevertheless, great and minor saints (*awliyā'*, pl. of *walī*) whose function is to reawaken the inner dimensions of the message and to adjust the tradition to novel historical circumstances. Many such saintly people, both men and women, have existed in Islam for the last fifteen centuries; but from among them great saintly reformers appear only periodically. They play the role of the Hebrew Prophets, though within the Islamic tradition. Speaking of them, the Prophet said, in a *ḥadīth*: "At the beginning of every century, God will raise up in this community a renovator of its religion."[5] This assumes, of course, that the process of decline natural to all cultures and peoples operates in an undulatory manner. Regeneration or renovation comes from reaffirming the original message with spontaneous spiritual insight.

The natural tendency of the guardians of the Law is toward an increasing formalism similar to that of the Pharisees in the days of the Christ. The teachings of the saintly reformers, who are the sages of the Path, act as a leavening influence, restoring the fullness of the revealed Message and thus preventing the formalism which comes over any religion that has been reduced to a *sharī'ah* without a *ṭarīqah*. Reducing a tradition to an exoteric legalism eventually results in the collapse of the top-heavy structures of the Law itself, unless spiritual reformation has taken place in time to prevent the interior disintegration of the Law.

The sequence of principles which establish a tradition is this: *Allāh*, revelation, religion, tradition, intelligence. That revelation originates in a Divine Source needs no explanation: the image, in the Islamic tradition, of Gabriel constantly visiting the Prophet to verify the Qur'ān and other aspects of the message is simply another way of saying that the message of salvation was under continuous divine supervision and guidance and was never left to the workings of chance and error. Religion, the result of the pact between Heaven and Earth contained in the revelation, is therefore what binds God to man and man to God, in beliefs, rituals, and moral practice. Since these bindings are multiple, we speak of the Islamic, Christian, or Hindu religions, all of which proceed from their respective revelations. Tradition is the religion transmitted in time and space, while keeping its supernatural element in a timeless and spaceless dimension of reality.

Tradition (*naql*) and intelligence (*'aql*) go together and are often cited together, almost in the same breath, by the religious authorities of Islam. This means that the word "tradition" should not be understood simply as the transmission of forms; it also implies man's awareness of their intelligible contents. The sense of tradition, in any case, while it does suggest transmission, must not be divorced from the discernment of its timeless essence.

Three Elements of Revelation

According to the Islamic tradition, revelation contains three elements that form the saving heart of a religion: *īmān* (''faith''), *islām* (''submission'', i.e., to the Divine Will), and *iḥsān* (''morality'' or ''spiritual life'') with the first two sometimes reversed in order. Later on, these will be more fully explained. For the moment, suffice it to say that they are the essential principles of religion, its basic states, corresponding to the states of a believer. *Imān* has to do with the beliefs of religion; *islām*, with the ritual observances; and *iḥsān*, with the moral or spiritual life and, by extension, with the aesthetic elements of the Message, its sacred art — which means that, at bottom, revelation also has an aesthetic message.

All of them form the nucleus of a religion and its traditional way of life, and are not in the least arbitrary. Man has a mind veiled by ignorance, and it must be purified by the articles of faith (*īmān*). He has a weakened will which should be regenerated or empowered to transcend itself through the rituals (*islām*). And his fallen life should be restored by the spiritual or moral code (*ihīsān*). His nature is composed of a mind, a will, and a life, and whatever their state, we should expect to rediscover the roots of his nature in the Knowledge, Power and Life of the Divinity. For *īmān*, *islām*, and *iḥsān* revive man's substance, giving it a measure of knowledge, power, and life it did not previously have, or better, removing the veils of spiritual ignorance, weakness, and death that the Fall engendered in man.

These three principles have exoteric and esoteric interpretations, to be sure, and are interrelated on both planes. A person's virtuous disposition (*iḥsān*) influences his faith (*īmān*) and ritual life (*islām*); his faith, if strong, can lead to a deeper practice of the virtues and ritual life; and his ritual life, through its diffusion of graces in his soul, can illumine his faith and provoke a deeper degree of virtue.

Whatever is true for an individual regarding the three principles is true also for a community collectively. Decadence or decline in a religion comes from a general weakness in the substance of the community, or a part of it, and this is manifested by an impoverishment of *īmān*, *islām*, and *iḥsān*. *Ghaflah* feeds the decadence actively or passively, and leads step by step to associationism (*shirk*), or paganism in all its forms, and this is not too far removed from disblief (*kufr*).

The Restoration of Edenic Consciousness

The revival of an individual comes through these same three principles. Likewise, the revival of a religious community (or *ummah*, of the Qur'ān) occurs when the principles are again manifested through the influence of saintly reformers and teachers whose spirituality permeates the hardened nature of the community, dissolving it sufficiently to permit the reappearance of those three principles in the souls of believers in much greater clarity. Initially, when revelation was brought into the world by the founder of a religion, it had a similar loosening effect on the fallen nature of the humanity it was first addressed to: it illuminated the darkened collective soul, making possible a new orientation of life. The Messenger himself, like Muḥammad, for example, had a spiritual radiance sufficient to banish disbelief and restore a prayerful life. That influence of the message allowed the beauteous life of the Spirit to permeate the souls of men and the things that surrounded their liturgical observance, so that art also could not but be part and parcel of the saving revelation.

The descent (*tanzīl*) of revelation, in response to the low points of human decline in a particular community, seems to arrest the momentum of the Fall by restoring awareness of the One that characterized mankind in the Edenic state before the expulsion. In fact, while revelation is a kind of recapitulation of the Edenic state under other conditions, it does not permanently stay the momentum of *ghaflah*. Forgetfulness is arrested long enough to allow the revelation to make a first impression, or sealing, of the collective psyche of the new religious community. There is a brief upward flow of spiritual aspiration that counters the downward movement of the Fall. After the period of revelation comes to an end, with the termination of the founder's mission, there follows an apostolic generation. What had been, during the revelation, a temporary reunion between Heaven and Earth, again becomes a gradually widening chasm between the two. This time, however, there are beliefs and practices in the new religion available for those who wish to undo the effects of the Fall. When the apostolic generation disappears from the midst of the community, the downward movement picks up speed and *ghaflah* spreads out, necessitating one of the periodic renovations which follow the declines.

Once the apostolic age has passed away, the regenerative role in Islam falls upon its many saints, men and women. They repeat the restorative effects of the initial revelation, but within the traditional matrix of the religion, revitalizing a moribund faith. This, no doubt, is the renovative role that all traditions assign to their saintly believers. But, just as there is a final point in the general history of mankind on earth beyond which no further major revelation will descend into this world, so, similarly, the renovative function of great sages, whose roles affect vast numbers of the faithful, must sooner or later come to an end. There is a reason for this: if the great revelations were to continue on after the Islamic message, there would be no Day of Judgment in the offing. Since there is a Day of Judgment, to which all religions point, then there must be a final message, which is what Islam considers itself to be. There must also be a final Messenger who sums up in himself the line of Messengers and Prophets going all the way back to Adam, and that is what Islam considers Muḥammad to be. In the same way, within the ups and downs of Islam, or of any religion, there must come a moment when the great spiritual reformers of the faith no longer can reach great numbers, and instead affect fewer and fewer believers. That is when the impetus of *ghaflah* begins to assert itself with greater and greater force. A turn for the worse takes place in Islam at that moment: decadence then becomes quite evident in all quarters and all aspects of life. However, even then the pious minority is unaffected by the all-pervading, insidious worldly drift of the community, for there is nothing deterministic or mechanistic about decadence, or the law of decline. The individual is always free to go down with the forgetful, if he chooses, or to go up with those who are mindful of the contents of revelation. In other words, every decline and rebirth, however small or great it might be, parallels the cyclical laws operating in the initial period of revelation. Sooner or later, however, only small minorities in a community can be reformed because of the widespread *ghaflah* among the great majority of believers.

One can easily conclude from all this that the Islamic traditional teachings have nothing to do with evolutionism in the modern sense, which holds that mankind and society improve with the passage of time: they evolve from lower to higher levels, the modern world representing the highest degree of progress. This prevailing evolutionistic notion affects practically every single domain of modern Western thinking, whether it be biological, social, artistic, political, historical, economic, or even theological. Nothing seems to escape the evolutionistic process. The Qur'ānic cyclical teachings, by contrast, are not at all evolutionistic. Quite the opposite: mankind and society degenerate as time goes by. Moreover, these Islamic teachings on the cyclical ups and downs of mankind, culminating in the Last Judgment, are in agreement with analogous doctrines found in other revelations, including the non-Semitic ones. In all of them, spiritual decline is universally recognized as having consequences for man's soul as well as his body. As the Qur'ān would put it: "We have created man in the most beautiful constitution, then We have brought him down to the lowest of the low, except for those who believe and do good works: for theirs is an unfailing reward" (Sūrah 95:4-6). This passage refers to man's original primordial nature, created in the image of God, which was blurred by the loss of the Edenic state.

The veiling of the inner Spirit by the fallen soul and body is the same as the blinding of the eye of the heart (*'ayn al-qalb*) temporarily or permanently. This clouding of the inner vision does not affect the immutable and transcendent Spirit in itself, no more than the dark clouds filling the sky affect the shining sun beyond them. In the long run, however, the loss of that spiritual vision of the Real leads to grave consequences for the overall nature of man, and for the cosmic milieu which is affected by whatever happens to him or emanates from him. Man's centrality in this world is a Qur'ānic teaching: this is why he is called the vicegerent (*khalīfah*) of God on earth, for the animals, plants, and minerals are peripheral in relation to him. He alone, of all creatures in this world, can consciously and actively know the Real with the vision of the Spirit which connects his soul to God.

Revelation furnishes the means for man to return to his Divine Source by unveiling, with the help of the revealed teachings and practices, the inner eye of the heart, so that it once again has the Edenic vision. The Spirit has always had that vision but man's darkened soul has prevented him from being aware of it. When the dark clouds hiding the sun are dissipated, one finds that the sun was always there, a radiant and silent witness to everything going on in the world. Likewise when man, following the message, removes the inner clouds and perceives once again the solar Spirit in the center of his being, he realizes that it had always been there, a silent and radiant Witness to all that went on before. In fact, it would seem that the restoration of the Edenic consciousness is the ultimate reason for revelation in the first place. It is man, not the Spirit, who has fallen from his former estate; it is man who has "devolved" from that paradisal mind through *ghaflah*; and it is man alone, who, with the help of *īmān*, *islām*, and *iḥsān*, can actively regain, or rediscover within himself, that Edenic stratum of his being which lies hidden within his unregenerate nature.

Ghaflah and the End of the Ages

The increasing intensity of *ghaflah*, as the end of mankind's sacred history approaches, does not mean that man is finally obliterated in the night of his own ignorance. It is true that the Last Judgment marks the terminal stopping point of the disequilibrium set in motion by the initial expulsion from Paradise. Each fall later on repeats, in its own way, the initial transgression that led to the original expulsion from a blessed state. But, regardless of the widespread capitulation to *ghaflah* as the end of the cycle looms, there will always be a small minority who, by virtue of their faith, can undo within themselves the traces of the original fall. That is why it cannot be said that all is darkness at the conclusion of mankind's earthly history.

Moreover, the Islamic tradition envisages a succession of events toward the end of the human cycle on earth which leads to the eventual triumph of Heaven over all darkness and subversion. In other words, Heaven is finally victorious and puts to flight the darkness which seemed to have temporarily gained the upper hand. We need not discuss the details of the "end of time", as the Islamic expression would have it. However, it is important to understand the general contours of the final scenes, just as it was important to grasp how things were in the beginning, for the two are interconnected. To understand the cumulative effects of the loss of the Edenic state, one must have some notion of the Last Judgment; to understand the conclusive character of the Last Judgment, one must have an idea of its causal relations with the loss of the Edenic world. Not that such notions are unique to the Islamic Message; their analogues can be found in all traditions. But they are expressed in a perspective which distinguishes each one from the others. Since *tawḥīd* is the basic tenet of the Islamic faith, everything is seen as revolving around its presence or absence, in an individual or a society, in a decline or a rebirth, in the Garden of Eden or the Day of Judgment. Perhaps it would be closer to the mark to say that, since all religions have an essential teaching on *tawḥīdawḥ*īd, they differ from one another in the manner in which they arrange their analogous elements.

One of the teachings that Islam has in common with Christianity has to do with the Messianic role of the Christ. Orthodox Islam asserts that the terrestrial cycle of mankind closes with the Second Coming of Jesus. Indeed, the Christ plays an important cosmic role in the world of Islam. However, neither he nor his mother Mary have the same traits which Christianity accords them: he is never the God-Man in a divine sense, which would go against the absoluteness of *Allāh*, the One without a second, who has no offspring or associates; and she is never the "Mother of God", for the Absolute has no parents or progenitors. Yet the Islamic tradition recognizes something exceptional in both Jesus and his mother, and agrees with the Christian teachings on the Virgin Mary that Jesus, like Adam, has no father: "Verily, the likeness of Jesus with God is as the likeness of Adam: He created him of dust, then He said unto him, 'Be!' — and he was" (Sūrah 3:59).

Islamic teachings assign to Jesus the function of the Messiah, whose Second Coming is at a time of great tribulation. One must not confuse the Messiah with another figure of eschatological significance, the *mahdī* ("the Rightly-Guided One"), a descendant of the Prophet Muḥammad who appears at the end of time, when troubles and subversion abound on all sides, and whose coming is also one of the articles of belief. He is perhaps a contemporary of *al-masīḥ ad-dajjāl* ("The False Messiah", the Antichrist). Most of the teachings on the *mahdī* and the Antichrist and the general "signs of the times" are to be found in the *ḥadī*ths of the Messenger and in certain verses of the Qur'ān. The "signs" are part of the admonitory events preceding the Day of Judgment and are sometimes included in the great confessions of faith (*'aqīdah*) that the orthodox theologians have composed for the mass of believers. They refer to the increasingly unstable condition of the world, and even to the rapid disintegration of the cosmic milieu, as the end of time approaches. The arrival of the *mahdī*, with his forces — to lead a Holy War is one of his functions — signals the manifestation of celestial powers on earth. But it is the Christ who puts an end to *ad-dajjāl*'s tyrannical government and false religion, and who takes the faithful with him into the Hereafter, leaving the awesome events of the last days to fall on the heads of the unfaithful.

The Day of Judgment

While the eschatological scenes depicted by the tradition are much more complicated than what has just been presented, enough has been said to give an idea of the principal terminal events. There follows the Last Judgment (*yawm al-qiyāmah*), when the gates of Heaven and Hell open to receive their respective inhabitants. Like the other Abrahamic faiths, Islam stops here in its cyclical account of the march of human events. In other words, the humanity which had played out its earthly existence, or its sacred history, from the Garden of Eden to the Day of Resurrection, has now been transported from this visible world to the invisible posthumous states of existence, celestial or infernal, so there is no longer any need to consider human existence on earth. True, Islamic cosmology agrees that the heavens and earth — the immediate cosmic milieu of this world — participate in the Judgment, with the end result that they will undergo a cosmic purification which restores their original integrity, removing the dross and infiltrations of impurity which had been the repercussions in Nature of man's Fall. But the teachings of the Islamic faith do not envisage the destiny of another group of people inhabiting the regenerated earth, as Hinduism and Buddhism do.

While the Indian religions — because of their teaching on transmigration (*samsara*) based on an impersonal causal law of action and reaction (*karma*) — can envisage the destiny of multiple humanities succeeding one another in this world as it undergoes successive dissolutions and purifications, Islam sees the overall cycle of only one humanity, as do Judaism and Christianity.[6] Previous or subsequent humanities do not enter into its picture of earthly human cycles. The fate of the present humanity, as measured by the posthumous Heavens and Hells, is the unique preoccupation of Islam. Accordingly, there is no reason for Islam to be concerned about other humanities prior to the present one or after it, the way the ancient Aryans, or Indo-Europeans, like the Greeks and the Hindus and Buddhists were. This is no doubt one reason why the Semitic traditions accentuate the Heavens and Hells with such force. For them, there is the humanity of this world, then there are the two posthumous conditions, Heaven and Hell, which can be chosen while still in this world. There are no prehuman or posthuman levels of transmigration in intermediate domains which the soul can traverse through repeated lives and deaths while working out its salvation through *karma*. Although the limbos and purgatories of the Semitic faiths approximate the intermediate states of Hinduism and Buddhism, they have never been stressed to any great degree in these traditions. In any case they have not been considered as goals worth striving for in their own right, or as states for vast numbers of souls who are neither hot nor cold, that is to say, who are not good enough for the Heavens nor bad enough for the Hells, but who merit something in between. That is why, once the Last Judgment takes place, Islam shifts its attention from this world to the Hereafter, where the Heavens and Hells begin their long-lasting periods of existence with their respective populations which had formerly inhabited the by now purified earth.

The Return to the Divine Source

To a certain extent, the story of humanity is not altogether ended once we get beyond the Day of Resurrection, for the Heavens and Hells also have their cycles of duration. Earlier on, mention was made that the entire created universe has its *ajal musammā* (''definite period'', referring to a cycle of duration, great or small). Let us recall the principle of *tawḥīd* in operation here: God alone is Eternal. Therefore, the universe, or the Creation, cannot be eternal alongside of God. That would make two Eternals, which of course is *shirk*. God is the First (*al-awwal*) before the Creation came into being, and He is the Last (*al-ākhir*) after the Creation in its entirety has ceased to be.

An immediate application of the principle of *tawḥīd* is this: the Hells, while long lasting, cannot be eternal, for that would make two or more Eternals. So there must come a time when their inhabitants, having undergone the process of purification, are withdrawn from them and sent elsewhere, eventually winding up in the celestial regions. The Heavens or Paradises are naturally more permanent than the Hells, but they also fall within the limits of the Creation and cannot, accordingly, be eternal alongside the Eternal One, for that would also make two or more Eternals — God and the Paradises.

One can say of the Paradises that by virtue of their nearness to God, symbolically speaking, they reflect Eternity in their own nature. That reflection is what makes certain Muslim theologians claim an eternal felicity for the Paradises: that felicity, being of divine origin, cannot end. However, on their own created levels of existence within the universe, the Paradises are not and cannot be eternal like the Divinity itself. If, on the other hand, one were to consider *Allāh* as the supreme Paradise in Himself, independently of the created Paradises just mentioned, then of course it would be true to say that Paradise is eternal, for it would be indistinguishable from God. Generally speaking, however, the theologians of Islam and the faithful make a clear distinction between the Paradises and their Creator, *Allāh*, as do most of the mystics.

The Paradises — or Heavens — occupy levels of reality that are evidently higher than man's but lower than God's. Like other revealed scriptures, the Qur'ān recognizes a hierarchy of descending levels of reality, beginning with the uncreated world of *Allāh* and ending with the world of man. The Qur'ān itself says that the blessed in the Heavens will abide in their state "so long as the Heavens and the Earth endure, except as the Lord willeth" (Sūrah 11:108). Obviously, the Heavens referred to here can be the physical heavens, but they also symbolize the paradisal states by virtue of their loftiness and purity. Just as one looks up into the physical heavens, one goes "up" into the spiritual Heavens. These are expressions which are perfectly intelligible in themselves because they are rooted in the nature of things. However, if taken literally, they can lead to a misunderstanding of Qur'ānic imagery. The Heavens in the abovementioned Qur'ānic verse include, therefore, the spiritual Heavens, whatever other meanings the verse can sustain. Those spiritual Heavens, where the blessed, the angels, and the Archangels are to be found, are reabsorbed at the end of their cosmic cycle back into their celestial Source in the uncreated world of *Allāh*. They are stripped of their "createdness" as they rejoin their limitless being in the uncreated Divinity.

We have seen that the Qur'ān envisages the beginning and end of the entire Creation, which is the ultimate meaning of this verse: "God has not created the Heavens and the Earth, nor that which is between them, except with the Truth and for a definite period" (Sūrah 30:8). This is a comprehensive statement which includes the Paradises, the Hells, and the physical universe. Not only does the verse announce the *ajal musammā* of the physical world, but also of the higher worlds as well.

The return of all things back to their Divine Source, or *Allāh*, is taught in the Qur'ān in different verses. When the Scripture says, for example, in this famous verse: "Verily, we are God's, and, verily, unto Him is our returning!" (Sūrah 3:109), we may draw numerous conclusions, to be sure, but they do not exclude the one already given. The return of all things back to their heavenly Origin in God implies the view that things emanate from God, while the Qur'ān seems to be teaching a creationist perspective that would have the world originate out of nothingness (*ex nihilo*) through divine fiat (*kun*, "Be!", the Qur'ān says). The theological schools of Islam tend, for the most part, to be creationist in their teachings on Qur'ānic meanings, out of fear that an emanationist perspective might compromise the purity and immutability — or the Eternity, if one will — of the Creator by engaging Him in the vicissitudes of the creative process.

But the fact that Islamic Neoplatonism, whether philosophical or even Ṣūfī, can discern an emanationist teaching in the Qur'ān, regardless of what others might think, and that ultimately the two apparently opposing viewpoints can be harmonized, should permit us to conclude that if things return to God they must first of all have issued forth from Him. This means that the final destiny of the universe is the return to *Allāh*.

The Outbreathing of the Compassionate

These remarks on the cycles, from individual human existence to the vast cycles of the Heavens and Hells, lead us to a consideration of the Ninety-Nine Names of the Divinity, the "Most-Beautiful Names" of *Allāh*, as the Qur'ān puts it. For the Ṣūfī contemplatives, the origin of the Creation lies in "The Outbreathing of the Compassionate" (*nafas ar-raḥmān*), a concept similar to that of the Divine Feminine Power (*shakti*) of Hinduism: it is the creative power of God to bring things into existence.[7] For Muslim theologians the omnipotence of God is the cause of the Creation. He did not have to create the universe; but if He did, it is because of the all-powerful nature of His Will. For Muslim philosophers, borrowing from the Greeks, the Creation proceeds by necessity from the absolutely Necessary, or God. But for some of the Ṣūfīs, it is the overflowing and beatific Love of the Compassionate (*ar-rahmān*) which causes the deployment of the "Most-Beautiful Names" of *Allāh*, such as the Creator, the Living, the Wise, the Truth, the Self-Subsistent, the All-Victorious, the Light, the Fashioner, and the Knowing, throughout the creative process, preserving, guiding, and eventually reintegrating the manifested world back into the Divinity, from which it came in the first place. The Names are merely verbal symbols of the differentiated aspects of the Divinity, in its Essence beyond all differentiation. They are like a halo of differently-colored rays issuing from a colorless center called *Allāh*, the Supreme Name.

Within the Divinity itself, there is not only an undifferentiated Essence but also a more extrinsic multiplicity of aspects, which we see in the Ninety-Nine Names of *Allāh*. This Divine Multiplicity is at the origin of the diversity of all things in the Creation, including the rich variety of peoples, races, and cultures found in our world, to say nothing of the many religions and their respective revelations. The incessant "Outbreathing of the Compassionate" not only brings the Creation into being but also, once the world is established, generates the variety of religions and their different perspectives. Still, the Divine Unity is in all of the Names, more or less as the solar light is in the variety of colors in the sun's rays. The metaphysical principle of the Divine Unity allows us to discern the unicity within the different religions, peoples, and races, restoring all things to their transcendent source in *Allāh*.

The metaphysical *tawḥīd* that underlies the different revelations is similar to the string which unites the many beads of a rosary or necklace, whereas the beads are like the diverse Divine Names. That notion, no doubt, is behind the Qur'ānic reiteration that the Messengers and Prophets are all speaking, in the final analysis, about the same absolute Oneness, *Allāh*. The different possible combinations of Names account for the diversity of religions, peoples, races, worlds, and even the experiences undergone by individuals and communities in their particular cycles, as they are subjected to the "radiations", so to speak, of the multiple Names of the Divinity.

That the very essence of the Deity is summed up in the Name *ar-raḥmān* ("The Compassionate"), which has connotations of infinite beatitude or love, means that the "Outbreathing of the Compassionate" (*nafas ar-raḥmā n*) is at work constantly in the preservation of the Creation, and especially so in the redemptive phases known as the revelations. These messages are outstandingly compassionate outbreathings of the Lord of the Creation, for they are manifestations or emanations of the Compassionate in moments of cyclical decline. The divine flux seems to operate in rhythmical pulsations, like the exhalations and inhalations of breathing, or the movements of the heart. The Islamic teaching on "the renewal of the Creation" (*tajdīd al-khalq*) at each instant is but a cosmic version of the same emanative principle at work on all levels.

The *nafas ar-raḥmān* which recreates the universe at every instant, and redeems the different fallen humanities with a revitalizing flow of the Names in a new message, is not simply a projection of the Compassionate. The world emanates from its Origin in view of an eventual return. This principle is already anticipated in the contemplative aspects of all revelations: the descent of the Qur'ān (*tanzīl*) is with a view to the ascension (*mi'rāj*) of the believer. In the end, everything that has been breathed out through the Divine Names must return to the One through the same Divine Names.

The character of the Divinity is defined in the opening consecrational formula to all the Sūrahs of the Qur'ān with the exception of the ninth: *bismi 'llāhi 'r-raḥmāni 'r-raḥīm* ("In the Name of God, the Compassionate, the Merciful"), a formula called the *basmalah*. The two Names, *ar-raḥmān* and *ar-raḥīm*, are derived from the same roots and differ in that God is *ar-raḥmān* in Himself, but *ar-raḥīm* in relation to the created universe. The two Names are considered to be apposites and thus they explain what *Allāh* is, both in Himself and with respect to the Creation. It is at least significant that these two Names are constantly repeated, not only at the head of the Sūrahs, but at the beginning of all necessary deeds, such as eating or drinking or writing or something else, as if to underline the true nature of the Divinity and its beatific presence in all such deeds.

The attractive force of *ar-raḥmān*, which is complementary to the "Outbreathing of the Compassionate", dissolves all resistance to itself. For that reason, all things seeming to move away from it, or to be distant from it, are eventually restored. The Islamic version of the Apocatastasis, or of the final restoration of all things, does not proceed merely from the notion of *tawḥīd*, in the sense that there cannot be eternal Hells because that would be *shirk*, but also from the ultimate nature of the Divinity in itself, as *ar-raḥmān*.

If revelations proceed from the merciful nature of the Divinity, then it should not be surprising that Muḥammad is described by the Qur'ān as "mercifulness" (*raḥmah*). It is through him that the Qur'ān came into this world and that the message of Islam was established among the Arabs. Now that we have seen how Islam views the role of the Messengers and Prophets, we must now turn to the Seal of the Prophets, to Muhammad as the Messenger of God (*rasūlu 'llāh*).

II
Muḥammad the Messenger

Abraham and Ishmael in Islam

When discussing Muḥammad's role as Messenger, we should keep in mind his connections with Abraham. The Abrahamic dispensation gave rise to four revelations, or messages, which have governed vast numbers of Semitic and non-Semitic believers. But, of the four — the Abrahamic, the Judaic, the Christian, and the Islamic — only the last three remain alive at the present day, the Abrahamic faith having gone the way of other extinct faiths, even though it survived in spirit in the remaining three.

The Abrahamic cycle constituted a decisive period for a great segment of mankind because it reintroduced monotheism in a Semitic world that had succumbed to polytheistic practices and beliefs, and it set the stage for the subsequent manifestations of monotheism in the other three traditions. In this regard, we know from Judeo-Christian and Islamic sources that Abraham's patriarchal role would have repercussions down through the ages: all three religions are connected to the great Patriarch in one way or another. Abraham is referred to in the Bible as the Father of believers (Genesis 17:5 and Romans 4:1) and the Friend of God (2 Chronicles 20:7), names acknowledged by Islam.

When the Old Testament speaks of God as saying to Abraham, "I will multiply thy seed as the stars of the heaven, and as the sand which is upon the seashore" (Genesis 22:17), this obviously applies not only to the Jewish and Christian peoples, but also to the Muslims. Indeed, from the Islamic viewpoint, the Abrahamic religion was unique in itself, and also distinct from the subsequent Jewish and Christian messages, for the Qur'ān states, clearly enough: "Abraham was neither a Jew nor a Christian, but rather, he was a true believer, submissive unto God" (Sūrah 3:67). The term *ḥanīf*, here translated as "true believer," has connotations of primordial purity. Those who followed the Abrahamic-Ishmaelite dispensation in Muḥammad's day were known as the *ḥunafā'* (pl. of *ḥanīf*). Abraham's message represents the primordial religion for the Semites, relatively speaking. As previously noticed, Muḥammad himself is seen by Islam as a latter-day version of Abraham; both were conditioned by the purity of the desert and nomadic culture. The relation between the two Prophets and their Communities is put in this fashion by the Qur'ān: "Verily, the mankind most worthy of Abraham are those who followed him, and this Prophet and those who believe" (Sūrah 3:68).

In the Western world, however, the link between Muḥammad and Abraham is largely unperceived. The Judeo-Christian tradition, its imagery colored by long association with the Bible, looks back towards Abraham through the lineage of his son Isaac, brought into the world by Sarah. Only brief mention is made in the Bible of Abraham's other son, Ishmael; the center of attention is obviously Isaac. Accordingly, the ancestral line of Moses and Jesus, the two great Messengers of the Judaic and Christian faiths respectively, proceeds from Abraham through Isaac, so that Ishmael and his mother Hagar are nowhere in sight.

Completely different is the perspective in Islam: here, Ishmael takes over the central role and Isaac is relegated to one side. It is as if, for centuries on end, the two lines of descent from Abraham had completely ignored one another until such time as the Ishmaelite descendants, mostly confined to the nomadic peoples of Arabia, exploded out of their desert homeland with a new message of *Tawḥīd* called Islam, which saw itself as a recapitulation of primordial Abrahamism and its Messenger Muḥammad as another Abraham.

The ties between the monotheism of Abraham and that of Islam are brought out in the traditional accounts on the origins of the Ka'bah, the sacred edifice in the Meccan sanctuary.[1] According to these accounts, Abraham and his son Ishmael were either the repairers or the builders of the Ka'bah: in either case, the Ka'bah would emerge as the oldest religious building in the world. Not only that, but many of the rituals of the pilgrimage to Mecca commemorate the diverse events occurring in the lives of Abraham, Ishmael, and Hagar in the Meccan valley. The biblical narratives of Hagar and her son Ishmael, especially after she was rejected by Sarah and left by Abraham to wander in the wilderness (Genesis 21:9-21), resemble their Islamic counterparts. Islamic sources specify that Abraham brought them to the Meccan valley and there left them to their own devices. Hagar's running to and from between the twin mounts of Ṣafā and Marwah in quest of water to give her dying son Ishmael is commemorated in the running between those two mounts by the pilgrims to Mecca; and the water she discovered is said to be the Well of Zamzam, considered a sacred fount to this day by all Muslims.

Abraham's mission, to put things in an Islamic light, was not confined to Haran and Canaan, or to the contiguous regions, as described by the biblical stories. On the contrary, although his sojourn in the Meccan area is ignored in the Bible, and therefore in the Jewish and Christian traditions, it is precisely the Meccan episodes of his life that Islam commemorates. Thus, Abraham and Ishmael are pictured in the Qur'ān as "raising the foundations of the Ka'bah" (Sūrah 2:127), which does not necessarily mean that they actually built the structure, for the traditional commentator, Ṭabarī (d. 923), when glossing this verse, gives other versions on the origins of the Ka'bah, connecting it to Adam and later to Abraham. The Ka'bah is said by the Qur'ān to be the first sanctuary founded on earth (Sūrah 3:96); the pilgrimage thereto was established by Abraham (Sūrah 22:26). The Qur'ānic "Station of Abraham", a stone on which he stood and supervised the work on the Ka'bah, is still a revered place within the sanctuary. A depression in the pavement on which the circumambulation is performed is said by tradition to mark the trough where Abraham and Ishmael mixed the mortar used in constructing the building. Between the semicircular wall on the pavement and the Ka'bah itself is a space where the graves of the Patriarch Ishmael and his mother Hagar are to be found.

An edifice of such a hoary antiquity could not but have a mystical radiance in the eyes of the faithful. It is not surprising, then, if we read in the work called *Akhbār Makkah* (The History of Mecca) by the ninth-century Arab, *al-Azraqī*, that there are celestial prototypes to the earthly Ka'bah. In the Islamic tradition, the Ka'bah is the navel or the center of the entire universe. Its ultimate prototype is the Throne of God: the circumambulation of the angelic hosts around the Divine Throne is reflected in this world in the circumambulation of the Ka'bah by the believers. Tradition would also have it that the Black Stone imbedded in one of the corners of the Ka'bah was a dazzling white in the earlier days of mankind, when the virtuous life was much more diffused than in later epochs. As time when by, and the sinful propensities of man were manifested, the stone got darker and darker, finally ending up black. This is but another way of showing the gradual spiritual decline following upon the Fall.

The world of Islam sees the Meccan bond in Abraham's life as being all the more precious in that his son Ishmael settled in northern Arabia, thereby spreading among the nomads there the primordial message of pure monotheism. Ishmael is considered by the Qur'ān to be both a Messenger and a Prophet (Sūrah 19:54), perhaps because he gave to the northern Arab tribes a message adapted uniquely to them. By the way, it is a moot point in Islam whether Abraham was ordered to sacrifice Isaac or Ishmael. Some say that the story in Sūrah 37:100 ff. refers to Abraham's offering of Ishmael either at Minā outside of Mecca, where a still-existing stone slab marks the possible site of the sacrifice, or else near the mount called Marwah. However that may be, the *'īd al-aḍḥā* ("The Festival of Sacrifice"), celebrated annually as a commemorative sacrifice on the tenth day of the month of pilgrimage both at Minā and throughout the Muslim world, is commonly associated with Abraham's sacrifice of Ishmael. For this reason, the latter is called *dhabīhu 'llāh* ("God's sacrificial victim"). The tenacity of the Islamic belief that it was Ishmael and not Isaac who was offered up, and that this was done in the Meccan region, and not in "the land of Moriah" (Genesis 22:2), seems to indicate that there might have been two offerings, one of Isaac and one of Ishmael. Since both traditions parted ways centuries before Islam appeared, there was never any meeting of minds on the issue by the partisans of each tradition.

Perhaps because of the patriarchal functions allied to his mission as a Prophet, Ishmael is thought of as the great ancestral figure, or the progenitor, of the northern nomadic Arabs. But the ancient Arabs had known other Prophets apart from Ishmael. They are mentioned in the Qur'ān and are generally outside the familiar biblical list of names. The Prophet Hūd, for instance, was sent to an ancient people called 'Ad (Sūrah 7:65 ff.) in southern Arabia; the Prophet Shu'ayb was sent to the Madyanites of the Sinai region (Sūrah 7:85 ff.); and the Prophet Ṣāliḥ was sent to the northern Thamūdites (Sūrah 7:73 ff.). Shu'ayb is sometimes assimilated to Jethro, the father-in-law of Moses (Exodus 3:1) and the priest of Midian; and the Thamūdites were apparently familiar as a historical memory to the ancient Greeks. Hence, when Ishmael appeared, he would not be the first Prophet sent to the Arabs.

Ishmael and his sons settled down among the ancient Arab tribes of those bygone days. Islam, as a matter of fact, agrees with the Old Testament that the Prophet Ishmael had twelve sons (Genesis 25:12 ff.); Muḥammad descends from either the first son, Nebajoth (Nābit in Arabic), or the second one, Kedar (Qaydhar). The description the Bible gives of Ishmael, incidentally, fits the Arab nomads quite well: "And he shall be a wild man; his hand will be against every man, and every man's hand against him; and he shall dwell in the presence of all his brethren" (Genesis 16:12). This must not be forgotten when trying to account for the extraordinarily divisive spirit that has always characterized the Arabs.

The northern Arab nomads, the Bedouins, traced their genealogy back to Ishmael through 'Adnān, whereas the southern Arabs, those of the Yemen, went back to a different eponym, *Qaḥṭān* (the Yoktan of the Bible, the son of Ebèr). Since this has a bearing on the Prophet Muḥammad's life, it is well to point out here that the ancient Arabs divided themselves into the

"Extinct Arabs", such as 'Ad, Thamūd, and others; the "Native Arabs", who are the southern Arabs, the Yemenis; and the "Arabicized Arabs", or the northern Arabs. Ishmael was not an Arab, but learned his Arabic from the southern Arab tribe of the Jurhum, one of the offspring of Qaḥṭā n, and is said to have married Jurhumite women, apart from the Egyptian woman mentioned in the Bible. In the Old Testament, we find that "under Ebar were born two sons: the name of the one was Peleg; for in his days was the earth divided; and his brother's name was Yoktan" (Genesis 10:25, and I Chronicles 1:19). Muḥammad's connection with Shem is through Peleg. The fact that the Prophet is among the Arabicized Arabs of the North means that he is of nomadic background, related to Ishmael, who was not an Arab by origin. The enmity, incidentally, between the northern and southern Arabs has probably something to do with the nomadic culture of the former and the sedentary culture of the latter. This hostility, of ancient origin, continued right into the early centuries of Islam, and is perhaps ultimately traceable to an original division of mankind into nomadic and sedentary peoples. It seems to be suggested in the story of Peleg and Yoktan, for in the former's days "was the earth divided".

Like all northern Arabs of his day, and especially the aristocratic tribal families, the Prophet Muḥammad had a family tree going all the way back to Ishmael through 'Adnān. This means that, in the eyes of the Muslims, Abraham was as much the forefather of Muḥammad through his son Ishmael as he was of Moses and Jesus through his son Isaac. 'Adnān's ancestral connections with the Prophet are agreed upon by Arab genealogists; things are less certain between 'Adnān and Ishmael, in the sense that there is no unanimity on the sequence of names. Of course, in speaking of Abraham as the forefather of Jesus, this is only a figure of speech: Jesus had no father, according to both the Christian and Islamic traditions. Christ's virginal birth was an accepted teaching in Islam, as previously stated.

As a result of all of these considerations, we can see that the associations between Islam and Abraham operate on various planes. First, there is the Islamic revival of the Abrahamic Message of *Tawḥīd* in its pure form; second, there is the ritual remanifestation of Abrahamism in the pilgrimage to the Sacred House in Mecca, a shrine directly connected with the hands of the Patriarch and his son Ishmael; third, and finally, there is the ancestral link between Abraham and Muḥammad.

Biographical Sketch of the Prophet

Innumerable traditional accounts of the Prophet's life exist, ranging from the ninth-century work, *Sīrat rasūli 'llāh* (*The Biography of the Messenger of God*), an edited version of Ibn Hishāam (d.c. 833) of the earlier biography by Ibn Isḥāq (d.c. 767), to the famous poems by the thirteenth-century Egyptian Ṣūfī poet, al-Būsīrī (d.c. 1296), called the *Burdah* (*Mantle Poem*) and the *Hamziyyah* (*The Poem Ending in the Letter Hamzah*), which are recited every year on the anniversary of the Prophet's birthday. In the biography of Ibn Hishām, we find a rather straightforward story with some miraculous events included to round off the picture, but with nothing that would explicitly refer to the Logos-nature of the Prophet; whereas, in the *Burdah*, we encounter both the historical Muḥammad as well as his celestial reality as the universal Logos. The majority of the traditional treatments of the Prophet's life revolve around these two extremes.[2]

Some notions about Muḥammad's life are certainly in order, if only to understand the subsequent remarks in their historical framework. His dates, to begin with, are 570-632, although the year of his birth in Mecca is not quite certain. He had been married for some fifteen years when, in his fortieth year (around 610), his mission as a Prophet and Messenger began with the reception, in the cave of Mt. Hirā' outside of Mecca, of the following revealed verses of the Qur'ān: "Preach in the Name of thy Lord who createth, createth man from a clot! Preach: And thy Lord is the Most Generous who teacheth by the Pen, teacheth man what he knew not" (Sūrah 96:1-3).

His mission thereafter is divided into a Meccan and a Medinan period. The Meccan one lasted from around 610 to 622, the Year of the Emigration (the first year of the Hijrah). It witnessed his first public teaching (around 613), whereas previously it had been private. It also saw the death of his first wife, Khadījah (620), after some twenty-five years of married life. The Meccan phase culminated in the persecution of the small band of Muslims and in their departure for Yathrib, later called Medina.

The Medinan epoch began in 622 and continued on until the Prophet's death in the year 632. This is the time when Muḥammad emerged as the ruler of his astonishingly expanding community. Battles fought between the Muslims and the Meccan pagans seesawed back and forth from the Muslim victory at Badr (624) to the Meccan victory at Uḥud (625) to the eventual conquest by Muḥammad of Mecca itself (630). After that, he became the undisputed master of all Arabia and lived to see tribe after tribe join his religion. It was during this Medinan part of his mission that the Prophet married a number of women, mostly for political and tribal reasons. He is said to have had perhaps nine wives. After the death of his first wife, Khadījah, he took other women in marriage, among whom was 'A'ishah (d. 678), the daughter of one of his companions, Abū Bakr, and the one whom he loved most of all. During his Farewell Pilgrimage to Mecca (632), the final verse of the Qur'ān was revealed: "This day," the Scripture says, addressing all of the Muslims, "have I perfected for you your religion and made My BLessing unto you complete, and have chosen Islam as a religion for you'' (Sūrah 5:3). Shortly after that, succumbing to an old illness, he passed away in the arms of his beloved spouse, 'A'ishah.

Such are the bare facts about the life of the Prophet. Within the tradition, all the events associated with him have historical and higher meanings, especially for the contemplatives. So, for example, the conquest by the Muslims of the pagan armies in possession of Mecca and its holy shrine, the Ka'bah, is the conquest by the Spirit and its virtuous forces of the passions, ignorance, and vices in control of the heart, the inner Ka'bah of man. Even the most insignificant remark of the Prophet has been taken in a symbolic sense by the mystics, but without this in any way abolishing the literal meaning.

Western Critics of the Prophet

Be that as it may, the Messenger has not fared well at the hands of his Western biographers, who see nothing particularly spiritual or mystical in either him or in the Qur'ān. There are some exceptions to this rule among the Western critics, and they are important, but they cannot by themselves stem the tide of rejection emanating from the others. Very often they reduce him to the role of a political, social, or historical personality devoid of any sacred dimension to his character or his mission. In more recent interpretations, he has been practically adopted by both Western and Muslim Marxists as one of their own. Under such circumstances, the traditional accounts of the Prophet are either ignored or treated in the light of the particular ideological system held by the biographer. In medieval times in the West, the critics of Islam and its founder were at least much more logical: Muḥammad was a false Prophet; the Qur'ān was a false Scripture; therefore, Islam was a false religion. His medieval critics knew perfectly well that two decisive questions had to be answered in advance by anyone evaluating the Islamic message, and that everything depended on how one answered them: ''Is the Qur'ān a revealed Scripture?'' and ''Is Muḥammad a true Prophet?'' They knew that, if they answered ''Yes'' on both counts, their entire doctrinal structure built on the uniqueness of the Christian message for all mankind would collapse over their heads. Their answers were ''No'' to both questions, and therefore they could conclude that Islam was not a true religion.

Fundamentally, the same questions exist today for anyone dealing with Islam. Understandably, the secularist scholars are more interested in reducing the Scripture and the founder of Islam to their own sense of values rather than grappling with issues which unconcern them. It is a completely different matter for the great majority of scholars handling Islam, for they are believers, mostly Christians, and some Jews. For them, there is no initial disbelief in transcendent, divine realities which would tarnish their treatment of the Qur'ān or the Messenger; but the Qur'ān and the Prophet continue to exist as stumbling blocks. In the case of the Jewish scholars, both Christianity and Islam are deviations from Judaism. If that is true for the founder of Christianity, who is generally seen by the rabbinical authorities over the centuries as a false Prophet, then it is even more so for both Muḥammad and the Qur'ān. At least the Christ had been a Jew with Messianic claims, whereas Muḥammad had never belonged to Judaism.

Christianity, for its part, accepts Judaism as a faith that played an anticipatory role in the First Coming of Christ, after which Judaism should vanish from the scene. But it has no such notion about Islam, for the latter tends to negate the definitive mission of the Christ. On that score alone, Islam cannot be viewed with a tolerant eye, as it were, by the Christian world, without this compromising the absoluteness of the Christian message.

To complete the picture, Islam views both Judaism and Christianity as valid messages of a celestial origin, like itself. Their founders, not to mention the other Prophets of the Abrahamic tradition, are saintly, inspired Messengers and Prophets, on an equal footing with Muḥammad. That attitude is held even by ordinary pious Muslims, and not just by learned theologians. Admittedly, it flows from the doctrine on the universality of revelation found in the Qur'ān. This in turn gives it a scriptural authority that imposes itself on all Muslims. But the proposition that all revelations proceed from the same transcendent Source and that the Prophets and Messengers are all inspired by the same Divinity and are spiritually equal in their wisdom and sanctity is much too self-evident and intelligible to be confined exclusively to the Muslim world.

It should be possible for both Jews and Christians to share in the same ecumenical attitudes of the Muslims without this in any way implying the abandonment of the essential beliefs of their own religions. But, if in principle this should be possible, in practice it has not been so for reasons having to do with the exclusivistic and polemical attitudes of their adherents. That is why the Prophet Muḥammad has been considered more as an obstruction for the Christians and the Jews than anything else, even though he descends from the same Abrahamic origins as they do.

The Spiritual Necessity for the Prophet's Mission

It would be instructive to explain the Muḥammad mission in terms of sacred history as a whole and of the particular period inaugurated by the Abrahamic message within the Semitic world. Revelation originates in a timeless, celestial Source, but its manifestations in this world obey laws associated with cyclical causality in a historical sense. We are obliged to account for the appearance of the historical phenomenon known as Muḥammad both in a universal way and also within the stream of the Abrahamic dispensation, if we wish to understand him aright.

Instead of looking at the flow of human history from Edenic to eschatological times, we can situate Muḥammad's mission within a much more restricted phase of the total story, that of the Abrahamic line of Prophets. We must then explain the terminal message of Islam within the Semitic world. If the Judeo-Christian message had been of a cyclically terminal nature, then this alone, it seems clear, would have obviated the need for the coming of Islam. It would not have appeared on the historical scene at all. Instead, there would have been a Judeo-Christian solution to whatever spiritual problems presented themselves at that time. Yet, the coming of Islam, and its eventually stunning successes all over the map of the Mediterranean regions, derive from a spiritual necessity that has to be elucidated. To put the question in other terms: Why was the Muḥammad mission spiritually necessary? For if it had not been, then Islam would have been a redundant religion without celestial support.

Allusions have already been made to the Message of the Christ as being primarily a spiritual Path (*ṭarīqah*) which contrasted quite vividly with the formalistic Law (*sharī'ah*) of Judaism. The early Christians included in their ranks many Jews who followed the Law and the spiritual message of the Christ without this in any way implying contradiction on their part. Eusebius (d.c. 340), in his *Ecclesiastical History*, remarks that, up to Hadrian's siege of the Jews (in the years 132-135), the first fifteen bishops of Jerusalem were of the Jewish faith, and "that their whole church at that time consisted of Hebrews who had continued Christian from the Apostles down to the siege." The English historian, Edward Gibbon, in *The History of the Decline and Fall of the Roman Empire*, says of that congregation of Jews presided over by the bishops of Jerusalem that they "united the law of Moses with the doctrine of Christ".

However, after the first century, the widening chasm between the Jewish and Christian faiths became a definitive rupture that could not be bridged. Neither the rabbinical nor the early Church authorities wanted to heal the breach. Instead, they deliberately provoked one another into the parting of the ways. Had that separation not taken place, then the Christian mystical message would have furnished the Jewish legalistic structures with a new lease on life. The spiritual Path of the Christ would have permeated the forms of the Jewish Law and given them, eventually, a purified and no doubt simplified character in keeping with the new universal faith. A synthetic perspective would then have arisen based on the abstract monotheism and exoteric Law of Judaism and on the esoteric contemplative Way centering around the God-Man and a mysticism of universal Love as contained in the message of the Christ. The two together would have formed an esoteric-exoteric tradition: they would have wedded the Christ-given *ṭarīqah* to the Mosaic *sharī'ah* in an organic whole that would have spread like wildfire throughout the Mediterranean lands.

There was no reason why that state of affairs should not have come about. Jesus said: "Think not that I came to destroy the Law or the Prophets: I came not to destroy, but to fulfill" (Matthew 5:17). His spiritual Path, in other words, rested on the Law and the Prophets and gave to them their deepest meaning. When the Apostles, meeting in council at Jerusalem, decided to refrain from imposing circumcision on the Gentiles (Acts 15:4; Galatians 5:2), it was more than a declaration that Christianity was not to be considered as a kind of Jewish sect. It was also a breaking away from the Law. The Pauline argument that whoever is circumcised "is a debtor to the whole Law" and that "Christ is become of no effect unto you, whosoever of you are justified by the Law: ye are fallen from grace" (Galatians 5:3-4), sounded the death knell to any moderate integration of Jewish Law into the mystical Way of the Christ.

A Judeo-Christian union would have rendered the coming of Islam unnecessary. The ethnocentrism of Judaism would have been diluted by the universality inherent to the Christian message of Love. The Christocentrism of Christianity would have been mitigated to proportions compatible with the Jewish beliefs in the absoluteness of the transcendent Divinity. But such was not to be and the two faiths went their respective ways. It was left up to Islam to effect the balance between the Law and the Path that the other two had rejected and to introduce a new perspective of pure *Tawḥīd.*

The Islamic contribution to Semetic nomotheistic doctrines lay in the principle, as was said, that *Tawḥīd* in itself of a salvatory nature. It has no need to be connected with a God-Man, as in Christianity, nor with a Chosen People, as in Judaism. It suffices unto itself as a means of salvation. Moreover, in its balancing of the Law and the Path lies the cyclical justification for the existence of the Islamic faith within the Abrahamic lands and for the historical appearance of its founder, Muḥammad.

Miraculous Events in the Prophet's Youth

Different ways of considering the life of the Prophet exist, but two important periods are self-evident in his mission. The first is his life up to the assumption of his role as Messenger; the second is his life after taking over that role. They are not of equal value, for the time involved in his Messengership is by far the more important of the two and certainly the one that produced the greatest fruits in the religion he founded. Nevertheless, the first period contains elements that are significant to the Islamic faith and that the tradition transmits from generation to generation as articles of belief.

While it is true that Muḥammad is not a God-Man within the perspective of Islam, tradition embroiders his birth with all manner of miraculous signs. Many of the biographical works on Muḥammad give numerous instances of the miraculous phenomena that the Prophet's mother Aminah and others witnessed before and after his conception and during his birth. Light issued from him when he appeared in this world, or his mother had visions of distant castles in Syria burning, or celestial visitors came to her. At the moment of giving birth to the Prophet, Aminah saw a light shine before her, in the mist of which were very tall women who surrounded her, saying: "We are Asiyah, the wife of Pharoah, and Mary, the daughter of 'Imrān, and these others here are houris." Asiyah and Mary are the two examples in the Qur'ān of feminine perfection (Sūrah 66:11-12), the former being the wife of Pharaoh, and the one who saved Moses (Sūrah 28:9), and the latter being the Mother of Jesus. Embellishment of his birth tales with miraculous phenomena is simply the Islamic way of testifying to the extraordinary nature of his character as the founder of a religion. It would have been strange if the Messenger had made his entrance into the world without celestial signs, and this is what the tradition wishes to teach with a certain ornamentation.

A clue to his character lies in the Qur'ānic thesis of his having been "chosen" for his spiritual mission. This implies a spotless soul free of the trammels of sinful impulses. Islamic dogma developed this scriptural concept into the important belief that Prophets and Messengers, being perfect saints, are beyond the impulses of sin or transgression. Impeccability in the Prophets does not militate against the existence of occasional imperfect actions. They are not sins: they are pedagogical lessons for believers in general. They proceed from Muḥammad's human side, not from his innermost being as the Logos, intermediate between God and man. The agony of Jesus in the Garden of Gethsemane, the hesitations of the Buddha after his Enlightenment under the Bodhi-Tree, and Muḥammad's own apparent confusion at the beginning of his mission all seem to belie the underlying "chosen" substance of the Messengers. The Messengers temporarily take on something of the fallen attributes of post-Edenic humanity. These trials or imperfections that come over the Messengers have a consolatory function in the life of believers in general, who would otherwise be overwhelmed by the perfection of sanctity and celestial wisdom in the founders of religion.

There are no doubt hidden significations in certain experiences within the lives of the Prophets and Messengers which have to be deciphered. According to Mahayana Buddhist teachings, the Buddha had no need for spiritual discipline to obtain Enlightenment. He had been enlightened from all eternity and merely recapitulated on earth the disciplinary aspects of the contemplative Path for the sake of others. Also, in Mahayana Buddhism the Buddha is considered under three different levels of reality, the *Dharmakaya* ("The Body of Essence", which is the eternal, Divine Reality), the *Sambhogakaya* ("The Body of Bliss", and this is the universal intermediate reality), and the *Nirmanakaya* ("The Body of Magical Transformation", which is the earthly, historical Buddha). The three "Bodies" are of decreasing reality, the true Buddha being the *Dharmakaya*, which has existed from all eternity. It manifests itself as this or that historical Buddha, who then recapitulates the way of salvation for everyone else's sake.

Something similar to the Buddhist doctrine can be said of all the Messengers and Prophets. Indeed, the ultimate nature of Muḥammad is the Real or God (*al-ḥaqq*), in keeping with what he said about himself: "He who has seen me, has seen God (*al-ḥaqq*)." He meant that, on the earthly plane, his form was a reflection of the transcendent Essence, which is the *Dharmakaya* of the Prophet. Further on down the line comes his transhistorical, spiritual nature as the Logos, the one he referred to when he said, "I was a Prophet when Adam was between water and clay." That is the *Sambhogakaya* of the Prophet. And finally, there is the *Nirmanakaya* of the Prophet, his historical or human form as the Arab Prophet.

Among the experiences undergone by the Prophet which seem to have a pedagogical signification for his community is the one called "The Splitting Open of the Breast" (*shaqq aṣ-ṣadr*). This took place when he was but a boy and prior to the death of his mother Aminah in his sixth year. Tradition says that the same, or similar, experience occurred at different periods in his life. The story is this, according to one account: While playing in the desert, he was seized by the Archangel Gabriel (or two angels, with golden utensils and a bowl of snow for purificatory purposes), thrown to the ground, his breast split open, and his heart removed and purified of a dark substance in it. After the purification of the heart, Gabriel returned it to its place, healed the Prophet's breast, and departed.

Symbolically, the event points to the removal of ignorance, represented by the dark substance, through the intervention of supernatural purification. The result is an unveiled or purified heart, source of impeccant conduct thereafter. The celestial agent in the story is Gabriel — or, in other accounts, angelic beings — who blot out the transmitted legacy of the Fall. There is something prototypal in the whole sequence of events: mystical rebirth is implied therein. Muḥammad's inward, celestial, and chosen nature makes his outward, human nature conform to this primordial purity by removing all obstacles to its radiance. In the process, the resulting impeccance (*'iṣsmah*) of the *rasūl* is a lesson to the believer of mystical bent that he, too, must restore in himself the Edenic image through the elimination of the darkened clouds that cover the inner eye of the heart.

Quṣayy and the Arabic Language

Muḥammad's own ancestral connections with the Ka'bah in Mecca should not be left unmentioned. We have already seen that Abraham and Ishmael, who figure in the Prophet's lineage, had a hand in the building or repairing of the Ka'bah. In his own day, when the edifice was in disrepair, Muḥammad himself (in his thirty-fifth year, around 605) helped in the work of restoration. But before his day, some five generations back, another ancestral figure, a certain Quṣayy, had been assigned the providential role of uniting the disparate tribal elements of the Quraysh into a force strong enough to capture Mecca and to settle down there. Under his powerful leadership, the Quraysh became the religious, cultural, commercial, and linguistic elect of Arabia. Quṣayy set about to regenerate, once again, the ancient pagan religious practices surrounding the Ka'bah, and Mecca reassumed its central position as the goal of pilgrims. In taking over the Meccan area, the Quraysh ended up by dominating the culture and the religious paganism of the Arabs.

The Prophet himself was born into the tribe of the Quraysh. His grandfather, 'Abd al-Muṭṭalib, the first guardian of the Prophet after his own father 'Abdullāh had died, was one of the aristocrats of Mecca and the overseer of the Well of Zamzam. Muḥammad's uncle, Abū Ṭālib, who took over the guardianship of the boy when he was around eight years of age, was likewise one of the leaders of the Qurayshg in Mecca and intimately bound up with the pagan religious ceremonies attached to the Ka'bah. Thus, the religious institutions of the pagan Arabs were already in Muḥammad's family line long before he himself undertook to reconsecrrate them in the name of Islam.

That was not all that Islam owed to Quṣayy. By settling the Quraysh in Mecca and its environs, he conferred a religious prestige upon them and also gave them a linguistic preeminence in Arabia that would have great importance later when the Qur'ān was revealed in the Quraysh style of Arabic speech. This is a matter of great weight and importance, for the ancient Arabs were a people obsessed with the purity and elegance of their speech. Language had a mysterious, even magical power which could provoke emotional reactions of the most explosive kind among both individual Arabs and entire tribes. The pre-Islamic Arabs had an extraordinary preoccupation with the Arabic tongue: its sounds, its stylistic arrangements, its imagery, its musicality, and its majestic rhythms. This preoccupation with the different aspects of their language explains their fascination with the Arabic of the Qur'ān.

Out of all the Semitic tongues known to us, Arabic is the latest to appear on the historical scene some fifteen centuries ago. It became the vehicle of a major revelation and culture. Yet, when it appears, it has the traits of an archaic Semitic speech.[3] While other Semitic languages, like Akkadian, Hebrew, and Phoenician, have suffered the loss of a number of elements postulated to have existed in their primordial ancestral source, Arabic is considered to have retained most of the original sounds and a good deal of the structural features of that ancient mother-Semitic. This is especially so for its highly inflected forms which would give rise to the present-day Arabic dialects, that are equally removed from the pure speech of the Quraysh of pre-Islamic and early Islamic times.

That such an inflected language could have been so close to the nature of the original source of the Semitic tongues and yet have maintained its primordiality is not immediately plausible. It becomes plausible when we recall that the Arabs who maintained the relative purity of their ancient speech were nomadic in lifestyle. They were cut off more or less from the surrounding civilizations with their urbanized centers and were insulated from them by vast and treacherous deserts wherein they found their sustenance and cultural habits as Bedouins. The all-encompassing desert, where time seemed to have come to a stop, preserved the archaic patterns of the ancestral Arabic tongue from succumbing to the depredations of time as it afflicts the speech of settled peoples and their sedentary cultures. The inflected speech of classical Arabic could still be heard in the ninth century among some of the nomadic tribes who had not had much intercourse with settled cultures, Arab or otherwise. Then, after that, it gradually retreated into the halls of learning, where scholars used it in their discourses and books, while the Arabic of the people turned gradually into the dialects of the present day.

Even so, the pre-Islamic Arabs were not uniformly pure in their language. On the contrary, the Arab homeland presented to the outsider a mosaic of tribes and dialects with diverse names, like Thaqf, Ḥanfah, or Sulaym. Each tribe was a community unto itself. Very often its tribal features included a special linguistic or dialect trait which made it approximate the Quraysh style of speech in purity or else removed it from that prestigious level altogether. By virtue of their preeminence in Arabia the Quraysh represented what could be called the King's Arabic. This was the *lingua franca*, not merely of poetical compositions, but also of commercial relations, military pacts, treaties, and general cultivated discourse. The aristocrats of Mecca maintained their purity of speech by the age-old habit of sending their offspring into the desert to dwell among the tribes who retained the most elegant and finest inflected speech. The Prophet himself spent a good deal of his early boyhood in the desert. He would be known for his eloquence, his speech being considered second only to the Qur'ān in purity and nobleness. The later Umayyads would also send their children into the desert to learn the pure speech of the nomads.

The Nature of the Ancient Arabs

Classical Arabic, best represented by its Quraysh models, reflects the contrasting qualities of the ancient Arabs on the eve of the Islamic revelation. It has a certain beauty and majesty, serenity and force, melody and rhythm that are the linguistic expressions of the explosivity and fatalism of the pre-Islamic Arabs. Volatile to an incredible degree, the Arabs were also capable of introspective resignation, as we see in some of their poets' reflective lines. Their existential poles were warfare and women, death and life, the sword and the beloved. Their poetry is saturated with extremes in chivalric warfare, passionate love, tribal honor, and moving descriptions of the desert world they knew so well, with its majestic rigors and seasonal beauties. Through all of their culture ran a strong sense of protocol and dignity, which can be rediscovered in the patterns and rhythmic movements of classical Arabic, not to mention the arabesques and geometric patterns of Islamic art later on. The cult of personal or tribal honor or glory is a constant element which none contested or called into question. It is only when the Prophet's time draws near that we begin to discern a premonitory awareness in some of the poets that incessant, internecine tribal warfare and glorification are not the goals of life. There is talk, in a poet like Zuhayr ibn Abī Salmā, who was raised in the Days of Ignorance, of peace and wisdom.

While the pre-Islamic age is called the *jāhiliyyah*, it has nevertheless a nostalgic atmosphere about it which derives in great part from its desert ambiance and from the fact that nomadism was then in league with nature and therefore culturally distinct from the urban centers of the surrounding Persian and Byzantine civilizations. The northern Arabs were fashioned by the desert. Theirs was largely a pastoral existence, their homes were black goat's hair tents near water wells and pasture lands for their camels, horses, sheep, cattle, and goats. They moved in circular patterns in their tribal lands under the governance of the seasonal fluctuations of rainfall, which in turn decreed where the pasture lands and water wells could be found.

Both the severity of the desert and the endemic warfare among the bellicose tribes eventually forged the Arab soul, habituating it to constant exposure to death from all directions. The poetic speech of the ancient Arabs has a magical eloquence, dignified beauty and wisdom both in form and content that were the fruits of their desert existence; it intruded itself even into the life of the little towns, such as Mecca. These fruits could not have emerged from a mediocre collective mentality. The desert never gave the Arabs a chance to be banal and trite. Abraham's biblical world of tents and nomadic movements and strong desert colors was still the world of the pre-Islamic Arabs.

It is probable that the Qur'ānic revelation caught the Arabs at the very peak of their nomadic culture. They had reached a perfect balance and tension in their traits of soul and language and attitudes that could be used in founding the new religion and in propagating it outside of Arabia. Out of all the Mediterranean peoples, the Arabs seem to have been the only vessels fit for the reception of the last revelation to appear in the world. True, their paganism was utterly uninspiring and even downright crass in its visual representation of their idols. This idolatrous ugliness, along with some of their other practices, had to go. But their positive qualities were something else altogether, and could be integrated into the revelation. The majestic beauty of their language, their innate sense of dignity and honor, their nobleness, their sensuality, and their volatile explosivity, all were a rare mixture possessed by no other people in the Mediterranean lands.

Because of their isolated nomadic culture, far from the corrupting influences of the cities in the civilized world, the Arabs had preserved the requisite qualities of soul which would make them the initial vehicle of the Islamic revelation. Islam in turn was largely conditioned by the ethnic genius of the Arabs themselves. The anthologies of Arabic literature, such as the tenth-century work, *Kitāb al-Aghānī* (The Book of Songs), by Abu 'l-Faraj al-Iṣfahānī (d. 967), which contains a good deal of pre-Islamic materials, reveals a world that has always evoked a nostalgic interest among Muslim scholars. It is not simply because pre-Islamic literature has a direct bearing on Qur'ānic studies that people are drawn to it. Rather, it is because the poets and figures of those days had a kind of wholeness and uniqueness, and even primordiality, that tied in perfectly well with the harsh beauty of the desert, even though they were pagans and had not yet rediscovered the notion of the transcendence of *Allāh.*

The Messengerhood of Muḥammad

Islamic mysticism has a famous dictum that says, "The color of the water is as the color of the glass," or "the vessel" (*lawn al-mā' lawn al-wi'ā'*). This is used to show that the Divine Reality, colorless like water, nevertheless takes on the coloration of whatever form it assumes, like water in a glass colored red, green, or blue. That is a law that is applicable to all celestial messages. The ethnic qualities of the ancient Arabs conditioned, or "colored", the colorless transcendent Spirit that manifested its nature in the Qur'ānic revelation. While it is true that the universal contents of the Qur'ān escape the limitations of its Arabic form, one can also say the exact opposite. As an expression of Arab ethnic genius, the Qur'ānic form necessarily delimits the Spirit to the extent that one takes into account only the "letter" of the Scripture, forgetting its spiritual symbolism.

That same spiritual law applies as well to the Messengers. They also express different aspects of the transcendent spirit while delimiting it in certain ways. Muslim sages, especially the Ṣūfīs, identify the Logos itself with Muḥammad, so that the other Messengers and Prophets emanate from the Logos-Muḥammad like rays of differently-colored lights from the unique solar orb. One could, of course, argue that the Logos is the Christ, or the Buddha, or Rama, and so forth, depending on the religion one has in view. All arguments would be equally valid inasmuch as each of the Messengers embodies only a particular aspect of the limitless nature of the universal Logos. No Messenger could possibly manifest, in his earthly form, the universal Logos in itself. Still, it is a fact that the different religions tend to see their founders as having a monopoly on the contents of the Logos in itself. It is as if they were not only the colored glass, but also the colorless water.

The Messengerhood of Muḥammad was conditioned by the fact that he was an Arab, and therefore that he was a Semite and not an Aryan like Gautama Buddha, or Rama, or Krishna in India. At the risk of belaboring the obvious, mention should be made of the principle that Messengerhood manifests itself in a variety of styles: saintliness can take on different colorations. Muḥammad could not have been a Messenger among his fellow Arabs with a style like that of the Buddha and yet have successfully completed his mission. On the contrary, it would not have prospered at all. The Buddha would have been totally out of place in the Arabia of those days. His yogic meditational approach to a nontheistic reality called Nirvana, which called for the renunciation of all pleasures and desires that kept the the wheel of rebirth (*samsara*) turning, was a spiritual possibility only in India. What the Arabs needed was a completely different style of Messenger, one who incorporated the pleasures or this world into the perspective of a pure monotheism centering around the theistic nature of *Allāh*. For this reason, Muḥammad's vessel was obviously of a different color from that of the Buddha's. But this should not make us forget that they were both "chosen vessels" of election, and that they represented the ethnic perfections and qualities of their respective peoples, the Semites of Arabia and the Aryans of India.

The Second Period of the Prophet's Life

The first period of the Prophet's life comes to a close in his fortieth year. During the first period, he was a monogamous merchant whose reputation as an upright and virtuous man of conciliatory and even-tempered dispositon made him a much-sought-after judge and arbiter of conflicts and contests. His time was about to come, and in an age of polytheistic Arabs his own pure monotheism was exemplary. His unitarian convictions bore fruit in his sincerity and truthfulness, his generosity and noble character, and in his wise discernment of men and of transcendent truths.

The second and more important period of his life began in his fortieth year, when his mission as a Messenger and Prophet was inaugurated by the Qur'ānic verses previously mentioned. It continued on until his death some twenty-three years later. This second phase, as we saw, is divided into two important epochs, the Meccan and the Medinan, the former lasting around thirteen years, the latter, then years.

Much has been said about the distinctions between the two periods. The Meccan verses of the Qur'ān are described as mystical and poetical, the Medinan as legislative and prosaic; the Meccan verses are indicative of a community caught up in an intense faith, the Medinan of a community which has waxed large in numbers and is in need of commandments and prohibitions; the Meccan verses are other-worldly, the Medinan, this-worldly. But perhaps it would be closer to the mark to describe the two as representing, in a predominant but not exclusive fashion, the esoteric and exoteric aspects of the Islamic revelation. The Meccan Sūrahs express the spiritual Path (*ṭarīqah*), and the Medinan the sacred Law (*sharī'ah*). These are general, schematic indications; in the Medinan period, we see Qur'-anic verses that are quite mystical too.

The Meccan days saw the beginnings of the Islamic religion, preached secretly at first for a few years. This was followed by the public preaching, and with it came the persecutions of Muḥammad and his followers by the Meccans, resulting in the emigration of the small band of Muslims to Abyssinia to find refuge under the Negus there. With the death of his wife Khadījah, and especially of his uncle and guardian Abū Ṭālib, an uncertain existence descended upon the Prophet. The Meccan chiefs resolved to put him to death. That is what provoked the Emigration (*hijrah*) from Mecca to the town of Yathrib by the Prophet and his small group of believers.

Before leaving Mecca, the Prophet underwent a spiritual experience that is of crucial importance both in dogmatic and mystical Islam. This is the famous Night Voyage (*isrā'*) by Muḥammad from Mecca to Jerusalem culminating in his Ascension (*mi'rāj*) through the seven Heavens to the Divine Presence. In its barest outline, the story goes as follows: One evening in Mecca the Prophet was bestirred by Gabriel, his constant companion, and led to a wondrous riding-mount called al-Burāq, which was white, with wings; it is said to have been the riding-mount of all the Prophets and Messengers. The medieval Persian miniatures of the *mi'rāj* often show the Prophet riding this fabulous mount while enveloped in flames, perhaps to indicate the illuminative nature of the spiritual voyage. Mounting it, and with Gabriel leading the way, he performed the Night Voyage to Jerusalem. Arriving there, he prayed with Abraham, Moses, Jesus, and a host of other Prophets. After descending into the infernal regions, the Prophet made his way back to Jerusalem and, from the boulder covered over nowadays by the Dome of the Rock, began his Ascension through the celestial sphere to the Divine Throne. After his descent, he remounted al-Burāq and returned that very night to Mecca, narrating the events to his followers and giving proofs of his voyage.

Orthodox Islam insists that the Night Voyage and the Ascension itself were in the Spirit, soul, and body, and not just in the Spirit. There is thus a similarity here to the Ascension of the Christ, which was covered by a cloud, whereas with the Prophet it was the night itself which veiled the absorption of the body into the soul and of the latter into the Spirit. There are also analogies between the *mi'rāj* and the Assumption of the Holy Virgin, to say nothing of the continual embodiments and reabsorptions of al-Khiḍr, one of the "Immortals" of the Islamic esoteric tradition, who resembles the Prophet Elijah who "went up by a whirlwind into Heaven" (2 Kings 2:11).

While the *isrā'* and the *mi'rāj* are dogmas of orthodox exoteric Islam that pious believers must adhere to, they are also teachings in the contemplative esoterism of the religion. The movement horizontally from Mecca to Jerusalem at night has relations with the self-extinction, "the dark night of the soul", that precedes the upward, vertical ascension of the Spirit. Indeed, the descent (*tanzīl*, which also means "revelation") of the Qur'ān is with a view to the eventual "ascension" of the believers from this world to the celestial abodes, which is what the process of salvation (*najāh*) involves. For the contemplatives of Islam, the Ascension of the Prophet was the prototype of the mystic's own spiritual ascension to *Allāh* via that ray of the Spirit connecting his soul to the Divinity. That is really what the Path is all about, except that in Ṣūfism the ascension is accomplished spiritually. On the Day of Resurrection, all believers "ascend" in resurrected and glorious bodies to await the judgment of grace or wrath, according to case. Thus, the prototypal voyage upwards of the Messenger of Islam applies to all members of his community.

Before leaving this all-important question of the *mi'rāj*, we might point out in passing that the Dome of the Rock is one of the first Islamic architectural marvels and that it symbolizes the finality of the Islamic message. First of all, the Rock covered over by the dome is precious to the Abrahamic dispensation because it was on this Rock that Abraham was to have sacrificed his son Ishmael. Secondly, the Dome of the Rock likewise stands over the site of the Temples of Solomon and Herod, a site formerly the heart of Judaism up to the destruction of the Temple in the year 70 by the Romans, in accordance with the prophecies of the Christ (Matthew 24:2; Mark 13:2; and Luke 21:6). And in Christianity the Temple of Jerusalem figured constantly in the life of the Christ, even to the point where his own sacred body was identified with the Temple (John 2:19-21). That Islam, which is the fourth dispensation within the overall Abrahamic tradition, should have wound up hallowing this very same spot is due to the tradition that the Prophet's footprint on the same Rock is the visible sign of his *mi'rāj*. It is this that caused the Caliph 'Abd al-Malik (685-705) to build the Dome of the Rock in 691. Jerusalem itself has eschatological signification for the entire Islamic cycle, especially when we consider the events of "the last days" and the traditional teaching that Mecca will be reabsorbed into Jerusalem, probably the Heavenly Jerusalem that descends after the cosmic purification has engendered "a new Heaven and a new Earth", as the Apocalypse would say.

To return to the Meccan period: during those days, Islam bore the imprint of a mystical message meant for a fervent minority of believers who found themselves in a hostile and aggressive world in which they were exiles. A *ḥadīth* of the Prophet makes that clear: "Islam began as an exile, and it will become an exile once again, as it was in the beginning. Blessed are those in exile!" That is with reference to the faithful at the beginning of Islam and at its end, when they are surrounded by an apostate world, and when they receive an augmentation of graces and blessings in compensation for the tribulations they underwent.

Things changed for the better in the Medinan years, in the sense that the Muslims themselves took over the reins of the city. The Prophet was faced with a completely different situation. Numerous new adherents to the faith called into being a code of commandments and prohibitions that would govern the community's ritual, moral, social and political activities. Islam, in other words, entered the world of fallen man and was bent on reforming or redirecting its energies in ways that were more or less in keeping with *tawḥīd*. Accordingly, the Medinan days saw the establishment and proliferation of rules concerning the Islamic state, society, warfare, marriage, divorce, commerce, the rituals, and a thousand other things which enter into the life of an *unmah* regulated by a sacred *sharī'ah*.

The Sunnah of the Prophet

That *sharī'ah* would not have been possible without the example and prescriptive instructions of Muḥammad himself. It is clear that he was to be followed and imitated by the faithful. Nothing was left to the inventive whims or fancies of the believers in general. The imitation of the Prophet's Norm, or Sunnah, in the performance of the rituals and in moral and social matters is what gives to the Islamic religion its rock-like stability throughout the ages. Of all the major religions still extant, Islam is the only one that is essentially the same now as it was in the days of its founder. As a result, the Muslim, whether in the Middle Ages or now, has nothing to invent or devise for himself. The manuals on Islam simply describe the beliefs and practices of the Prophet, as embodied in his Sunnah. The Muslim seeking a pious life merely follows the patterns established by the Prophet; the fervor he brings to his religion is what enlivens those patterns and gives them their inner life.

The Prophet consciously set out to create a Sunnah consisting of words and deeds transmitted to posterity by his companions, such as Abū Bakr, 'Alī, Abū Hurayrah, not to mention his wives, such as 'Ām'ishah and Zaynab. The resulting Sunnah has a kind of crystalline structure in the moral and religio-social domain. It is a revealed mold of behavior that furnishes order, harmony, and equilibrium to the soul of the believer, that had previously been formless and unregenerate. From thence on, the Muslims would conform their intentions and actions to the Sunnah bequeathed by the Prophet to his community.

That Sunnah was the necessary complement to the Qur'ān. The two go together, the Scripture providing a static doctrine of *tawḥīd*, while the Sunnah gives a dynamic or active method of realizing the Idea of Oneness in daily life. Put somewhat differently, the ultimate content of the sacred text is really the doctrine of pure *tawḥīd*, while the ultimate practice of the Sunnah is really the remembrance of *Allāh*, or *dhikr*.

Nothing is more contrasting to the Sunnah of the Prophet than that of the Buddha. The latter is an example of a purely Aryan Messenger; he has no connections whatsoever with the Semitic world of the Prophet, to say the least. The Buddha, with his clear-cut, serenely rational teachings, seems strange and completely out of place in the igneous and impassioned atmosphere of the Arab nomads of bygone days. The Sunnah of the founder of Buddhism was purely contemplative and meant almost exclusively for monks, even though some provisions were made for laymen during and after the Buddha's mission. This clearly was not the case for the Sunnah of the Prophet which contained a mystical or contemplative essence, as in Buddhism, as well as prescriptions for the life of action that applied to the *entire* community. There were no laymen in Islam.

Within the Abrahamic tradition, the mystical message of the Christ is the only one similar to that of the Buddha: both established a purely spiritual Sunnah for their respective communities and left no sacred Law, no *sharī'ah*, for the mass of believers. The *Sangha* ("community") of the Buddha was independent of the Hindu Law. As was said earlier, the Christ brought only a *ṭarīqah* initially based on the Jewish Law; but this symbiosis did not last long. Christianity broke away from that original foundation and, after the fourth century, had to devise its own social code patterned, this time, on the models provided by Roman law and administration. This was not a sacred Law, in the Judaic or Islamic or Hindu sense. But it was a necessary expedient, given the need for rules to govern the mass of believers who were now subject to the Church operating in a Christian State. The essentially mystical message of the Christ perpetuated itself in the bosom of both the Eastern and Western Churches through their monastic institutions. These were designed to preserve some semblance of contemplative discipline within an ecclesiastical structure, one becoming more and more exoteric with the passage of time. On the eve of the Islamic message, the mystical contents of the Christian faith were still evident here and there in the monastic communities. But the official Church had by then evolved into a dogmatico-legalistic formalism that seemed, ironically enough, to reduplicate the legalism of the Jewish faith in the days of Jesus Christ.

If we compare the strictly mystical Sunnah of the Christ with the Sunnah of the Prophet, the latter seems to be an all-englobing Norm containing both esoteric and exoteric elements. The former seems quite simply esoteric, as is evident from the Gospels and the early history of Christianity. That being so, the very character of Christianity could not but provoke all sorts of disequilibriums in the social body as time went by. After vast numbers joined the faith, they introduced the law of quantity into the Church. Incomprehension, sectarianism, heresies, dogmatic reformulations, and constant disputations over the Christological mysteries were the inevitable bitter fruits of an esoteric Way that had to be severely compromised and considerably diluted in order to become the religion of the masses.

The Islamic message, embodied in the Qur'ān and the Sunnah was an absolutely necessary reaction to the state of affairs in a Christendom that after six centuries had yet to settle down doctrinally or even socially. For instance, the thesis that the Christ had but one will, or Monotheletism, broke out in the Eastern Church in the very year of the Hijrah (622) and was espoused by the Emperor Heraclius (d. 641), whose caesaropapism in itself provoked reactions from the Western Church. This was the final Christological heresy and almost undid the entire work of the Fourth Ecumenical Council of Chalcedon (451) which had established the divine and human natures of the Christ. It was not until the Third Council of Constantinople (680) that this heresy was put down, shortly after the blockade (673-678) of the great city by the Umayyad Muslims, who were now moving into North Africa and Central Asia with the new monotheistic faith that would conquer the greater part of the known world.

Islamic responses to what was going on in the Christian world can be seen in numerous domains. The Trinitarian teachings of the Church, for example, were counterbalanced by the pure and strictly monotheistic faith of Islam. Its metaphysical and theological *tawḥīd* reaffirmed the absoluteness of the One without a second. Likewise, the one-sided Christian emphasis on the mystical Way, heavily compromised and weighted down by dogmatic and legalistic armature, was compensated for in Islam by the appearance of a Law and a Path flowing from the same revelation. If, in the Christian world, we find a growing chasm between the sacerdotal authority and the increasingly large numbers of laymen, in the Islamic faith this dichotomy was abolished by the imposition of sacerdotal functions on all believers as a matter of right. Again, there are no laymen in Islam and there is no secularist world divorced from religion. The monastic ideal of Christendom, with its cult of chastity, resulting in the desacralization of the sexual life and the denigration of marriage, was rejected by Islam. The matrimonial Sunnah of the Prophet led to the sacralization of sexuality and the exaltation of marriage. But one could go on in this fashion. Enough has been said to show that Islam has to be understood, in great part, as a kind of divine response to the state of affairs existing in Christendom that threatened to engulf the entire known world.

The entire Islamic community can not operate under purely contemplative rules, even if the Sunnah contains mystical prescriptions for a minority. Considering that tens of thousands of Arabs joined the banners of Islam in the Medinan years, we should not be surprised to find that the *ṭarīqah* of the faith applied only to a small number among the companions of the Prophet, such as ʿAlī, Salmān al-Fārisī, or the People of the Verandah (*ahl aṣ-ṣuffah*). Excluded from this inner mystical circle around the Messenger were such persons as Muʿāwiyah (d. 680), the later founder of the Umayyad Dynasty, who was initially one of the Prophet's secretaries and sometimes ranked as a companion (*ṣaḥābī*), or Abū Mūsā al-Ashʿarī (d. 657), another companion and one of the umpires at the Battle of Ṣiffīn between the Caliph ʿAlī and Muʿāwiyah. Excluded also from any connections with the contemplative Way would be the mass of believers who entered Islam in the Medinan years. That the *sharīʿah* makes its appearance then, and even takes on a rather complex religio-social nature, signifies the entrance of Islam into the domain of quantity. For the multitudes who embraced Islam in those days, the faith was devoid of any mystical or contemplative facets. It was simply a Law governing human actions. During this very period, we sense the first manifestations of tension between the exoteric and esoteric levels of the religion. But the presence of the Messenger in the midst of his community dissolved all problems and kept the synthetic vision of the message alive. But that tension was there just the same. After his death it would intrude itself into the substance of the community and finally break out, a century or so later, into the classical division of the Islamic tradition into an esoteric *ṭarīqah* and an exoteric *sharīʿah*. The former identified with Ṣūfism presided over by the Shaykhs, while the latter identified with the schools of jurisprudence (the *madhhabs*) watched over by the religious authorities, the *ʿulamāʾ*.

Exoterism in the Prophet

An argument can be made that the nature of Muḥammad's mission forced him into positions favoring the Law. The exoteric part of his message is what immediately concerned the generality of believers. Left to fend for themselves were the tiny contemplative minority, or the esoteric elect. It is true that both the Qur'ān and the Sunnah make ample provision for the mystical minds of Islam. In addition, their own discernment could be counted on to restore the proper perspective, that of the Spirit over the letter of the Law, whenever things got out of hand.

While this is no doubt true, the fact of the matter is that both the Qur'ān and the Sunnah seem to tip the balance toward the exoteric forms of the religion. The result is that the exoteric mind — for exoterism is, after all, in the mind of the believer — would be hard pressed to see anything more in the Islamic message than what is in the literal meaning of the text. This is not peculiar, of course, to the Muslims. It is a blindness widespread among the believers of all religions, but especially so among the Semitic faiths. If the Qur'ānic revelation itself takes it into account, all the more reason why the Messenger should do so in his Sunnah.

One of the immediate results of all this is that the Sunnah of the Prophet is fairly easy for the ordinary Muslim to follow. The Christ, on the other hand, is the sublime teacher of the inner life. His Sunnah is purely spiritual and only an elite can follow it. The Christ said that "The Kingdom of God is within you" (Luke 17:21), and he divulged, during his mission, the mysteries of the *ṭarīqah* ("the mysteries of the Kingdom of God" mentioned in Luke 8:10, or of "the Kingdom of Heaven", in Matthew 13:11). In the process, his nature as the Incarnation of God shone through him and was exteriorized in the innumerable miracles he performed. But all of this put him out of the reach of imitation by believers in general. The style of Muḥammad was the exact opposite. If his Sunnah was to be followed by all Muslims, mystical or not, then he had to be imitable even by the humblest of the faithful. That is what we see, and that is what gives to the Prophet an earthy nature, in contrast to the sublime character of the Christ. That earthiness of the Prophet veiled his inner spiritual life and made him an easily accessible model for his community. At the same time, it made his spiritual Sunnah something that the ordinary believers, including many of their religious authorities, do not easily perceive.

Given the Prophet's stress on the exoteric traits of the Islamic religion, it is not surprising that both he and his religion should be seen by outsiders as devoid of any depth. That is what his Western critics really have in mind when they fail to see anything mystical — or, what amounts to the same thing, spiritual — in either the Qur'ān or the Messenger. A kind of unexceptional nature is attributed to the religion that goes hand in hand with a legalized sensuality created by the Sunnah of its founder. Modernist Muslims — and even, truth to tell, the fundamentalists — are of no help at all in clarifying things. Their superficial and at times even alarmingly fragmented versions of the faith combine to give the lie to anyone affirming the spiritual depths of *tawḥīd*.

One of the historical ironies of our times is that both the Western critics of Islam and the modernist Muslims and fundamentalists are agreed that there is nothing particularly mystical in either the Qur'ān or the Messenger. Ṣūfism has therefore no place within the Islamic religion. Neither the modernist Muslims nor the fundamentalists can grasp why it is that certain Westerners are interested in the Ṣūfī Path and not in their particular versions of Islam. Of course, for the Western critics, Islamic mysticism owes its origins to non-Islamic sources, since neither Muḥammad nor any of his companions had any spiritual realization, and thus they could not have transmitted a mystical Path to later generations of Muslims. But, as was said, the Prophet's emphasis on the exoteric nature of his Sunnah leaves the door open for his eventual Western critics to disregard his inner life.

The Evaluation of Muḥammad

At the end of his mission, in the tenth year of the Hijrah, the Prophet made the Farewell Pilgrimage to Mecca. That city had been reconquered, Islam had spread to the four corners of Arabia, and hundreds of thousands, if not millions, of Arabs had rallied to his cause. In a famous sermon given on Mt. 'Arafāt outside of Mecca to a great multitude of the faithful, he summed up the beliefs and practices of the religion he had brought to them and enjoined upon them the fear of God. During that Farewell Pilgrimage, the last verse of the Qur'ān was revealed (Sūrah 5:3). It was clear to all that his mission had ended. Shortly thereafter, upon his return to Medina, he fell ill and passed away surrounded by his great companions, some of whom would become the first Caliphs of the early Islamic Empire. He was buried in Medina, and there is where his shrine, source of blessings to the believers, stands to the present day.

Since his time, throughout the Islamic world, there has been a very profound cult of love for the Prophet.[4] This, of course, in no way implies that he is worshipped as a God-Man, for the perspective of *tawḥīd* militates against the divinization of Muḥammad either in his historical or in his trans-historical spiritual reality as the Muhammadan Light (*nūr muḥammadī*). Rather, the love that the pious and knowledgeable Muslim has for the Messenger is a reverential admiration and a loving gratitude. The admiration is because of the perfections of servanthood which Muḥammad embodied in his person and which permitted him to be the recipient of the Qur'ānic revelation and the Exemplar of Islam. The gratitude of the Muslims towards him is because of the Qur'ān and the Sunnah he left behind as legacies for his community and as the instruments of salvation for the hundreds of millions, and even billions, of human souls who have followed in his footsteps for the last fifteen centuries.

The critics of Islam have often pointed to the apparently luxuriant sensuality of the founder of that religion as a kind of defect or imperfection that belies his actual sanctity as claimed by the tradition. It has to be admitted, first of all, that the pre-Islamic Arabs were indeed a people whose earthiness and sensual proclivities left their stamp on their poetry and customs and also on the Qur'ān and the Sunnah of the Prophet himself. A radiant concupiscence governed the life of those Arabs. It was an ever-present glow that could turn into an intoxicating passion by even trifling provocations. It reigned, like an implacable invisible spirit, over men and women to the same degree. Its expressions in Arabic literature, while frequently straightforward and even stunningly realistic, are ennobled, more often than not, by the beauteous qualities of the Arabic language itself. To deny the rather massive sensualism of the ancient Arabs would be quite pointless. They indulged their pleasures in "wine, women, and song", as the expression goes, with a unmeasured enthusiasm that was utterly beyond the capacity of their syncretistic pagan religion to control.

If Muḥammad had not had a sensual element in himself, a certainly earthy propensity, it is highly doubtful that he could have served as a model for his community. Even so, one must not exaggerate his sensuality. In his youth, right up to his twenty-fifth year, he was known for his chaste nature, and this at a time when his fellow Arabs were indulging themselves at every turn. He was married to Khadījah, his first wife, who remained his only wife for a quarter of a century; she would be the mother of practically all of his children. This is hardly the image of a man who shared in the licentious and incontinent habits of the Arabs in those days.

On the other hand, through his Sunnah, Muḥammad did reveal how the carnal pleasures of the married state could be integrated into the salvific framework of the Law by conditioning them with religion. It is this no doubt that gives to the Prophet and to the religion he founded a kind of sacred sensuality that restores to sexuality as such its noble nature and allows it to play a significant role in the process of sanctification. "Marriage," according to a *ḥadīth* of the Prophet, "is half of a man's religion" the other half being good character resulting from the discipline and perfection in the virtues that both spouses engage in. Accordingly, Muslim saints tend to be married men or women; Christian saints, by contrast, tend to be monks or nuns, the vow of celibacy being an almost indispensable aspect of sanctity in most of the traditional Churches of the East and the West. The fact that

Muḥammad was not only married but also polygamous after his fiftieth year means that the person conditioned by the notion that sexuality has something sinful about it, and who associates saintliness with chastity, will invariably consider the Prophet as having a blemished soul precisely because of his indulgence in the pleasures of the flesh. But in Islam that indulgence is in conformity with a sacred Law that determines its nature and is considered by the faithful to be of celestial origin.

The Prophet has also been taxed with having a vengeful and even unforgiving nature, as when he put to the sword the Jewish tribe of the Qurayẓah. But here also we must remember that, unlike his contentious and bellicose fellow Arabs, Muḥammad was known, even as a youth, as a trustworthy and just arbiter between conflicting parties. Until well into his fifties, when the Battle of Badr took place (624) — the first battle of Islam — his life was by and large that of a peacemaker. When he finally took Mecca (in 630), he could have avenged all the wrongs committed against him and his fellow Muslims by the Meccans, but instead he pardoned them all, citing as his model the Prophet Joseph towards his brothers. He was indeed rigorous, like the Prophets of the Old Testament, but showed considerable generosity and leniency throughout his mission. The betrayal of the Prophet and his community by the Qurayẓah is another matter altogether: this was a traitorous deed calling for an exemplary manifestation of justice, not for turning the other cheek.

We should not forget that the Western critics of Islam, who tend to be of the Christian faith, have been conditioned by the sublime and even dramatic life of the Christ. In comparison, the Prophet Muḥammad seems strangely ordinary and even uninspiring. Because of his indulgence in carnal joys with a number of wives, his early life as a merchant, his use of warfare in the name of religion, and his founding of a faith that seems to make numerous concessions to the passions of mankind and that requires only a rather elementary morality, the Prophet does not appear to have the same refulgent spirituality as the Christ. The dramatic death of the Christ through crucifixion, while darkness was over the land and the veil of the Temple was rent, is simply overwhelming. The death of the Prophet in the arms of his beloved wife ʻĀʻishah seems to be in keeping with the rather simple nature of the religion he established. In Islam all dramatic moments are dissolved with a fatalistic perspective that situates all persons and events in the range of the omnipotent power of the Divine Will.

The Messenger of Islam appears to be defective when seen in the light of the Christian tradition. We must not forget, however, that the Islamic tradition, while it accepts all the Messengers and Prophets as being spiritually perfect saints, nevertheless sees exterior differences and perhaps even deficiencies in some of them. The fact that the Christ never indulged in the pleasures of the flesh and that the message he brought is lacking in a sacred Law has not gone unnoticed by Islam. Quite the opposite, for the Islamic traditional teachings would have it that Jesus is the Messiah, and that when he returns at the end of time he will marry and judge according to revealed Law. In other words, the sublime asceticism of the Christ and the utter absence of a sacred Law in his spiritual message constitute two drawbacks in the eyes of the Islamic tradition which have to be done away with somehow before he can have the completeness that the Prophet of Islam has.

All of these considerations show how relative the criticisms of foreign religions and their founders can be. For the Christian, the abstinence of the Christ in sexual pleasures and the pure morality of his spiritual Path combine to suggest that the indulgence of the Prophet Muḥammad in carnal relations and the simple and undemanding morality of his sacred Law are signs of an imperfect religion. For the Muslim, the reverse is true. Because the Messenger consecrated sexuality and brought a comprehensive *sharī'ah* that covers all aspects of daily existence, something is lacking in the person of the Christ, and something is wrong in his Sunnah that will have to be put to rights in the last days when he returns as the Messiah.

It is perhaps not necessary to point out that the ascetical nature of the Christ was not an inhuman absolute. He blessed the marriage at Cana, he was often accompanied by women during his mission, not to mention his love for Mary Magdalene. An ascetical attitude is not incompatible with a love of the opposite sex, as we see in the relations between St. Paul and St. Thekla, and in the Agapetae of the early Church, who lived in spiritual love with men while remaining celibate. The life of indulgence is also not an absolute. The Prophet was continent before his first marriage at the age of twenty-five. During his mission, when he was married to a number of wives, he gave evidence of ascetical tendencies, as during his fasts and his late nightly vigils. In the history of Ṣūfism, there are numerous saints who have abstained from all carnal relations either permanently or for certain periods of time, as do all the faithful at proscribed hours during the month of Ramadan.

The question of the presence or absence of a sacred Law in a given religion is also a complex problem. A spiritual Path suffices unto itself, as we can see in the Desert Fathers of Christianity, the Buddhist monastic tradition, and indeed in all contemplative Ways, including Ṣūfism, which has absorbed certain elements of the *sharī'ah* into its structures. The Law, on the other hand, does not and can not suffice unto itself and is in need of the Path to fulfill it, as the Christ put it (Matthew 5:17). Yet, it is true that without a sacred Law a given community is subject to disequilibrium. At the same time, the formalism that is natural to the Law, when left to its own tendencies in the hands of the Pharisees, creates opposition to the Path and ends up by extinguishing the life of the Spirit ("For the letter killeth, and the Spirit giveth life").

If the traditional teaching on Muḥammad as a historical Messenger and universal Logos are unconvincing, we can always resort to the well-known words of the Christ, "By their fruits ye shall know them" (Matthew 7:20), to evaluate him.[5] The fruits of the Islamic message brought by the Prophet are there to be assessed: the thousands of saints, both men and women, who have laid claims to him for over fifteen centuries; the incredible regenerative nature of his mystical Path in century after century; the dazzling artistic and architectural achievements of Islamic civilization; the profound intellectual and spiritual writings of its great sages, among the greatest mankind has ever seen; the explosive power of its imperial dynasties, like the Ottomans and the Umayyads; its literatures in Arabic, Persian, Turkish, and other languages; the actual persistence and loving devotion to his Qur'ān and Sunnah for over a millennium and a half by hundreds of millions of souls who have sung his praises and chanted the Qur'ān he brought; and the real impoverishment that would have come over the entire world without such fruits must all be borne in mind when attempting to assess the founder of Islam.

No one, in the last fifteen centuries, can compare with him in the establishment of a religion and culture that would rule the lives of untold numbers of human beings, not only in this world, which goes without saying, but in the Hereafter. One would therefore be justified in concluding that the tradition was right all along in affirming that Muḥammad would be the last *rasūl* and that his religion would be the last message sent into this world before the coming of the Day of Judgment. Since his day, in point of fact, there has been no one who could even remotely match him in spiritual fruits nor has any religion arisen that could rival the miraculous efflorescence of the message he left behind.

III
The Nature of the Qur'ān

The Descent of the Qur'ān

In Islam, the Qur'ān is said to be a miracle (*mu'jizah*). Indeed, it is considered the greatest miracle that *Allāh* wrought through Muḥammad. There were other miracles that he manifested, both great and small, but this one is unanimously deemed to be the Word of God for his community. The miraculous nature of the Qur'ān does not lie in its grammatical or syntactical or linguistic characteristics, for these can be quite easily imitated. It is rather the Divine Presence in the Qur'ānic letters and sounds which is the "miracle" in question, and this is inimitable. That mysterious Presence within the form of the Scripture radiates graces and benedictions which are sensed by the knowledgeable and pious Muslim whenever he chants the Qur'ān or hears it chanted. Neither the worldly Muslim nor the non-Muslim can know anything about those graces, for the Qur'ān is said to open its inner meanings and benedictions only to the worthy among the faithful. Westerners who hear the Qur'ān chanted in one of the orthodox styles can of course appreciate the aesthetic shock which comes from the stately rhythm of the recitation. This does confer a kind of intuitive awareness of a certain supernatural element in the Book. Deeply pious Muslims also receive the same aesthetic waves of beauty and majesty emanating from their Scripture, but these faithful go on from there to feed on the inner dimensions of "the Miracle" that elude the outsiders.[1]

The Qur'ān is said to have descended into this world on the Night of Power (*laylatu 'l-qadr*) toward the end of the month of Ramaḍān, the ninth month of the lunar calendar. This was a "descent" (*tanzīl*) into the spiritual heart of the Prophet while he was meditating during Ramaḍān in a cave on Mounṭ Hirā', not too far from Mecca. That vertical descent of the Qur'ān was exteriorized in the piecemeal revelations which came out of him, prompted by this or that circumstance, in the course of the twenty-three-year period of his mission.

To understand all of this, we must go into the teachings on the nature of the Qur'ān. In the early generations of the religion, these teachings were fraught with weighty consequences and produced considerable tension and turmoil within the community before the light of intelligence intervened to resolve their apparent contradictions.[2] First of all, there is the celestial Qur'ān of Islamic dogma, the one said to be Uncreated (*ghayr makhlūq*). Because it is uncreated, it corresponds to the level of the Divine Reality itself. The Uncreated Qur'ān is clearly beyond all limitations, so that we cannot speak of its "letters" and "sounds" except in the sense of prototypal realities, or metaphysical essences, as the Ṣūfīs do in their writings on this particular theme relating to the Qur'ān.

Then there is the created Qur'ān, namely, the one with the "letters" and "sounds". This was exteriorized during the above-mentioned twenty-three years of Muḥammad's Prophethood and it circulates among the believers as Scripture. If the Uncreated Qur'ān is limitless, the created Qur'ān is limited, more or less as the essence of a form is limitless in comparison with the form that manifests it in a particular manner.

We have to imagine the "descent" of the Qur'ān as an emanation of the Uncreated Qur'ān from its source in *Allāh* downwards, in a vertical sense, into the heart of the Prophet. The created Qur'ān is a kind of horizontal manifestation, in the form of letters and sounds, of that limitless essence called the Uncreated Qur'ān. These are not two Qur'āns, to be sure, for the created Qur'ān is the formal crystallization of the infinite reality of the Uncreated Qur'ān. But we can, and we must, speak of two different levels of reality. There is the Divine Reality of the Uncreated Qur'ān and there is the earthly reality of the created Qur'ān. When Islamic dogma talks about the "miracle" (*mu'jizah*) of the Qur'ān, it is clearly referring to the presence of the Uncreated Qur'ān within the letters and sounds of its created form. The insistence by certain Ḥanbalī dogmatists of early and medieval Islam that the very letters and sounds of Qur'ānic Arabic were themselves "uncreated" can be understood as a confusion of planes, the uncreated and the created. The Islamic argumentation resembles, in its own way, the Christological propositions on the nature of Christ. These were finally resolved at the Council of Chalcedon (451), which declared Christ to be "true man, true God". Just as Christianity had to dispute over a long period of time over "the Word made flesh", so similarly Islam had to argue at great length over the true nature of the Qur'ān, "the Word made book".

The final solution was a combination of the two propositions on the Uncreated and created natures of the Qur'ān.

The descent of the Qur'ān from the uncreated plane of reality to the created was through the luminous ray of light of the Holy Spirit, personified by Gabriel, the Archangel of revelation and the tutor of the Prophet. The Qur'ānic revelation had spiritual, psychical, and physical consequences on the Prophet. The spiritual influences flowed from the presence of the Spirit itself within the Prophet's innermost being. This in turn affected his soul, or his psyche. His thinking, his memory, his imagination, his feelings were all suffused with the imprint of the Qur'ānic revelation. But things did not stop there, and the overflowing of the soul affected his physical nature, his very body, sometimes plunging him into an ecstatic trance which dominated him totally. The descent of the Qur'ān, in other words, was from the Spirit to the soul to the body: the Word moved down by way of his Spirit, then it spilled into his soul, and finally into his body. On one occasion, when certain verses of the Qur'ān were being revealed, the Prophet's body became so heavy that the camel he was sitting on sought vainly to support the increasing weight by adjusting its legs; by the time the revelation ceased, its belly was pressed against the earth and its legs splayed out.

Stories on the "weightiness" of the Qur'ānic Word are meant to point to the total involvement of Muḥammad in the process of revelation. Nothing of his nature was left out of the dominating influence of the Spirit. The stories also presume a purity of receptivity to the divine Word in the Prophet. Such a receptivity was possible only by virtue of his supreme sanctity and wisdom. The descent of the Qur'ān came into a pure soul without any obstacles to tarnish the radiance of revelation.

The Messenger had no control over the flow of revelation. The Qur'ān came to him independently of his will; he could neither hasten the coming of the verses (*āyāt*, pl. of *āyah*) and chapters nor postpone it. The reality of revelation was experienced by him both subjectively and objectively. Subjectively, there were all sorts of interior psychical experiences of a theurgical nature announcing the coming of a revelation, such as the tinkling of bells, voices and the like. When a particular revelation came, this was often accompanied by ecstatic states that overwhelmed him and extinguished his outer man. Even so, one cannot reduce the Qur'ānic revelations to subjective realities. Objectively, they overpowered him and were totally independent of his desires. The objective nature of the reality is clearly seen in the fact that the Qur'ānic words often address the Prophet in the second person: "You must do this," or "You must do that," and so forth. These are words stemming from a divine Source that Muḥammad knew to be utterly distinct from himself. To put things somewhat differently: they are revelations from an objective Reality which he experienced subjectively.

In the beginning, when the Qur'ānic revelations began arriving, Muḥammad had hesitations and felt anguish. But neither the hesitations nor the anguish had anything to do with his convictions; he was absolutely certain over what he knew to be true regarding God and creatures. The hesitations were over his mission to the Arabs: how was he to carry out his task among them, given the intensity of their paganism? These hesitations, uncertainties, and even anxieties, in the lives of Prophets and saints, on the eve of their missions in the world, represent no doubt their self-effacement before the immensity of their tasks. Sooner or later, after the initial qualms, Heaven rallies to their cause. This happened to Muḥammad, and from then on he was given to understand that he would never be left alone when carrying out the celestial instruction he was entrusted with. When that awareness of heavenly backing came over him, he was unwavering to the end.

The Arrangement of the Qur'ān

The bit-by-bit revelation of the Qur'ān was dependent on external circumstances which provoked the arrival of this or that verse. An incident or a particular event involving the Prophet, his companions, his wives, or even his enemies, could cause the revelation of a verse, a group of verses, or of an entire Sūrah of the Qur'ān. A vast domain of Qur'ānic studies, which delves into the "causes of revelation" (*asbāb at-tanzīl*), that is to say, the circumstances surrounding particular revelations, has been created by the religious authorities of Islam to give historical or nonhistorical explanations for the Qur'ānic verses. This is not to imply that the events or circumstances themselves are the causes of revelation, for that would be tantamount to saying it is creatures who predetermine the Divine Will. While Islam insists that the Qur'ānic revelation is of divine origin, it is understood that the creaturely circumstances which elicited this or that verse were themselves predetermined by *Allāh*. In *fine*, the revelation and the causes of revelation are ultimately reducible to celestial origins.

As the Qur'ān was revealed in this piecemeal fashion, the Prophet would indicate to his companions where to place a particular verse or Sūrah within the body of the Scripture revealed up to that point. Since the ancient Arabs had astonishing memories, a trait which their nomadic culture reinforced with its emphasis on oral literature, the retention of the Qur'ānic verses presented no problems. As a people, they were used to memorizing vast quantities of poems, tribal histories, sayings, and a host of other orally-transmitted materials. To this day, there are millions of Muslims who have memorized the entire Qur'ān or else large portions of it. The rhythmical nature of Qur'ānic prose lends itself to memorization. We have to bear in mind that the Qur'ān must be memorized to a greater or lesser extent by all Muslims to fulfill their ritual obligations. The five daily prayers, for example, cannot be recited save in sacred Arabic and only from memory while facing the *qiblah*. The Islamic religion itself gave a powerful stimulus to the natural penchant of the Arabs of those days to memorize everything. The Arabs, in their turn, communicated that same stimulus to all the non-Arab Muslims.

No other sacred Book in world history can match the Qur'ān in actual diffusion among believers or in real usage on a daily basis. It literally circulates like a kind of life-giving scriptural blood within the minds of millions of Muslims. It nourishes their thinking, in varying degrees, in an hourly fashion, so that no other people have been more "People of the Book" (*ahl al-kitāb*), as the Qur'ān would put it, than the Muslims. In the days of the Prophet, the early Muslims would recite entire portions of the Scripture as part of their ritual duties until late in the evening, following his example. This became a practice which pious Muslims in later generations would follow. Constant recitation of Qur'ānic Arabic in fulfillment of ritual obligations was one way of perpetuating its form throughout the centuries following the initial revelation.

Apart from memorization of the Scripture as it was revealed, the companions of the Prophet also had recourse to writing for the preservation of the text. A host of writing materials, from papyrus to palm leaves to leather, and so on, came to be used. But none of these Qur'āns written down by the early Muslims in Muḥammad's time has come down to us, nor would they have had any importance when weighed against the authority of oral transmission. It is the correct oral transmission of the Qur'ān that has always held the central role in the preservation of the authentic scriptural form. In every generation following Muḥammad's, we find innumerable reciters of the Qur'ān (the *qurrā'*). Great authorities among them have exercised a teaching function that perpetuates the rules and prescriptions governing their particular school of recitation. Oral transmission has a preeminence in Islam that is similar to what one finds in the other great traditions of the East, as in Hinduism, for example, that stresses the oral retention of the Vedas.

Tradition maintains that Gabriel, the Archangel in charge of revelation, would appear to the Prophet each Ramaḍān throughout the course of his mission to review the Qur'ān with him up to the latest revealed verse. The intention behind this traditional narrative is really to show that the integrity of the Scripture was not to be left in human hands, however saintly. Rather, the Qur'ānic text was entrusted to the guardianship of the Spirit at every step of the revelatory process. What this means is that, while the arrangement of the verses and Sūrahs of the Qur'ān seems to be the work of the Prophet himself, it is in reality the work of the Spirit acting through Muḥammad. That is what the imagery of Gabriel's reviewing the Qur'ān with the Prophet really points to. Seen in this light, the Qur'ān as the Word of God has not only a divine origin but also, once revealed, a divine preservation.

The arrangement of the Sūrahs, and even of the verses, does not follow the order of the successive revelations in time and space. Chronological arrangement of the scriptural text is not observed, nor was it meant to be observed. As the revelations came, the Messenger would indicate to his companions, or to his scribes, where to put the particular Sūrah or verse then revealed. In this fashion, additional verses to a particular Meccan Sūrah would be revealed in the Medinan epoch. Similarly, some of the Medinan Sūrahs have verses revealed at different times. In general, when the Sūrahs are described as being Meccan or Medinan in origin, this means that they were revealed in those cities; but in some cases this origin refers only to the predominant number of the verses.

The Written Collection of the Text

Since the Prophet had his scribes, there were written collections of the Qur'ān in his day, but they were incomplete.[3] The process of revelation went on almost to the very end of his life, so that the written versions (whether among the companions or others) could not have been definitive. When we remember that the Qur'ānic revelation is not in chronological order, we can easily perceive that no complete edition of the Qur'ān could have had general circulation before the death of Muḥammad. Some versions would have been more and some less complete than others. While this holds true for the written text, it does not hold true for the oral version. At the death of the Prophet, tens of thousands of Arabs had memorized the Qur'ān, including the last revealed verses. This should not be forgotten when reflecting on the transmission of the Qur'ānic Scripture, which at that moment in Islamic history was less a text or written reality than it was an orally transmitted revelation. True, there were written versions, but these did not have the same weight as the Qur'ān carried in the hearts of the Muslims. Nor must we think that its existence in their memories was like that of their poems, proverbs, or other varieties of their profane literature. On the contrary, the Qur'ānic verses had a sacred presence in their souls which set them apart from the worldlier kinds of Arabic prose and poetry they cultivated with enthusiasm and even with inspired eloquence from time to time.

The first written collection of the entire Qur'ān was made in the time of the Caliph Abū Bakr (d. 634), the immediate successor to the Prophet. He reigned for two years, when some of the bloodiest battles of early Islam took place, resulting in the death of innumerable Muslims who knew the

Qur'ān by heart. Fearing that the integrity of the Qur'ān might be compromised with the disappearance of so many Qurān-knowing believers, he ordered that a copy of it be made. After his death, that copy was kept in the home of Ḥafṣah (d. 665), a widow of the Prophet and daughter of the Caliph 'Umar (d. 644), the second great Caliph of the early Islamic State.

It was in 'Umar's reign that the Muslims expanded into the non-Arab world and mixed with them. The mingling of Arabs and non-Arabs affected the correct pronunciation of the Qur'ān and threatened its integrity, creating some anxiety; but nothing was done during the ten-year rule of 'Umar. By contrast, things got out of hand during the Caliphate of 'Uthmān (644-656). By this time, the Arabs were reporting too many variations and lapses from the pure speech of the Quraysh in the pronunciation of the Qur'ān by both Arabs and others. To put a stop to this decadence and eventual threat to the purity of the Qur'ānic text, the Caliph 'Uthmān ordered a commission of trusted companions to draw up the official version of the Qur'ān. This was to be done in the Quraysh style of speech, in which it was revealed. It was to be checked against the versions in the memories of other companions as well as against the written copy preserved in the custody of Ḥafṣah. This was done; official copies were sent out to the provinces with the understanding that this Quraysh version henceforth was to be the unique standard for the Qur'ānic text everywhere, and since 'Uthmān's day the Muslim world has had only one version of the Qur'ān.

The 'Uthmānic recension was really the diffusion of the same Qur'ānic text as found in Ḥafṣah's copy, which had been compiled by the Caliph Abū Bakr in accordance with the completed revelation left behind by the Prophet at the time of his death. 'Uthmān's version, in other words, is the same as the version revealed to the Prophet. 'Uthmān neither added to the Qur'ānic revelation nor took anything away. In his recension of the Qur'ān, he was motivated precisely by the desire to preserve the original revelation exactly as it was and to put an end to the incorrect pronunciations and grammatical or lexical variations that were cropping into the sacred text in his day. The 'Uthmānic recension of the Qur'ān is not properly speaking a recension in the sense that, out of several variations, he chose the one which seemed, critically speaking, the best of all. There was no critical evaluation of the Qur'ānic materials available in his time which would help the committee of companions compose a new Qur'ān more or less in agreement with what they thought the Prophet left behind. Quite the contrary, there was a revealed Qur'ān, which the Caliph 'Uthmān and thousands of other Arabs, including the members of the committee, all knew. This Qur'ān agreed with the written Qur'ān in the possession of the Prophet's widow Ḥafṣah. What 'Uthmān and his committee did was simply to make sure, through long investigations, that they were not in error on any point regarding the Qur'ān they knew by heart and which conformed to what others knew by heart also. Once their investigations confirmed this unanimity, they made sure that the Quraysh form of the Qur'ān would prevail over the entire community. It is this which constitutes the "recension" of 'Uthmān.

The Recitations of the Qur'ān

While the work of 'Uthmān eliminated the mispronunciations and other errors which had crept into Qur'ānic recitation, it did not impose a unique chanting style, or a special mode of reciting the Qur'ān, on the entire community.[4] During his lifetime, the Messenger had permitted variations in chanting styles. These continued after his death and even after the 'Uthmānic recension of the Qur'ān. They became the bases on which the different Qur'ānic schools of chanting could be distinguished from one another. Eventually, as time went by, the diverse styles of Qur'ānic recitation, with complicated rules for pronouncing the vowels and consonants of the Book, not to mention other phonetic laws governing words and sentences, were reduced to seven. At the present day, these seven chanting styles (*qirā'āt*, pl. of *qirā'ah*), all of which go back to the Prophet himself for their validation, are recognized as the traditional correct ways in which the Muslim may recite the Qur'ān as a source of grace. The idea behind this is that the Qur'ān cannot be recited or chanted in just any way one chooses, but that one must follow the orthodox patterns of recitation. This liturgical chanting of the Qur'ān must not be confused with reading or meditating on the Scripture nor with the ritual use of the Qur'ān for the prescribed five daily prayers or for other rites. The chanting of the Qur'ān is of course a ritual in the sense that it is a sacred act. But it is independent of the Five Pillars of Islam and is a kind of superogatory deed that transmits special graces and benedictions coming from the sacramental quality of the Qur'ānic letters and sounds. It is to this liturgical chanting of the Qur'ān that the seven chanting styles refer. It is true, nevertheless, that many Muslims, even in the performance of their five daily ritual prayers, employ a style of reciting Qur'ānic Sūrahs which resembles the chanting or psalmodizing of the Christian Scripture.

One must not confuse these chanting styles with the variant readings of the received text that the Prophet permitted in his day to make the Quraysh Arabic more palatable or less foreign to some of the Arab tribes whose dialects were distinct from the Quraysh speech. These variant readings tended, by the very nature of things, to fall by the wayside as Islam moved through history. They were preserved in learned works as relics of earlier usage by some of the Arab tribes. They represented concessions made by the Prophet to tribal speech differences by way of rendering the Qur'ān more in keeping with accustomed ways of speaking and comprehension.

With the 'Uthmānic recension, a considerable blow was given to these variant readings. It is obviously their existence in the provinces and their usage among some of the companions themselves in the distant centers of Islam that made for a certain strong reaction when the 'Uthmānic Qur'ān was imposed as the definitive version for the community as a whole.

The Qur'ān and the Christ

The Muslim world has always had the same Book from its beginnings down to the present day. There is no other canonical text of divine origin in the Islamic religion: the Qur'ān alone is the revealed Book from cover to cover. This contrasts with the New Testament, which does not originate with the Christ but comes after his time. It is not uniformly a "revelation" (*waḥy*) in the Islamic sense of a direct manifestation of the Divine Will in the form of a saving message. It is instead both "revelation" and even less than that, or "inspiration" (*ilhām*), which is an indirect and less authoritative scriptural text. We can find the latter in some of the Pauline epistles, when St. Paul speaks on his own authority. The fluctuating nature of the New Testament does not infringe upon its celestial contents, for it remains a sacred scriptural work. But it does permit us to contrast its heterogeneous provenance with the homogeneous nature of the Qur'ān. The uniqueness of the Qur'ān for the Islamic community, its sacramental role within that world, are in contrast with the diversity of Christian Scriptures, both canonical and noncanonical. It has a function similar to the central role played by the Christ in the Christian world, for his presence is perpetuated by the Eucharistic sacrament. The spiritual nature of the Qur'ān is that of the Word made manifest, like the Christ. But the New Testament does not have a sacramental reality, for it is a kind of scriptural afterthought. Within the Christian world, it is secondary to the Divinity of Jesus; but, in the world of Islam, Muḥammad is secondary to the Divine Presence within the Qur'ān.

The contrast between Islamic and Christian scriptures is also to be found in their liturgical languages. On the one hand there is the Arabic of the Qur'ān, which is invariable and the same for the entire Islamic world, while on the other hand there are the diverse liturgical languages of the Christian religion, from Latin to Greek to Syriac to Slavonic. None of the scriptural languages is in the Aramaic or Hebrew used by Jesus. The sacred Arabic of the Qur'ān is the language in which the revelation took place. It is in this language that the ritual obligations of Islam are carried out by Muslims of the most diverse ethnic origins. The sacramentality of the Qur'ān is seen precisely in this sacred Arabic, which is the vehicle for the Divine Presence. The letters and sounds of the visible and audible Scripture ("the created Qur'ān") are the supports for the Uncreated Qur'ān of celestial nature.

What could be most contrastive between the two religions than the fact that the Word in Islam is a Book whereas in Christianity it is a Person? Mystical esoterism in Islam, which is Ṣūfism, speaks of the spiritual reality of Muḥammad as the Word itself, the Muḥammadan Logos intermediate between God and man. This sounds somewhat like the mystical view of the Christ as Word of God. But that is an esoteric interpretation of the Logos which has little pertinency outside the mystical or contemplative life of the religion. Even so, the Muḥammadan Logos, unlike the Christ as Word, is never given divine status, for *Allāh* has no associates or peers who share in the divine nature. Consequently, the Qur'ān as verbal crystallization of the Word is really the equivalent in Islam of the person of Jesus in Christianity. Since the Word is a Book in Islam, the arts in that religion revolve around nonrepresentational, calligraphic reproductions of Qur'ānic verses. In Christianity the iconography centers around the Person of the Word, Jesus Christ; hence the representational nature of its arts, that give to the Saviour a human imagery.

Holy Statements and the Qur'ān

We should bear in mind that the Qur'ān represents a kind of "divine speech" coming through Gabriel to the Prophet, but that it is not the only such transcendent speech in Islam. Tradition attributes to the Prophet thousands of statements (*aḥādīth*, pl. of *ḥadīth*) which he made on his own authority. These, while they are inspired, represent his own words. Several hundred of these "statements" are not really from him; they are instead words originating with the Divinity and spoken through him. Because of that exceptional character, they are called "holy statements" (*aḥadīth qudsiyyah*).[5] Dealing for the most part with the mystical or spiritual life of the believer, they belong to the esoteric or Ṣūfī teachings of the faith more than to the exoteric. Muslim authorities distinguish between these "holy statements" and the Qur'ān by observing that ritual prayers can be performed only with the Qur'ānic text, not with the *aḥadīth qudsiyyah*. They also say that before physically handling the Qur'ān one must be in a state of ritual purification, whereas such is not the case when handling a collection of these *aḥadīth*. Their object in making these contrasts is to establish a kind of objective distinction which would isolate the Qur'ān from any association with similarly revealed words transmitted through the Messenger. The exact number of these "holy statements" has never been determined; they can be found in the canonical collections of the *ḥadīth*-literature as well as in other, equally authoritative works. But their existence proves that there is more in the Islamic concept of "revelation" (*waḥy*) than first meets the eye.

Qur'ānic Commentaries

As in other religions, Islam developed an extensive exegetical literature (*tafsīr*) on the Qur'ān.[6] Every single consonant and vowel, every word and sentence, has been examined and explained from different angles, now historical and grammatical, now mystical and theological, and so on. The range of the exegetical literature on the Qur'ān is quite vast. Every current of thought in the traditional Muslim world wanted to base its principles or fundamental notions on the Book. Given the synthetic nature of the Qur'ān revelation, it is easy to discern gnostic, theological, cosmological, and spiritual contents to the sacred text that would be developed into more intricate systems of thought by particular exegetical schools.

The commentaries can be divided into esoteric or exoteric, with some partaking of both aspects of the Islamic tradition. The exoteric commentaries, like those of aṭ-Ṭabarī (d. 923) and al-Bayḍāwī (d. 1286), explain the verses with a view to reconstructing the circumstances that caused them to be revealed in the first place. They add whatever is necessary to a grammatical or linguistic understanding of the text, sometimes going rather deeply into the etymological ramifications of words.

The esoteric commentaries, like that of Ibn al-'Arabī (d. 1240), are generally from the Ṣūfīs, who are concerned with giving spiritual interpretations of the text and who seldom linger on the external, literary significations.[7] These are not arbitrary mystical explanations which would do away with the literal meaning of the Qur'ān. The rule in Ṣūfism is that the literal text should remain intact, superimposing on it loftier significations connected with the inner life of the Spirit; the esoteric commentary would then give it a depth of meaning that had not been initially apparent. The esoteric commentary adds nothing to the text in an artificial fashion; it merely explains the interior dimension or profound spiritual content that was already there from the beginning.

Even so, because of the technical terminology used by the Ṣūfis, their commentaries remain in circulation mostly among those Muslims interested in the contemplative or mystical life. To be sure, all Ṣūfī works are really exegetical observations on the verses of the Qur'ān. Some of these works, like the popular treatises of al-Muhāsibī (d. 857) and al-Ghazālī (d. 1111), are really expositions of Qur'ānic verses strung together to form coherent books that are read by great numbers of the faithful. So it can be said that Ṣūfi explanations of the Word are not always confined to the mystically inclined. But Ṣūfī commentaries, especially those technical in nature, do not have the force of authority in the community at large as do the commentaries penned by the eminent authorities of exoteric Islam. This is understandable, given that such commentators, by their very exoterism, embody in their writings a kind of inspired norm for the generality of believers. The faithful look to these commentaries for the definitive explanations of the Qur'ānic verses. For their part, these authorities transmit a mass of materials that the tradition has passed on from generation to generation. In the case of the aforementioned aṭ-Ṭabari, the tedious recitation of facts and details can thwart a reader's efforts to make his way through his commentary from cover to cover. This is not so for such inspired commentaries as that of al-Bayḍāwi, who richly deserves the praise he has gained over the centuries for his intelligent handling of the traditional data.

There is a considerable chasm between a purely exoteric explanation of a Qur'ānic verse and an esoteric one. With the former, we reamin imprisoned within the literal signification of the text, wondering if there is anything else beyond the straightforward meaning of the words. With the latter, we fly in a spiritual sense, for we leave the verbal forms and enter the world of essences through the symbolism intrinsic to the words of the Qur'ān. But one must not think that such mystical or anagogic interpretations of the Word are subject to whimsical movements of the mind. There are rules and objective principles that enter into the authoritative Ṣūfi glosses on the Sacred Text. The criteria for these more spiritual commentaries on the Qur'ān are obviously very subtle and cannot, as a result, be accessible to everyone. It is precisely because their principles of interpretation repose on spiritual realities that the orthodoxy of Ṣūfi commentaries is much more difficult to grasp. They are all the more easy to reject as unorthodox, accommodative, farfetched, and the like if the evaluation of a Ṣūfi commentary is made by a person of an exoteric disposition of mind. In that case the tradition is reduced to the level of his understanding, which is more or less fundamentalist or literalist, and therefore limited.

Apart from these two levels of interpretation, the esoteric or spiritual and the exoteric or dogmatico-theological, numerous other approaches to the Word exist in Islam. Schools of numerology have arisen that employ the numerical values of the letters, words, and sentences of the Book to arrive at different conclusions, mostly of a cosmological nature. Divinatory and even theurgical practices associated with the Sūrahs and verses of the Qur'ān exist also. In all epochs the faithful have resorted to them for healing sicknesses, both physical and mental, for removing states of distress and anguish, and for peering into the future. There are hermetic interpretations, employing the symbolism of astrology and alchemy, which delve into the cosmogonic and cosmographic aspects of the universe, combining the Semitic contents of the Qur'ān with the formulations of Greek wisdom in a harmonious synthetic manner, for both the Greeks and the ancient Arabs shared in a relatively common cosmos.

Whatever the value of these special approaches to Qur'ānic hermeneutics, they are secondary in relation to the exegetical works of the

Ṣūfīs and of the doctors of the Law, or the *'ulamā'*. It is the great commentators throughout the ages who have kept the traditional teachings of Islam alive, whether they are the mystical teachers of Ṣūfism or the religious scholars of exoteric disciplines.

The Qur'ān by itself does not fully divulge its meaning. It has both literal and symbolic verses; it presupposes a considerable awareness of the laws of Arabic grammar and rhetoric; and it seems deliberately vague and somewhat imprecise and even contradictory on a number of occasions.

The first hermeneutical remarks on the verses of the Qur'ān come from the Prophet Muḥammad himself and are contained in the *ḥadīth*-literature. In his own day, it was necessary to spell out some of the hidden or implicit meanings of the Book, which would not have been necessary if merely knowing Arabic were sufficient to grasp the contents of the Qur'ān. After him, the exegetical remarks of the companions play an important role. Such companions as 'Alī ibn Abī Ṭālib (d. 661), and others, transmitted orally a wealth of materials of a hermeneutical character, for they knew the inner dimensions of the text at first hand. Later generations would develop more specific interpretations of the Qur'ānic revelation. In the eighth and ninth centuries, we see the rise of the esoteric and exoteric schools of exegesis, which we can recognize historically as the early period of Ṣūfism, representing the Path, and of Ḥanbalism, Shāfi'ism, Mālikism, and Ḥanafism, representing the Law. They are the two fundamental dimensions of the Islamic revelation, the ones that would govern the outlook of the community for well over a thousand years thereafter.

Fundamental Teaching of the Qur'ān

The essential thesis of the Qur'ān is of course the affirmation of the Oneness of the Divinity, *Allāh*. His transcendence and immanence are particularly evident in the famous Ninety-Nine "Most-Beautiful Names" (*al-asmā' al-ḥusnā*) of God that are scattered throughout the sacred Book and constantly repeated in numerous verses. The Divine Unity, or *Tawḥīd*, is inculcated into the reader's mind through the diverse accounts of the Prophets and Messengers, particularly of the Abrahamic line, found in Sūrah after Sūrah. From the time of Adam on to the days of Muḥammad, the Prophets and Messengers have only one function, namely, to preach *Tawḥīd* to their respective communities. The Qur'ān pictures the lot of those communities who live in keeping with *Tawḥīd* as coming under the dispensation of Divine Mercifulness. Those communities who fall away from *Tawḥīd* come under the rigorous, punitive measures of the Divine Wrathfulness. Mercifulness is particularly evident in the periods of revelation, as in the days of Abraham, Moses, Jesus, and Muḥammad. Wrathfulness comes into view at the cataclysmic upheavals and the cosmic perturbations that accompany the end of a decadent people, when they are punished for their sins and especially for their "associationism" (*shirk*), the very opposite of *Tawḥīd*. Divine Wrathfulness is especially evident in the last days of all humanity, the end of the world, when the Day of Judgment terminates the force of the ancestral Fall and ushers in the definitive posthumous states of existence in the Heavens and Hells.

The Qur'ān stresses, as a corollary to *Tawḥīd*, the remembrance of *Allāh* (*dhikr*). *Tawḥīd* stands in need of a method of actualizing it in one's life, a spiritual method that will permit one to remember the Divine Presence as often as possible in the course of one's life. Thus, *dhikr* encompasses all those practices that dissolve the fallen state of man, his *ghaflah*, and that restore in him the grateful remembrance of *Allāh*. Among those practices, going from ritual prayer to meditation, the one most aptly termed *dhikr* by the Qur'ān itself is the discipline of invoking one of the Ninety-Nine "Most-Beautiful Names" of the Divinity both orally and mentally. The Divine Names of *Allāh*, being sacred, exercise a sacramental influence on the soul of the believer. They burn out of him the tendencies towards *ghaflah*, which are at the bottom of all rebellion and sin. They allow his primordial or Edenic nature (*al-fiṭrah*), veiled by the effects of forgetfulness, to come once again to the surface of his mind, bringing with it the peace and graces and wisdom that lie hidden under the strata of fallen human nature.

Allāh in the Qur'ān

As with the other scriptures of the world, the Qur'ān speaks of certain central themes: God, the Heavens and the Hells, and Man. There are other concepts also, such as Eschatology, but these can all be subsumed under one or another of the central notions. Scripture must speak about the Absolute, in this case *Allāh*, because the process of decline and decadence blurs man's view of the real nature of the Divinity. The same *glaflah* that produces wrong thoughts about God also reduces man's moral vision of the consequences of his acts in a posthumous sense. The meaning of life is distorted through the aberrations of passion and ill-conceived deeds. Accordingly, Scripture speaks of the Heavens and Hells awaiting those who either live in keeping with the Spirit or who choose not to do so. Finally, Scripture has to mention Man: what he is, why he is here, where he came from, and where he is going. *Ghaflah* tends likewise to force man to live more and more in the superficial facets of his being and to ignore the spiritual life altogether.

The Qur'ān does not have a developed, abstract metaphysical doctrine on the nature of the Absolute similar to the highly intellectual propositions we find imbedded in such Hindu scriptures as the Upanishads. Nor does it have a theological system comparable to what can be found in the New Testament. But it does have germinal principles that, later on, would give rise to metaphysical and cosmological notions. In any case, the nature of the Divinity, or of *Allāh*, is essentially depicted in the Qur'ān through the medium of the Ninety-Nine Names, such as the Merciful, the Living, the Wise, the Creator, the One, the Most-Holy, the Guide, and the Light. From such Divine Names, there emerges the description of *Allāh* as having both an impersonal divine nature as well as a personal one. *Allāh* is an impersonal essence in an undifferentiated sense, and He is the personal Lord of the Universe in a differentiated way. However, most of the Names are applicable to the personal Divinity.

Like other scriptures, the Qur'ān uses a spatial symbolism to describe the relationship between *Allāh* and His Creation. When the text speaks of God as being transcendent, it says He is "beyond the Universe" and hence beyond or outside of the ephemeral and transient world, for *Allāh* is Eternal and not subject to the change and flux of the cosmos. This is the Transcendence or Incomparability (*tanzīh*) of *Allāh*, for nothing in the impermanent world can be compared to Him. To say that the Divinity is beyond or outside of the world is not really to localize God so much as it is to indicate that He is Immutable and not involved in the impermanency of created things.

If Transcendence were the only teaching of the Qur'ān with respect to *Allāh*, the inevitable result would be the desacralization of the world, for there would be God "up there", so to speak, and the world "down here", with a chasm between the two which would be unbridgeable. Muslim theologians come fairly close at times, in their eagerness to skirt any possibility of having God pantheistically involved in the flux of created things, to declaring the doctrine of *tanzīh* to be the unique teaching of the Qur'ān. In their minds, there is a cautious and prudent resolve not to allow the generality of believers to fall into error by bringing God into the world, and even into themselves.

But Transcendence is not the only Qur'ān doctrine. There is also Immanence or Comparability (*tashbīh*), so that things in this world are comparable to the nature of *Allāh*. For example, the light we find here is comparable to the Light in Him, and so on. His Light is reflected in earthly light; they are comparable because of the identity of essence between them, even though they are different in their respective planes of reality. From this perspective, God is "in" or "inside" the world, not beyond or outside it. If He is in the world, then there is symbolism or comparability, for His near Presence cannot but manifest itself in creatures. The proximity of *Allāh*, who is the Hearing and the Seeing and who, according to the Qur'ān, is closer to man than his jugular vein, refers to His being within the world and therefore within man.

Ṣūfism tends to have a doctrine based more on the Immanence of *Allāh* than on His Transcendence. With the former, the Divine Reality is accessible to man, for the Divine Presence is within him; with the latter, there is a certain distance and inaccessibilty to God. Immanence does not mean that the Divinity is caught up with the impermanence of the world or that it is localized "within" the world. The two aspects of *Allāh* go together and are mutually corrective. Two of the Ninety-Nine Names are the Interior (*al-bāṭin*) and the Exterior (*aẓ-ẓāhir*), which have numerous possible interpretations undoubtedly, but they can also refer to the Immanence and Transcendence of *Allāh* respectively.

The traditional arrangement of the Names into Names of Essence and Names of Quality or Attribute is but another manner of describing the total nature of *Allāh*. This becomes even more evident when one realizes that the Names of Quality are themselves divisible into two categories, the Names of Majesty, which are masculine and wrathful, and the Names of Beauty, which are feminine and merciful. From this one may conclude that the divine nature of *Allāh*, as far as the undifferentiated Oneness is concerned, transcends the dualistic polarity of the Names of Attribute, while at the same time taking on a prototypal Masculinity and Femininity towards the Creation in the Names of Majesty and Beauty.

There is thus no reason to reduce the divine character to an ultimate masculine principle, or even to an ultimate feminine principle. *Allāh* transcends both, while at the same time appearing as both on a more extrinsic plane. In the Qur'ān, if the pronominal references to God are nevertheless masculine, and not feminine, or not masculine and feminine on alternate occasions, this is perhaps a perpetuation of biblical usage as found among the Abrahamic traditions of Judaism and Christianity. Since Islam sees itself as a remanifestation of the Abrahamic desert-like faith, which was patriarchal and not matriarchal, the religion bequeathed by Muḥammad to his community is necessarily patriarchal through scriptural injunction. That patriarchal nature in turn is based on a metaphysical reality in God, namely, the masculine reality of the Divinity, which of course does not exclude the feminine.

The Qur'ānic revelation enjoins upon the faithful to address the Absolute through the use of the Divine Masculinity manifested in the aforementioned pronominal forms. It does not sanction addressing God through the use of the Divine Femininity, as we see in certain forms of Hinduism. Accordingly, it is not the patriarchal tribal institutions of the ancient Arabs that imposed a masculine interpretation of God; it is rather that God has a prototypal masculine nature that reflected itself in the patriarchal systems of the Abrahamic people. These included the Arabs, however decadent they might have been at the time of the revelation, when the masculine references to *Allāh* were imposed upon them as the prescribed ways of addressing God.

There is God on the one hand and then there is the Creation on the other, the two being quite distinct in the Qur'ān and yet not absolutely cut off from one another. As was said, *Allāh* transcends His Creation and yet is within it, preserving it, guiding it, and watching over His work, at every instant. As the Creator, He brought the world into being out of nothingness, which is the Islamic and the Judeo-Christian teaching. All three religions are anxious to preserve intact the liberty of God to create the world without being forced by necessity to do so. Creationism, or the emergence of the world out of nothingness, and not emanationism, which is the emergence of the world out of the Divinity through necessity, as the Greeks taught, is therefore the Qur'ānic view on the origin of things. At least this is apparently the case on a first look at the text; but, as was previously noted, the fact that certain Ṣūfī sages, under the influence of Neoplatonic notions, have seen no contradiction in interpreting the Qur'ānic cosmogony along creationist and emanationist lines simultaneously seems to suggest that the last work on the verses of the Book dealing with the origin of the universe is not strictly creationist in an absolute sense.

Heavens and Hells

The second of the several previously mentioned central themes in the Qur'ān has to do with the Heavens and Hells. These are cosmic realities independent of man's terrestrial plane of existence, though no doubt not hermetically sealed off from his earthly life. They represent states awaiting him in the Hereafter, and even here and now he establishes a causal relationship with them that is decisive at the hour of death. Like other scriptures, the Qur'ān draws attention in manifold ways to the effects of man's behavior in this world upon his life beyond the grave.

Since the Heavens and Hells described by the Qur'ānan are situated in definite cosmic spheres within the vast, all-englobing sphere of the Creation, we must take a look at the structure of that Creation. We see that the created world is an immense Cosmos containing concentric spheres within it, and that the whole resembles the cosmography of the ancient Semites, with the result that there is nothing particularly novel in the Islamic universe. It is a seven-tiered system rising up from the Earth, which is the central point of reference. The perspective is geocentric; and as one moves vertically upwards one penetrates the different Heavens, arriving finally at the Divine Throne. All of this is represented visibly by the stellar bodies moving in their appropriate spheres within the heavenly vault and culminating in the Empyrean of fixed stars wherein is the divine abode. The cosmology of the Qur'ān, both regarding cosmogony and cosmography, is conceptually simple at first glance but extremely complicated when seen fully developed. It has the apparent simplicity of a diamond as well as the complexity of the multifaceted colors and lights of a diamond when examined from all angles. The *ḥadīth*-literature brings out even more the intricacy of the Islamic Cosmos; later on, when Greek, Persian, and other elements are brought into the picture, an additional increase in detail results. But the essential, germinal Qur'ānic notions remain intact nevertheless.

The loftier, upward levels of the universe are the spiritual abodes of the souls who gain salvation and of the angelic and archangelic realities. We can speak of them as being the Paradises wherein the beatific vision of God is the ultimate reward of the saved. Between the Earth, wherein man dwells, and those celestial spiritual regions, there are other supra-terrestrial domains, subtle, invisible, and having within them animated entities or powers, known by the Qur'ān as the Jinns, that are both good and evil. They must not be confused with the angelic powers or intelligences higher up in the spiritual domains.

The same multitiered system is used for depicting the lower regions of the Universe, the Hells. Starting once again from the Earth, one must now move vertically downwards. It is in the various strata of these lower worlds that one finds the souls suffering from the pains of damnation. Infernal spirits, the devils of different sorts, and Satan, who is the personification of rebellion and subversion abide therein. In the more detailed descriptions of these regions which one finds in the later periods of Islamic history, the Hells are peopled by human souls inhabiting different abodes of perdition and by a vast array of devils or demons in accordance with a complex system of hierarchy centered on Satan. That hierarchy mirrors in a subversive manner the hierarchy of God, the angelic hosts, the Paradises and their inhabitants.

The Heavens and Hells of the Qur'ān are depicted with a concrete and even sensual imagery that must not be taken literally. They are interpreted as actual places by the mass of the faithful, and perhaps this has been the inevitable consequence of the imagery itself. The paradisal gardens of Eden, the Houris, the chaste mates, the goblets of gold, the fruits and drinks, the cool shades, the flowing rivers, the fountains, the carpets and cushions and thrones, are some of the images for the Heavens. The blazing fire, the boiling water, the shades of dark smoke, the garments of fire, the maces of iron, the roasting skins, the liquid pitch, the bitter food, the marching in chains, are some of the images for the Hells. To say that these are nothing but symbols of the posthumous worlds, beatific or infernal, is not to explain them away. In these invisible worlds, or in these conditions of being, there are realities that no doubt correspond to the concrete things just mentioned. These are images that seek to picture the Hereafter in sufficiently strong enough colors to awaken in the believer a yearning for the celestial regions and a repugnance for the infernal ones. The contrasts between the Heavens and Hells are sharp and are meant to reach the imagination of the faithful and pull them out of the spiritual lethargy produced by forgetfulness. The terrifying descriptions of Hell should block the downward movement of the soul and force it to redirect its will upwards toward Heaven, which is described with attractive colors. That is the way the imagery works in periods of spiritual awareness and rebirth; in periods of decline and stagnation, the imagery is obviously inoperative and perhaps even implausible to the worldly-minded Muslim.

Man as Vicegerent of God on Earth

The final theme of the Qur'ān is that of Man, who is called the vicegerent (*khalīfah*) of God on earth because of his central or axial nature in relation to the animal, plant, and mineral kingdoms. His centrality comes from the consciousness that his Spirit has of the Oneness of the Divinity. Out of all the creatures in this world, he alone has the possibility of consciously knowing and loving *Allāh* directly and concretely, not simply theoretically and mentally. His primordial nature (*al-fiṭrah*) is that of an unveiled Spirit that radiates wisdom and sanctity throughout his soul and body. That seems to have been his state before the Fall. The veiling of the Spirit by the layers of ignorance is not an absolute and irredeemable condition. Revelations "descend" into the world with methods for unveiling the inner Spirit. The unveiling is sufficient at least to permit salvation at the hour of death for the faithful. In the case of the saintly mystics, the unveiling can go quite far, even unto union with God, as the Ṣūfīs would say.

Man's centrality has cosmic reverberations on the world around him, depending on his spiritual state, which may be good or bad. The Qur'ān describes chastisements inflicted on entire communities, great or small, as a result of their departure from revealed norms. They were overwhelmed by cosmic perturbations and cataclysms of one kind or another. The Day of Judgment is unique in the sense that whereas previous chastisements, apart from the Fall, the Dispersion of mankind, and the Deluge, seemed to have been confined to particular communities and not to have enveloped mankind as a whole, the Day of Judgment encompasses all mankind. The entire earthly plane of existence then goes through the transmutative fire of universal purification.

Such are the general themes of the Qur'ān. The stories of the Prophets and Messengers, the moral lessons, the descriptions of the Edenic paradise, the eschatological accounts of the end of the world, the innumerable verses dealing with social, economic, matrimonial, military, political, and ritual matters, are all meant to supplement these basic themes. The Qur'ān presupposes that its germinal principles and ideas will be given greater amplification in the future commentaries, and that is indeed what we find upon examining the traditional hermeneutical literature of the faith.

Translations

The polyvalent resonances and meanings contained in the sacred Arabic of the Qur'ān are things which cannot be translated.[8] Given the particular Semitic nature of Arabic, the translation of the Qur'ān into a European tongue necessarily leaves out those rich associations of meanings intrinsic to Qur'ānic Arabic words. All translations are said to be betrayals. This is doubly so for translations of the Qur'ān; most of them are rather flat and platitudinous, even when they are more or less faithful to the literal meaning of the Scripture. This is due precisely to the absence of those resonances or associations of ideas that the Arabic text would produce in the mind of the Muslim who is at home in his religion.[9]

Westerners are not normally drawn to the Qur'ān in translation, whereas they might be drawn to the *Bhagavad Gita* when translated from the Sanskrit, or to a sermon of the Buddha when translated from the Sanskrit or to a sermon of the Buddha when translated from the Pali Canon. The reason for this is simple enough. Both the Sanskrit of the *Gita* and the Pali of the Buddha's sermon are Aryan languages. They are still within the thought patterns of the Westerners' own Indo-European world, which has a mental style of its own, quite distinct from the patterns of Arab thought, which derive from the Semitic world, and even from a nomadic form of Semitic culture. The Westerner expects a well-ordered, sequentially-arranged text with chapters and verses marshalled in such a fashion that there is a kind of logical movement having a beginning, middle, and end. But that is not what he finds in the Qur'ān. Quite the contrary, the sacred text is without any logical order at all and moves like the Bedouins in the desert within repetitious and monotonous circles. It is like the endless arabesques and geometrical motifs decorating the walls of a mosque. There is neither rhyme nor reason to the structure of the Sūrahs and verses. Frequent discontinuities and abrupt changes in subject matter are the general rule, not the exception. The whole is a faithful reproduction of the Arab soul at its noblest and most forceful; we see similar traits in the poetry and prose of pre-Islamic Arabs. Thus the Qur'ān mirrors the ethnic qualities of the Arabs of those days, as it had to do if it were to be an effective instrument of revelation. So long as one understands this, there is no reason to decry the apparent limitations of all translations of the Qur'ān.

The Arabic Qur'ān

In Arabic, the Qur'ān is completely different, particularly when it is chanted in one of the traditional styles. Then the beauty and majesty of the sacred text come through in the rhythmical intonations of the chanting. The latter opens up the receptive soul to the *barakah* ("grace") of the Book or to the aesthetic radiance of the Qur'ān. Even if one does not understand the words at all, there nevertheless seems to be a kind of spiritual magic in the scriptural recitations that can be felt by both insiders and outsiders to the faith.

The Qur'ān is divided into one hundred and fourteen Sūrahs of decreasing length, so that the shorter ones are towards the end of the book. Each of the Sūrahs begins with the *basmalah* ("In the Name of God, the Compassionate, the Merciful"), with the exception of the ninth, said to be really a continuation of the previous Sūrah. Since the Sūrahs are of unequal length, the number of verses varies from Sūrah to Sūrah, the total number being, according to one school of recitation, six thousand two hundred and thirty-six in all. Because the Qur'ān is meant to be recited ritually, it has been divided into thirty sections of equal length, allowing the reciter to finish it in a month, or into seven sections, enabling him to finish the book in one week. For all of these recitational details the usual Qur'ān has a number of signs indicating not only the section number but also, with the body of the text, all manner of abbreviations and punctuational indications that show the reader how to render the proper liturgical recitation. The professional Qur'ānic chanters know the entire text by heart together with all of the innumerable rules governing their particular school of recitation.

Ritual recitation is done in sacred Arabic, according to the tradition, and this is binding on all Muslims, be they Chinese, Turks, Arabs, Persians, Africans, or others. One must not confuse sacred Arabic, which is really classical Arabic in scriptural form, with the Arab dialects of the present day. The latter are all equally removed from Qur'ānic Arabic. Nor should that Qur'ānic Arabic be confused with literary Arabic, as if somehow that type of written Arabic also partook of the sacredess of Scripture. It is the Arabic of the Qur'ān that is sacred, not Arabic in general. Because the revelation came in the form of a book it is this particular Arabic Book that is the foundation of the Islamic tradition, not Arabic as such.

While Arabic partakes of the prestigious quality of Qur'ānic Arabic, its usage as a universal literary vehicle for the Muslim world gradually diminished after the early centuries of Islam. Other languages arose in different parts of the Islamic world that eclipsed the literary exclusivity of Arabic. After the tenth century, Persian arose; later on, Turkish would emerge as yet another vehicle for Islamic expression. These three, Arabic,

Persian, and Turkish, are the principal literary expressions for the Islamic world. Nevertheless, in all three of these cultures, the Qur'ān was central to their way of life, as we can see in the magistral beauty of the *Mathnawī* of Jalāl ad-Dīn Rūmī, the great Persian Ṣūfī poet of the thirteenth century, whose work has been called a sort of Persian Qur'ān.

Because the Qur'ān must be recited in Arabic, Qur'ānic schools for children arose in the days of the Prophet to teach them the text by memorization. These schools have continued down to our own times. One can actually be illiterate and yet know the Qur'ān by heart, for one memorizes the sounds of the Scripture. Generally, however, in these schools for children, some reading and writing is also taught. It is at an early age that Muslims begin assimilating the Qur'ān. Many go on to learn the entire text from beginning to end until it forms part and parcel of their mental substance. Muslims think Qur'ānically, a trait especially evident among the pious and intelligent believers. In the daily life of the faithful, Qur'ānic verses are constantly being recited in the ritual prayers, in the liturgical chanting of the Scripture, and in the give-and-take of social activities and conversations, particularly in those milieus where religiosity is rather strong and perfectly well understood. But even among profane and impious Muslims, one is always surprised at the occasional Qur'ānic phrases they give vent to, even almost in spite of themselves, as if the force of the religious culture was too strong for them to arrest in themselves.

Interpretations of the Present Day

Unlike the Bible in the contemporary Christian world, the Qur'ān remains to the present day uncontested in the community.[10] No one would dream of applying to the Qur'ān the same "higher criticism" that Westerners gave to their Bible in the nineteenth century. This reduced the authority of the Bible for vast numbers of cultivated people, and in some cases even abolished all belief in its inspired nature. There is no similar "critique" of the sacred text in Islam. To find within the Christian world an attitude comparable to that of the Muslims toward their Scripture, one would have to go back a couple of centuries or so in Western history. Then the mass of Westerners still had a homogeneous faith in the Word of God. Afterwards came the rise of modern secularist civilization, with its plethora of conflicting ideologies. The Christian religious culture of the past then gradually disappeared from the scene, taking with it that unquestioning faith in the integrity of the Bible. Today, only certain Christian fundamentalist Churches which accept the inerrancy and infallibility of the Bible would be comparable to what one finds throughout the world of Islam.

Even when the process of Westernization has gone quite far in particular regions of the Islamic world, the Scripture remains unquestioned. This is largely because Western critiques of the Qur'ān are often seen as so many affirmations of Western "imperialism" of a cultural kind, which seeks to undermine Islamic culture and subjugate the Muslims to Western values. But these are simply defensive reactions, mostly emotional, sometimes even contradictory. Moreover, even supposing that these reactions were valid, the fact of the matter is that Islam is in real need of reexamining itself in the light of the Qur'ānic teachings of a traditional character.

Modernist interpretations of the Qur'ān are all alike in rejecting or ignoring the traditional ones and in upholding different Western notions on evolutionism, or republicanism, or Marxism, or feminism, or scientism, or socialism, or progressivism, or some other thesis drawn from modern Western civilization. The West produces such notions with a frequency that betrays the unsettled and unsettling nature of modern man's mind. In the hands of such modernists, the Qur'ān can be twisted to say almost anything they want. This in itself proves the infinite protective value of the traditional exegetical literature. While those commentaries of the past might have had different levels of depth and application, they never betrayed the integrity of the scriptural Word.

One would have thought that the contemporary fundamentalist Muslims' interpretation of the Qur'ān would represent a considerable improvement over the modernists' view of the sacred text. In fact, the fundamentalists of the present day are not at all like their counterparts in Islam's Middle Ages. The latter lived in a traditional world, a civilization with its own intellectual and spiritual teachings which were reflected in the philosophical, theological, and mystical doctrines of the religion. It was a homogeneous cultural matrix that affected the fundamentalists of those days, including the Ḥanbalīs who tended not to like any speculative interpretation of the Qur'ānic text at all and fought everyone engaging in such interpretations. But the Islamic *Weltanschauung* of those times pervaded everyone's mind, including the thinking of those who wanted no particular speculation on the *āyāt* of the Qur'ān that called for some kind of rational grasp.

Things have changed as a result of the collapse of that old traditional civilization. The modern Western world has brought its ideas, its constantly-changing ideological systems, and its secularistic values to the Muslim world. A fundamentalist of the present day is quite different in mental formation from his medieval counterpart. He lacks the understanding of the traditional Islamic doctrines, to begin with. Even when he is exposed to them, he sees them in the light of the different thought systems of Western origin floating about in the collective soul of the present-day Muslim world. Where he is close to the traditional Muslim intellectual is in his dependence on the literal meaning of the Scripture. The great sages of the past also had to start from the literal or self-evident meaning of the verses before they went on to the anagogical exegesis they had in view.

What is needed in the Islamic world today is a greater comprehension of the traditional teachings, from the metaphysical to the philosophical to the theological to the cosmological, and so on. Many of those hermeneutical efforts of the past lie buried in unedited manuscripts. The scholastic intellectual terminology of Islam is no longer current among the cultivated layers of society, and is instead confined to a very small minority. The vicious cycle of fighting Western notions with more Western notions in recent generations had made the intellectual heritage of the community seem almost like a buried treasure. And yet it is only in that legacy of the past that Islam can hope to find its regenerative impulses.

Traditional interpretations of the Qur'ān of the present day can be found in the different Ṣūfī orders, particularly the ones which are spiritually alive and have authentic teachers. Here one finds the perennial exegesis without betrayal; it reappears in all of its spiritual and intellectual depth and totality. But this is an esoteric hermeneutics that is not easily penetrated by the outsider and especially the modernist or fundamentalist Muslim of the present time, whose premises are often quite distinct from the traditional exegetes of Islam. There is a marked reluctance in the modernists, whose fundamental orientation of thought is derived from one or another of the contemporary Western schools, to look into the legacy of the traditional Islamic culture of the past. The fundamentalists, for their part, like the Salafīs of Egypt and elsewhere, merely cling to the surface meanings of the text. Their minds are colored likewise by the Western modes of thinking that enter into their passive psyches by the implacable ubiquity of the modern world.

Only the traditional spiritual exegetes of the contemporary Islamic world offer intellectual continuity with the perennial Qur'ānic hermeneutics. Fortunately, many of the traditional commentaries on the Qur'ān have been reprinted in recent times. These perpetuate the all-important gnostic, theological, and philosophical works of early and medieval Islam. Likewise, one sees a general effort nowadays to rediscover the actual traditional heritage of the community. Ṣūfī intellectuals should take a much more visible role in explaining to their fellow Muslims the contents of the Qur'ān in terms they can understand without violating the spiritual tradition of the community. Otherwise, the interpretation of the Qur'ān will fall more and more into the hands of the modernists and fundamentalists. The former have no regard for the depths and heights of the tradition; the latter have little regard for anything beyond the literal meaning of the sacred text.

In previous epochs of decline, Ṣūfī spiritual and intellectual exegetes furnished the interpretations of the Scripture that went beyond the purely literal meanings. They thereby met the needs of those Muslims who knew there was more to the Qur'ān than meets the eye. With the passage of time, and the increasing complexity of the intellectual heritage of Islam, Ṣūfī interpretations became in their turn quite complicated, even amazingly so. The rather imposing hermeneutical edifice of Ibn al-'Arabī (d. 1240), who is known as *ash-shaykh al-akbar* ("The Most-Great Master"), is definitive in its interlacing unification of the metaphysical, cosmological, theological, spiritual, juridical, and psychological doctrines of the traditional Islamic world. No other author before or after him in Islam can match the Andalusian sage in volume and quality of production. Just as the *Summa Theologica* of Saint Thomas (d. 1274) represents a definitive intellectual formulation of the Western Christian teachings, so the great works of the *shaykh al-akbar* are definitive for the intellectual tradition of Islam. The Muslim world should not be content with repeating what that eminent Ṣūfī had to say. A tradition recognizes spiritual originality and requires only that one not betray the universal truths imbedded in the revelation. This already casts a veil of suspicion over the modernists' and fundamentalists' exegetical efforts. The present-day exegetes faithful to their heritage should bring out the spiritual implications of the Qur'ān for their fellow Muslims and even readapt the traditional scholastic terminology in such a way that it can be understood once again with clarity.

The rediscovery of the spiritual interpretation of the Qur'ān alone can awaken either the first stirrings of the contemplative life or an understanding of the traditional teachings of religion. That understanding would be sufficient to enable Muslims to handle the modern world around them — and inside their minds — with a certain immunity to its spiritually lethal emanations.

The Scripture of a people is what gives meaning to their earthly existence. In the traditional civilization of the past, the Muslims watched over their Book to make sure that its expositors held fast to the precious legacy transmitted to them by pious ancestors. The ideas of modern man, such as those on progress and secularism, had not yet eaten into the spiritual fabric of the culture. In the past, everyone was more or less protected by the surrounding traditional civilization. It radiated its glories in the arts and architecture, in the political and military fields, in the societal manifestations of Islam, and in the lives of their saintly contemporaries, both men and women. This is no longer the case. Because it is not, the spiritual interpretation of the Qur'ān is needed yet once again. To be effective that spiritual exegesis has to be within the traditional doctrinal framework. Otherwise it will go the way of the modernists and fundamentalists of recent times, some of whose works already seem dated and meaningless and in any case have no bearing on the real spiritual malaise which has descended on *dār al-islām* like the night.

IV
The Spiritual Path of Ṣūfism

Ṣūfism is the spiritual Path (*ṭarīqah*) of Islam and has been identified with it for well over a thousand years. It must not be confused with any of the sectarian movements of religion in either the Sunni or *Shī'ī* world. On the contrary, it is comtemplative in nature and goes beyond sectarian beliefs. It has been called ''Islamic mysticism'' by Western scholars because of its resemblance to Christian and other forms of mysticism elsewhere. Unlike Christian mysticism, however, Ṣūfism is a continuous historical and even institutionalized phenomenon in the Muslim world that has had millions of adherents down to the present day. Indeed, if we look over the Muslim world, there is hardly a region that does not have Ṣūfī orders still functioning there. Even in the Russian communist empire of Central Asia, and in spite of the repressive measures against the Islamic communities, we find great numbers of the faithful belonging to one or another of the Ṣūfī orders under the direction of their teachers or guides in the Way. The Ṣūfī meeting-place (*zāwiyah* in Arabic, *khānaqāh* in Persian), where the master holds forth with his disciples, still exists all over the Muslim world. Throughout its long history in the midst of the Islamic community, Ṣūfism has influenced the spiritual life of the religion to an extraordinary degree; there is no important domain in the civilization of Islam that has remained unaffected by it. Caliphs, sultans, great religious scholars, philosophers, theologians, architects, poets and men of letters in general, to say nothing of the other classes of society, have all been drawn to the Ṣūfī way of life. Suffice it to say that Ṣūfism considers itself as the very heart of the Islamic religion, not as something peripheral or accidental to the vitality of the faith. To understand this, we have to grasp the nature of the spiritual esoterism of Islam. In other words, to appreciate the function of Ṣūfism in Islam, we really must distinguish between the esoteric and exoteric dimensions of religion.

Esoterism and Exoterism

Ṣūfism sees itself as the spiritual essence of the Islamic religion.[1] It is concerned primarily with the mystical contents of the Qur'ān and the Sunnah of the Prophet, which are the two foundations of the Islamic faith. All religions, of course, have a mystical message addressed to a small minority of believers who are spiritually inclined by nature, and in Islam these are the Ṣūfīs. As a result, the revelation of Islam as well as the Sunnah of the Prophet are subject to two dimensions of understanding, the esoteric mystical way and the exoteric religious way. The former is confined to a contemplative minority who come from all walks of life; the latter embraces the great mass of believers and their religious authorities.[2]

Revelation, whether it be the Qur'ān, the Bible, or the Vedas of Hinduism, contains these two levels of understanding because it is addressed to a community of believers of greater or lesser discernment. These two ways of looking at revelation are really two ways of looking at religion, for a religion such as Judaism or Islam or Hinduism proceeds from an initial revelation which establishes the new faith in the world. Since the Ṣūfī mystic is concerned with the spiritual realization of the truths ofthe Path in this life, he will see in the revealed Scripture and in the Sunnah of the Messenger those teachings and practices that lead to the love and knowledge of the Divinity. He will consider this love and knowledge of God to be the very summit, or even the very heart, of religion, all other views being less profound, or exoteric by comparison. In other words, his is the contemplative life which seeks to contemplate God through the spiritual vision resulting from union with the Divinity.

To reach that union, the person of mystical or esoteric tendencies is prepared to submit himself to the guidance of a teacher, the Shaykh of the Ṣūfī Path. That teacher is respected and followed because as the real master he is considered to have experienced in himself the truth of the mystical way he teaches to others. Before his realization, he himself had been guided by his own Shaykh, and so on back to the founder of the Islamic religion, the Prophet Muḥammad, who established the spiritual Path in his religion. Founders of religion, in fact, embody in themselves the esoteric (*bāṭinī*) and exoteric (*ẓāhirī*) aspects of their religion. Thus, the esoteric or mystical way of Ṣūfism derives its validation from the Messenger himself. It was Muḥammad who furnished the teachings and practices that the later masters of the Path would readapt to changed circumstances as the religion moved through the corridors of history and underwent vicissitudes of all kinds. Indeed, the principal doctrine of Islam, or *Tawḥīd*, is the fundamental teaching of the Ṣūfī Path in one form or another. And the essential practice of Islam, that of *dhikr*, or the remembrance of God that dissolves the forgetfulness of fallen man, is likewise the characteristic method of spiritual concentration in Ṣūfī.

Not everyone in Islam seeks the contemplation of God here and now as do the Ṣūfī mystics. But everyone must engage in action, including the mystics. For that reason, the exoteric facet of the Islamic faith is concerned primarily with the commandments and prohibitions controlling human action. It is, after all, through the rules governing good deeds of all sorts that the believer merits the posthumous Paradises and it is through the nonobservance of those rules that the impious are threatened with the posthumous Hells. In principle, the contemplation of God should be for all men, but in practice this is simply not the case because the majority of believers are not at all drawn to it. Yet no one can abstain from action, not even for a moment. Everyone, contemplative or not, must therefore engage in action, which means that everyone is under the reign of the Law, or should be, while in this world, for the Law (*sharī'ah*) contains the principles of action. Observance of the Law, in view of salvation at the hour of death through entrance into Paradise, is the goal that exoteric Islam has set for itself. Salvation (*najāh*), understood as the beatific state in the Hereafter, is the aim of the Law. It is that goal which confers meaning to the believer's actions while he is still in this world. Without the prescriptions of the sacred Law, the believer would not know quite how to go about obtaining that posthumous state of felicity called salvation.

The Ṣūfī mystical perception of the contents of revelation is spiritually deeper than that of the exoteric faith. This follows from the fact that the contemplative mind of the Ṣūfī esoterist is not restricted to the letter of the Qur'ān, to its literal meaning. He discerns far more in the words of the Qur'ān than does the ordinary believer, the exoterists. When the scriptural text says that *Allāh* is the "light" of the heavens and the earth (Sūrah 24:35), the conventional religious authorities and the great mass of believers will not perceive immediately that this has any bearing on themselves or even that there is a relationship between the Divine Light of God and the physical light of the stellar regions or of the sun and the moon. By contrast, the mystically-minded person will discern that the divine Light in the spiritual heavens is the same Light found within his own heart. That heart can be opened or "unveiled" by the teachings and methods of the Ṣūfī Path. He will know that, because of the Fall, the "eye of the heart" (*'ayn al-qalb*), which is really the Spirit within him, has been veiled by ignorance and forgetfulness in his soul. Under the guidance of his Shaykh, he can burn away the veils of ignorance through self-purification, which results from the techniques of concentration he has learned from the master. When those veils are removed, the inner Light radiates throughout the soul of the Ṣūfī adept, sanctifying him and preparing him for union with *Allāh*, source of the Divine Light.

A revelation such as the Qur'ān cannot be reduced either to its esoteric or exoteric meanings, for the two can be found, as was said, in the Messenger who brought the religion to begin with. But the generality of believers do not operate on both planes, as do the mystics. For the majority of believers, and this includes their religious leaders, neither the Qur'ān nor the Prophet has anything mystical or esoteric that they could discern with spontaneous ease. On the contrary, they tend to reduce the Scripture and the Prophet to their level of comprehension and to reject whatever goes beyond that. Nevertheless, Ṣūfism does not seem to maintain that the limitations of the exoteric comprehension of either the Qur'ān or the Messenger are permanent and ineradicable in all persons. Rather, they affirm that such limitations might only be temporary and eradicable in some persons. A mystical argument unperceived previously by a believer might, upon awareness, have the effect of effacing the mental blocks to his understanding of the deeper nature of the Qur'ān and the Prophet. If that purification of the mind continues long enough in him, a whole new dimension — the esoteric, in fact — is discerned by him in the Islamic message and even in the entire world around him which he had not known formerly. Since the conventional forms of religion are exoteric and therefore limited, only the mystical or esoteric perspective can bring out the total scriptural truth. As a matter of fact, only the mystical teaching can reconcile both the exoteric and the esoteric way of looking at things, something that exoterism could not do without lethal consequences for its own perspective.

We can say of Ṣūfī mysticism that it is the esoteric interpretation of Scripture because it insists on the spiritual symbolism that goes unheeded in the usual literal interpretations of exoteric Islam. Yet the two complement one another even though they are not on a plane of equality. By virtue of its contemplative nature, Ṣūfism is superior to ordinary religiosity based on action. All traditions are agreed that the contemplative life is superior to the active life. At the same time, the esoteric dimension of revelation is clearly superior to the mere literal interpretation of the text. It includes that meaning as the point of departure for deeper, spiritual interpretations, which only Ṣūfī esoterism can extract from the Scripture.

Ṣūfī mysticism is likewise synonymous with spirituality because the mystic is looking for the perfect love and knowledge of God through spiritual realization. The spiritual domain has to do with the Spirit and its operations in the soul of man or in things. Certainly one can be spiritual without having the mystic's desire for union with God. But since the perfection of the spiritual life lies in that knowledge and love of God, one might conclude that the Ṣūfī mystic seeks the fullest spiritual life in this world. It is in this sense that the Ṣūfī Path (*ṭarīqah*) can be defined as the total spiritual life of Islam.

Within Ṣūfī mysticism, as in other religions, we see different approaches to God. To the extent that the Path is governed by the knowledge of God (*ma'rifah*, "gnosis"), we can speak of intellectual or even of philosophical mysticism. In Islam, the previously-mentioned Ibn al-'Arabī (d. 1240), the great Ṣūfī of Andalusia, is a good example of this type of gnostic mystical sage. In the Western world, the intellectual mystic is exemplified by Plato and Plotinus among the ancient Greeks, and Origen, Clement of Alexandria, and Meister Eckhart in Christendom. They were all characterized by a certain intellectual discernment that did not, of course, exclude the love of the Divinity, but that defined man more in terms of intelligence than in terms of his devotional attitudes.

The other varieties of mysticism, both in Islam and in other religions, revolve around nonintellectual, devotional ways of approaching the Divine Reality. They are not gnostic in nature, but they do have the love of God as their first consideration. Gnosis does of course integrate the attitudes of love into its discipline. In Ṣūfism, *ma'rifah* presupposes that the individual has cultivated all of those virtues having to do with reverential respect for the Divinity or with the love of God. Without those virtues, there can be no *ma'rifah*, which is why the Ṣūfī masters have written numerous manuals describing the virtues that the person bent on mystical realization must have. Because *ma'rifah* is the fundamental goal of the *ṭarīqah*, it gives a certain gnostic coloration even to those Ṣūfī who are primarily God-lovers. It is even possible that most of the mystics of Islam, as in other faiths, follow a way of love more than a way of knowledge.

Because it deals with spirituality in all of its depth, the *ṭarīqah* of Ṣū ufism is the purest form of Islamic esoterism. But lesser forms of esoterism exist also, especially in Shī'ism and in some of the cosmological schools of thought. However, they do not have the universality of Ṣūfism. Rather, they occupy a domain somewhere between the pure esoterism of gnosis and the exoterism of the Islamic Law, its *sharī'ah*. In reality, the exoterism of Islam is that *sharī'ah* and the theological dogmas that go with it. Throughout the centuries, the overwhelming number of Muslims have been governed by the dogmatic beliefs, the ritual observances, and the moral legislation found in the *sharī'ah* and its accompanying theological propositions.

We must understand that the *sharī'ah* of Islam, like the *ṭarīqah*, is also based on the Qur'ān and the Sunnah of the Prophet. The difference between the two is that the *ṭarīqah*, as was said earlier on, perceives the mystical contents of the Islamic message while the *sharī'ah* is concerned only with the commandments and prohibitions of the faith. Both aspects of Islam have their own institutional authorities. The Ṣūfī Shaykhs are the guides or masters and they exercise a spiritual authority in their particular orders. The authorities of the *sharī'ah*, the *'ulamā'*, exercise a religious leadership within their lands. No single, overall religious authority for the entire Islamic world, comparable to the Vatican in Rome for Catholicism, exists anywhere in Islam. Instead, one finds throughout the long centuries of the faith that the orthodox tradition is upheld by an ensemble of like-minded teachers, and they are either esoteric or exoteric, or both at the same time, like the great Ṣūfī of Baghdad, 'Abd al-Qādir al-Jīlānī (d.1166).

From time to time conflicts between the two domains have broken out as a result of the incomprehension or the hostility of the *'ulamā'* and the provocative remarks or deeds of the Ṣūfīs. Saintly Ṣūfīs have always had a great following among the people at large, who have been drawn to their charismatic natures. But while Ṣūfī teachers have often had *'ulamā'* among their disciples, the general rule has been that the religious scholars have kept their distance from the Shaykhs and their followers. Nevertheless, the tradition has always recognized the legitimacy of Ṣūfism as representing the spiritual message of the Islamic revelation, and eminent religious authorities in different epochs have maintained this recognition.

The division of labor between the Ṣūfī Shaykhs and the religious leaders with respect to the Islamic revelation has been due to the fact that the contemplative life in Islam has always been independent of the *'ulamā'* from the very beginning. That independence contrasts with the historical development of mysticism in Christendom, where the mystical sages have been subjected to the authority of the official Church from the early days of Christianity. The very notion that a spiritual master could function independently of the Church hierarchy and ecclesiastical control or that such a master alone has sole authority on the life of the Spirit in man is foreign to the mentality of the Western Roman Catholic Church. Only in the Eastern Orthodox Church, especially in its mystical tradition called Hesychasm, which has had its own institutions, doctrines, and masters for centuries on end, can we discern anything similar to the Ṣūfī institutions of Islam. The image of the *staretz*, or the spiritual guide, in the Russian Church recalls the image of the Shaykh in the Ṣūfī tradition. Therefore, the monastic institutions of the Western Church in recent centuries are not comparable either to the Hesychastic tradition of the Eastern Church or to the Ṣūfī institutions precisely because they lack the doctrines, the methods of spiritual concentration, and the all-important chain of masters which all integral and authentic spiritual Paths have always had.

The Origins of Ṣūfism

The mission of Muḥammad was that of a Messenger (*rasūl*) and Prophet (*nabī*) and presupposes perfect wisdom and sanctity in him. But because he was a Messenger, he could not have been concerned exclusively with the esoteric Path, for he also had an exoteric message for the generality of his followers. Later on, the Ṣūfīs would look back on the Prophet as the first "Universal Man" (*al-insān al-kāmil*) of Islam. However, he is in a class by himself as Prophet and Messenger, and the same can be said of his companions, who had special functions in the apostolic generation of the tradition. Even the followers (*tābi'ūn*), such as al-Ḥasan al-Baṣrī (d. 728), or the early 'Alid Imāms up to and including the eminent Imām Ja'far aṣ-Ṣādiq (d. 765), seem to have played important roles in transmitting what the companions received from the Prophet. Accordingly, from the Prophet to the companions to the followers, we do not discern a predominantly mystical or esoteric bent in any one of them. Even 'Alī (d. 661), the legendary and charismatic companion of the Prophet, has an exoteric-esoteric mixture in the sermons, letters, and poems attributed to him that reinforce the notion that the roles of the early leaders of Islam addressed the entire community — not just the mystics or just the believers. Only with the passage of time, and especially after the generation of the followers had left the scene, do we begin to notice a gradually increasing separation of the two domains of Islam, the Path and the Law. The original eso-exoteric symbiosis of Islam bifurcated more and more in the early eighth century. Already, in the days of the Sixth Imam, Ja'far aṣ-Ṣādiq (d. 765), we hear of the term "Ṣūfī" for the first time among the ascetics and devotees of early Islam.[2]

Ṣūfism seems to have surfaced as a term synonymous with the *ṭarīqah* of Islam in the eighth and ninth centuries. The word "Ṣūfī" was used to refer to the person who was attached to Ṣūfism, which was known as *taṣawwuf*, a word meaning "to put on a woolen garment", but which came to mean "to adhere to esoterism". While numerous other terms were used to designate those who followed the Path, the Ṣūfī as such was the one who had reached the end of the Path of sanctification and was a sage, a saintly man. Once the term Ṣūfī and the like appeared historically on the scene to identify the follower of the Path, Ṣūfism and *ṭarīqah* became synonymous thereafter. In that critical period of Islam, a number of causes converged to allow for the identification of Ṣūfism and *ṭarīqah*.

In the first place, while the Path had existed from the time of the Prophet up to its assimilation with Ṣūfism, its gnostic core was not easily discernible among the innumerable ascetics and devotees of the time who belonged to the different sects. Most of them were not interested in gnosis as such, but they were interested in their asceticism and devotional life. Indeed, they made asceticism and the devotional life the very nature of the spiritual life. Consequently, the initiatic Path, with its gnostic goal, was hidden in the midst of these ascetics. They generally wore garments made out of wool (*ṣūf*) and held themselves aloof from the rich, spoiled, and decadent high society of the cities of the Muslim world, whose sumptuous garments betrayed the loss of the primitive simplicity of early Islam over a century before. White, woolen garments had been used by the Prophet and his companions and were associated with the earlier Prophets. In wearing them, the ascetics were maintaining the example (Sunnah) of the Messenger of Islam. At some point after the middle of the eighth century, the followers of the integral Path of gnosis came to be associated with woolen garments. This was not just simply in the sense of wearing them like the ascetics of the epoch but in the sense of actually being related to wool, which is precisely what the simple meaning of Ṣūfī is (''someone related to wool''). The extended meaning of the term, of course, denotes the follower of the *ṭarīqah* and even the saint who has reached the end of the realizational Path. From then on, as was said, Ṣūfism and its related terms came to be applied exclusively to the seekers of *ma'rifah*. Since they insisted that this was indeed the integral Path bequeathed by the Prophet to his community, in contrast to the way of the ascetics that was devoid of gnostic goals, Ṣūfism and the Path coincided.

Secondly, Ṣūfism arose to denote the esoteric Path precisely at the time that the different schools of the exoteric Law arose. They began to call themselves by different names, such as Ḥanbalī, Mālikī, or Ḥanafī, and to develop into permanent currents of jurisprudential thought within Islam. Attached to them were the early dogmatic formulations of the theologians on the Essence and Attributes of God, predestination and free will, or the nature of the Qur'ān. The exoteric aspect of Islam soon grew into a body of teachings, practices, and moral legislation, all under the watchful control of the *'ulamā'*. The rise of Islamic exoterism in an institutionalized fashion provoked the rise of Ṣūfī esoterism, with its own Shaykhs, its own practices, and eventually its own institutions. From that very period on down to our times, we will find the two levels of authority in operation throughout the Muslim world, the Ṣūfī Shaykhs and the *'ulamā'*.

Thirdly, the historical evolution of Shī'ism probably played a role in the appearance of Ṣūfism on the Islamic scene. During the first century or so of Islam, the first six Imāms of the Shī'īs (from the Imām 'Alī to the Imām Ja'far aṣ-Ṣadiq) were among the great authorities of early Islam. They are also claimed by the Sunnī world as members of their own tradition; and the later Ṣūfīs claim them too. Neither the Sunnī nor the Ṣūfī authorities refer to the Imāms as having vital roles to play within Islam because of their importance to Shī'ism. On the contrary, they tend to ignore their Shī'ī connections. The fact that the 'Alid Im̄ms are the most important descendants of the Prophet in the first century or more of Islam is something that gives added prestige to their mission within the community. But it was the esoteric role of the early Imāms within Shī'ī circles that probably contributed another reason for Ṣūfism to make its case public. The Shī'īs were beginning to develop theological ideas about their Imāms that had a semimystical ring about them and which generated a cult of love toward the Imāms that we do not find in Sunnism. It was necessary for Ṣūfism to make quite certain to everyone that what was happening in the Shī'ī world toward its Imāms had nothing to do with the *ṭarīqah* and could therefore be ignored or even refuted. Indeed, after the eighth century, the remaining Imāms of Twelver Shī'ism (so named because of its twelve Imāms) no longer have the universal function of the early Imāms and tend to preside solely over the Shī'ī world.

Finally, Ṣūfism had to arise if only to permit the masters of the Path to affirm their independence of the doctors of the Law. Had they not done so, then the *'ulamā'* would have succeeded in imposing themselves as the unique arbiters of things Islamic. In that case, the Islamic religion would have reduplicated the same monopolistic tendencies we find in the official hierarchy of early Christianity; the latter had crushed all movements that attempted to go beyond its magisterium. A number of valid Christian gnostic teachings were thereby eradicated on the score that they belonged to the suspected heretical domain of Gnosticism. From that time on, the Church was always on its guard against any gnostic leanings among its mystics. In the Muslim world, no such effective monopoly over the contents of revelation was permitted the *'ulamā'* by the Ṣūfīs. Often, the Ṣūfīs speak of the exoteric authorities (*'ulamā' aẓ-ẓāhir*) as having a limited view of the Scripture because they tend to reject the symbolic content of revelation, or the spiritual realities imbedded in the words of the text. The limitation of exoterism is thus in the mind of the exoterist. The Ṣūfīs are saying something like this: Only the *ṭarīqah* confers a universal spiritual perception of Scripture; through the vision of the Spirit, the sage can penetrate into the inner realities of the Qur'ān and the Sunnah of the Prophet. This is tantamount to saying that the limitations intrinsic to the guardians of the Law cannot but influence their view of things. Whatever might be their piety, their virtuous dispositions, their religious erudition, and their noble aspirations, the religious authorities of Islam have a constricted vision of the Islamic message.

Conflict and Reconciliation

In the eighth century, there was no hostility between the partisans of the Law and those of the Path. Nothing scandalous came from such God-loving saints as Rābi'at al-'Adawiyyah or contemplative sages like Dāwūd at-Tā'ī or Ma'rūf al-Karkhī. Their version of the Path was not too far removed from the norms established by the numerous ascetics of the day. But after the collapse of the Umayyad Dynasty and the rise of the 'Abbāsid, the religious leaders themselves began to feel their way into the institutional structures of the State. They now had access to the power and authority of the rulers.

It is during the ninth century that the *'ulamā'* showed an increasing antagonism toward the Ṣūfī Way and its adherents. Admittedly, some of the early Ṣūfīs acted in a manner that was bound to provoke reactions, and perhaps they did so deliberately, more or less like a bull in a china closet. Probably this was the Ṣūfīs' way of showing their independence of the religious authorities. By deliberately provoking their ire, the Ṣūfīs revealed a combative side to the Path that caught their opponents off guard.

First attempts at reconciliation between the Law and the Path now come to the fore in the works of al-Muḥasibī (d. 857) and al-Ḥakīm at-Tirmidhī (d. 892). They represent the more sober schools of Ṣūfism in contrast to the ecstatic expressions of such Ṣūfīs as Abū Yazīd al-Basṭāmī (d. 874) and others, who tended to shock everyone by their remarks and behavior. But those ninth-century efforts at reconciliation would be short-lived. The simmering hostility of the *'ulamā'* against the followers of the Path finally broke out with great violence and brutality at the end of the ninth and in the beginning of the tenth century with the case of the martyred mystic, al-Ḥallāj (d. 922).[4]

His ecstatic expression, *ana 'l-ḥaqq* ("I am the Truth," or by extension, "I am God"), brought the full force of the Law down on his head. Other deeds and words had issued from him over the years. The religious council of Baghdad accused him of blasphemy. He had been persecuted for years by all the religious leaders acting in unison in hopes of breaking once and for all the Ṣūfī tendencies to escape the control of the religious authorities. He was imprisoned, maltreated, and finally strung on the gibbet in Baghdad for his blasphemous, or seemingly blasphemous, words, which resemble those of the Christ ("I am the Way, the Truth, and the Life"). But, far from having broken the back of Ṣūfism, the sacrificial death of al-Ḥallāj served rather to shock everyone into a reevaluation of Islam itself.

Once again, the task of reconciliation was assumed by a saintly Ṣūfī of the tenth century, Abu Ṭalib al-Makkī, the author of *Qūt al-Qulūb* (*The Nourishment of Hearts*). That work would remain popular in pious circles down to recent times. It would be used extensively by the famous reformer and sage, al-Ghazālī, the eleventh-century Ṣūfī whose own work of reconciliation between the Path and the Law, *Iḥyā' 'Ulūm ad-Dīn* (*The Revival of the Religious Disciplines*), would become the best-known of all the reconciliations and perhaps the most important one. It spelled out in simple language and in well-organized volumes the two dimensions of Islam, the Path and the Law. Direct, mystical knowledge of God was preached in the work as the very summit of the Islamic life. While al-Ghazālī was not the first to show the compatibility between the Path and the Law, his work is a masterful presentation of the totality of the Islamic religion. Other authors in later centuries would also write books on the *sharī'ah* and the *ṭarīqah*, but his work would always be held as constituting a landmark in the relations between the Law and the Path.[5]

Ṣūfī Institutions

In the early centuries of Islam, none of the great Ṣūfī orders (*ṭuruq*, pl. of *ṭarīqah*) of later times existed.[6] Instead there were limited circles of Ṣūfī Shaykhs and their disciples, and these small communities would perpetuate themselves for several generations, gradually fading into other Ṣūfī circles or else dying out altogether. The Shaykh of a community would sit in a corner (*zāwiyah* literally means "corner") somewhere — his home, a cave, a mosque, or a fortress — with his disciples seated around him in circles. That was done in imitation of the Prophet and was part of his Sunnah; so it was not peculiar to Ṣūfism. The religious teachers also sat in the midst of circles when imparting lessons in their homes or in mosques. Later, as time went by, an institutional structure peculiar to Ṣūfism appeared. This was the official-looking *zāwiyah* (the *khānaqāh* of Persian Ṣūfism) which was exclusively for the Ṣūfī master and his disciples. Some of them became imposing and even luxurious buildings in medieval Islam, housing armies of Ṣūfī adherents. They were not, of course, the only places where one could find Ṣūfī teachers and their followers; but they did represent the integration of Ṣūfism into the social fabric of Islam. When the great Sunnī chiefs of State, like the sultans or Caliphs of the eleventh century, began to champion orthodox Islam, they built numerous religious schools (or *madrasahs*) for instruction in the disciplines of the *sharī'ah*, and *khānaqāhs* for promoting the cause of Ṣūfism. The Saljūq Turks, for example, and the Ayyūbid sultans of Egypt saw to it that both institutions were constructed in their domains.

The *madrasahs* and the *khānaqāhs* became the centers for learning the two dimensions of orthodox Islam, the exoteric and the esoteric. Inevitably, with the rise of magnificent Ṣūfī meeting-houses supported by the State and containing facilities for great numbers of Ṣūfī initiates (*fuqarā'*, pl. of *faqīr*, "poor man", or "initiate"), a certain worldliness set in, more or less as in the rich monasteries of medieval Europe at the time. For that reason, we often find the real Shaykhs of the Path holding forth in private *zāwiyahs*, away from the State-supported institutions.

Every land sooner or later developed its own *zāwiyahs* of all shapes and sizes, official or private. Those that were sponsored by the State had Ṣūfī Shaykhs who were officially appointed to them. In the elaborate protocol developed in the medieval courts and which lasted down to recent times in the Ottoman Empire, the Shaykhs were given special titles, special salutations, special robes, and were headed by the "Shaykh of the Shaykhs". He represented his colleagues before the rulers and the other officials of the State. Many of the rulers of Islam had their own Ṣūfī teachers to whom they showed reverential attitudes of respect and admiration.

It goes without saying that among these innumerable Shaykhs, few could be taken as being authentic teachers of the Path. The price of the institutional acceptance of Ṣūfism by Islamic society was precisely the presence in the Muslim world of *khānaqāhs* and *zāwiyahs* that were not spiritually vibrant. There were also vast armies of wandering dervishes who were not all authentic seekers of the Path. On the other hand, there were *khānaqāhs* and *zāwiyahs* that were alive with real teachers, and among the wandering dervishes there were, to be sure, saintly persons and genuine seekers of the Path. Around the tenth century we begin hearing of frauds, not only among the teachers, but also among the seekers; their number increased with the passage of time, so that it became necessary for the authentic Ṣūfī masters to write descriptions of the true teachers for the benefit of the innocent or the inexperienced, and even to lay down rules for Shaykhs and their disciples in general.

All of these institutional forms of Ṣūfism and its widespread diffusion among the people at large have to be borne in mind in order to understand the tremendous influence it has exerted on every single facet of Islamic life, from the arts to music to literature to popular dancing to architecture to poetry to calligraphy to folklore, and so on. By the eleventh century, when al-Ghazālī (d. 1111) turned to Ṣūfism to save his soul, the world of Islam had already been worked over by these numerous popular expressions of Ṣūfism: the Ṣūfī saints and their charismatic deeds were well known and loved by the people, and even by some of the doctors of the Law. Let us remember that the classic molds of Islamic civilization had already been largely established in the eighth century, especially after the 'Abbāasids came to power; and it is into these molds that the Ṣūfī genius flowed with a certain relative ease among the people. The ground of Islam had been well churned over by Ṣūfism and had yielded considerable spiritual fruit everywhere. Ṣūfism was not, in other words, an exotic or tangential element of the Islamic world, as the term "mysticism", in the pejorative meaning it has today, might lead us to believe. It was, instead, an all-pervasing reality that touched everyone, even the scoffer and critic of the Path. When al-Ghazālī went off in search of a teacher to show him the way to God, he was not on some wild-goose chase: members of his family were Ṣūfīs, the institutions of Ṣūfism were everywhere in sight, and he knew more or less what he was looking for. All of this he recorded later in his autobiography, *al-Munqidh min aḍ-Ḍalāl* (*The Redeemer from Error*);[7] and when he wrote his famous reconciliation of the Path and the Law, the *Ihyā'*, it was addressed to the intelligent Muslim of his day who knew already quite a bit about things Ṣūfī.

The Thirteenth-Century Revival

All of these strands in the societal manifestations of Ṣūfism came together in the thirteenth century, when Islam witnessed the spiritual eruption of innumerable new Ṣūfī orders that would last, as living presences within the framework of the community, down to our own days. These were the orders, such as the Suhrawardiyyah, the Mawlawiyyah, the Shādhiliyyah, the Chistiyyah, the Aḥmadiyyah, and many others, named after their founders, that would play such a vital role in the revival of the spiritual life of the Muslim world, not only in that epoch, but in succeeding ones. Already, in the twelfth century, the Qādiriyyah, founded by 'Abd al-Qādir al-Jīlānī (d. 1166), had spread over the face of the Muslim world, spanning the continents; and a number of other, lesser orders had likewise come into view. But it was reserved for the thirteenth century to witness the explosive nature of Ṣūfism in the century-long manifestations of its spiritual and intellectual vitality.

From then on, the term *tarīqah* would refer simultaneously to the mystical Way in general and to the specific Ṣūfī orders in particular. Ṣūfism itself would mean the teachings and life within the different orders, each of which colored Ṣūfism in a specific manner. The literature of each order, apart from its own style of life and protocol, would further distinguish it from the others; in the course of time, the Shādhilīs of North Africa, the Chishtīs of India, and the Naqshbandīs of Central Asia, just to name these, developed into total systems or, if one will, total religions that were somewhat different, at least externally, from one another by virtue of their unique rearrangement of the elements held in common by all the Ṣūfī orders. While at bottom there was only one generic Path, or one inner reality common to all the orders, externally there was a considerable differentiation, more or less as the spokes of a wheel are separated at the rim but converge closer together and finally unite within the hub.

And since Ṣūfism has a universal appeal, the orders themselves sooner or later took on popular expressions, incorporating vast numbers of the population into their *zāwiyahs* and *khānaqāhs*. Millions of Muslims throughout the length and breadth of the community rallied to the different brotherhoods. Some of the orders, such as the Rifā'iyyah, soon became associated with unusual practices and procedures, such as walking through fire, skewering the members' cheeks with fine knives or daggers, and the like, that confined their membership to special segments of the people. But these forms of Ṣūfism were exceptional, the norm being the devotional and contemplative practices of, say, the Qādiriyyah, or the Shādhiliyyah, and their branches.

For the vast numbers adhering to the Ṣūfī fraternities, the contemplative life was certainly not the attracting influence; this was confined, as always, only to a tiny minority clustered around the spiritual guide. Instead, it was the devotional life of the orders that drew them. Once in the brotherhoods, they were in turn influenced by the saintly members, who were perhaps not numerous, to be sure, but whose lives were exemplary and in any case manifested the fruits of the "remembrance of God" (*dhikru 'llah*). This is a point that should not be forgotten: the authentic Shaykhs of the Path were often surrounded by saintly disciples who exerted a considerable influence on everyone else in the order, not only through the hierarchic arrangements found in each brotherhood, but through their own spiritual example or radiance. It is through its saints and sages that Ṣūfism has had its most direct influence on the community. The presence, all over the Muslim world, of innumerable Ṣūfī saints' tombs that are shrines and often pilgrimage centers, drawing great numbers of the population at particular periods every year, proves that their influence was not confined simply to their lifetimes. The popular response, in building the shrines to begin with, must have been based on some awareness of the value of their sanctified souls.

Inasmuch as the orders took on the totality associated with the religion as a whole, there resulted a kind of reduplication of the same diversity of outlook found in the Islamic faith. We perceive, first of all, a small minority of pure contemplatives constituting the uppermost stratum of an order, and they would be the most intimate disciples of a given spiritual teacher. Second, there would be those disciples who were much more devotional than gnostic in mental substance. Third, and finally, there would be the seekers who belonged to an order largely because of its opportunities for them to be within a religious community that was much more pious and less worldly than what existed in the usual Islamic society. Outside the fringes of an order, among the uninitiated, would be the innumerable pious Muslims who sympathized with Ṣūfism and its adherents and who were drawn to those who were particularly saintly.

As can be seen, although the goal of ṣūfism is gnostic, the adherents of a given order are not all bent on a gnostic realization. So long as the teacher of the Path is himself a gnostic, his *zāwiyah* or *khānaqāh* is characterized as having a gnostic bent, and at least the intimate disciples of the master have a gnostic orientation. But this does not impede his instructing disciples less given over to the gnostic viewpoint. That is exactly what we find among many eminent Ṣūfī teachers over the centuries, especially those whose radiance affected both a rigorously contemplative minority as well as a mass of less contemplative disciples. From the thirteenth century on, the Ṣūfī communities tend to have this type of stratification, from pure gnostic esoterism, on the one hand, to a kind of eso-exoteric piety and religiosity that is hardly distinguishable from what one finds among the exoteric milieus of Islam.

The variety of talents in the Ṣūfī orders explains why so many of the *'ulamā'* of those days, and down to recent times, belonged to one or another of the Ṣūfī fraternities. Apart from the fact that, like everyone else, they were affected by their fellow religious scholars' affiliation to Ṣūfism, which induced a conformist tendency that could not easily be resisted, they found in at least the pietistic levels of Ṣūfism something that agreed with their own legalistic and even moralistic interpretations of Islam. This is not to say that the *'ulamā'* were always bent along formalistic lines; some of the great Ṣūfīs, such as 'Abd al-Qādir al-Jīlānī, of the twelfth century, were much preoccupied with the study of Islamic jurisprudence and the Law in general, so that they too were "religious authorities" in addition to being "spiritual authorities". But it can be said that the general formation of a religious scholar created a natural propensity toward legalism and dogmatic exoterism that would make his affiliation to Ṣūfism rather suspect, if we did not already know in advance of the multiple layers of orientation in the ranks of the Ṣūfī adherents.

The productions of *ash-shaykh al-akbar* ("The Most-Great Shaykh"), Ibn al-'Arabī (d. 1240), the Andalusian Ṣūfī whose mission spanned the Western and Eastern regions of the Islamic world, were part and parcel of the revival of the Islamic message through Ṣūfism in the thirteenth century.[8] His hundreds of books and treatises on Ṣūfism represent an intellectual legacy that incorporated into the Path the Neoplatonic or Greek forms of wisdom that had already, since the ninth century, crept into the styles of thinking of Muslim intellectuals affected by the translations of Greek philosophical works into Arabic. The sacred wisdom that results from *ma'rifah* is organically related to the substance of faith (*īmām*) as a kind of summit to it or as the definitive capping of faith. It is possible to talk about gnosis while remaining within the pale of simple faith. It is also possible to talk about it with an elaborate theosophical or philsophical structure, which is what the *shaykh al-akbar* does in his voluminous production, particularly his *al-Futūḥāt al-Makkiyyah* (*The Meccan Revelations*), in many volumes, and in his small but important work called *Fuṣuṣ al-Ḥikam* (*The Bezels of Wisdom*).[9] These are written with a gnostic viewpoint that oversees the spiritual and cosmological and philosophical ramifications of Ṣūfī esoterism.

The unique esoteric doctrine of the *shaykh al-akbar*'s school is called *waḥdat al-wujūd* ("The Oneness of Being"), which is a metaphysical version of *Tawḥīd* that affirms the fundamental thesis that all beings derive their reality from the One and, when stripped of their contingency, are reducible to the absolute Being of *Allāh*. At bottom the being of creatures and the Being of God is one and the same thing. The charge of pantheism has been hurled at the exponents of *waḥdat al-wujūd* because they seem to be saying that God and the world are one. But that is only so in appearance. What is really being said is that there is essential — not material — identity between the beings of this world and the pure Being of God. In other words, their being, which allows them to exist in the first place, comes only from the Being of *Allāh* and, in the final analysis, is essentially the same thing.

As was said, this is actually a metaphysical view of *Tawḥīd* that lies behind the Prophet's remark, "He who has seen me has seen God," which could be taken in a purely pantheistic way, if one interpreted it literally, like the *ana 'l-ḥaqq* ("I am God") of al-Ḥallạj. In both cases, the identity of their being with the absolute Being of the Divinity is what must be understood, not only in a metaphysical sense, but also in a spiritual manner, as a kind of affirmation of the Supreme Identity that is engendered through gnostic realization. This represents, both metaphysically and spiritually, pure esoteric *Tawḥīd*.

The *shaykh al-akbar*'s immense codification of the esoteric disciplines directly and indirectly connected with *taṣawwuf* served as a kind of readaptation of the Islamic message to a much more analytically-minded humanity. Not everything he has to say is immediately concerned with *ma'rifah*, which is, after all, the essence of the Ṣūfī Way. Instead, he casts his net rather far out to encompass numerous cosmological disciplines, such as alchemy and astrology, that are only tangentially related to the Path, although he presents them in their esoteric dress. His works would have great influence, not only on Ṣūfī, but on Islam in general for centuries on end, and indeed, are still influential.

A more popular version of *waḥdat al-wujūd*, but at the same time much more intimately bound up with the spiritual life of *ma'rifah*, is the great Persian didactic poetical work, the *Mathnawī, by Jalāl ad-Dīn Rūmī* (d. 1273), a contemporary of Ibn al-'Arabi and founder of the Mawlawiyyah, the "whirling dervishes". This vast composition, in eight books, has circulated on all levels of society in the Eastern Muslim world, wherever Persian culture has gone, and embodies the most brilliant mystical teachings in a poetical form that is consistently inspired. The philosophical mysticism of Ibn al-'Arabī and the poetical mysticism of Rūmī are but two of the different genres used by thirteenth-century Ṣūfism to effect a spiritual reanimation of Islam that would be the literary counterparts to the eruption of Ṣūfī orders all over the face of the Islamic world. All of these literary works and the new Ṣūfī brotherhoods together constitute a spiritual revival much more analytical, much more discursive, much more openly esoteric and spiritual and philosophical or theosophical than we see in earlier times. Not only the brotherhoods established then, but also the esoteric doctrines that were promulgated in the light of day, have withstood the test of time and endured to our day. In more ways than one, it is possible to speak of the Ṣūfī literary and spiritual fruits of the thirteenth century as forming, in their ensemble, a veritable spiritual message that would govern the general outlook of the Islamic civilization and affect all facets of society for centuries.

For the Islamic faith, the definitive ascendancy of thirteenth-century Ṣūfism, with its gnostic and devotional spirituality that included all aspirations, kept the door of spiritual realization open to its seekers for centuries, right into the twentieth century. It had no need to hide the Path under a thicket of dissimulative practices and teachings. The Caliphs, the sultans, the amirs, and even many of the religious chiefs of the later States, often had their own Ṣūfī teachers whom they consulted regularly. The Path was everywhere in evidence; the many Ṣūfī orders had millions of adherents coming from all ranks of society. This was the case for centuries on end; it represents a diffusion of mystical elements within the life of the community that enabled it to retain its traditional structures long after their analogues in the West had begun to crumble, and even to disappear, under the dissolving influences of modern Western civilization.

The Ṣūfī orders have exercised a regenerative spiritual effect on the community through the influence of its saintly adherents in a kind of rhythmical up-and-down fashion. The vitality of Ṣūfism depends largely on the presence in its midst of real masters and disciples of serious disposition. Each order presents a different face, country by country. Thus, an order like the Qādiriyyah, which can be found from Western Africa all the way to China, has numerous Shaykhs and *khānaqāhs* or *zāwiyahs*; in Central Asia alone, it has hundreds of thousands of members. It is inconceivable that, at every epoch, such an order would be uniformly regenerative and influential. Nor does Ṣūfism ever make the claim that such is indeed the situation; on the contrary, it affirms that the vitality of an order in a particular city or region or province or country depends exclusively on the presence in its midst of a teacher with spiritual credentials that are authentic and more or less evident to others. Now, the Shaykhs one encounters in the different *zāwiyahs* of the Muslim world cannot all be of such a type, yet the Ṣūfī tradition accords these more or less formalistic Shaykhs a measure of authority, reserving for the real Shaykhs the unique role of guiding seekers to spiritual realization. When, therefore, an order has one or more authentic masters of the Path, then the regenerative functions of Ṣūfism can be perceived in a particular area, as in North Africa, for example, in the first quarter of the nineteenth century when Mawlay al-'Arabī ad-Darqāwī (d. 1823), founder of the Darqāwā, lived and instructed his numerous disciples, some of whom became great teachers. Elsewhere, the same order may have

Shaykhs who are purely formalistic and simply preserve the institutional life. What determines the appearance of a living Ṣūfī master in a given place is hard to say. Certainly the French Occupation of Algeria, with its deleterious effects on Islamic culture there, did not impede the flowering of Ṣūfī spirituality under the guiding hand of one of the greatest Shaykhs in the history of Islam, Aḥmad al-'Alawī (d. 1934). He was the founder of the 'Alawiyyah, which became in due time the source of renewed spiritual vitality in other parts of the Islamic world, and even outside of it as the Shaykhs who trained under his direction came to their own elsewhere.

The Silsilah

When the Ṣūfīs say that the esoteric Path is based on the Qur'ān and the Sunnah, they are really saying that the Path is revealed, that it is not of human invention. Fallen man cannot devise either his own means of salvation or his own mystical way leading to union with God. The teachings and methods leading to realization must therefore be of supernatural origin. It is this concept of the revealed origin of the Path that lies in the Ṣūfī initiatic chain of transmission, or the *silsilah*, which connects the Ṣūfī masters of the present day with the Messenger of Islam in a master-to-master line.

For the scores of Ṣūfī orders (the *ṭuruq*) in existence today, their *silsilahs* demonstrate the initiatic succession through the centuries. They reveal the orthodox regularity of the initiation, should any questions arise on that score. They function more or less like the regularity of sacerdotal ordination in the Church, conferring the right of administering the sacraments to the priest or clergyman. They are also an indirect confirmation that Ṣūfism is an ongoing transmission of teachings of an orthodox Islamic esoterism that has to be rediscovered and relived through actual spiritual realization under the guidance of experienced and authentic teachers in each generation. While the Ṣūfīs have written an immense quantity of prose works and poems, the Path as such is not to be found in books. It is to be found only with the living Shaykhs, and that is another truth that the *silsilah* indirectly reveals. That the *silsilahs* begin historically with the founder of Islam attests to this living transmission, to this predominantly invisible and oral character of the *ṭarīqah*.

Generally, in the initiatic line of transmission of a given Ṣūfī order, such as the Qādiriyyah or the Shādhiliyyah, one finds the names of the Shaykhs of that order in unbroken succession from the Messenger to the latest one in our days. But the Messenger himself did not originate the Path. It came to him, according to tradition, from Gabriel, the archangel in charge of revelation. The supernatural nature of the Path is indicated in the *silsilah* by putting Gabriel's name before that of the Prophet, and the Name of *Allāh* before that of Gabriel.

The *silsilah* also guarantees that the initiatic pact (*bay'ah*) between the

Shaykh and his disciple is valid. That *bay'ah* is given to the disciple upon entering the Path and is referred to in the Qur'ān as the *bay'at ar-riḍwān* ("The Pact of Divine Satisfaction"). It is an initiatic reality inaugurated by the Messenger at a certain moment in his mission. The Ṣūfīs describe it as an initiation into the life of the Spirit and even as a "second birth", but in a spiritual sense. In reality, it is the transmission by the master to the disciple of the *barakah muḥammadiyyah* ("Muḥammadan Grace") and is the esoteric Islamic equivalent to the mystical explanations of the nature of Baptism that one finds among certain theologians of the Christian tradition. The *bay'ah* is an esoteric ritual of the Path that confers regenerative graces and empowers the initiate to follow the Path under celestial protection and guidance.

The Messenger did not transmit to those mystical companions of his like 'Alī or Abū Bakr or Salmān al-Fārisī the *bay'ah* alone. He also transmitted his esoteric teaching on *Tawḥīd* as well as the method of concentration called the invocation of God, or *dhikru 'llāh*. Both the teaching on *Tawḥīd* and the practice of the *dhikr* represent the fundamental pillars of the ṭar*īqah* along with the *bay'ah*. As was said previously, the Qur'ān is ultimately reducible to the doctrine of *Tawḥīd* just as the Sunnah of the Prophet can be summed up in the spiritual method of the *dhikr*. Whatever might be the doctrinal ramifications of *Tawḥīd* (and they can be metaphysical, theological, spiritual, or the like), it remains the fundamental teaching of Ṣūfism throughout the ages. In like fashion, the phrase *dhikru 'llāh* is applicable to a complex ensemble of ritual and moral and invocatory practices in both exoteric and esoteric Islam, and yet it is clear that the essential type of the "remembrance of God" in the Path is the invocation of the Divine Name, *Allāh*, or one of the other Ninety-Nine Names of the Divinity.

What is startling in Ṣūfism is how the doctrine and the method represented by *Tawḥīd* and *dhikr* grow out of the original revealed message and proliferate in complexity with each passing century. Perhaps this is a response to the gradual loss of the intuitive perception of scriptural truths that characterized the first generations of Islam. The *silsilahs* of ṣūfism demonstrate this law of increasing complexity indirectly: they show only the names of the successive teachers after the Prophet; but one has only to imagine the period, historically speaking, of the later masters to see the law of proliferation at work. As the centuries go by, the Shaykhs pile on more and more details and explanations in their books, as if they felt that the simple Qur'ānic allusions had to be supplemented with rather complicated intellectual developments before the deeper intuitive layers of their disciples' minds could rise to the surface.

It is probably a law of growth in all of the religions that they move from what is germinally or synthetically simple to what is increasingly analytical or complex. That certainly applies to their respectivè esoteric Ways. This is quite evident in the immensely complicated formulations of Ṣūfī esoteric teachings found in the works of the Andalusian Ṣūfī Ibn al-'Arabī (d.1240). By the time he came upon the Ṣūfī scene, Islam had undergone some six centuries of growth and development: from the germinal seed planted by the founder to the vast tree that is represented by the works of the Andalusian sage, Islam experienced all sorts of historical events, such as the importation of Greek Neoplatonic thinking and the rise of diverse rationalistic and dogmatic schools. Yet, the Ṣūfism of Ibn al-'Arabī, when stripped of its nonessential elements, is the same *Tawḥīd* and *dhikr* of the Prophet's time; it is just that he was addressing a much more complicated mental substance by then.

That cyclical law of increasing doctrinal differentiation must be borne in mind when pondering over the successive names of Ṣūfī masters found in the *silsilahs*. Arabesques or geometric ornamentations on mosque walls can be either simple or rather complex, filling entire walls, without losing their aesthetic unity. The same law of complexity based on a real unity occurs in Ṣūfism, but in a spiritual manner. Complexity is not syncretism, for the latter represents an ill-arranged hodgepodge of teachings with no real unity. Even when the Ṣūfīs are eclectic, drawing now from Neoplatonic or now from Hindu formulations, they retain that spiritual unity. Their eclecticism is organic and compatible with the integrity, or let us say the *Tawḥīd*, of the Islamic revelation.

In a very striking fashion, the *silsilah* reveals likewise the central role of the Shaykh in Ṣūism. In other words, the *ṭarīqah* is a master-to-master transmission. The reverential attitudes toward the Shaykh expected of his disciples make sense when we realize that he embodies the Path as such in his very person. The Shaykh is the Path, as some Ṣūfīs would say, and the Path is the Shaykh. He is considered to be representative of the Prophet for his age and endowed with a certain spiritual infallibility in guiding his disciples toward union with the One. Thousands of masters, great and small, have existed in the long history of Ṣūfism, and each has to be imagined with his or her disciples. Their presence in the midst of the Islamic community goes a long way toward explaining the remarkable spiritual fruits of the faith in terms of saintly men and women, works of art and architecture, literature, music, and everything else that went into those great moments of Islamic culture in days gone by when the tradition was still intact. While it is true that the contemplative life taught by the Shaykhs to their disciples might seem useless to an age of utilitarianism, it is well to remember that their influence on the world around them was often immensely useful in a thousand different ways in leading to the Hearafter.

The *silsilah* also conveys to us the meaning of tradition in its supernatural and historical manifestations. The Shaykhs were living historical personalities but their instruction had to do with the domain of the Spirit. They inherited the traditional forms of Islam and its Ṣūfī message, but it is through their spiritual insight that they made fresh, original, and spontaneous adaptations of the historical tradition to their times.

Dozens of Ṣūfī orders today all have *silsilahs* going back to the Messenger of Islam. What those *silsilahs* are really saying is something like this. The Islamic message, whether exoteric or esoteric, comes from the transcendent Spirit. That same Spirit continues its work within the community through the inspired Shaykhs of the Path and the great religious authorities of the Law. But since Ṣūfism is most especially concerned with the spiritual Path, it is among its saintly guides that one will always find those direct inspirations of a celestial nature. It is these inspirations that maintain the complete message of the original Qur'ānic revelation and the Sunnah of the Prophet within the traditional framework and prevent them from disappearing altogether as a result of the forgetfulness (*ghaflah*) that overtakes the community with increasing power as time goes by.

The Critics of Ṣūfism

Ṣūfism has not received favorable treatment at the hands of either the modernists or the fundamentalists of the Muslim world. The Kemalist revolution in Turkey, for example, whose secularist nationalism was borrowed from the West, wiped out not only the visible institutional structures of Ṣūfism but also eradicated as many of the forms of Islam as it could. All of this was done in the name of progress, republicanism, nationalism, and secularism. But it could not give Ṣūfism the final blow, and it still survives in Turkey. Russian communist imperialism in Central Asia has likewise sought to destroy Islam and its Ṣūfī foundations, but it too has not been able to efface them, in spite of over half a century of the most violent persecutions and atheistic propaganda, to say nothing of the closing down of thousands of mosques. Anti-Ṣūfism is also strong among the different fundamentalist movements of modern times in the Near East. While the modernists reject the traditional Ṣūfī teachings because they seem medieval and constitute a block to the imposition of Western thinking and institutions on the Muslim world, the fundamentalists reject them because they seem like accretions on the purity of Islam, which they wish to restore to the community. There can be no doubt that, as a result of the efforts of both camps against Ṣūfism, the societal structure of the *ṭarīqah* has been seriously undermined and impaired.

The Path seems to have retreated from the public scene as the Muslim world has increasingly succumbed to the process of Westernization or to the various puritanical movements of the present day. The traditional teachings have receded more and more from the consciousness of the cultivated Muslim. In the process, the contemplative Path seems archaic in the thinking of the modernist or it seems like a terrible deviation in the minds of the puritanical sectarians.

Modernist Muslims get most of their arguments against Ṣūfism from Western scholars who generally consider the Ṣūfī Path to be foreign to the Islamic religion as such. Needless to say, fundamentalist Muslims would agree with them. Western investigators, looking for its origins outside Islam, have referred to Hinduism, Christianity, Shamanism, Neoplatonism, and the like, hoping to establish a historical causality that would account for the eruption of Ṣūfism within the Islamic community. If there is no mysticism to be found in the early period, then clearly it is not part of the substance of the religion, but an accident, so to speak, that came later on and from other sources.

Westerners are partially right when they say that there is no Ṣūfism in early Islam. The word "Ṣūfī" and its cognate terms, as we saw, do not come into view until after Ṣūfism emerges into the light of history around the middle of the eighth century and establishes itself as a permanent institution in the Islamic community. However, to conclude that the Path did not exist because certain words did not exist would be a gross generalization, to say the least. It is this nonexistence of Ṣūfism as a term at the origin of Islam that has made for the rejection by most Western specialists, and some Muslims, of Ṣūfism as an integral part of the Islamic message. But, as was said previously, when one understands the distinction between the term "Ṣūfism" itself and the reality of the *ṭarīqah* to which it refers, then the absence of the term in the days of Muḥammad and his companions does not of course mean the absence of the *ṭarīqah*.

If the absence of the term is what causes the Western scholar to reject the spiritual Path as being an element in the Islamic revelation, he can look elsewhere for the origins of Islamic spirituality. But for a Muslim to say that there was no spiritual Path in the days of Muḥammad that later on became known as Ṣūfism, would be another matter altogether. We know that, historically speaking, there have been Muslims who have said as much. They are really saying either one of two things. One, there was no spiritual Path at all in the Islamic message in the days of the Prophet; but this is tantamount to saying that his religion is devoid of all real depth, for an Islam without a Path is precisely that. Two, there is a spiritual Path in Islam, but it did not become Ṣūfism until later on. If that is so, then the religion is reduced to a shadow of its real self once again, for we see nothing in Islam that can approach the stunning spirituality of the great Ṣūfī saints or sages. Let us recall that for the Ṣūfīs the *ṭarīqah* is the spiritual heart of the Islamic religion.

The mystical contents of either the Scripture or the Prophet's life are not immediately self-evident. Islam has a rather dry and muted spirituality couched in an Arabic nomadic style that is indirect, elusive, suggestive, and evocative. The formulations of that spirituality have to be penetrated through an intuitive perception that enters into the essence of the Semitic speech of the Arabs. The few Western scholars who have accepted the thesis that the Qur'ān has mystical dimensions are aware of the problems facing the outsider — Muslim or non-Muslim — to Islamic spirituality.

No straightforward Yoga can therefore be found either in the Qur'ān or in the Prophet's life that would refer directly to the existence of a contemplative Path. By contrast, clear-cut expressions of the Path can be pointed to in the teachings of the Buddha, for example who has quite a bit to say on meditational practices. Similarly, the *Bhagavad Gita* of Hinduism is a marvelous scriptural summary of the many facets of the Path and its different yogic practices. But in Islam we do find nevertheless an indirect Yoga in the Scripture and in Muḥammad, meaning here a spiritual teaching or discipline, a way of concentrating on God. Now, that kind of Islamic Yoga has to be extracted from the inner layers of the Qur'ān and the Sunnah. Not that the Scripture and the Sunnah are devoid of all overt mystical flashes, for they do exist. It is just that they must be correlated through a lengthy process of meditation, more or less as the Ṣūfīs themselves do, that such luminous expressions are turned into inexhaustible sources for the inner life of the Spirit.

That the Ṣūfī interpretations of Qur'ānic doctrines have much in common with non-Islamic forms of esoterism, such as Neoplatonism, for example, should not surprise us. The metaphysical, spiritual, and other aspects of the different mystical Paths of mankind's religions cannot but speak of the same realities in more or less the same fashion. The Paths in the various religions may start out from widely-separated points, but they converge upon the same Absolute in the end. In so doing, they traverse inner worlds that are strikingly similar. Besides, the Ṣūfīs may have borrowed a number of Neoplatonic formulations, but this does not mean that the spiritual Path of the Islamic faith begins with those borrowings. Given the universality of spiritual esoterism, it is inevitable that borrowings by the Ṣūfīs from Neoplatonism, Hinduism, or other traditions take place. Moreover, Neoplatonism as such entered into the cultural stream of Islam through the translations of Greek wisdom into Arabic and was part and parcel of the Islamic philosophical tradition. Neoplatonic esoterism could not but give to the synthetic expressions of early Islamic thought a more analytical and detailed perspective that would be needed by later generations. We must remember not to confuse the borrowings from Neoplatonism or other systems of thought with the actual spiritual reality of Ṣūfism derived from the revelation and the Messenger.

If the Ṣūfī formulations are in agreement with non-Islamic mystical teachings, such as the Hindu Vedanta and Chinese Taoism, we should not be surprised.[10] The metaphysical and spiritual teachings of the various mystical Paths of mankind point to the same Absolute, of course, in different ways. It is not just that *Allāh* in Islam, *Brahman* in Hinduism, and the *Tao* in the Chinese tradition are different Divine Names for the same transcendent Real. It is that even the more extrinsic facets of the Real are more or less concordant among the various esoteric traditions. For example, the all-important esoteric teachings that within the Divine Nature itself there is a metaphysical distinction between the personal and impersonal Divinity is to be found in the Qur'ān, when we consider the Ninety-Nine Names of *Allāh*. In exoteric Islam, we hear almost only of the personal Divinity, the Lord of the Universe, and rarely of the impersonal Divine Essence; but that is because exoterism tends to reduce its consideration of the Ninety-Nine Names to those having an anthropomorphic quality. Now in Ṣūfism both the personal Divinity and the impersonal Essence — the Absolute in itself — are taken into account in the total doctrine of the Path. This is why the impersonal nature of the One, which is infinite and unconditioned and absolute, is the same as the abstract, ultimate reality to which Advaita Vedanta, Mahayana Buddhism, and Taoism refer in their teachings. It is more than likely that when Islam sees *Tawḥīd* as underlying the different revelations given to the world, so that Islam is merely a reconfirmation of what was previously revealed, it is really of that ultimate, non-anthropomorphic Divine Unity that it speaks, not of God in His personal nature as Lord of the Creation, possessed of anthropomorphic aspects. The abstract, nontheistic Divine Unity permits the integration even of Buddhism into the perennial message of *Tawḥīd*. But that is a proposition that ordinary, exoteric Islam cannot make: it identifies God with the personal Lord, who creates, sustains, and guides all creatures and worlds. Since Buddhism, with its Nirvanic reality, is nontheistic in its description of the Absolute, it will seem to the Muslim exoterist as pure disbelief or atheism — a godless religion.

Apart from Western scholars who generally divorce Ṣūfism from its Islamic roots for different reasons, there are also other Westerners, mostly young people, who are interested in Ṣūfism as a mystical Way and who also strip it of its Islamic framework. This Western interest in Ṣūism has drawn the ire not only of modernist Muslims, who look upon all of this with disfavor, but also of the puritanical conservatives. Since the latter exclude the mystical life as having any bearing on the Islamic religion, Western interest in Ṣūfism is bound to seem irrational, to say the least. Recall that Ṣūfism is the deepest and most spiritual reality of the Islamic religion; therefore, to speak of Ṣūfism on the one hand and of the Islamic religion on the other is not really exact. Ṣūfism cannot be cut out of Islam by some kind of artificial surgery. Ṣūfī masters themselves, throughout the centuries, have always insisted on the proper integration of the *sharī'ah* of the religion into the *ṭarīqah*. They would not have done this if they had felt that exoteric Islam were not vital to Ṣūfism or esoteric Islam. Consequently, those Westerners who give the Way of Sufism serious consideration in their lives would do well to ponder the example of the Shaykhs of Ṣūfism who, after all, had good reason to claim that the Law and the Path complement one another.

Muslims who are stunned that Westerners should be interested in Ṣū fism but not in Islam — or in their versions of Islam — are committing the opposite mistake. Whereas the Westerner of would-be Ṣūfī inclinations rejects the *sharī'ah* in favor of the *ṭarīqah*, the puritanical Muslim rejects the *ṭarīqah* in favor of the *sharī'ah*, or of a certain view of the Law. But we do not find anywhere in the tradition that the believer is excused from leading a spiritual life so long as he follows the Law, as if the Law sufficed unto itself. A degree of spirituality is demanded of everyone looking for salvation (*najāh*). When speaking earlier of the three principles of the Islamic tradition, namely *imān* ("faith"), *islām* ("submission"), and *iḥsān* ("virtue"), which are also the three states of the Muslim, we noted that *iḥsān* also means "spiritual life", among other things. If therefore the spiritual life is demanded of everyone, rejection of the *ṭarīqah* is a grave mistake. For that reason, the Imām al-Ghazālī (d. 1111), one of the eminent authorities of the Sunnī tradition, has very severe reprimands for those pharisaical Muslims who would reduce Islam to the external form of the Law and banish the Ṣūfī Path altogether from the revealed message.

For the traditional Muslim intellectual, an Islam without Ṣūfism is simply a heterodox version of the religion that cannot last for very long without sooner or later collapsing from its own dead weight. Throughout the centuries of Islam, there have been many eminent doctors of the Law who have understood perfectly well that the religion cannot survive without the spiritual light furnished by Ṣūfism. One has only to examine the many antitraditional interpretations of Islam coming from the modernists and others of the present day to see that the *'ulamā'* who championed Ṣūfism were utterly right, and that an Islam without the Path disintegrates into mutually destructive deviations from the original revealed message. These subversions obscure the road to salvation for many Muslims and reduce the grandeur of Islam to yet another banal ideology of modern times.

That the mystical life is still possible in the Islamic lands is due to the continued presence of Ṣūfī masters, and this alone guarantees that the religion of Islam will not utterly succumb to the unsettling influences of modern Western ideology. It is indicative of the power intrinsic to an authentic tradition like Islam that it still has teachers of the Way leading to spiritual realization. In spite of the intense efforts of one or two generations of modernists to do away with the inherited traditional forms of the faith that have prevented these Westernized Muslims from being completely at ease in the Muslim world, authentic Ṣūfī teachers can still be found, and the great mass of the faithful continue to live within the confines of the religious culture that has survived into our day. The living masters and their Ṣūfī orders represent the last bastions of the original religion in all of its depth and fullness, the last strongholds of *Tawḥīd* and *dhikr* in their plenary intellectual and spiritual contents and radiance.

V
The Sacred Law of Islam

The Sharīʿah

We have seen that the *ṭarīqah* is based on the mystical contents of the Qur'ān and the Sunnah, its fundamental orientation being that of the contemplative life. The sacred Law of Islam is the *sharīʿah*, and it is also based on the Qur'ān and the Sunnah, but it is nonmystical in character, and therefore it concerns itself exclusively with the active life.[1] While the *ṭarīqah* seeks union with God in this life through spiritual knowledge and love, which is what is meant by gnosis (*maʿrifah*), the *sharīʿah* seeks salvation (*najā*h) through posthumous entrance into Paradise and the resulting beatific vision of God. Ṣūfism strives after union with God here and now through spiritual concentration; the Law prescribes for believers the commandments and prohibitions they must observe if they are to obtain that salvific state after death. It is not so much that the Ṣūfīs look down upon the beatitude of posthumous salvation as it is that they look up to the ultimate Source of all beatitude, the paradisal One in itself, beyond the created Paradises of Islam.

The superiority of the contemplative life over the active life, of the *ṭarīqah* over the *sharīʿah*, is due to the all-comprehensiveness of the former as against the latter. It is due also to their respective goals, the Path having spiritual union or identity with the Divinity as its aim, while the Law envisages a kind of separative but blissful state of posthumous salvation in the created Paradises, not in *Allāh* Himself. This is not to say that the *ṭarīqah* functions independently of the *sharīʿah* for the Law is an integral part of the Path, and indeed, every believer, whether contemplative or not, must observe the Law. The Ṣūfī insistence on the Law shows that the sacred Legislation is indispensable in the overall framework of the Path. It is sometimes forgotten that the reverse is also true: the Law is in need of the Path. While not everyone is obliged to contemplate God, no one is exempted by revelation from living more or less in conformity with the Spirit. After all, the spiritual Path of Islam could not have been revealed simply as an exotic element of the revelation for the sake of a chosen few, the rest being allowed to ignore spirituality altogether. But in practice the *ṭarīqah* has been confined to a minority in the Muslim world since the beginnings of the religion because the spiritual life has not been the immediate goal of the majority of believers. From time to time, under the influence of great saints, the substance of the community has been ignited spiritually and has exploded in the miraculous manifestations of Islamic civilization, only to subside once again when left to the dead weight of its own forgetfulness and worldliness.

While the Meccan period introduced the mystical Way into Islam, the Medinan period brought the Law into existence. The rallying to the Islamic faith of vast numbers of Arabs in the Medinan epoch of the Prophet's mission is in itself an immediate cause for the elaboration of the Law. But the fact that Islam does have a sacred Law covering both individual and collective life and that this Law is deemed to be of supernatural origin implies that, from the very beginning, the religion set out to distinguish itself from the Christian world around it, which had no sacred Law. It is only later, after the days of the Emperor Constantine (d. 337), when Christianity became the religion of the State, that we see an attempt to integrate Roman Law into the Church, with mixed results. But in any case this is not the same thing as the *Sharī'ah* of Islam, which originated in the Islamic revelation itself, as did the *ṭarīqah*. That sacred Law of Islam has been the principle of stability and equilibrium in the Muslim world since then. It integrates all social life into its prescriptive norms, the Sunnah of the Prophet having ritual, matrimonial, military, financial, domestic, political, hygienic, and social aspects, to say nothing of his spiritual or mystical Sunnah. By contrast, the absence of a *Sharī'ah* in the nascent Christian religion meant the nonintegration of society into the Christian mystical Way (which only monks and nuns could really follow). No religion can address a people without making some attempts at social legislation. The Christian rejection of Jewish Law, done in the name of the mystical Way of the Christ, therefore had to become the Christian acceptance of Roman Law. The result was that the Church assumed an almost antimystical attitude in its formulations and in its draconian ferreting-out of all possible gnostic teachings that menaced its newly-acquired official positions of an exoteric nature.

Imān, Islām, and Iḥsān

The most elementary form of the Law is the *shahādah*, containing both the First and the Second Testimonies of Faith, just as this is the most essential formulation of the Path. Acceptance of the twofold *shahādah* is what defines the Muslim and, in a sense, constitutes the salvific core of the Islamic message. The remaining prescriptions of Islam revolve around the *shahādah*, so to speak. But they do not have its absoluteness, for it is the unique sacred formula of Islam that gives immediate expression to the teaching on the Divine Unity and on the Messengerhood of the Prophet. At the same time it serves as a means of mental or oral prayer that conveys grace to the believer's soul. The two Testimonies go together; rejection of the one is rejection of the other. Thus, there is a complementarism between them like that between the Qur'ān and the Sunnah.

While the *shahādah* is the most elementary expression of the Law, and even of the Path, the Sunnah of the Prophet has laid down certain minimal practices that, if followed faithfully and with the right intention (*niyyah*, guarantee salvation (*najāh*). To describe these, one has to go into the nature of religion, the foundations or principles of religion (*anfās ad-dīn*), namely, *īmān* (''faith''), *islām* (''submission'' i.e., to the Divine Will), and *iḥsān* (''morality''). These correspond, respectively, to the beliefs, the ritual practices, and the moral code that we find in all religions, and not just simply in Islam. They are principles that apply simultaneously to the religion and to the individuals and the community that follow it. Every religion, in other words, like every believer, has teachings about God and the other transcendent realities; every religion has revealed ritual observances that are said to be sources of grace; and every religion has moral precepts that affect the individual and society in general. *Imān*, *islām*, and *iḥsān* have esoteric and exoteric interpretations, even though, in certain Ṣūfī works, the third principle, *iḥsān*, is reserved for the Path because of its relations with spiritual virtues. The three are conditions or states either of the religion itself or of its followers. The first two, *īmān* and *islām*, are sometimes reversed, but in any case, the vitality or lack of vitality of Islam is dependent on these three conditions.

The individual Muslim's religion and the Islamic community in general rise or fall in accordance with the depth or shallowness of the three. They have scriptural backing in the Qur'ān and represent a kind of hierarchy of ascending nearness to God. Islam takes its name from the principle of *islām* primarily because it is from this condition that the Five Pillars of Religion (*arkān ad-dīn*) flow forth. They are the ritual forms of Islam that engage the Muslim's active nature, and are therefore the visible or external manifestations of his faith, or his response to the contents of his faith.

In a famous *ḥadīth* on these principles of religion, Gabriel is pictured as coming to the Prophet to interrogate him on them one by one. In response to the question on *īmān*, the Prophet answered that it is faith in God, His Angels, His Books, His Messengers, the Day of Judgment, and in the predestination of good and evil. These six articles constitute an elementary creedal formulation that, later on in Islam, would be given greater elaboration, particularly in dogmatic theology. By the phrase "His Books", the multiplicity of revealed messages is affirmed, all of which come from the same Source. Similarly, by "His Messengers", the equality of the Messengers before God and the fact that there have been numerous chosen vessels of revelation are to be understood. The "faith" (*īmān*) described here is a system of beliefs but it is also the interior faith that goes beyond formulations — which is the deeper meaning of the word — as we see in the works of the theologians and the Ṣūfīs.

When Gabriel asked the Prophet to explain the next principle, *islām*, he answered that it is these things: the Testimony of Faith (*shahādah*), the five daily ritual prayers (*ṣalāh*), the fast of Ramaḍān (*ṣawm Ramaḍān*), alms-giving (*zakāh*), and the pilgrimage to Mecca (*ḥajj*). These are the famous Five Pillars of Religion (*arkan ad-dīn*). They sum up the fundamental sacred practices for gaining salvation and are considered to be sources of grace or blessings (*barakāt*). A sixth one, the Holy War (*jihād*), is a disputed pillar, although it does show that Islam considers warfare — in accordance with the prescribed rules, to be sure — as part of the general redemptive observances in which the believer may engage.

The Pillars of Religion are carefully detailed in the Sunnah of the Prophet. They are not acceptable except when carried out with the right intention (*niyyah*). This in itself immediately removes them from the onus of mechanical action and puts them in the category of living piety. That intention must square with the spiritual intention of the Prophet when performing them. The rites of Islam cannot be carried out in just any way nor for just any reason. There is a kind of rock-like stability to the Islamic religion that comes from the fact that these Pillars of Religion have remained invariably the same as when first performed by the Prophet. Their purificatory value comes from the inner graces they project into man's soul; indeed, the Prophet described the five daily ritual prayers, for example, as comparable to five baths in a stream of water.

We need not go into a detailed description of each of these sacred acts, or rituals, but a brief account would be helpful in gaining some notions on the simple structures of the *sharī'ah*. The *shahādah* has already been explained as the fundamental expression of Islamic faith, esoteric and exoteric. Yet it also has a ritual usage, not only as a kind of prayer uttered over and over again in the mind or with the voice, but as the formula the would-be Muslim must utter to verbalize his adhesion to Islam in the presence of witnesses. It is this utterance that makes him into a Muslim. Similarly, the *shahādah* is pronounced in the ear of the newly-born child, just as it is uttered in the ear of the deceased: the *shahādah* accompanies man's entrance into this world and his exit from it.

Ritual prayer (*ṣalāh*) is performed five times a day, in the early morning, at noon, in the afternoon, at sunset, and in the evening. These prayers are called by their respective moments of the day, as "the early-morning prayer" or "the noon prayer", and so on. One must be in a state of ritual purification before engaging in prayer, and this is acquired through the major or minor ablutions prescribed by the Sunnah, depending on the source of impurity. The believer, facing the direction of Mecca indicated by the niche (*miḥrāb*) in a mosque or known in advance by him if he is praying outside of a mosque, goes through certain ritual postures and gestures, such as standing, inclining, prostrating, and sitting. These constitute one complete unit of prayers, the five daily prayers having anywhere from two to four such complete units. The prayers are drawn from the Qur'ān, each unit having at least the opening Sūrah of the Qur'ān, the *Fātiḥah*, to which another, short Sūrah is added, depending on the unit being performed. Sacred Arabic alone is used in ritual prayers, either aloud or in an inaudible voice, and these have to be learned by heart, for the prayers cannot be performed with a book in hand. Regulations as to dress, eye and hand movements, irregular motions, and the like, complete the ensemble of prescribed recitations, postures, and gestures, all of which have been set down by the Sunnah of the Prophet. While all of this seems impersonal, in reality the ritual prayer is a kind of daily reaffirmation of man's role as vicegerent (*khalīfah*) of God on earth, praying on behalf of all creatures. Personal prayer (*du'ā'*), in which one supplicates the Divinity in one's own language, is done after the completion of the ritual prayer and has introductory and concluding formulas in Qur'ānic Arabic. It is in this personal prayer that the individual cultivates intimacy with God.

The fast of Ramaḍān involves abstaining from all food and drink and conjugal relations between early dawn and sunset. Since Islam operates on a lunar calendar, the fast can fall in the middle of the summer, at which time it is particularly rigorous. It is a remarkable fact of social life that the observance of Ramaḍān is rather widespread in the Islamic world. Even those who are not normally pious have been known to observe the fast. Perhaps this is due to its occurring once a year: it is like a yearly purification of the soul, that otherwise would be burdened by the weight of *ghaflah*.

Alms-giving, or *zakāh*, is the legal percentage of one's wealth given yearly to the poor. If one's wealth is in money, for example, the *zakāh* given is around two and one-half percent after taxes. If one's wealth is in other forms, the *zakah* follows complicated directions established by the *sharī'ah*. *Zakāh* also is a purificatory rite that affects not only the wealth of the person giving it, but also his inner nature: a charitable disposition is thus encouraged, which combats any inclination towards a tight-fisted attachment to worldly possessions. Moreover, its yearly occurrence in a legal fashion leads to the cultivation of nonlegal forms of *zakāh*, or charity toward one's neighbors in a general way. While Ramaḍān represents a kind of renunciation of the world, if only temporarily, *zakāh* has to do with the eradication of one's egocentric attachment to possessions.

The pilgrimage to Mecca, the *ḥajj*, is to be performed toward the end of one's life, if possible. The Ka'bah, the sacred edifice in Mecca, is the center of the pilgrimage, which yearly draws hundreds of thousands of Muslims. The various elements of the pilgrimage, *dhu 'l-ḥijjah*, the last in the lunar calendar, are commemorative of events in the lives of Abraham, Ishmael, and Hagar when they were in the Meccan region. The tenth of the month, for example, is the Feast of Sacrifice (*'īd al-aḍḥā*), celebrated simultaneously throughout the Islamic world by the sacrifice of animals in commemoration of the animal sacrifice Abraham was allowed to make in place of his son (Ishmael or Isaac, according to the Islamic source one has in view).

Such, then, are the Five Pillars of Religion as seen in summary fashion, and without regard to their esoteric contents, which the Ṣūfīs have brought out in their numerous works. They are the characteristic rituals of the faith and are what most Westerners associate Islam with, and with good reason, for these are the rites that all Muslims perform, either individually or collectively. It should be remembered that it is in these Pillars that we see the social traits of the religion in a clear-cut fashion. Islamic culture has always been attuned to the Pillars, for the traditional world revolved around them, and the governments made provisions of all sorts to guarantee that the fulfillment of these Pillars was not obstructed in any way. The arts and architecture of Islam, the traditional clothing of the Muslims, the societal protocol, and even the daily and yearly rhythms of life, have arisen largely for the sake of these Five Pillars of Religion. When one talks about the *sharī'ah* insofar as it has a salvific nature affecting even the most humble Muslim, it is about these Pillars that one should speak. No wonder, then, that they occupy a central position in the Law, for they are the strict minimum required of the believer intent upon saving his soul at the hour of death.

Returning now to the principles of Islam, the third and final one is *iḥsān*, or morality, both in a civic and exoteric sense as well as in a spiritual one. When Gabriel asked the Prophet to define *iḥsān*, the latter answered: "It is that thou shouldst adore God as if thou sawest Him; for if thou seest Him not, He in any case seest thee." The *ḥadīth* implies that the vision of God, which is purely spiritual, yields the fruit of adoration: one adores or loves what one knows or sees. Both knowledge and love are implicit in the *ḥadīth*. Consequently, this particular principle of the religion is the one to which the Ṣūfīs devote considerable attention, whereas in exoteric Islam it receives purely moral applications. By "spiritual morality", the inner life of the Spirit is meant. That is why *iḥsān* concerns esoteric Islam in particular. Nevertheless, conventional morality, as preached by the *sharī'ah*, is a form of *iḥsān* and derives from the moral teachings of the Qur'ān and the Sunnah. These teachings are embodied in those diverse actions comprised in the commandments and prohibitions of the sacred Law that are factors making for the equilibrium of society.

The Ḥadīth

The Sunnah deserves our attention at this point in the discussion on the Law of Islam. The Sunnah is a record of what the Prophet said and did on innumerable occasions and is the Norm of conduct for the pious and intelligent Muslim. During the Prophet's lifetime, his Sunnah was a living reality, observed and followed by his companions down to the tiniest details. After his death, the Sunnah was transmitted by the companions both in word and in deed, not just merely in words. Their own style of living was based on the style of the Prophet, which was what he expected. The transmission of the living example of the Prophet by the companions, the "followers", and the inspired authorities of early Islam, obviously did not suffice to maintain the integrity of the Sunnah. It had to be codified, along with so many other things vital to the faith, in the eighth and ninth centuries. This was done in the great *ḥadīth* collections of the time, such as the *Ṣaḥīḥ* (*The Sound*) of al-Bukāri (d. 870) and the similarly-named work of Ṃuslim (d. 875). The principle employed by the transmitters of *ḥadīth* was that of tracing out the line of transmission (*isnād*) connecting the collector or transmitter of later times with the Prophet through a series of reliable intermediaries, whose names figure in the line. The Prophet's remark forms the content (*matn*) of the *ḥadīth*; but before reaching the remark, the listener or reader has to go through the *isnād* of names that generally ends with a companion who had heard the Prophet's statement.[2]

This is a tedious way of proceeding, but the *isnādic* principle is characteristically Arab. It perhaps has direct connections with the pre-Islamic transmission of oral literature, such as poetry and tribal histories, as we see among the narrators of those days. It influenced practically all the other genres of Arabic literature in the first few centuries, and crops up, for example, in such domains as history and biography. The principle was of varying importance in those fields, but it was of crucial significance for the collecting of *ḥadīths* inasmuch as the Sunnah of the Prophet reposed on them. Since there were thousands of *ḥadīths* in oral circulation among numerous transmitters, the collector, such as al-Bukhārī, had to make a choice of those that were to be included in his compilation, and those would be the ones he considered authentic. The authenticity of a *ḥadīth* was determined by a host of objective biographical criteria relating to the transmitters, their characters, their death dates, and by evaluations of their general trustworthiness, as well as by the content of the *ḥadīth*, namely, its conformity to the spirit of Islam as understood by the collector. In the course of time, the Sunnī tradition would consecrate six of these collections as the canonical ones, "The Six Books," with that of al-Bukhārī being considered as second only to the Qur'ān in its importance for the Islamic faith. Other collections were made, of course, but they would not have the same authority as those of al-Bukhārī or Muslim. The Shī'īs also had their own compilations, transmitted through the line of their Im/$mams, but these are of importance only in Shī'ism.

The *ḥadīth* are of two types, the *ḥadīth nabawī, "a ḥadīth* related to the Prophet", wherein he speaks on his own authority; and the *ḥadīth qudsī, "a holy ḥadīth*", wherein the Divinity is said to speak through the Prophet as previously noted. The overwhelming number of *ḥadīths* are of the former type, the latter being several hundred or more in number. The Sunnah, accordingly, is largely made up of *ḥadīths* drawn from the Prophet's own inspired authority, while the "holy *ḥadīths*" seem to be concerned mostly with mystical or spiritual lessons.

There is no exclusive subject matter to the *ḥadīths*: they cover an incredible diversity of fields, such as religious beliefs, Qur'ānic commentary, eschatology, ritual observances, hygiene, medicine, cosmology, marriage, the family, warfare, morality, etiquette, to say nothing of historical and nonhistorical materials. Through them we know how the Prophet lived, even in his most intimate moments, for he was to be imitated down to the tiniest detail; and through them we have additional light thrown on the Qur'ānic texts.

While the orthodox tradition agrees on the canonicity of the principal compilations of *ḥadiths*, it also agrees that the *ḥadīths* are of different categories of reliability. They vary from those that are rare or weak to those that are good or generally accepted by the different authorities. The canonical collections represent nevertheless a perspective that was held in common by their compilers and that could not but exclude whatever went counter to it. This is not to say that they are largely responsible for creating the general contours of the Sunnah by eliminating whatever was incompatible with their view of things. But it is true that the figure of the Prophet that emerges from their *ḥadīth* collections is nonmystical and imitable. Now, that was not of their invention. We can already sense that the Qur'ānic teachings on him portray the same image. Other sources on the Prophet, such as the early biographical and historical works, leave us with a similar impression. The Prophet's own style of living in general likewise leads us to the conclusion that he preferred keeping his inner life to himself while outwardly appearing humanly normal, the better to be imitated by everybody. Thus, the considerable mass of *ḥadīths* excluded from the received corpus allows us to conclude that the view of the prophet that the canonical works wanted to transmit, to say nothing of their view of Islam, was in general exoteric.

Within the Islamic orthodox tradition, the canonical compilations of *ḥadīths* go uncontested. That has been the case for centuries, so that they resemble the incontestability of the Qur'ānic text. At the most, there might be hair-splitting distinctions around the variant readings, but reconsidering the soundness of the canonical collections is something else altogether. While the *ḥadīths* do not partake of the revealed nature of the Qur'ān, they do share with it a certain stability and even immutability within the context of the tradition as a whole. They have, in other words, a sacredness of their own, and it is this which prevents them from being considered as merely profane. In modern times, only Western scholars and modernist Muslims have sought to demolish the integrity of either all or part of the canonical works, depending on the critic. But they are not of one mind, nor can they be, and very often their conclusions are mutually contradictory, to say nothing of their premises. They share only one thing, namely their opposition to traditional authority, and they appeal to similarly-minded Muslims, as well as to those who are wavering in their faith.

The Madhhabs

While the *sharī'ah* is based fundamentally on the Qur'ān and the Sunnah, other principles are also taken into consideration by the religious scholars when seeking to arrive at conclusions on any given legal point. The consensus (*ijmā'*) of the notables of the community is a principle that can intervene when neither the Qur'ān nor the Sunnah offers a solution to a problem. Still another principle, that of argument by analogy (*qiyās*), is available when the others fail. These four principles of jurisprudence came into play as the community expanded outside of its Arabian homeland and entered into contact with novel situations not mentioned in the Qur'ān nor in the Sunnah but that could be handled by either consensus or analogous reasoning.

The codification of the Law in the eighth and ninth centuries came about because of a need for manuals and treatises on jurisprudential matters. The various schools of jurisprudence, the *madhhabs*, which arose in that epoch were founded by individuals of independent or personal authority (*ijtihād*), whose interpretation of how the principles of jurisprudence applied to particular questions was not always the same. Their differences, however, were seen in a positive light, in accordance with the dictum, "The differences of the religious authorities are a mercifulness from God," which banishes the possibility of the tyrannical rule of one *madhhab* over the whole Muslim world. While there were many *madhhabs* circulating in early times, eventually the four great *madhhabs* of the present day emerged as the orthodox schools of jurisprudence. They were named after their founders, Mālik ibn Anas (d. 795), ash-Shāfi'ī (d. 820), Aḥmad ibn Ḥanbal (d. 855), and Abū Hanifah (d. 767), their *madhhabs* being, respectively, the Māliki, the Shāfi'i, the Ḥanbalī, and the Ḥanafī.

These *madhhabs* have become, in the course of time, characteristic of certain regions of the Islamic world, the Mālikī being strong in North Africa, the Shāfi'ī in Egypt, the Ḥanafī in Turkey and Pakistan, while the Ḥanbalī has a very limited diffusion in parts of the Near East and the least number of adherents. The four *madhhabs* recognize one another's orthodoxy; the muftis of each school give their formal legal opinion (*fatwā*) in accordance with the rules of their *madhhab*. The tradition maintains that, since the founders of the *madhhabs* exercised absolute authority, this same independent or absolute *ijtihād*, cannot be exercised by later muftis, who have only a relative *ijtihā*d, the "gate" of *ijtihād* in an absolute sense having been closed at the time of the founders of the reigning *madhhabs*. But one finds later figures, like as-Suyūti (d. 1505), claiming the same absolute independent authority as earlier ones, which does not mean that they upend the conclusions of the founding fathers. Quite the contrary, they arrive at the same results, which in effect lends credence to the statement that the "gate" of absolute authority was closed in early Islam, the same investigations leading to the same results, at least regarding the essentials of the Islamic Law. In nonessential matters, the later muftis are free to pursue a relatively independent judgment within the framework of their particular school. They cannot now, for example, reexamine the necessity for observing the Pillars of Religion and thus overturn the traditional practice, but they can issue *fatwās* on more peripheral matters. Even so, the traditional muftis are not to be confused with modernist Muslims, especially of the extremist type, who would like to reexamine everything and even to start all over again from scratch. Nor must they be confused with the Shi'i muftis who operate under their own rules, independently of the orthodox schools of Sunnism.

The *ṭarīqah* represents the inner life of the Spirit, and is consequently not something that the religious scholars delve into when discussing the Law in their works. That is a domain reserved for the Ṣūfī authorities, and it is a fact that, after al-Ghazālī's reconciliation of the Law and the Path, this division of tasks has been observed. But the Ṣūfīs have nevertheless quite a bit to say about the Law and its prescriptions. This is undoubtedly because their disciples must act or engage in different types of action while in this world. Such action brings into play the principles of the Path, or the virtues, as well as the diverse kinds of action defined by the Law. As previously stated, the active life has results not only in this world but in the Hereafter; there is a causal connection between one's deeds in the present life and one's posthumous condition. It is not so much that the acts themselves lead to positive or negative consequences as it is that they reflect the inner state of the soul, the heart, and it is this which is judged. For that reason, the intention (*niyyah*) of the believer in carrying out a particular action is what really counts in the eyes of Heaven. People see only the external deed, not the intention rooted in the heart, which may or may not be sound. To assure that the intention preserve a generally correct tendency, the works of the faithful must be lined up with those of the Prophet as expressed in his Sunnah. This implies that the external deed as well as the inner attitude toward it should correspond to what the Prophet established in the Sunnah. The inner attitude is correct when the right intention (*niyyah ṣāliḥah*) is present in the heart. In that case the external act, as judged by men, may actually be imperfect, but it is given celestial approval by virtue of its sincere intention. The inner intention is therefore the principal element in the life of action, not the acts themselves, or as a *ḥadīth* of the Prophet would put it: "Actions are to be evaluated only by their intentions."

Like other sacred Laws governing mankind, the *sharī'ah* has commandments and prohibitions addressed to the individual and society, the commandments detailing what has to be done, the prohibitions describing what must be avoided. Between these two extremes, which carry posthumous implications having to do with salvation and damnation, there are other categories of actions that the *madhhabs* have examined. They are concerned particularly with the ritual and moral observances of the Law, and these categories we can already see delineated by Muḥammad and his companions. Fundamentally, the Law speaks of five types of action, the obligatory (*farḍ*), the recommended (*mandūb*), the tolerated or indifferent (*mubāḥ*), the reprehensible (*makrūh*), and the prohibited (*ḥarām*). The different *madhhabs*, while agreeing on the essentials, sometimes differ on the category of a particular deed and on the lightness or severity or even the absence of the punishment that is to be meted out for violations of the prohibitions of Islam and even for failing to observe the obligatory prescriptions. It is in this interpretation of the commandments and prohibitions of the faith by the different *madhhabs* that we can discern a particularly eloquent testimony of the principle that "The differences of the religious authorities are mercifulness from God." All flexibility would have disappeared from the juridical evaluations if the five kinds of deeds were similarly treated by the authorities of the great *madhhabs*.

The different types of action, from the obligatory to the prohibited, have formed the substance of jurisprudential works and have been given wide recognition in all spheres of Islamic life and society since the origins of the religion. Just as Christianity has propagated an awareness of the Ten Commandments throughout Christendom, so similarly Islam has spread an awareness of the five kinds of actions wherever it has gone. That awareness has been intensified by the fact that the religion tends to encourage the Muslim to assume his own sacerdotal functions, which in turn implies knowledge of what is obligatory or prohibited. The *sharī'ah* of Islam, in essence, is especially concerned with these varieties of commandments and prohibitions because they affect the immediate equilibrium of the community as a whole, keeping it within the bounds of religion as interpreted by the religious authorities, and directing the fallen nature of society into a direction that is compatible with the saving content of the revelation.

It is the *madhhabs* that confer a certain uniformity to Islamic Law throughout the Muslim world. The *sharī'ah*, when residualized into the Five Pillars, is strikingly homogeneous from one end of the Muslim world to another. It binds all Muslims together as the unifying principle of their external actions. Islamic Law, however, being sacred, is not comparable to the profane Law that exists in the Western world. No atheist would observe the *sharī'ah*, for its commandments and prohibitions have to do, not only with man's life in this world, but with the consequences of his deeds in the Hereafter. Western Law, by contrast, can be observed by disbeliever and believer alike, its code having nothing to do with the life to come. Like Islamic Law, which has the equilibrium of society in view, Western Law also seeks that equilibrium. But there the similarity ceases, the *sharī'ah* being concerned also with the posthumous world, in terms of reward and punishment. Moreover, the content of the two legal systems is not the same, the Islamic Law having elements that the secularist Law of the West does not have, such as liturgical or ritual prescriptions, or the religio-social etiquette governing human relations, and so on. Not having a secularist view of life, which separates society from the religion, the *sharī'ah* integrates into the religion all the necessary activities that together form man's individual and social existence. In this respect, one has to look beyond modern Western legal codes to find the analogues to the Islamic Law in the sacred legislation of Judaism and Hinduism. It is this awareness that the legal system of Islam is sacred and exclusive to Muslims that brought into play the rights of religious minorities, such as Christians and Jews, to follow their own ritual and personal statutes as *dhimmīs*, or individuals having a special protective covenant (*dhimmah*) with the Muslim authorities. This was a brilliant solution to the question of the multiplicity of religions under the domination of Islam, and represented a particular application of the Qur'ānic doctrine on the universality of revelation.

The 'Ulamā'

While it is true that Islam has no priests or sacerdotal class, and that the Muslim is his own sacerdote, the fact of the matter is that there has always existed a well-informed and pious minority of authorities whose knowledge of the principles and practices of the religion placed them heads and shoulders above the others. Because of their comprehensive knowledge of the *sharī'ah*, they were consulted by the mass of believers. After the first century of Islam, they formed the ranks of the *'ulamā'*, or the religious scholars, who became an important socio-religious class in society and in the workings of the State. With the establishment of the 'Abbāsid Dynasty, in the eighth century, they became full-fledged members of the Government, assuming in particular the judicial functions. It is the *'ulamā'*, in the technical sense of a body of religious scholars, who would take on the special duties of codifying, preserving, and interpreting the *sharī'ah*.

While the *'ulamā'* are religious scholars, their ranks are further subdivided by their particular specializations. The muftis are those who are empowered to deliver *fatwās*, or legal opinions, on different subjects. The *qāḍīs* are the judges of Islam, who adjudicate in matters of the Law. The *fuqahā'* are the jurisconsults whose field of study is Islamic jurisprudence (*fiqh*). In the traditional Islamic world, their authority was considerable. They were ranked according to a certain hierarchy, which is still the case here and there, given that there are thousands of them with unequal talents.

Their formation was mostly in the religious institutions, the *madrasahs* of Islam, many of which still exist in the various parts of the Muslim world. It is in these schools that they pursued the programs of religious studies, requiring years of dedication, to gain a diploma that would entitle them to function officially as *'ulamā'*. In the past, they wore special dress, had special posts and titles in the Government, and in general wielded no small degree of influence. It is they who are the religious authorities of Islam and guardians of the Law. That they can become pharisaical and puffed up in their erudition to the point of rejecting the *ṭarīqah*, or Ṣūfism, is clear from any consideration of their history within the community. But one must not exaggerate in relegating all of them to the ranks of the Pharisees, for some of the greatest in every generation were members of Sūfī orders. In any case, it is not the Law as such that is decried by the Ṣūfīs; it is the limitations of the *'ulamā'*, who are the exoterists par excellence of Islam. Great Ṣūfīs have also been authorities on the *sharī'ah*, so it is not the study of the Law that leads to the constricted outlook of exoterism; it is an attitude of mind in the exoterist as such.

The State in Islam

After the passing away of the first four Caliphs ("The Rightly-Guided Caliphs," *al-khulafā' ar-rāshidūn*), who were the companions of the Prophet, there gradually developed a symbiotic relationship between the State and the religious authorities that continued down to recent times. The reason for this is that the State itself is covered by the Law.[3] It is not above it and the ruler is as much subject to the Law as his people. Attempts have been made to describe the traditional Islamic State as theocratic in nature, and this is true on condition that it be understood that there are no priests in the religion. Because there is no secularism in Islam, there is no separation of Church and State. Everything falls under the rule of the Law, including the State, and to this extent Islam is a nomistic religious system. It is because of its nomism that Islam, as a civilization, rapidly developed the fruitful interaction between the State and the *'ulamā'*. There was a division of labor between the political authorities and the religious authorities in the sense that the former occupied themselves with the State, the latter with Religion.

The nomistic character of Islam permits a wide variety of political institutions to flourish. Nevertheless, it is clear, both from the career of the Prophet Muḥammad and the age of the "Orthodox Caliphs" (632-661), Abū Bakr, 'Umar, 'Uthmān, and 'Alī, that there is a fundamental tendency in Islam toward monarchic as opposed to republican or democratic forms of Government. To begin with, the Prophet did not rule and reign by democratic acclamation or by some kind of republicanism among the ancient Arabs. Arab egalitarianism was not opposed to tribal aristocracies and Muḥammad's style is that of a desert monarch with a prophetic mission. His monarchic tendencies, although couched in the harsh simplicity of Bedouin culture, and not in regal pomp and glory, came from the mission assigned to him as Prophet and Messenger. This was absolute and admitted of no republican derogations of the Islamic revelation. Moreover, his companions who ruled after him were just as monarchic as he was and little disposed to tamper with the revelation for the sake of democratic compromises with the people. We can see this with striking clarity in the whip that the Caliph 'Umar carried about with him on all occasions; and he is looked upon by later generations as somehow embodying the ideal ruler. In truth, the very institution of the Caliphate presupposes a monarchic outlook not only in the first four Caliphs but in the later ones. Finally, the nomistic structures of the religion envisage a State that has an executive power and a judicial power, but not a legislative one that could compromise the sacred legislation derived from the Qur'ān and the Sunnah. The executive power, historically, might be one of innumerable variations on a monarchic theme — Caliph, Sultan, Amir, Shah, King, Maharajah, and the like — that ruled either by hereditary or elective customs. The judicial power, by contrast, was strictly in the hands of the religious scholars, who watched over the Law and interpreted it. But legislative functions vested in a body of individuals who could formulate laws on their own that would erode the integrity of the *sharī'ah* are not to be found in the nomocracy of the religion.

The executive's functions have to do with those duties that concern the State inwardly and outwardly. He must implement the *sharī'ah* as interpreted by the religious scholars — and it is here where the symbiotic relationships between the State and Religion come into the picture — within the confines of his State, which leads to interior equilibrium. He must also engage in Holy War (*jihād*) or have treaty relations with neighboring, non-Muslim States, in view of an eventual state of peace. Whatever he is, a Caliph, a Sultan, or a Shah, he can come to power by heredity or by force of arms; but in either case he is as much subject to the Law as is the lowliest of his people. Muslims are under obligation to obey him so long as he does not contravene the Law. Throughout the centuries, they have always shown great tolerance toward their rulers and have allowed them considerable leeway in their private morality. Just as there have been good kings and bad kings in Christendom, so there have been good and bad Caliphs or Sultans in the Muslim world. A king of the measure of Saint Louis (d. 1270) has his counterpart, in saintliness and political acumen, in the Ayyūbid Sultan Salāḥ ad-Dīn (d. 1193), the Saladin of the Crusaders.

The great figurehead of Islamic political theory is of course the Caliphs (*khalīfah*). The theory would have it that, since there is only one Islamic *ummah*, there should be only one Caliph who reigns over it as "the shadow of God on earth". Since the death of the Prophet, there has always been a Caliph in the Islamic community, at least up to recent times. For some fourteen centuries, Caliphs succeeded one another as good or bad rulers or simply as reigning monarchs who did not rule. Then the entire institution was brought to an end by the Westernized Turks in the 1920s, who proceeded to strip Turkey of its Islamic institutions in the name of republican secularism. Since those days, the Islamic world has had no Caliphal institution that would give it a semblance of unity. More often than not, especially after the early centuries, the Caliphs reigned rather than ruled, while the true rulers were the Sultans or others. But whether reigning or ruling, the Caliphs, even when reduced in their powers to practically nothing at all, still commanded the affections of the generality of Muslims, more or less like the Papacy in Rome stirs the hearts of Christians. When the modernist Turks struck down the age-old institution, there was a traumatic reaction through the world of Islam, as was to be expected.

Sunnism and Shī'ism

The question of the Caliphate leads to another problem, that of the Imāmate, the former having to do with Sunnism, the latter with Shī'ism.[4] Sunnism is the Islam of the overwhelming mass of Muslims, whereas Shī'ism is a special deviation from the Sunnī mainstream and is followed by a small minority in the Islamic world. The origins of Shī'ism can be situated among the partisans (*shī'ah*) of 'Alī. Even during the lifetime of the Prophet, they gathered around 'Alī because of his charismatic radiance. Later Shī'īs assert that 'Alī was designated as his successor by the Prophet. It is also affirmed that he was of the "People of the House" (*ahl al-bayt*), along with his wife Fāṭimah (d. 632), and their sons Ḥasan (d. 669) and Ḥusayn (d. 680). It is they who form a prestigious line from which would issue the descendants of the Prophet, and whose eminence in this respect should have been given prime consideration in the choice of a successor to the Prophet. The Shi'ī theses were based on all sorts of evidence, advanced with a certain assurance, that the Prophet had indeed chosen 'Alī as his successor. Subsequent Shī'ī theology would envelop these assertions with a semimystical doctrine on the Light transmitted from the Prophet to the Shī'ī Imāms and on their religio-political infallibility (ʿsmah) as religious leaders. For the Shī'īs, therefore, the Imām 'Alī should have been the rightful head of the community and the hereditary Imāmate the only kind of political governance. For the Sunnīs, the head of the community was the Caliph (*khalīfah*), and the Caliphate was normally elective, even though the Caliph ruled with monarchic power under the *sharī'ah*.

'Alī did not rule (656-661) until after the deaths of the first three Caliphs, and even then it was not by hereditary right. Nor did his reign show any of the signs of the religio-political infallibility predicated of the Imāms by the Shī'ī doctrinaires. His son, the Imām Ḥasan, abdicated the Caliphate. The other son, the Imām Husayn, who claimed the Caliphate, was killed at the Battle of Kerbela (October 10, 680) by the forces of the Caliph Yazid. That day (the 10th of Muḥarram in the Hijrī calendar) has been commemorated every year since then with mourning and lamentation among the Shī'īs, a practice one does not find in the Sunnī world.

The triumph of Sunnism over Shī'ism relegated the Shī'ī version of Islam to the peripheral status of a minority movement that became increasingly isolated from the mainstream of the community in proportion as it absolutized the role of its Imāms. There was now added a mystique of love for the Imāms that eclipsed the central role of the Prophet as founder of the religion. Joined to that mystique was a cult of suffering, in emulation of the suffering of the Imām Ḥusayn at Kerbela and of the other rejected Imāms. "Shi'ism is thus not only a teaching about the Imām 'Ali's right to succeed the Prophet, but it is also a mystique of Love covering all the Imāms."

This is especially so in Twelver Shi'ism, which ends its line with the Twelfth Imām, Muhammad al-Mahdi, who disappeared in 940, becoming the "Hidden Imam" (*al-imām al-mastūr*) in the process, and who will return as the Mahdi at the end of the ages.

The Sunnī tradition has always insisted on the crucial role played by the first four Rightly-Guided, or Orthodox, Caliphs of Islam, including the Imām 'Alī, in preserving and watching over the Islamic religion transmitted to them by the Prophet. It does not permit the disparagement of any of these Caliphs, for they were all morally intact in character. Individually, they might have made mistakes in political and other matters, but this is more or less inevitable in the give and take of ruling. However, they were all companions of the Prophet in an intimate fashion, and this in itself implied a certain spiritual role for each one that could not have been carried out by persons of suspected morality. Consequently, while Shī'ism insists on the uniqueness of 'Alī to the degree that it calls into question the moral integrity of the first three Caliphs of Islam, Sunnism ascribes to all four the virtues of "the Orthodox Caliphs".

Sunnism also recognizes the special function of the "People of the House" (*ahl al-bayt*), at least up to the Sixth Imām, Ja'far aṣ-Ṣadiq (d. 765), as authorities in the eso-exoteric facets of the Islamic revelation. But they are not seen, of course, in the special fashion envisaged by Shī'ī teachings. The religious authorities of Sunnism as well as the Ṣūfīs cite the Imāms, not as Shī'ī personalities purveying Shī'ī teachings, but as descendants of the Prophet well-versed in the religion he left behind. They were not the only ones who exercised the role of authoritative guides to the community, nor were they the only descendants of the Prophet. There were other, equally authoritative teachers, such as al-Ḥasan al-Baṣrī (d. 728), not to mention other descendants of the Prophet. But the early Imāns, by virtue of their prestigious lineage, their knowledge of the Law and the Path, and the cyclical needs of Islam for patriarchal leadership in preserving intact the message of Muḥammad, could not but have a religious role to play that the later Imāms, who lived long after the classic contours of the religion had been established, did not have.

The Shī'ī Twelver *madhhab* differs from the Sunnī *madhhabs* in small details, so that the *sharī'ah* in both camps is more or less the same. Nevertheless, the Sunnī tradition as a whole has never accepted the Twelver school of jurisprudence as part and parcel of orthodoxy because of the creed (*'aqidah*) of the Shī'is, considered irregular in the eyes of Sunni authorities. Now, it is the creedal belief that distinguishes one Muslim from another in orthodoxy. This holds true even among the Sunnīs, as witness the interminable conflicts between the Shāfi'īs and the Ḥanbalīs, not with regard to their respective *madhhabs*, which were mutually considered orthodox, but with regard to their respective *'aqīdahs*. The former were largely of Ash'arī persuasion, the latter of fundamentalist and nonspeculative tendencies. At some point in the early history of Islam, certain *madhhabs*, like the Shāfi'ī, were identified with certain *'aqīdahs*, such as Ash'arism, a form of orthodox Sunnī theology. So, similarly, the Twelver *madhhab* came to be identified with the theological thinking of Shī'ism and was consequently declared to be an aberration by Sunnism and rejected as an expression of Islamic jurisprudence.

It is possible that Shī'ism represents a kind of dogmatico-theological expression of fragmentary aspects of the total spiritual Path in Islam. This would account for its resemblances to Ṣūfī esoterism and for its mystical teachings, both devotional and intellectual, regarding the Imāms. It is not that the early Imāms themselves created such teachings. They were bent on preserving the integral nature of the Law and the Path as transmitted to them by the Prophet, not on devising novel theological and semiesoteric formulations on their Imāmate, which is what their partisans did. In doing so, the latter absorbed fragments of the esoteric Path, which they identified with Shī'ism, compromising the integral contemplative Path of Islam. Partly because of that identification, the *ṭarīqah* was forced to surface as Ṣūfism and to declare its independent nature. Shortly thereafter even the Imāms of the Shī'īs ceased having the catholicity of the early ones and took on instead an increasingly Shī'ī coloration that isolated them from the Sunnī world and confined them to a Shī'ī matrix.

It is also this intrusion of an esoteric or mystical element into the theological considerations on the Twelve Imāns that gives to Shī'ism its similarities to Christian teachings on the Christ. He is the sacred Intermediary (*wāsiṭah*) between Heaven and Earth, to use Shi'i terminology borrowed from the *ṭarīqah* of Islam. But there is only one Imam in Christianity; there are Twelve in Shī'ism, or in the Twelver form of Shī'ism. The cult of penitential suffering, the mystique of love towards the Intermediary who is still mysteriously present, and the long-awaited eschatological triumph of the suffering Imām in his glorious return in messianic times, are so much alike in the two communities that Shī'ism has sometimes been described as a Christian form of Islam, or Christian Islam. This in no way implies Christian influence on Shī'ism, the Shī'ī truncation of Islamic esoterism being sufficient to explain the origin of its sectarian teachings on the Imāms.

If the origin of the teachings can be explained, the spiritual need for such teachings is another matter altogether. That need was not only questioned by Sunnism but actually rejected largely because the cult of the Imāms detracts from the centrality of the Prophet. The cult tends by its very nature to go against the grain of Sunnī Islam as a whole. True, the cult of Ṣūfī saints in the Sunnī world is comparable to the Shī'ī attitude toward the Imāms. But it is spread out over thousands of saints' shrines, impeding thereby the concentration of cosmic functions in any sacred duodecimalism, as we see in Twelver Shī'ism. Also, it is relativized beforehand by the preeminence given to the Prophet over all the other saints of Islam in both exoteric and esoteric Sunnism. Sunnī rejection of Shī'ī teachings and practices on the Imāmate condemned Shi'ism, whether moderate like the Twelvers, or extremist like some forms of Ismā'īlism, to exclusion from the bosom of the community. Nevertheless, from time to time, Shī'ism has experienced impressive intellectual and cultural flowerings, as among the Safavids of Persia (1502-1736), that belie any attempt to reduce it to a backwater sectarianism without inner vitality.

The Holy War

We may return now to the *sharī'ah* itself to consider the question of Holy War (*jihād*), which is sometimes construed as the sixth Pillar of the religion.[5] Unlike Christianity, which spread throughout the Roman Empire under the cover of its far-flung legal, administrative, and military system, and had only to move along the byways and highways of the excellent Roman road network in order to preach the Word, Islam had to unsheathe its sword from the very beginning to establish itself in Arabia and to carry its message to the non-Arab world. Warfare was not a matter of choice for the Muslims. They were enjoined to fight by both the Qur'ān and the Sunnah, so that the *jihād* has a binding quality to it, in the eyes of the Law, whenever the integrity of *dār al-islām*, or parts of it, is menaced, or whenever there is felt the need to spread the faith through the force of arms. The fighting prescribed by the *sharī'ah* is not an end in itself, for the goal of warfare is eventual peace through treaty arrangements, and not perpetual warfare. Nor is the *jihād* to be conducted outside the framework of rules and conditions established by the Law, which restricts the amplitude of the fighting and seeks to protect the noncombatants. But this is not to say that all wars in the history of Islam between Muslims and non-Muslims have been fought in conformity with the rules set down in the Law and interpreted by the religious authorities. There have been many wars that were in violation of these rules. Such infringements or violations of the rules of Holy War were more or less inevitable, since Muslims have never had any qualms about engaging in warfare and Islam has tended to create a combative disposition that is all the more explosive and unbridled in that the Qur'ān itself sanctions fighting and even urges the believers to draw the sword against disbelief.

The revelation took the ancient Arabs as they were, an extremely volatile and warlike people with a certain chivalric and magnanimous character. Without changing the positive traits of their impulsivity and passional nature, Islam sublimated their warring instincts by incorporating them into the structures of the Law. The Arabs embodied the characteristic combativity of

Islam and even transmitted something of its igneous psychism to the other people who joined the religion. Warfare, in those days, was not peculiar to Islam alone: the Christian Byzantine Empire and the Persian Zoroastrian Empire had been locked in battle for some time before Islam appeared on the scene. Like all religious civilizations, Christianity, once it became the religion of the State after the fourth century A.D., did not hesitate to use the sword.

Islam was born as a combative faith in the midst of a Mediterranean world that was torn by strife and warfare. But its combativity is for the sake of an eventual equilibrium and peace, or for the integration of a community of disbelievers into its message. Nevertheless, it can be said that, while the religion has indeed spread by the sword, it has mostly spread by persuasion and example, and continues in this latter fashion to gain converts to the present day. Although the notion of warfare sanctioned by revelation might seem strange to the outsider, one has to remember that Islam takes human nature as it is, with all of its passional attachments, and seeks to penetrate it with the idea of the Divine Unity as much as possible. It seeks to convert the warring instincts into a spiritual force that is compatible with the Islamic message. It is better to control the fighting instincts with religious injunctions which keep them within the pale of the Law and in view of man's last ends than it is to give vent to them without restraint and with purely worldly goals in view. At least that is one way of looking at the Qur'ānic sanctioning of warfare on behalf of Islam.

We should also recall here the distinction made by the Prophet between the "lesser *jihād*", or military warfare, and the "greater *jihād*", or spiritual warfare. The latter pits the virtues in man's soul against the vices and passions with a view to the ultimate triumph of the Spirit within man over its interior enemies. The peace of soul that follows the round of spiritual battles in the "greater *jihād*" is the contemplative prototype of the peace that should follow the military warfare of the "lesset *jihād*." The Qur'ānic view of *jihād* permits of its interpretation in a military as well as in a purely spiritual case. While a Muslim may be prevented from engaging in the "lesser *jihād*", no one is really exempt from the "greater *jihād*", for the whole question of salvation revolves around the successful outcome of the inner warfare in man's soul, right up to the hour of death. It is perhaps for this reason that Ṣūfism has quite a bit to say about the spiritual warfare that must take place within man's soul to undo the effects of forgetfulness and ignorance and to permit the luminous raying-out of the victorious Spirit.

The Islamic Marriage

Another aspect of the *sharī'ah* that has provoked Western criticism of Islam is the institution of marriage, especially in its polygamous features.

Needless to say, polygamy has not been peculiar to Islam; Judaism has had it, as witness the wives of David and Solomon, and a kind of *de facto* polygamy has existed in other traditions of the world, even when the sacred legislation, as in Hinduism, honored monogamous arrangements. Moreover, the Islamic Law simply regulated multiple marriages, as well as concubinage; but it does not force polygamy on the men, must less concubinage, since its principal view of marriage tends to be that monogamy is normative for the community, not polygamy.

Marriage in Islam is seen as a contractual agreement within a religious framework. But it is not a purely contractual or legal affair devoid of religious connotations, otherwise the Messenger would not have said, "Marriage is half of a man's religion." Yet it is true that the institution does not have the sacramental characteristic that one finds in Christianity, even though marriage is seen as a source of *barakah* for the parties concerned. Let us recall that the sacramental marriage is indissoluble, whereas this is not the case for marriage in Islam.

The motivating cause of union — matrimonial and carnal — between the spouses is said to be love. This is a Qur'ānic thesis that affirms the primacy of love as the cause of marriage, not simple reproduction. Nevertheless, the religious authorities, almost unanimously, interpret marriage as primarily reproductive in nature and as a means of perpetuating the species. Since popular opinion seems to agree in general with that interpretation, the matrimonial institution revolves, in great part, around this function. That does not mean that love between the spouses is nonexistent, but only that it is not given the weight one might think it should have as the causal element of union. Other traditions agree that the reproductive function of marriage has prime consideration, especially for the carnal act, as we notice in Christianity, Judaism, and in other, more Eastern religions.

The fact that Islam views the carnal act as not merely the source of pleasure but also as a source of *barakah* means that sexuality has positive connotations and is not associated with sin, as we see in the Christian world. There is nothing absolute in this distinction between the two faiths, but the fact remains that the Christian teaching on the transmission of Original Sin through the sexual act has been decisive in coloring that faith's attitude towards carnal love. The sexual purity of both the Christ and the Virgin Mary is significant in this respect. In Islam the consecration of carnal love in marriage by the Sunnah of the Messenger dissolves all possible sinful associations with its pleasurable nature and elevates it almost to the rank of a ritual and even to a criterion of faith. The pious man is the one who follows in the footsteps of the Prophet by observing his matrimonial Sunnah. The dictum in both Hindu and Buddhist Tantrism that "Whatever makes a man fall can also make him rise" led to the reconsideration of the symbolism of sexuality in a positive sense as conducive to spiritual life rather than as being a block to it. Such a notion has a kind of generalized Islamic application: That which makes a man fall, such as the sexual act, can also make him rise by virtue of its having been sacralized by the Prophet in his Sunnah. Henceforth, sexuality became a powerful element in the process of man's salvation. The apparent sensuality and earthly nature of the Prophet, seen in this light, restores to sexual union something of its symbolic power.

While the Law of Islam permits marriage with four women and also concubinage with those women captured in war as part of the booty, it is clear from the Qur'ān that man cannot do justice to more than one wife. Why, then, does the *sharī'ah* allow polygamy to exist? For one thing, the sensual activity of the male lends to some men a polygamous bent that has been recognized by the most diverse cultures of ancient and medieval times, and even institutionalized in some, particularly among the ranks of the aristocracy. Rather than allowing this sensuality in the male to run riot, obeying nothing but its own impulses, the Law of Islam sets down a polygamous framework within which to give it a certain control. As with the combative passions that are expressible in Holy War, so in this domain also, that of sexual passions, Islamic Law confers a conscious mold on the formless instinct of man in order to keep him within the structures of religion.

For another thing, the decimation of the male population of Islam through Holy War in the seventh century or so, and even in later expansions, would have led to anarchism in social life. Numberless widows and orphans would have been unprotected by husbands and fathers had the *sharī'ah* not already made provisions for polygamy by anticipation. Islam sanctioned the *jihād*, to the point where the State made its way in the world with sword in hand. The religion could not have spread with such astonishing speed had there been no Law covering the Holy War, which in turn obliged it to have provisions for polygamous marriage so as to maintain the social equilibrium of the community.

Finally, Islam sought instinctively to avert the institution of the "mistress" that shadows the monogamous character of marriage in Christianity by permitting overtly polygamous arrangements within its sacred legislation and thus cutting at the root of the problem.

As a sacred bond between the spouses, marriage is seen by the Law as a lifelong or permanent union, requiring the consent of both parties in the presence of witnesses. But the Law likewise undertakes to set down those conditions that can lead to divorce. While it is true that the Prophet said, in a *ḥadīth*, that "nothing is more hateful to God than divorce," nevertheless it is permitted for a number of reasons, ranging from impotence to nonsupport. If it occurs, the woman keeps her dowry. Divorce courts have existed throughout the history of Islam, largely to adjudicate whatever legal complications result from dowry and other problems in a divorce. In principle, the divorce can be initiated by either the man or the woman; in practice, it is the man who does so through the formula of repudiation. Each of the *madhhabs* in the Sunni world has a wealth of details on all phases of marriage and divorce, as can be well imagined, so that the simplicity of the matrimonial and divorce proceedings of Islam is only an appearance.

The Role of Women

Compared to pre-Islamic women, who had few rights, the Law of Islam conferred on women new rights, such as the abolition of female infanticide, property rights, and dowry rights which cannot be touched upon divorce. Nevertheless, Islam does not preach the equality of the sexes. The feminist notion that one finds in Western secularist cultures are not to be found in the Islamic tradition as such, and wherever one does find them in the East is the result of the process of Westernization. Rightly understood, Islam preaches a number of attitudes toward women, and not just one, as might be thought. There is, first of all, the subordination of women to men; secondly, the equality of both before God; thirdly, a certain superiority of women to men, at least regarding the symbolism or spiritual value of women.

When Islam preaches the subordination of women to men, it does so in common with all the other great traditions, such as Hinduism, Buddhism, Christianity, Judaism, Confucianism, and so on, all of whose scriptures or legislative codes have that feature. But the Qur'ān refers to that superiority as being ''a degree'', which certainly does not imply total or absolute subordination in all domains. Instead, a limited, social subordination is taught that gives to the man the role of paterfamilias, and that does not militate against a woman having qualities of superiority in spirituality, intelligence, or culture. Probably that social superiority of men came from the fact that, in the Qur'ān, they are considered to be the guardians or protectors of women. In fact, the patriarchal nature of Islam is manifested in the guardianship of the man over the woman. So much so is this the case that only on very few occasions do we actually find women rulers in the history of the faith. The entire patriarchal tradition of Islam harbors a kind of antipathy to the rule of women, no doubt because of scriptural criteria that are decisive but also because of the Sunnah of the Messenger, that is purely patriarchal, as in the *sharī'ah* which flows from both the Scripture and the Prophet's example.

Proof that in Islamic teachings there is equality of men and women, and not just subordination of the latter, lies in their participating in the same human nature and having immortal souls that will be judged at death. This is a spiritual equality that both share in, for both must work out their salvation, and not merely the men. Hence, the commandments and prohibitions of the *sharī'ah* fall equally upon the women in view of the life to come, for the Paradises are open to them also, as is the road to saintliness. Throughout Islamic history, we find many minor and great women saints, such as Sayyidah Nafīsah (d. 824) of Egypt and Rābi'at al-'Adawiyyah (d. 801) of Iraq, to say nothing of the myriads of pious, saintly women, all of whom were conscious that the sanctification of their souls was something to which they had equal access alongside of men. While the search for saintliness is binding on both sexes, it is evident that it does not do away with the previously-mentioned social subordination of woman to man. In other words, there is an intrinsic equality of the sexes, regarding their souls when facing God, that exists within an extrinsic framework of subordination of women to men. Even if one interprets that equality as a kind of complementary role each sex has toward the other or as functions that each sex fulfills and that complement the functions of the other sex, it still remains true that the *sharī'ah* retains the subordination of women on a social level as a normative rule, as we can see throughout the Sunnah of the Prophet.

Islam also sees a third attitude toward women, namely, the superiority of women over men. This is especially true in the spiritual life, as we see in the cases of some Ṣūfī women who were the guides in the Path for men disciples. The poets in the various Islamic tongues talk of women more or less as if they were "idols" to be looked up to and respected, if not adored, for their beauty, their virtues, their noble qualities, and their representing in a concrete fashion the Eternal Feminine. We discern this in the many legends associated with the love story of Majnūn and Laylā. The great women saints of Islam, many of whose shrines are still visited by the pious, are superior by virtue of their sanctity and wisdom. And their superiority is due to their spirituality as such, not to their beauty and charms, so that the Eternal Feminine manifests itself in them in a mystical style. This is not incompatible with feminine beauty, as we find in the example of Fāṭimah, the daughter of the Prophet and the wife of 'Alī, who is said to have had great saintliness and beauty. On a lesser plane, but still within this ambiance of superiority, is the position of mothers over their offspring, who must show them respectful affection and look up to them as the inferior to the superior. Nevertheless, the general attitude of Islam has been that of subordination due to the self-evident patriarchal character of the religion, with all that this implies in the way of cultural habits and modes of conduct. Feminist ideas, which in the West are based on secularist notions of life, to say nothing about indifference to the traditional scriptural teachings or their reinterpretation to fit modern notions, have come into the Islamic world through the influence of Westernized Muslims. In reality, Western feminism can only take root in a totally secularist society, a condition that has not been reached yet anywhere in the Islamic lands; and that is why the patriarchal culture of the religion still holds sway.

Economic Aspects

Teachings in regard to the economic institutions of Islam can be extracted from the Scripture, the *ḥadīths*, and the works of religious authorities over the centuries.[6] One must also add the evidence of the institutions themselves that encompass financial, commercial, and trade activities of all sorts. The traditional economic life of the community was based on agricultural and artisanal activities that cannot be compared with the capitalistic, socialistic, and other types of economic systems engendered by modern Western industrial civilization. They had religious underpinnings completely lacking in their Western counterparts. Capitalism and communism, for example, which are the two main camps of the modern West, are both hostile to the Islamic modes of economic behavior, but in different ways. The fact that Islamic Law permits the accumulation of wealth and the holding of private property, to say nothing about the entrepreneurial system and the free market for the determination of prices, would seem to give the Islamic system a resemblance to the capitalist way of doing things and to remove it altogether from the socialist theories and practices of the modern West. But while Islam seems closer to the Western capitalist way of life, its Law prohibits the taking of interest (*ribā*), and this establishes a sharp distinction between Islam and the interest-taking facets of modern Western capitalism. However, there is still another distinction: the *sharīʻah* imposes on all those who possess wealth, great or small, the various obligations of legal alms-giving on a yearly basis, or *zakāh*, already mentioned among the Pillars of Religion, which is not the same as taxation. The accumulation of wealth is not therefore restricted by the Law, but all wealth is subject to the provisions of *zakāh*, and this introduces a charitable disposition into the community and restrains the acquisitive passions.

Since the means of production and the distribution of goods were largely in entrepreneurial hands, as we see in the traditional civilization of the past, unprincipled rapacity and greed were discouraged by the prohibitions of the *sharīʻah* against usury and by its commandments on legal alms-giving. The conditioning of the economic life by a religious framework mitigated somewhat the imperfections and faults that are to be found in all sorts of material gain and production. It is this mitigation of the evils resulting both from the production of wealth and its distribution in society that the *sharīʻah* has in mind, not the abolition of it altogether, which would be a complete impossiblity in a society of imperfect men.

While Islam is basically egalitarian in its religious nature, this should not lead to confusing such egalitarianism with the proletarianism and demogogic democracy of modern times in the West. The distinction between the social classes is no doubt abolished in the various ritual manifestations of the religion, as we see in the ranks of the faithful in mosques or in the common pilgrim's garb worn by everyone on the pilgrimage to Mecca. But this does not constitute a denial of the normal hierarchies of society, nor does the egalitarianism of Islam level the believers into one anonymous rank. The egalitarian principle of Islam is based on the thesis that all men possess an immortal soul created by God and that they are equally responsible before their Creator for its posthumous state. That this does not conflict with the principle of spiritual aristocracy can be seen in the Qur'ānic verse, "Verily, the noblest among you, in the sight of God, is the most God-fearing" (Sūrah 49:13). This in effect establishes the distinction between the religious elite and the generality of believers, already visible in the days of the Prophet.

The fraternal and communal attitudes instilled by Islam are not the same as the camaraderie of the communist or republican systems of the West. The reason is that the Sunnah of the Prophet contains a rather elaborate code of conduct (*ādāb*) which establishes hierarchies and distinctions among believers and rules for eating, drinking, speaking, walking, greeting, leave-taking, and the like. In their aggregate, these rules are meant to reform the chaotic substance of man and to transform it into its primordial nature, its *fiṭrah*, as it was when made in the image of God. Observance of Islamic *ādāb* creates attitudes of dignity, piety, nobleness, and sincerity that are man's responses to a sacred presence in his fellow man. It is this which prevents Islamic fraternalism from descending into the crass comradeship of certain Western materialistic ideologies that strip man of his immortal Spirit and reduce him to his animality. Likewise, Islam has always recognized the distinction of social classes and has never preached the active hostility of the lower classes against the higher, or what is nowadays called "class struggle", with purely economic and materialistic motives. The *sharī'ah* of Islam, through its prescriptions for *zakāh*, and the moral strictures of the faith, prohibits any such hostility. It encourages instead harmonious relations between the social aristocracy and the lower classes, to say nothing about the relations between the ruler and his subjects.

The Poor and the Rich

Yet, within the general religious atmosphere produced by the influence of the Law and the Path on society as a whole, there is a tendency to favor the poor as against the rich. This is not because their poverty is intrinsically laudable as such, but because it induces a nonacquisitive, religious life without distractions. The Prophet himself lived in a state of poverty that had a certain dignity and beauty which derived from the spiritual message of his religion. He set an example of simplicity and nonattachment to material goods in view of the "remembrance of God" (*dhikru 'llāh*). In so doing he encouraged a frugal existence, a kind of religious poverty, that permitted the dictates of faith to be followed without the distracting influences of a life dedicated to the piling up of wealth. It is not, therefore, poverty as such that is favored, but religion: it is the religious life that counts, not one's poverty or wealth.

The mendicant orders of Ṣūfism used poverty as a discipline in the Path, but not as an end in itself. It was meant as a deliberate pruning away of nonessentials in the life of the contemplative so that he could devote himself with greater ease to the inner demands of the Path. But the Ṣūfī orders never assumed that this was the only approach to spiritual realization. Thus we find other Ṣūfī methods that do not prescribe external poverty, nor do they require the seeker to leave his post in society, whether he be rich or poor, young or old. Their perception of things is that what counts is not one's external wealth or poverty but one's interior spiritual poverty (*faqr*) in the face of the infinite richness of the Divine Presence, and this produced a necessary detachment toward all external conditions. It is that spiritual poverty alone that is absolute in the Path.

The favoring of the poor in some of the prescriptions of the *sharī'ah* does not mean that, because of their poverty, they are exempt from the other observances of Islam having to do with sanctification of the soul. That is binding on all, rich or poor, and is not a luxury limited only to those who have the means and the time to be religious. On the contrary, since Islam views the pious and God-fearing or God-loving or God-knowing believer as the flower of the faith, or as the norm for the community, or even as the axial creature in this world, there is no cult of the average man or of the generality of believers, whatever might be their social rank in society. On the contrary, it is they who revolve around the saintly poles of their religion. Like other scriptural texts, the Qur'ān has nothing but praise for the pious religious minority, out of whose ranks are drawn the spiritual aristocracy of Islam. This elect can come from any walk of life, as we see in the hagiographical literature of the religion. That is indeed the fundamental hierarchy of Islam. It is the distinction between the spiritual elect (*al-khāṣṣah*) and the generality of the believers (*al-'āmmah*), having connotations of superiority and inferiority in a spiritual sense that refer respectively to the saintliness of the former and the worldliness of the latter. While Islam has traditionally permitted different types of hierarchy, in the social, military, political, and other spheres, the spiritual aristocracy has been normative, as witness the long line of Caliphs and Sultans who would consult with saintly men or women ascetics and sages while showing them deferential respect and honor.

The Law and Decadence

All of these considerations on the Law of Islam should not make us forget that it represents the exoteric level of the revelation, and that it does not suffice unto itself, for the spiritual esoterism of the Path alone provides the fullness of the message. That the Law can become an end in itself and wind up destroying the life of the Spirit might seem like a contradiction, at first glance, for it is sacred and should in principle conduce to salvation when properly followed. Yet it is a matter of historical experience in all religions that exclusive preoccupation with legal matters, proliferation of ritual observances, and hair-splitting and punctilious distinctions in the moral code lead eventually to a stultifying legalism, ritualism, and moralism, respectively, which cannot but stifle the intuitive spiritual consciousness of man. When St. Paul said that "the letter killeth, but the Spirit giveth life" (2 Corinthians 3:6), he meant by this that the Jewish Law had been superseded by the Path revealed by the Christ. But there is also implicit in the statement the notion that the Law in itself has an intrinsically mortal tendency, and this can only be when its provisions are carried to excess and result in pharisaism, which extinguishes the life of the Spirit.

As strange as it might seem, spiritual decadence is manifested not only in the absence of the Law, leading to socio-religious anarchism, but also in its presence as an inflated legalism devoid of inner life. We can perceive the latter in the Jewish Sanhedrin which sent Jesus to the Cross or in the *'ulamā'* of Islam whose fundamentalism has led them to persecute the Ṣūfī saints in the name of the Law as in the famous case of al-Ḥallāj (d.922), martyred by the religious authorities of Baghdad. From this, one may conclude that an Islam reduced merely to its *sharī'ah*, and stripped of all influences coming from the Path, is in danger of cutting itself off from its source of regenerative vitality. For the same reason, a Ṣūfism that is shot through and through with the endless ramifications of the Law ends up by being a kind of spiritualized legalism, but a legalism nevertheless. That is in contradiction with the intrinsic nature of the Way. Nevertheless, it is true that, in the history of Islam, there is a widespread, intermediate type of Ṣūfism that is neither purely contemplative and mystical Ṣūfism, nor merely exoteric legalism, though it tends toward the latter. It arose from a propensity to multiply the observances of the Sunnah on the score that this is indeed what the message of Islam calls for over and beyond the Five Pillars that represent the "golden norm" of the religion. If the phrase "Ṣūfī exoterism" were not a contradiction in terms, it would be applicable to this particular species of Islam.

In the history of Islam, observance of the Law is subject to the cyclical rhythms of decline and rebirth that one finds in all religions. Since the Path and the Law are interrelated, the revival of the Path through the mediation of Ṣūfī saints and teachers has an influence on the observance of the Law. While numerous ups and downs have occurred in the various periods and dynasties of Islamic history which impinge on the observance or nonobservance of the *sharī'ah*, the general movement of believers has been toward increasing worldliness and therefore toward the gradual domination of forgetfulness (*ghaflahs*) over the flow of human events. The *ḥadīth* of the Prophet to the effect that every generation after his would be worse than the preceding one reflects this law of general decline. That decline is halted from time to time by the appearance of a great renewer (*mujaddid*), for in another *ḥadīth* the Prophet is pictured as saying that God will raise up in the community a renewer of its religion at the beginning of every hundred years. That seems to contradict what was previously said, but only in appearance. The renovation or renewal (*tajdīd*) in question affects fewer and fewer people, until finally the end is in sight. In the case of Islam, the end corresponds to the Day of Judgment. With the decline of the community, there is a corresponding decline in the observance of the Law, and the pious minority becomes quite small in the process. That is exactly what we find in the present-day decadence of Islam. What is peculiar to our times in the Muslim world is that the modernist "reformers" seek their ideas from the non-Islamic world whereas the traditional reformers have always depended on the inspiration furnished by the revealed message and the criteria established by Islamic spirituality. In the past, the worldly and the impious merely ignored the Law and had absolutely no illusions about "reforming" Islam to make it fit their particular conceptions or styles of living.

Nonobservance of the Law leads to the dissipation of spiritual life, but legal formalism also has a negative result in that it shuts out the light of the Spirit. Excessive formalism represents an opaque substance that cannot be penetrated. It results in the absence of the virtues in the doctors of the *sharī'ah* themselves and is probably produced by an initial hardening of their psychism, which in turn affects how they handle the Law. That is a point that is often forgotten by those who would reintroduce the *sharī'ah* into the public life of Islam without simultaneously instilling in mankind, and in themselves, the practice of the spiritual life (*iḥsān*, among the three principles of religion). The routine observance of the *sharī'ah* will not revive a people if the concomitant spirituality is absent. Those who feel that imposing the Law, or their version of the Law, on all and sundry is the best way to reform society seem to forget that the Law without the inner spiritual attitudes ends up by obstructing the very reformation they seek. That is exactly what happens when the Law is detached artificially from its connections with the Path and taken as an end in itself.

In the long run, all attempts to reform the Islamic world without the spiritual criteria furnished by the tradition end up by deforming the Islamic message itself or else reducing it to a shadow of its former self. The modernist reformers, through their rejection of the traditional norms and authorities, create deviated forms of Islam; the fundamentalist reformers, through their reintroduction of the Law without spiritual content, impoverish the faith. All of this proves that the Path is an indispensable element in the life of the Islamic community, without which even the Law becomes formalistic legalism devoid of inner graces and blessings.

VI
The Islamic Intellectual Tradition

The Synthetic Nature of Revelation

The Qur'ānic revelation is a synthetic message that does not really espouse any particular school of thinking. Instead, its verses contain the germinal ideas that later would be elaborated by the different schools of Islam into systems that at times were mutually exclusive or complementary. All scriptures, of course, have the same synthetic nature. They function as revealed messages that will guide the destinies of great masses of believers having different levels of scriptural understanding and appreciation.

It follows that the Qur'ān was not meant for a small minority of mystical contemplatives alone nor merely for the majority of the faithful, but for both categories simultaneously. As a result, nothing contrasts more with the Qur'ān than the intellectual and gnostic character of the Hindu scriptures known as the Upanishads, revealed to a tiny contemplative minority of Brahmins. Because these Hindu texts were addressed to individuals of pure spiritual substance, they discuss directly the realization of the Self (*Atman*), the meditational technique of the Path, and other purely esoteric teachings that only individuals taught by masters could effectively understand and carry out in their lives.

Had the rigorous theosophical esoterism of the Upanishads been the unique content of the Qur'ān also, then the mass of the faithful would have been cut off from the redemptive message of *Tawḥīd*. Even those mystical devotees of Islam whose spirituality is not based on gnosis (*ma'rifah*) would have been left out of consideration. What we find, instead, is that the Qur'ān has a message addressed to a great variety of spiritual vocations. Although the gnostic content of the Qur'ān represents the zenith in the hierarchy of spiritual levels, the mystical depths of the text cannot be reduced to the intellectual perspectives that result from gnosis. Devotional mystics, with their love of *Allāh*, also find in those depths the needed inspiration for their viewpoint. This means that the Qur'ān, unlike the Upanishads, does not deal openly and directly with the theme of *ma'rifah*, preferring instead to hide it in the midst of ascetic and devotional injunctions of the most diverse kinds. Patience, sincerity, trust, detachment, and a host of other virtuous dispositions that characterize *iḥsān* ("virtue"), are demanded of the contemplative on the way to *ma'rifah*. Because the virtues are both preparations for gnostic realization and its fruits, they tend to veil their ultimate roots in *ma'rifah*.

The esoteric and exoteric teachings on the Qur'ān and the Sunnah are the original systems of thought, so to speak, that emerged from the primitive message of Islam and the ones most directly connected with the question of salvation (*najāh*). Salvation for the Path is here and now through spiritual realization; salvation for the Law is posthumous and involves no mystical union with God in the blissful Paradises. Other differences exist between these two systems of thought, but their direct bearing on salvation as such is what makes them so essential for an understanding of the religion. They are intimately bound up with the teaching and practice of the faith as it was revealed. That cannot be said of later systems of thought that developed in the course of the Islamic system and are to be situated between the two extremes of the Path and the Law, which are central to the religion. The Qur'ān encourages believers to reflect on the "signs" (*āyāt*) that God has put in the universe and that "they meditate on the creation of the Heavens and of the Earth" (Sūrah 3:191) with their minds. The fact that later theologians and philosophers referred back to different Qur'ānic verses for the validation of their theses proves that they detected no intrinsic limitations to the revealed Word. On the contrary, they felt that it was sufficiently universal in nature to contain a variety of viewpoints.

In the days of the Messenger and his companions, there were no systems of theology (*kalām*) and philosophy (*falsafah*) because the revealed Word was still fresh and powerful. Faith, in all of its different levels, had not yet strayed from its synthetic vision of things. Later on, of course, when such forms of intellectuality appear, they would be integrated into the tradition as a whole. When they first appear, however, they seem redundant to the faith as such. After the demise of the apostolic generation of the companions (*aṣḥāb*) and their followers (*tābi'ūn*), we encounter these nascent schools of thinking, which gradually become more important as the community moves away from its origins. Something happened in the world of Islam which made for the rise of such intellectual disciplines that seemed to be outside the *Tariqah* and the *shari'ah*. To understand what happened, we must first examine such notions as reasoning and rationalism, or the Spirit and intellect, for they are basic to the whole intellectual legacy of the Islamic religion.

Intellect and Reason

The Arabic term *'aql* is sometimes translated as "reason" and sometimes as "intellect" or its cognates, such as "intelligence". There is a profound difference in these two aspects of the *'aql* because reasoning, which is the work of the reason, is not the same as intellection, which is the work of the intellect. We are told that the intellect resides in the subtle, invisible heart of man, and that as such it is synonymous with the Spirit (*ar-ūḥ*). It operates directly and intuitively with the reality it knows, whereas man's reason, situated in the subtle brain, operates indirectly and discursively, through the reflected light of the intellect or the Spirit. The Ṣūfīs often compare the intellect to the sun and reason to the moon that reflects the light of the sun.

The Qur'ānic teachings on the heart (*al-qalb*) as the seat of spiritual vision or blindness refers to the *'aql* in the sense of intellect. This holds true likewise for the Ṣūfī doctrine on the "eye of the heart" (*'ayn al-qalb*), which is either blinded through ignorance or sees through mystical perception. In fact, in all spiritual traditions, the heart is the innermost center of man's being. It is there where his Spirit, which is like a ray of light, connects him with *Allāh*, the luminous Source of all things. When the Prophet said that "the first thing God created was the Intellect," he did not mean by that rational faculty, or reasoning, in man. He meant instead the universal Intellect at the center of the entire universe. Man's intellect derives from that Intellect like the rays of light projecting from the solar orb. As we saw earlier, Ṣūfism establishes an identity among such terms as the universal Intellect, the Spirit, the Muḥammad Light, and the Logos, which are intermediate spiritual realities between God and man. Those realities have no direct bearing in Islamic exoterism, but they are of great importance in the mystical Path. At the same time, they reveal that a term like the *'aql* under discussion can have different meanings according to context.

As reason or reasoning, *'aql* refers to man's rational power, his reflective thought which functions with the light borrowed from the Spirit in the heart. So long as reasoning and man's other faculties, such as his memory or imagination, align themselves under the controlling influence of the solar Spirit, there are no problems. Man then manifests his Edenic mind, his primordial nature (*fiṭrah*), such as he was before the Fall. But when reasoning cuts itself off from the authority of the Spirit, interior anarchy arises.

The tendency of man's rational power to reject subordination to the Spirit is one of the fruits of the Fall, according to the Ṣūfīs. This leads directly to rationalism, which is dependence on reasoning alone to arrive at conclusions. It rejects both the authority of the inner Spirit within man and the authority of the same Spirit as it manifests itself in Scripture. This is a twofold rejection that leaves no room for a transcendent solution to the problems posed by a reasoning that is left to its own devices.

At what point reasoning becomes rationalism is something that is not easily determined. The former is positive when it is obedient to the Spirit; the latter is negative because of its rebellion against the Spirit within man and in revealed Scripture. For the authorities of the Path and the Law, rationalism is seen as spiritually lethal to man's last ends. But here we must take note of an unfortunate confusion between rationalism and the rational operations of the mind in the thinking of some of those authorities. Because the transition from reasoning to rationalism takes place in a no-man's land difficult to demarcate, their rejection of rationalism is at times tantamount to rejecting reasoning as such, and even man's pure intelligence, which they confuse with reasoning. That confusion is easily done because the same word, *'aql*, applies to both the reason and intelligence. Under those circumstances, faith and reasoning would be considered as almost hostile to one another instead of being mutually supportive. The hostility, real or fancied, between faith and reasoning would have long-term results on the intelligibility — and even the unintelligibility — of Islamic dogmatic theology, as we shall see later. For the moment, let us turn to the rise of Islamic theological thinking as such, to see how it came about and what role it played within the community.

Islamic Theology

Islamic theology *(kalām)* did not arise until long after the community had gone through a number of intellectually unsettling experiences that called for some kind of response to defend the articles of faith derived from the Word of *Allāh.*[1] In the early epoch of Islam, there was a sort of primitive theology that revolved around jurisprudence and the simple dogmas of the religion. It has sustained by numerous references to the Qur'ān and to the *ḥadīths* of the Prophet, but it was neither systematic nor speculative. It proved to be insufficient when the Islamic faith began to enter the troubled waters of rationalism a century or so after the death of the Prophet (632).

Reasoning on purely theological themes arose at the same time as the first great readaptation of the Islamic message in the eighth and ninth centuries. We have only to recall that this was the period that saw the appearance of Ṣūfism, the different schools of jurisprudence, the codifications of grammar, lexicography, the *ḥadīths*, and of so many other disciplines vital to the faith. This was likewise the period when the cultivation of Greek wisdom came about through the translation into Arabic of all sorts of texts on philosophy, medicine, mathematics, astronomy, logic, and the natural sciences. A veritable cascade of intellectual disciplines drawn from non-Islamic sources came into the cultural life of the community. It was only natural that all of this fermentation should provoke rational investigations into Qur'ānic theses of different sorts. There had been a loss of the primitive spiritual vision of things, a decline in the faith of the community. This was not the result of the intrusion of Greek or other non-Islamic modes of thought into the mental life of the Muslims. Rather, the decline itself led to the cultivation of Greek thinking. At the same time there was an upward tendency, which accounted for the simultaneous splitting of the tradition into its Ṣūfī esoterism and the exoterism of the *madhhabs*. The downfall of Islam produced a much more analytical frame of mind, a more rational orientation. It was this that led to the use of Greek wisdom, which likewise was more analytical and discursive in nature than had been the thinking of the Islamic world previously. With the passage of time, Greek thinking, now Islamicized, would contribute to the intellectual regeneration of Islam. But in the eighth and ninth centuries, rational consideration of certain Qur'ānic notions was a characteristic of an Islamic school known as Mu'tazilism, a kind of speculative system of theology that had latent rationalistic tendencies.

Mu'tazilism

The early sects of Islam, such as the Khārijīs and the Murji'īs, were mostly concerned with religio-political matters, especially on the claims of the different parties to the succession to the Prophet. Mu'tazilism was a schismatic school founded by a certain Wāṣil ibn 'Atā' (d. 748) in the city of Baṣrah, a cultural center of the Muslim world in those days.[2] The school was the first manifestation of reasoning on purely theological themes, such as the questions on predestination and free will or on the Attributes and the Divine Unity. Its members, the Mu'tazilīs, called themselves "The Partisans of Unity and Justice" (*ahl at-Tawḥīd wa 'l-'adl*). They did so because they denied the existence of the Attributes, such as Power, Life, and Knowledge, on the score that the uniqueness of the Eternal Unity would be menaced otherwise. If both the One and the Attributes are eternal, they claimed, associationism (*shirk*) would result from the plurality of the Attributes. They insisted that God was Just towards His creatures, punishing them only for those evil deeds they committed. But He was not Himself the origin of evil, for the Mu'tazilīs accepted the teaching on free will of the sect known as the Qadarīs and rejected the predestinarianism of the other sect known as the Jabarīs.

The Mu'tazilīs could have maintained that the Divine Unity is absolute and that the Attributes pertained to a more extrinsic aspect of *Allāh*, preserving in that fashion the integral nature of the Divinity as impersonal essence and personal Lord of the Universe. But the rationalistic tendency in their thinking forced them to the wall and made them reject the existence of the Attributes. Later on, certain medieval Ṣūfī doctrines would preach the coexistence, so to speak, between the impersonal Unity of *Allāh*, the Divine Essence in itself, and *Allāh's* personal nature as Lord of all beings and things. For them, it was a question of degrees of reality within the Divinity. But for the Mu'tazilīs no such degrees within God were rationally conceivable, and the only solution was to reject outright the actual reality of the Attributes. This immediately created a confrontation between them and the Sunnī authorities. That was even further exacerbated by the Mu'tazilī contention that the Qur'ān is a created thing, that is to say, that its letters and sounds pertained to the world of creation, not to the uncreated world. Now the latter assertion was a dogma among the religious authorities of Sunnism, especially Aḥmad ibn Ḥanbal (d. 855), founder of the Hanbalī school of jurisprudence. The teaching on the Uncreated Qur'ān was a question of faith, not of reasoning, for the Ḥanbalīs and the other Sunnī schools of thought. What nettled them was that the Mu'tazilīs assumed an air of rational independence in arriving at their denial of a cherished traditional dogma. They therefore considered Mu'tazilism as a dangerous schismatic movement that undermined the articles of faith through rational procedures. The Mu'tazilīs eagerly absorbed the Greek modes of rational discourse, especially logic and dialectic, and that training gave to their argumentation a rather disciplined character not possessed by their opponents. The latter were content to cite Qur'ānic chapter and verse with tireless ease, thinking that this was sufficient as a rebuttal to all Mu'tazilī thinking.

Eventually, the power of the Mu'tazilīs grew by leaps and bounds until it culminated in the reign of the enlightened Caliph al-Ma'mūn (813-833), who declared Mu'tazilism to be the official religious teaching of the State. This was a public acknowledgement that reasoning had rights of its own alongside those of faith. His rule witnessed an astonishing effervescence in the intellectual life of the Muslim world, which continued on into the reign of the Caliph al-Mu'taṣim (833-842).

The future course of Ḥanbalī dogmatism was probably determined by the temporary triumph of the Mu'tazilī sect in the days of those Caliphs. All who opposed Mu'tazilism were officially persecuted. Aḥmad ibn Ḥanbal himself was maltreated and scourged in the presence of the Caliph al-Mu'taṣim because of his refusal to accept Mu'tazilī teaching on the created

Qur'ān. His refusal to waver from belief in the Uncreated Qur'ān led eventually to an intransigent attitude among later Ḥanbalīs on a number of dogmatic points that brought down on their heads a good deal of hostility from those Muslim authorities who used reasoning to back up their faith. The Mu'tazilīs were the first Muslim thinkers to attack the Ḥanbalīs. Their persecution of those who went counter to the teachings of Mu'tazilism left an indelible mark in the minds of the Ḥanbalīs, almost as if they saw the whole issue as Reason persecuting Faith. The Ḥanbalī tendency toward a blind and unthinking faith was accordingly reinforced by those early traumatic experiences. Unfortunately for the history of Islamic intellectuality, the issue was not quite so simple as that between Faith and Reason. The Mu'tazilīs were Muslims, after all, who believed in their religious principles. Their rationalism might have been carried to excess in some directions, but they did have faith. They were the champions of a thinking faith as opposed to the unthinking faith of the Ḥanbalīs.

In its totalitarian moves to impose itself on the community, Mu'tazilism reveals that rationalism can be just as fanatical and harsh as fundamentalist faith. However, it is sometimes forgotten that the Mu'tazilīs were not rationalists after the fashion of the irreligious figures of modern Western thought. They were religious men who used reasoning, and even intelligence, to grasp theological points. That some of the early Ṣūfīs were accused of being Mu'tazilīs because of their dialectic shows that reason, when used intelligently, is compatible with faith.

The short-lived victory of Mu'tazilism soon gave way to the proclamation of Sunnism as the official teaching of the State in the reign of the Caliph al-Mutawakkil (847-861). This was not the end of Mu'tazilism, for it continued on for quite a while. The toppling of Mu'tazilism made the cultivation of philosophy and even any tendency toward simple rationality highly suspect in the eyes of Sunnī religious authorities. Yet, some of the Mu'tazilī views would be integrated later on into the orthodox formulations of theology. Their thesis, for example, on the created Qur'ān would be combined with the dogma on the Uncreated Qur'ān to produce the final word on the total nature of the Islamic Scripture. That being so, Mu'tazilism was not devoid of a certain measure of truth, which it expressed rationally. It could be that a tendency toward rationalism is inherent in Aristotelian syllogistic thinking. Perhaps this was what constituted the danger of Mu'tazilism or even of Islamic philosophical works in general, in the eyes of the champions of faith, who confused rationalism with rational discourse, as was previously said.

There is also a danger in the irrationality of the believers who stand fast on faith alone, to the exclusion of reason. This is evident, for instance, in the affirmation of the Ḥanbalīs that the letters and sounds of the Qur'ān are uncreated, so that the Qur'ān one sees and hears is indeed the Uncreated

Qur'ān. The violent battles between the Ḥanbalīs and the other schools of orthodox Sunnism in the Middle Ages on this very point show that the Mu'tazilīs were at least partially right in opposing Ḥanbalism. The faith-impregnated will of Ḥanbalism saw no need for any speculation on the articles of belief through the use of reasoning. It was sufficient to have faith in the Word of God without trying to interpret it rationally. The suspension of man's intelligent thinking in understanding the Scripture was an act of faith in the sacramental nature of the Qur'ān.

Orthodox Scholastic Theology

It would have been impossible for Islamic dogmatists to continue systematically refusing the support of reason indefinitely without sooner or later alienating the best minds of the community. Since man has a rational power, the use of reasoning to uphold the contents of faith is only normal. To accuse a saintly Ṣūfī like al-Muḥāsibī (d. 857) of Baghdad of harboring Mu'tazilī tendencies merely because of a certain dialectic clarity in his works is to risk eventually the spiritual well-being of the community for the sake of blind dogmatism. Rationalism is indeed mortal to the tenets of faith, but such is not the case for reasoning that is subject to the influence of the Spirit, as was said. What the early Muslim authorities possessed was a dogmatism without any reasoning at all. This they wished to impose on all and sundry in the Islamic world of the Mu'tazilīs, the philosophers, and the Ṣūfīs.

Had they succeeded, Islam would have been turned into a monolithic fundamentalist faith devoid of intelligible contents. But they were prevented from doing so by a number of convergent historical strands of the time. First of all, the claims of the exoteric *'ulamā'* that they had a kind of monopolistic control on the Islamic revelation and were therefore the guardians of orthodoxy were rejected by the Ṣūfī authorities of the Path. We have only to recall that Ṣūfism was surfacing everywhere then precisely to contest this reduction of Islam to its most external shell, devoid of all spiritual depth. Once Ṣūfism had established its case, it was no longer possible for the *'ulamā'* to assume that they were the only ones to interpret the message of Islaṃ. From then on, they had to share authority with the Ṣūfī masters, whether they liked it or not. Second, the Mu'tazilī might have seemed excessive in their rationalism to the dogmatists, but they nevertheless forced the Sunnī authorities to come to grips with the different Mu'tazilī propositions, so that something had to be done. It was not possible to continue the practice of citing verse and Sūrah of the Qur'ān or *ḥadīths* of the Prophet to silence all opposition for the simple reason that the Mu'tazilī theses were rationally persuasive. Third, the Muslim philosophers such as al-Kindī (d. 866) were now culturally important figures. They had harmonized Plato and Aristotle with Islamic teachings to the point where the truths of philosophy were claimed to be compatible with the truths of religion. This could hardly be a threat to the faith, in that case, but rather a powerful support for the faith of the intelligent believer. Finally, the Islamic religion itself was now far removed from the pristine days of its youth. Too many sects had arisen, too many questions had been asked since the demise of its founder to permit the dogmatic authorities to be complacent and self-assured. There was a real need for the systematic formulation of the dogmas in a positive sense. It was no longer sufficient to reject what was dogmatically false. Reasoning now had to be used to defend what was dogmatically true so that the believers would know exactly what they must adhere to with a certain system.

It was in the tenth century that scholastic theology (*kalām*) came to the fore in the defense of the faith with some of the weapons of reasoning. The crystallization of Sunnī scholastic theological thinking took place in the works of al-Ash'arī (d. 935), al-Māturīdī (d. 944), and aṭ-Ṭaḥāwī (d. 933). Because al-Ash'arī is one of the first theologians to employ the dialectic of the Mu'tazilīs, and even to turn it against them, he is considered the founder of orthodox scholastic theology in Islam. His school of thought, Ash'arism, is sometimes called orthodox Islamic theology, as if the other theological schools were somehow outside the pale. In reality, Ash'arism is but one of the different schools of Sunnī theology. Generally, it has been associated in times past with the Shāfi'ī *madhhab*. Another school, that of the Māturīdīs, was also part and parcel of the orthodox theological tradition, especially among the Ḥanafīs of Central Asian lands. The school of aṭ-Ṭaḥāwī was Egyptian in origin. While Ash'arism had been the most prestigious because authorities like al-Ghazālī (d. 1111) belonged to it, Māturīdism had really had a great deal of influence, winding up by infiltrating Ash'arism itself. The latter, nevertheless, spread in all directions and soon became the *kalām* that was taught everywhere, its last great exponents being al-Faḍālī (d. 1820) of Egypt and his commentator al-Bayjūrī (d. 1844). Both used the intricate scholastic terminology that had evolved in the millennium separating them from the beginnings of Islamic scholastic theology.

Side by side with these scholastic forms of theological thinking that were somewhat speculative, there were also the Ḥanbalī nonspeculative theological positions based on the dogmas of Islam. These were embraced by Ḥanbalīs and some Muslims belonging to the other *madhḥabs*, who preferred an unquestioning faith to the speculations of scholastic theology. When speaking of Islamic theology as a tradition, one should remember that Ḥanbalism is part of it. Its nonspeculative stance was of course anathema to the Ash'arīs, and the two schools were constantly at loggerheads, but even so it was an integral part of the theological tradition as a whole.

Ash'arism

Al-Ash'arī himself had been an adherent of Mu'tazilism.[3] The dialectic tools he had learned from that sect were used by him to destroy the Mu'tazilī theses and to defend the articles of faith. Combining the argumentation of reason with the contents of tradition he created the *kalām* known as Ash'arism. Previously, the religious authorities had not been able to refute the Mu'tazilīs with more than just Qur'ānic argumentation. There was no *kalām* then, but only a rudimentary dogmatic theology that eschewed all rational formulations in defense of the accepted beliefs. Now, with the advent of Ash'arism, a measure of rational argumentation entered into the unthinking faith of earlier times. It was not so much an improvement as it was a means of warding off errors from the creedal formulations of Islam, a kind of systematic reinforcement of the right dogmas of a salvatory nature.

It is said that Ash'arism held to a middle ground between the extremes of nonspeculative dogmatism on the one hand and Mu'tazilī rationalism on the other. There is a kind of truth in that observation. But what is certain is that Ash'arism did not always seek a middle ground in all matters, nor could it have done so without betraying Islamic beliefs in the end. For the Mu'tazilīs, let us remember, such Attributes as the Divine Knowledge, Will, Life, or Power, were nonexistent because only the Divine Essence was intrinsically One. If one admitted their existence alongside the Unity, there was a risk of association, as we saw previously. What to do? The Ash'arī solution to the question of the Attributes or Qualities and the Essence was in the formula, "They are not He, nor are they other than He." What this infelicitous expression meant was that the Attributes were not the Divine Unity as such, for then there would be multiplicity in the Essence, an unthinkable proposition. Nor were they other than the Essence, for then they would coexist outside of it as independent realities, which was associationism. Perhaps the Ash'arī expression was simply a roundabout way of declaring the impotence of dogmatic theology.

Between the partisans of free will and those of predestination, Ash'arism produced a kind of mitigated predestinarianism. It allowed man a certain power over the acquisition of his deeds but not over their production, for they are predestined and produced or created by God. This likewise was an attempt at a middle ground between free will and predestination; but in reality, when all is said and done, it is practically indistinguishable from the latter. The Qur'ān preaches both free will and predestination in different, conflicting verses. To reconcile both requires a subtle juxtaposition of the notions on the Divine Omniscience that knows all things in advance and the Divine Omnipotence that creates things in their proper place and time, including man's free will, which operates within certain limits. But even a limited free will was dangerous in the eyes of the Ash'arīs since it implied a productive and creative power in man (*shirk*) that competed alongside the similar power in God, as if there were two creative powers in the world. Far safer was it to espouse the primacy of the Divine Power and have done with it, even though this risked ascribing to *Allāh* the responsibility for man's deeds. Such a constant and obsessive preoccupation with the Divine Power eventually led the Ash'arīs to reject secondary causes in the production of natural phenomena. This was done in order to make the unique causal Power of *Allāh* stand out all the more. It is not fire that burns, therefore, for this would be to ascribe to a secondary cause the power that belongs to God alone. It is in reality *Allāh* who infuses instantaneously into that fire the igneous property of burning. An original and even dynamic view of the creative Power of God developed out of this reduction of all causality to the unique Cause. This was "the renewal of the creation" at every instant, which has God creating spontaneously with each passing moment everything that would be attributed to secondary causes in the natural sciences. The invincible radiance of the Divine Power was felt by Ash'arism to be much too omnipotent to allow any suggestion of associationism to enter the picture through the consideration of secondary causality that might detract from the uniqueness of the Divine Cause of all things.

Ash'arism retained the thesis of dogmatic Islam on the Uncreated Qur'ān, but it rejected out of hand the Ḥanbalī notions on the uncreated nature of the letters and sounds of Scripture. It thus upheld the Mu'tazilī thesis on that point while at the same time preserving the dogma of the Uncreated Qur'ān. The latter is the spiritual prototype of the created Qur'ān that is recited and heard. This final solution to the vexing problem of the actual nature of the Qur'ān did not put an end to the Ḥanbalī views. But it certainly recognized that reasoning, whether Mu'tazilī or otherwise, was right in holding that the letters and sounds of the Qur'ān could not themselves be eternal without falling into absurdity.

Similarly, Ash'arism rejected all grossly literal interpretations of the Qur'ān. But it did not sanction the speculative interpretation, or the metaphorical explanation, of such Qur'ānic imagery as God's eyes, face, hands, feet, sitting on the throne, and other anthropomorphic expressions. The Ash'aris asked for a suspension of intelligence here: one must accept such imagery without asking any questions (such as, "How does God sit on the throne?"). Nor must one draw any comparisons between God and human qualities, which was the thesis known as Comparability (*tashbīh*). This meant that the fundamental tendency of Sunnī theology would be largely in the direction of the Incomparability (*tanzīh*) of *Allāh*. He cannot be compared with anything in the created world. Incomparability showed, of course, the transcendence of the Divinity in relation to the universe. In that fashion, *Allāh* would not be subject to the flux and transformations that occur in the world. Comparability, by permitting that *Allāh* be compared with creatures in qualities and the like, risked introducing pantheism into the minds of the believers, which was the error of identifying God with the world. In promulgating Incomparability as its dominant view, Ash'arism was in a sense going by the general drift of Qur'ānic doctrine. But the Scripture also teaches Comparability, as when it speaks of God as being "the Light" of the Heavens and the earth, so that the complete teaching would be both Incomparability and Comparability. That Incomparability corresponds more to the nature of the exoteric mind is self-evident, whereas the perception of the symbolic nature of forms, a trait of the esoteric mind, makes for the mystical recognition of the rights of Comparability.

In all the other dogmas of Islam, such as the teaching on the Ascension (*mi'rāj*) of the Prophet, or on the events of the Last Day, Ash'arism took no "middle ground" whatsoever. Instead, it transmitted faithfully what the pious ancestors considered as the saving truths of the religion. One may conclude thus that the speculative theology of al-Ash'arī was rather limited in nature. Its later defenders would indeed amplify its contents to a certain extent but never to the point where the dogmas of Islam themselves would be exposed to the light of rational analysis. Māturīdism was somewhat more tolerant of rational discourse, as witness its thesis that man has a free will, and later on its arguments would influence Ash'arism. But it also maintained a strict adherence to the articles of faith in the Sunnī tradition.

The 'Aqīdah

The importance of Ash'arism, accordingly, for the religious equilibrium of the community, lies not in its speculative theology, which was rather narrow, but in its creedal formulations.[4] It is the Ash'arī Creed (*'aqīdah*) that had such a powerful influence in maintaining the mass of the faithful within the precincts of orthodox Islam. This is not simply the creedal text attributed to al-Ash'arī himself but also the numerous other creeds composed by eminent Ash'arīs of succeeding generations and centuries. They were couched in scholastic terminology with the passage of time. Some were reduced to poetical compositions for the sake of easier memorization. There were Māturīdī creedal formulations also, to say nothing of the Ḥanbalī creeds. All of these creeds were meant to provide verbal crystallizations of the saving truths of Islam extracted from the revealed message. The early creedal formulations of Islam could only say what the faith was not, and hence they tended to be rather defensive toward the heresies of the Mu'tazilī It was left for the scholastic theologians of the tenth century, beginning with Al-Ash'arī and his contemporaries, to give complete dogmatic expressions that covered all of the essential saving truths of the revelation as seen from an exoteric viewpoint. This was the primary need of the community as a whole, given the inroads that Mu'tazilism had made on the integrity of the dogmas. On the other hand, the need for speculative theology was clearly of secondary importance.

It was through those creeds that Sunnī exoteric orthodoxy spread itself among the faithful. The creeds expressed the salvific essence of the religion with respect to the nature of God, the angels, revelation, the Prophets, the Day of Judgment, and so on. There was no one particular creed common to the entire Islamic world and therefore equivalent to the Apostles' Creed or the Nicene Creed in Christianity. Instead, over the centuries, certain confessions of faith composed by eminent traditional authorities have been held in great esteem, such as those of aṭ-Ṭaḥāwī (d. 942), al-Ghazālī (d. 1111), an-Nasafī (d. 1310), or in more recent times the creed of al-Faḍālī (d. 1820). These are the articles of faith of Sunnī traditional orthodoxy and are to be distinguished from Shī'ī creedal formulations that apply only to the Shī'ī minority of the Islamic world and those particular differences with mainstream Islam are rejected in advance by Sunnī authorities.

Dogmatic formulations seem to be a characteristic of the Semitic religions. We do not see them in the Chinese, the Hindu, or the Buddhist traditions. In Christianity and Islam, confessions of faith appear in response to opposing and seemingly false propositions which, if allowed to spread unchecked, could undermine true religion. While dogma is a verbal formulation of a saving truth, it cannot possibly contain all aspects of the truth. That totality is the business of the esoteric tradition of a religion, as we see in some of the Greek Fathers or in a Meister Eckhart of the Christian Church, and in the eminent Ṣūfīs of Islam. But dogmatic theology, while it defines the fundamental beliefs of religion and establishes the general contours of the exoteric tradition, has a tendency to become dogmatism. This is the same as reducing the contents of revelation to particular dogmas and holding these to be the only contents of the initial message. Now, that is equivalent to judging the revealed and total truth with the constrictive vision of exoteric minds and the verbal formulations of dogmatic truth. What prevented Islamic exoterism from actually becoming the uniquely orthodox perspective is that, from the beginning, the esoteric aspect of Islam clashed head-on with the gradually increasing possessive claims of the *'ulamā'* over the revelation and won the day for the spiritual claims of the Path to the same revelation. With the triumph of Ṣūfism, the very concept of orthodoxy in Islam, in the sense of "true doctrine", was widened to include the doctrines of the Path, which went beyond the limitations of dogma, and that spoke about the spiritual contents of the Islamic revelation. Gradually, the *'ulamā'*, the guardians of exoteric Islam, took on a very diminished air in the eyes of the Ṣūfīs. The latter began referring to them as the "partisans of the shell" because they were concerned only with the external forms of the religion, and were characterized by limited mentalities that saw only fragmentary aspects of the revealed message. The Ṣūfīs were looking at things from the all-englobing perspective of the integral Path of *ma'rifah*, which made the dogmatism of the *'ulamā'* seem very narrow-minded by comparison. That such a restricted formalism escaped being heterodox altogether is due to the fact that the dogmas of Islam, for all their conceptual limitations, are verbal expressions, after all, of saving truths. So long as the *'ulamā'* upheld them, they could not be accused of harboring false ideas.

It therefore comes as a stunning surprise when we learn that some of the best creeds of Islam were written by Ṣūfīs. Al-Ghazālī (d. 1111), already mentioned, formulated his confession of faith in Ash'arī terms; and the founder of the Qādiriyyah, 'Abd al-Qādir al-Jīlānī (d. 1166), whose *'aqīdah* is Ḥanbalī, includes even the standard Ḥanbalī teaching on the uncreated letters and sounds of Qur'ānic Arabic, which Ash'arism rejects out of hand. Apart from these, other eminent Ṣūfīs have written *'aqīdahs* with greater or lesser diffusion in the Islamic world. All of this seems to contradict what was said in the preceding chapter, but only in appearance. In his work entitled *al-Ghunyah*, al-Jīlānī gives us, first, a general view of exoteric Islam, its beliefs and Law, and then, in the second part, a summary of the teachings and practices of the Path. If only the first part existed, one would have thought him a Ḥanbalī fundamentalist; the second part, plus his other works, belie all such limitations, for there we see his spiritual esoterism manifest itself.

A solution to this problem lies in the *Futūḥāt al-Makkiyyah* (*The Meccan Revelations*) of the Ṣūfī Ibn al-'Arabī (d. 1240), whose *madhhab* originally was that of the Ẓāhirīs, a literalist school. In the introductory chapters of this great work, he gives an *'aqīdah* for the generality of believers, that is to say, one that is quite literalist and with no interpretative or speculative elements. Then, after that, he gives an *'aqīdah* for the elect, which is really no longer a dogmatic creed, as was the case for the first one, because at this point dogmatism begins to dissolve into esoteric truths that are of a more subtle nature. And finally, he mentions that there is an *'aqīdah* for the elect of the elect scattered throughout the pages of his compendium of esoteric teachings. This no doubt refers to the metaphysical and spiritual teachings of the Path that are beyond all possible dogmatic formulations. In other words, there are three levels to orthodox teachings, in the mind of Ibn al-'Arabī, that increase in subtlety as one ascends from the literal or formal plane and passes through an intermediate doctrinal plane to arrive finally at the metaphysical teachings of *waḥdat al-wujūd* ("Oneness of Being"), which cannot be expressed in dogmatic terms at all. The *'aqīdah* for believers in general is what they need in the way of elementary saving beliefs, and these are the teachings having to do with exoterism; beyond this are the teachings of the esoteric Path of increasing refinement.[5]

When the likes of an al-Ghazālī or an 'Abd al-Qādir al-Jīlānī write *'aqīdahs*, therefore, this does not mean that they limit the truths of the revelation simply to those dogmas. Being Ṣūfī, their own spiritual esoterism allows them to dissolve the limitations of dogma and to transcend them in contemplative vision of the realities of the Path. But their *'aqīdahs* for the generality represent compassionate attitudes on their part toward believers so as to keep their faith within the confines of a simple orthodoxy. Moreover, that Ṣūfīs should descend to the level of composing confessions of faith for the people is illustrative of an important truth. Esoterism is all-englobing in its interpretation of the revelation, which means that it encompasses the exoteric truths likewise. Hence the Ṣūfīs can write creeds without any pangs of conscience, all the more so in that they are anxious to preserve the simple faith of the community. But the opposite of this is not true, namely, that the exoteric *'ulamā'*, or exoterists in general, can englobe the universal truths of Ṣūfī esoterism in their beliefs. This shows that the guardians of the Law have a restricted view of the revelation.

In all of these dogmatic facets of the Islamic religion, one perceives positive and negative fruits for the faith as a whole. On the positive side, it is clear that the rise of scholastic theology and its creedal expressions was necessary to maintain alive the saving nucleus of beliefs that would otherwise have disappeared under the constantly erosive influences of Mu'tazilism. Whether the particular fashions in which the Ash'arīs, the Mā turīdīs, and the Ḥanbalīs went about distilling those creedal elements out of the corpus of materials furnished by the Sunnī tradition was indeed the right solution is another questions altogether. One can conceive of better ways of regarding the questions of the Divine Essence and Attributes, and of the interrelationships between the Divine Omniscience and free will, and so on. In other words, Islamic dogma is a way of looking at the Islamic message: it assembled together certain elements and rejected others, which is the special prerogative of all dogmatism.

On the negative side, once scholasticism had made its choice, this was then interpreted as the only choice and inevitably turned into a verbal absolutism that was binding on everyone. When one sees even the Ṣūfīs espousing Ash'arī, Ḥanbalī, and Māturīdī creeds, and bending their spiritual teachings to conform to the dogmatic exigencies of the religion, it is easy to conclude that there is a natural expansionist imperialism in all dogmatism and that it sets the pace, so to speak, for all systems of thought. Setting out to delineate the elementary truths of Islam in dogmatic forms, the Ṣūfīs became the victims of their own charitable dispositions when that very same theological dogmatism invaded their own domains and forced them to concede considerable ground to it. We see something of this in the *Yawāqīt wa 'l-Jawāhir* (*Sapphires and Gems*) of the Egyptian Ṣūfī, ash-Sha'rānī (d. 1565), a summary of the teachings of the Andalusian Ṣūfī, Ibn al-'Arabī

(d. 1240). The Egyptian master, while holding fast to the preeminence of Ṣūfism, bends over backwards to make the *shaykh al-akbar*'s thinking conform to the dogmatico-legalistic Ash'arism of his epoch, a *tour de force* that would have been out of the question for a pure gnostic Ṣūfī like an-Niffarī (d. 965).

Looking at things schematically, one might say that Islamic scholastic theology has a tendency to see God as Power, while Ṣūfism sees Him as Love, and Islamic philosophy, as Wisdom. Of course, Ṣūfī gnosis also has its cognitive elements having to do with Wisdom. But insofar as these aspects of the Path are suprarational, the Ṣūfīs themselves speak of Love, by way of setting that gnosis apart from merely rational knowledge of God. The fact that the theological positions of scholasticism are largely structured on the Divine Power and even inclined to define God in that sense means that, from the very beginning, there was an intrinsic orientation to this way of thinking. There can be no doubt that the Qur'ānic revelation stresses, again and again, the omnipotential nature of the Divinity. That in no wise means that it defines God as primarily Omnipotent, for among the Ninety-Nine Names, there are those that have to do with the Divine Beauty, or the loving and merciful nature of God.

Perhaps exoteric theology, which maintains an attitude of separation between the Creator and creatures in this world and in the Hereafter, was instinctively drawn to a consideration of the Omnipotence of God out of an unconscious awareness that a theology based on the Divine Love or the Divine Knowledge would have broken the barriers between God and the Creation. That is what happened with the Ṣūfīs and the Muslim Neoplatonic philosophers. In the end, any form of *Tawḥīd* which menaced the official theological theses that posited an irreducible separation between God and man was declared to be a species of pantheism and counter to the Islamic message. We see this accusation in some of the belligerent religious authorities, like the Ḥanbalī canonist, Ibn Taymiyyah (d. 1328), who condemned such Ṣūfīs as Ibn al-Arabī, al-Ḥallaj, and others who preached *wahdad al-wujūd* in one or another of its variations.

Islamic Philosophy

When one moves from theology (*kalām*) to philosophy (*falsafah*) in the Islamic tradition, one has the impression of entering a deeper world of intelligibility.[6] This is not because revelation restricted theology, but because the theologians restricted the intelligibility of their interpretations of what the Islamic message said, while the philosophers had no such qualms over the use of intelligence. If there was no theology in early Islam, the same can be said of philosophy. Both arise as a result of the questioning attitudes of the postapostolic generations and the introduction of Greek thinking through translations into the cultural life of the Islamic community. The questioning attitudes were the outcome of the gradual rise of an inquisitive outlook that stirred Islam. The translations of Greek works — and also of other foreign works — would not have been possible without the preliminary inquisitiveness. Once they were introduced into the substance of Islam, they engendered further reflection and mental interrogation, not to say agitation, into the minds of Muslims.

Since Islam was meant for the non-Arab world also, and not just for the Arab, it is unlikely that its originally Bedouin cast was meant to remain forever as its fundamental cultural expression. Quite the opposite, it seems clear that the intermarriage of the Arab conquerors, such as the companions, with women of foreign origin was a kind of presage of what the future Islamic culture would be like, a symbiosis of Arab and non-Arab traditions. The fourth and last Orthodox Caliph, 'Alī (d. 661), spent a great deal of his time in Kūfah, which was under Persian cultural influence. Although the sermons attributed to him by later compilers might not all be exactly his words, it is obvious in some of them that his Arabic is much more analytical and expanded than the Arabic of the Prophet. He was aware of a certain philosophical terminology in usage in Kūfah, for this crops up in some of his teachings, to say nothing about his comprehension of Persian administrative matters. In other words, the companions knew that adjustments had to be made in all domains, intellectual, matrimonial, cultural, administrative, and political, in order for the early Islamic civilization to take root and grow. Some of them, like 'Alī, were gnostic sages whose esoteric perspective permitted them to perceive in the non-Islamic cultures the elements needed for the germinal formation of the future world of Islam. The Arabs of their day had no civilization, in the sedentary sense of that word. They had a culture, but it was nomadic, and of course they had the new message of Islam. For Islam to become a civilization, it had to draw from all the sedentary peoples it conquered, particularly from the Persian civilization, which it conquered in its entirety.

One has to bear in mind that the Arab conquests were two-way movements: the Arabs conquered sedentary cultures in the name of Islam and were themselves conquered by the non-Arab cultures. The religious and cultural ferment of that first century or so of Islam, when the Islamic civilization was beginning to take definitive shape, is reflected in the translations from Greek and other languages that began entering the mental horizons of the cultivated Muslims. That the Umayyad prince, Khālid ibn Yazid (d. 704), was already a student of alchemy barely a generation after the death of the Caliph 'Alī is a sign that Islam was not destined to be simply a religion for nomadic Arabs. It is in this context that one must situate the rise of Islamic philosophical thought.

The Content of Islamic Philosophy

Like European philosophy until modern times, Islamic philosophy oscillates between Platonism and Aristotelianism. These were the two poles of ancient Greek wisdom, with Neoplatonism a kind of synthesis of both. While Neoplatonic thinking seems to dominate in the Muslim world, Aristotelianism had its great representatives, such as Ibn Rushd (d. 1198), the Averroës of the Christian world. In any case, Aristotelianism was always present whenever logic was studied. The content of *falsafah* in Islam was more or less in antiquity: metaphysics, logic, natural sciences, mathematics, and medicine. But the individual philosopher (*faylasūf* or *ḥakīm*) added to these disciplines all sorts of other fields, such as music, alchemy, history, astrology, and so on, depending on his talents. In the case of such minds as that of Ibn Sīnā (d. 1037), the Avicenna of Western history, we are in the presence of great knowledge and erudition, as can be seen in his *Shifā'* (*Healing*), a philosophical encyclopaedia that embraced numerous domains of learning.

Mention should be made that the philosophical sciences remained always somewhat outside the pale of the traditional disciplines, such as Qur'ānic commentary, jurisprudence, the science of *ḥadīth*, scholastic theology, grammar, lexicography, rhetoric, and literature. These were also known as "the disciplines relating to the Law" because they were more immediately connected with the exoteric Law than the "foreign sciences", of which *falsafah* was one. Due in great part to the anti-intellectual aspects of Islamic dogmatism itself, philosophical thought was always seen as somehow extraneous to the Islamic message, if not actually dangerous. When we realize that Ibn Rushd himself thought of philosophy as being an esoterism only for an elite, while the *sharī'ah* was for the faithful in general, we can sense that *falsafah*, even among its practitioners, was rather special.

Unlike theological thought in Islam, which was confined to the Muslims, philosophical thought, by virtue of its disinterested nature, had a much more universal air to it. Muslims, Jews, and Christians could cultivate it within the Islamic world without feeling that it was inimical to their religious interests. Averroism, for instance, is simply the Christian world's version of the philosophy of Averroës, or rather, of his particular remarks on Aristotle, which are abstract and universal in content. The intellectual universality of *falsafah*, its impersonal and disinterested regard for the truth, and its detached attitude toward the forms of any religion, made it all the more suspect in the eyes of Muslims. Ṣūfīs, as well as doctors of the Law, felt themselves in unfamiliar surroundings, if not lost, when entering the world of *falsafah*. Whether we consider the abstract sciences or the natural sciences of the well-informed *ḥakīm*, they seem not to have anything to do with the ultimate goal of salvation or with the religious life in this world. At least that is the way philosophy was regarded by most of the *'ulamā'* and the Ṣūfīs. For that reason, it was never admitted into the inner sanctuary of Islam but remained something of an outcast. Yet it could not be altogether rejected, for the simple reason that Islam itself was in need of its laws of logical thinking, its terminology, and its intellectual abstractions on a host of metaphysical and cosmological problems. Indeed, the more one examines the traditional world of Islam, the more one realizes how much it owes to Greek *falsafah*, even if the partisans of that world, such as the doctors of the Law and many of the Ṣūfīs, had their reservations about philosophy as such.

The Development of Falsafah

In the early period of Islamic philosophical thought, that of the translators of the eighth and ninth centuries, *falsafah* emerges as a distinct field and invades all domains of thinking. Later, from the tenth century on, scholasticism arises in Islam as a style of expression in both technical terminology and approach. Theology, *taṣawwuf*, and the cosmological disciplines of various types absorbed Aristotelian and Neoplatonic elements into their systems. Thus they consecrated Greek wisdom within Islam. In the Sunnī world, the assimilation of Neoplatonic modes of thinking into the Ṣūfī teachings of the school of Ibn al-'Arabī (d. 1240) was the death knell for the potentially rationalistic orientation of Islamic Aristotelianism. The latter, with its cultivation of logic and syllogistic forms of thought, tended to imprison reasoning within a limited framework. Neoplatonism, by comparison, was much more open to intellectual intuitions which went beyond the purely rational functions of the mind. Averroism actually moved over into the Christian medieval world through the translations from Arabic into Latin and emerged as an essential element in the nascent scholasticism of the thirteenth century in the Western Church. The triumph of Aristotelianism in Christendom meant the gradual demise of Christian Neoplatonism. The opposite took place in the Islamic world of that time. Islamic Neoplatonism won out over the purely Aristotelian tendencies represented by the works of Ibn Rushd. *Falsafah* in its Aristotelian form now faded from the scene in Sunnī lands because it had been fully integrated into the mystical, theological, and cosmological thinking of medieval Islam by the thirteenth century. What is more, the gnostic doctrines of Ṣūfism now made all philosophical speculations — whether Aristotelian or Neoplatonic — seem beside the point, at least in appearance.

Here we should remember that it was precisely in the thirteenth century that Ṣūfism witnessed the eruption of numerous fraternities all over the lands of Islam. Such Ṣūfī orders as the Shādhiliyyah or the Suhrawardiyyah, which saw the light of day then, would last down to our times and have tremendous influence on the spiritual life of the community. Their presence everywhere rendered the cultivation of philosophical discourse somewhat redundant. If the direct vision of God is made possible through Ṣūfism, then discussing Him without spiritual vision becomes suspect, which was what the philosophical approach was, or seemed to be.

As if the mystical implications of the universal presence of Ṣūfī orders in the Muslim world were not enough, the great outpouring of esoteric teachings in the works of Ibn al-'Arabī was a powerful factor in the suppression of philosophical discussion. Philosophy in its Aristotelian character was neutralized and even silenced within the Sunnī world. Quite different, however, was the situation in the Shī'ī domains. A resurgence of *falsafah* in an eclectic dress took place in the Safavid Persia of the seventeenth century with the school of Mullā Ṣadrā Shīrāzī (d. 1640). Whereas the Sunnī Ṣūfī tradition had absorbed *falsafah* into its gnostic doctrines, the Shī'ī thinkers absorbed Ṣūfism into their philosophical, or theosophical, system. This brand of philosophy would remain in the Shī'ī community down to recent times, thus testifying to the presence of a philosophical school in Islam after the days of Ibn Rushd.

Philosophy and Religion

Thinkers like al-Kindī (d.c. 850), who was "The Philosopher of the Arabs", or the Turk al-Fārābi (d. 950), or the Persian Ibn Sīnā (d. 1037), had no pangs of religious conscience in cultivating philosophy. For them, it was but a form of truth. Therefore, it could not but uphold scriptural truth, which was revealed. But here one should remember that the Muslim sages accepted only such Greek wisdom as was compatible with the Islamic notion of *Tawḥīd*. Since the Divine Unity is an abstract concept, so to speak, and not accessible to representational imagery, Greek philosophical abstractions were all the more welcome because they reinforced the fundamental thesis of Islam. Moreover, only those aspects of Greek thought that were squared with the spiritual perspective of Islam were brought into the cultural stream of the community. Polytheistic traits of the ancient Greek tradition were filtered out in the monotheistic sieve of Islam. What resulted from all that was a purified Greek wisdom that was perfectly in harmony with the general tenor of the faith, or so the Muslim philosophers thought.

When they came into Islam, the abstract and natural sciences of the Greeks were seen as simply different fields of the human spirit that reflected, each in its own way, the Divine Unity itself. Because of this integration of all of the diverse disciplines into the perspective of *Tawḥīd*, we can speak of an Islamic philosophy as such.

After the apostolic age of Islam, the spirit of inquiry expanded into the most diverse areas. Consequently, the introduction of philosophical thinking into the culture of 'Abbāsid times obeyed that expansive movement of the collective soul of the Muslim world. At the same time it was a tendency that reflected one of the many ways in which Muslims carried out Muḥammad's command: "Seek knowledge, even if it be in China." One could argue that the knowledge he had in mind was connected more with religion than with philosophy. Yet, the pursuit of philosophy, like the study of grammar, *ḥadīth*, Qur'ānic commentary, or even literature, was but a way of preparing oneself for man's life in the Hereafter. If the literalist or crassly anthropomorphic versions of the faith are to be included in what is generally called Islam, then the philosophers' versions have at least an equal right to be heard.

One reason why philosophical enquiry was suspect among the religious authorities is that it seemed to encourage the use of reason (*'aql*). In their view, reason eroded the dogmas of religion. That was what had happened in the days of the Mu'tazilīs before the rise of Ash'arism confronted the dogmatists with a kind of orthodox theological thinking. Confusion between a reason (*'aql*) that cannot reach God and a spiritual intellect (likewise *'aql*, as we have seen) that can have direct access to Him is not because the exoteric theologians misunderstand the contextual meaning of the word *'aql*. It is rather the result of their indifference to either of the two faculties in man. They preferred instead to rely on the light provided by faith (*īmān*), submission (*islām*), and morality (*iḥsān*), the three foundations or principles of religion. Mu'tazilism had exposed the limitations of the reasoning faculty, or the *'aql* confined to the discursive, reflected power in man. Dogmatic theologians knew little if anything about the other *'aql*, the heart-intellect, which intuits the Divinity through direct, luminous knowledge. That kind of perception was related to the teachings of the Path on the nature of the "heart". We see all of this discussed in the works of the early Ṣūfīs such as al-Ḥakīm at-Tirmidhī (d. 898) or in the later ones like al-Ghazālī (d. 1111). In his book on the revival of the religious disciplines (the *Iḥyā'*), al-Ghazālī discusses at some length the purification of the intelligence situated in the subtle, invisible heart of man. This is the unveiling of the eye of the heart, allowing it to see the Divine Reality, which vision engenders absolute certitude as one of its many spiritual fruits. That is all part and parcel of the mystical esoterism of Islam which the doctors of the Law affected to ignore because of their assumption that there was nothing in the revelation beyond the dogmatico-theological teachings they espoused.

Islamic Neoplatonism

In the long run, Islamic Aristotelianism could lead to a rationalism that threatened the revealed truths and rejected direct knowledge of spiritual realities. Its syllogistic types of reasoning and its preoccupation with the empirical objects of knowledge encouraged the nonmystical perception of things. Quite different was the case for Platonism in its form as Neoplatonism, for it preached actual intellective union with the One. This is quite evident in such a work as *The Theology of Aristotle*, translated into Arabic for the Caliph al-Mu'taṣim (d. 842) and revised by the philosopher al-Kindī himself. The latter had been a companion of the 'Abbāsid Caliphs al-Ma'mūn and al-Mu'taṣim in the days when Mu'tazilism reigned as the official religious teaching of the State. The title of the work must not mislead us, for it is not Aristotle's. In reality it is a translation of some of the *Enneads* of Plotinus (d. 270), the founder of Neoplatonism and the sage known to the Muslims as *ash-shaykh al-yūnānī* ("The Greek Master"). Neoplatonism sought to harmonize the Platonic and Aristotelian perspectives. The fact that it is attributed to Aristotle shows that the Platonic and Aristotelian positions were not mutually incompatible in the eyes of the Muslim philosophers.

Neoplatonism was an explicit doctrinal expression of the esoteric philosophical tradition of the Greeks. It has the merit of conveying to the reader in rather clear terms the goal of philosophy. This was the purification of the soul (*psyche*), caught in the opaque hylic or material world, so that the intellect (*nous* in Greek, *'aql* in Arabic) could return to its luminous Divine Source. The ascensional flight of the intellective ray back to the pure Being of God was the aim of the spiritual life of man.

In Neoplatonic teaching, which would be integrated into Islamic philosophy, the One gives rise to the Divine Intellect by a process of emanation. That Intellect in turn generates the World Soul, which connects the material or hylic level of existence to the spiritual. The three Hypostases (the One, the Intellect, and the World Soul) are emanational principles, in descending order. They account for the origin of the universe and the resulting imbedding of the soul in the material world. All of these principles would be assimilated into the Islamic metaphysical and cosmological teachings extracted from the Qur'ān, the *ḥadīths* of the Prophet, and the remarks of the early Muslim sages. The intrusion of Indo-European or Aryan concepts into the Semitic imagery of Islam was possible because of the concordance that could be found in the esoteric teachings of the Mediterranean religions. The main difference is that Aryan teachings introduced a much more developed analytical framework into the synthetic outlook of the Semites.

The three Hypostases, in the reverse process of reintegration back to the One, also serve to show man how to disentangle his soul from the darkness of matter. Through the purification of his *nous*, he returns to the Divine Intellect and, from there, to the One. That, in essence, is what Neoplatonic gnosis is all about. As such, it is a doctrine that could not but square with its Semitic counterpart in the Islamic message, as we see in Ṣūfism. Given that both the Greek and the Islamic mystical teachings refer to the same realities, but in different fashions, it is not surprising to find analogous expressions in both. This is especially so as we approach the more abstract notions surrounding the metaphysical principle of the One. Pure *Tawḥīd* in Ṣūfism has the same impersonal nature we find in the One of Greek esoteric thinking.

Where Ṣūfism divorces itself from Neoplatonic thought is in its alliance of pure doctrine with the methodology of spiritual realization. Greek esoterism seldom if ever refers to the question of the mystical technique of concentration on the One, except perhaps in the occasional exposition of the spiritual virtues. On the contrary, the Greek sages, unlike their Ṣūfī counterparts, tended to confine their discussions to the elucidation of purely doctrinal matters. They seemed anxious to restrict the spiritual method of realization to the oral tradition of the teachers and therefore to keep it out of the reach of the uninitiated. Therein lies the danger of Neoplatonism in contrast to Ṣūfism: it risks being a purely speculative system. In a work like *The Theology of Aristotle*, it is taken for granted that only theory will be discussed, not practice or what pertains to the mystical art of concentrating on God. Accordingly, in the hands of a person of noncontemplative mind, such a work becomes an exercise in purely exoteric philosophy, as the Greek adepts would say, and loses the fullness of its esoteric character. It is the absence of the mystical life in the philosophers that made the Ṣūfīs criticize philosophy as such, forgetting that the great Turkish philosopher al-Fārābī (d. 950) combined both Ṣūfism and Neoplatonism. It was not, then, the philosophy that was lethal to the life of the Spirit, but it was the absence of the life of the Spirit.

The Influence of *Falsafah* in Islam

The debt owed by the Islamic world to its eminent philosophers, and therefore to Greek wisdom, is truly incalculable. Without the influence of Greek dialectic in the clarification of concepts and precision of definitions, it is doubtful if Islam could have had sufficiently universal intellectual formulations to back up its obvious spiritual treasures of a Semitic nature. The religion was evidently not meant simply for the Semites, in this case the Arabs. Otherwise, its wars of conquest at the very beginning would not have encompassed Berbers, Armenians, Persians, or other non-Semitic peoples. Had the monotheistic message of Islam remained only among the Arabs, bottled up in Arabia, then probably it would have had no need for the Aryan wisdom of the Greeks and would have been content with its Semitic modes of expression. It would have been more or less like the earlier, pre-Christian monotheistic teachings of the Arab Prophets such as Hūd, Shu'ayb, Ṣāliḥ, or the Arabicized Ishmael, progenitor of the Northern Arabs. But in mingling with Aryans in Persia and elsewhere, the Arabs themselves were Aryanized to a certain degree. Hence, they too were in need of the intellectual clarifications that Greek wisdom was able to impart to the Semitic faith of their forefathers. The Arabs were not immune to the decline that took place in the early century or so of the religion. The codifications taking place then were not meant simply for the non-Arab Muslims. Quite the contrary, the very conquests of the Arabs transformed their nomadic culture into a sedentary civilization that absorbed elements from the great Persian and Byzantine imperial systems. All of this interior psychological readjustment of the Arab soul to the exigencies of the new Islamic civilization meant that the Arabs also had to absorb the more analytical approach of Greek thinking.

For many of the religious authorities and Ṣūfīs of early and medieval Islam, the thought that Islam might be indebted to the more precise and nuanced thinking of Greek wisdom was simply out of the question. Islam had no reason to call upon the supplementary light of *falsafah*. For the theologians, philosophy was but another form of Mu'tazilism: it tended to deal with rationalistic propositions and to reduce the sacred dogmas to the level of profane notions. If many of the fundamentalist theologians of Islam, like the Ḥanbalīs, rejected already even the speculative processes of Ash'arism as being concessions to the requirements of a weak faith, then philosophy had no chance whatsoever. It was a dangerous exercise of reasoning that threatened faith and led to doubts, hesitations, and even to disbelief.

Nevertheless, one finds great philosophers in Islam like Ibn Rushd (d. 1198) who were also eminent religious authorities of admirable piety and moral integrity; they were the exceptions to the rule that the *'ulamā'* and *falsafah* do not mix. In his important work entitled *Tahāfut al-Falāsifah* (*The Incoherence of the Philosophers*), al-Ghazālī (d. 1111) showed that ideas circulated among philosophers, which were counter to Islamic dogmas, and which had to be refuted by reason. He had in mind such philosophical concepts as the eternity of the world, the impossibility of the resurrection of the body, and the like. In reality, his book is a proof that reason can be employed to destroy reason. That principle accounts for the existence of a point-by-point retort made later by Ibn Rushd in his *Tahāfut at-Tahāfut* (*The Incoherence of the Incoherence*). But by then it would be too late to resuscitate interest in philosophical studies within the Sunnī world of Islam. Through his different works, al-Ghazālī had pointed to Ṣūfism as the definitive solution to philosophical doubts and spiritual hesitations stemming from the sickness of reasoning uncontrolled by faith in scriptural evidence or by the light of the Spirit in the heart.

The case of al-Ghazālī is illustrative of the inner malaise that had come over many of the best minds of his day. His doubts, his anguish, his disbelief, his search for the peace of God, which he reveals to us in his famous spiritual autobiography, *al-Munqidh min aḍ-Ḍalāl* (*The Redeemer from Error*),[7] were not confined to him alone. They must have invaded the souls of innumerable religious scholars, theologians, philosophers, authors, and others in his generation. They were not sure how to put the disease of uncontrolled reasoning to rest. Nor did they know how to obtain the spiritual certitude that alone could burn through all the disquietudes of the soul and bring "the peace of God, that passeth all understanding".

Al-Ghazālī became a model for those who faced these inner problems and sought to resolve them. He was a kind of chosen vessel who had to experience the depths of despair, then the fire of purification, and finally the blissful union with God that brought illuminative knowledge and peace. After a spiritual crisis that pushed him to the edge of the abyss, he set about to examine the teachings of the dominant schools of his time. One by one he investigated the claims of the scholastic theologians, of the philosophers, of the Isma'īlī "esoterists" of Shī'ī Islam, and of the Ṣūfīs. When he studied Ṣūfism, he perceived that it was not just a teaching about *Allāh* but also, and above all, a method of spiritual realization that had to be actually experienced by the adept himself. Leaving Baghdad, he set out as a seeker of the Path in Syria and, under the guidance of masters, eventually found the luminous peace he had sought. Shortly afterwards, he penned his famous *Iḥyā'*, which presented the Path and the Law as complementary aspects of the same Islamic message and that definitively established *taṣawwuf* ("esoterism" in the Ṣūfī sense) as the pinnacle of *Tawḥīd*.

In criticizing the different philosophers, the *Munqidh* added yet another nail to their coffins. They had already been under the attack of the dogmatists and religious authorities of earlier times. Now, with the appearance of the *Iḥyā'*, the philosophers were excluded altogether from the ideal *dār al-islām*. From that point on, they had to justify their problematical existence in diverse ways. The claim of Ibn Rushd that *falsafah* was esoteric in relation to the Law was precisely such a justification. Failing that, the philosophers could turn the tables on the Ṣūfīs by absorbing Ṣūfism into their own philosophical systems. We see this in "the philosophy of Illumination" (*ḥikmat al-ishrāq*) of the Illuminationist school founded by Shihāb ad-Dīn as-Suhrawardī (d. 1191). This was a system of thought that combined Islamic Neoplatonism, Ṣūfism, and even Persian Zoroastrianism into a kind of philosophical esoterism. By keeping within the framework of Neoplatonism, Illuminationism had the advantage of moving within the general drift of Islamic thought. That thinking was suffused increasingly with a Ṣūfī coloration as the Middle Ages wore on. Aristotelianism, by contrast, found a ready audience only in the Christian scholastic theology of the epoch. It had been progressively squeezed out of the Western Islamic community by the combined pressures of both the scholastic theologians and the Ṣūfīs. Never again would Aristotelianism reappear in its pure form within the confines of Islam, Sunnī or Shī'ī.

One is constantly surprised to discover in the writings of the eminent Ṣūfīs of medieval Islam, such as Ibn al-'Arabī (d. 1240), that they are themselves the exponents of a philosophical mysticism owing a great deal to the terminological influence of Neoplatonism within the Islamic intellectual tradition. The explanation of this apparent contradiction in those very Ṣūfīs who condemned Islamic philosophy is simple enough. Once philosophy was admitted into the culture of the community, it was Islamicized by all sorts of writers. A prose stylist like al-Jāḥiẓ (d. 868), for example, introduced its vocabulary selectively into his works of a popular nature. Similarly, the widely-known but anonymous philosophical work of the tenth century, *The Treatises of the Brethren of Purity* (*Rasā il Ikhwān aṣ-Ṣafā'*), gives us a simple but lucid overview of the Islamic cosmos seen in the light of philosophy and its ancillary disciplines. Works like these could not but spread abroad the use of philosophical terminology derived from Neoplatonism in its Islamic guise. By the time the great medieval Ṣūfī sages appear on the historical scene, a widespread scholastic intellectual tradition of Neoplatonic colors is to be found in the cultural fabric of the community. It is this which allows an Ibn al-'Arabī to criticize the philosophers while himself expounding a philosophical mysticism. He could not have written as he did without the centuries-old legacy of Islamic philosophy that he inherited. While he protests that his writings on *taṣawwuf* are not to be construed as philosophy, he makes use of philosophical modes of exposition in his *al-Futūḥāt al-Makkiyyah* (*The Meccan Revelations*) and in other works. In attenuation of his seemingly contradictory position, we have to bear in mind that philosophy as such is ambiguous when we contrast its Neoplatonic and Aristotelian aspects. As already pointed out, Neoplatonism is an esoteric Greek doctrine. It is much more analytical and systematic than the Semitic esoterism of early Islam, to be sure, but both nevertheless are pointed in the direction of gnosis. Aristotelianism, for its part, is more of a tool for argumentation and ratiocination and in any case is certainly not an esoteric teaching. It can be integrated into gnostic forms of thought, as we see in certain aspects of Neoplatonism. It is thus reasonable to conclude that Ibn al-'Arabī and other Ṣūfīs merely lumped the two versions of Greek wisdom together into the same general category of *falsafah* when disclaiming any role as philosophers. From a certain point of view, they were indeed philosophers, exactly as Plotinus and other Greek mystical sages who preached the intellective vision of the One as the goal of the contemplative life. That was what the Ṣūfī gnostics themselves were saying, in their own way.

But the adherents of Ṣūfism do not in general see the positive facets of philosophy. They do admit that the philosopher can perceive truths from time to time. However, the negative traits of philosophy neutralize such truths, and this is so because the philosopher's reliance on reasoning alone blocks in advance his direct perception of the absolutely Real through the use of the inner eye of the Spirit. Likewise, even though the philosopher may occasionally articulate truths, the fact that he does not follow a way of sanctification means that such truths are inevitably caught up in the unregenerate mental substance of his psyche and are consequently compromised in their effect. Moreover, while it is true that philosophy speaks about God and other transcendent realities, most philosophers do not envisage the spiritual realization of the Divine Unity through gnosis as an indispensable element of their discipline. Instead, they confine themselves to a purely theoretical or conceptual consideration of metaphysical truths without seeking to remove the inner blindness of their heart-intellects, which is what gnosis has in view.

Such arguments against *falsafah* and its exponents are effective only if there is general agreement beforehand that the mystical vision of God is necessary before one can speak about Him with consistent authority. There must also be agreement on the part of everyone that within Islam only the Ṣūfīs have such a direct, concrete knowledge of the Divine Unity. This implies that every body else speaks about God through the indirect light of Scripture, seen with the eye of Faith or Reason, or both at the same time. Ṣūfī argumentation of that kind took quite a while before it became fully persuasive. It did so through the gradual penetration of its esoteric notions into all levels of society and into all fields of endeavor, including the literary arts and genres. When such prose stylists as Abū Ḥayyān at-Tawḥīdī (d. 1023), who was also something of a philosopher, speak admiringly of the Ṣūfīs and even imitate the tone of their devotional style, as he does in his *al-Irshādāt al-Ilāhiyyah* (*Divine Directives*), this shows the spiritual pressure exerted by Ṣūfism. Similarly, the case of the philosopher Ibn Sīnā (d. 1037), an Aristotelian in his formative years and a Neoplatonic mystic later on, reveals that the sages of *falsafah* could be caught up in the contemplative atmosphere of Islam.

It was left for al-Ghazālī (d. 1111) to draw the conclusions on *falsafah* and to spell out the priority of the Ṣūfī Way over all other modes of thinking. The Ṣūfī *ma'rifah* that he speaks of had been in the spiritual culture of Islam for centuries before his time and that of his detractor Ibn Rushd (d. 1198). If Ibn al-'Arabī (d. 1240), the *shaykh al-akbar* of the Ṣūfī tradition, could not convert the Aristotelian Ibn Rushd to the idea of *ma'rifah*, this was by then of no consequence for the future of Islam. Ṣūfism was everywhere in evidence: the immense literary production on esoteric themes by Ibn al-'Arabī would not have been possible if his audience had not had long preparation. Even the contemporary of Ibn Rushd, the Ḥanbalī canonist and preacher Ibn al-Jawzī (d. 1200), could not reject Ṣūfism or the Path in general. In his *Talbīs* Iblīs (*The Devil's Deceit*), he confines his criticism to those Ṣūfīs who seemed to exaggerate or to break the customary norms of the community.

Little by little the Ṣūfī arguments against *falsafah* gained ground and finally triumphed. But they did so by assimilating all the positive features of Greek wisdom, especially in its Neoplatonic version. Ṣūfism left to one side those aspects of Greek thinking that had no immediacy for the contemplative life, such as logic, mathematics, the natural sciences, and medicine. Greek metaphysical and epistemological notions that had a bearing on gnostic speculations on the Divine Unity were by their very nature usable. It was largely through the diffusion of the innumerable works of Ibn al-'Arabī that the integration of Neoplatonic thought into Ṣūfism was most effectively actualized. Hundred of works issued from his pen on metaphysical, spiritual, cosmological, eschatological, and initiatic speculations based on the integrative principle of *Tawḥīd*. It was an eclectic system that had a spiritual unity and not at all a syncretism without interior harmony and concord. His intellectual and spiritual work would dominate the Sunnī world of thinking for centuries on end, and even move into the Shī'ī lands.

Other forms of Ṣūfism rejected the scholastic armature or the philosophical style of expression. They preferred instead the nonspeculative approach to gnosis. Their teachers expounded the depths and interrelationships of *īmān* ("faith"), *islām* ("submission"), and *iḥsān* ("virtue"), the perfection of which leads to *ma'rifah*, their greatest fruit. In abstaining from philosophical speculation, this type of Ṣūfism harks back to the simpler esoteric structures of earlier Islam. There was no philosophy then, but only the *sharī'ah* and the *ṭarīqah*; so there should be no need for it now. But in reality there was a vital need for the philosophical argumentation of certain brands of Sufism. Those contemplatives who had been formed by the medieval scholastic intellectual tradition and the philosophical culture of the day had to be addressed in a style congenial to their formation. That accounts for the doctrinal complexity in the works of Ibn al-'Arabī and his school of thought. The complexity of argumentation was designed to remove the ensemble of mental patterns in the mind of the contemplative that impeded the smooth flow of intuitions arising from the simplicity of his inner being.

While philosophy in its usual sense retreated from the Sunnī world, it remanifested itself, as was said, in a dress related to Twelver Shī'ism. This was the Shī'ī philosophical school of Mullā Ṣadrā Shīrāzī (d. 1640).[8] It preached an eclectic system containing *falsafah*, Ṣūfism, Illuminationism (*Ishrāqiyyah*), and Shī'ī mystico-theological elements. The whole formed a theosophical teaching that brought its practitioners into direct conflict with the more dogmatic Shī'ī doctors of the Law in Safavid times in Persia. That school would last as a philosophical tradition down to recent times in the world of Shī'ī Islam and would draw some of its intellectual apparatus from the Sunnī Ṣūfī, Ibn al-'Arabī. The latter had absorbed philosophical elements into his system of Ṣūfism, and now his Sūfism was absorbed into the philosophical structures of the Persian Shī'ī thinkers who had created the latest version of Islamic philosophy.

The discovery that the Muslim world had not lost its philosophical tradition after the days of Ibn Rushd has reversed the usual view of Islamic cultural history. Far from disappearing, philosophical speculation continued on and emerged once again in the Persia of Safavid times. Indeed, Islamic philosophy was the intellectual foundation to the impressive Safavid accomplishments in the arts, architecture, and the sciences. This was a cultural flowering of Islam that was contemporaneous with the brilliant achievements of Islamic civilization among the Ottoman Turks and the Mughals of India.

In the present-day Islamic world, a struggle between the exponents of the traditional Islamic *falsafah* of millennial history and the partisans of modern Western philosophies has seesawed back and forth. In the works of the Shī'ī school of Persia and the Sunnī philosophical esoterism of Ibn al-'Arabī, we find an extraordinarily rich intellectual heritage that is directly related to Islam, which is certainly not the case for modern Western philosophical thought. Capitulation to Western modes of thinking is in line, however, with the modernists' rejection of the Islamic tradition in general. Conservative Muslims differ from them only in being slower in the process of surrendering to the modern Western industrial civilization in all of its aspects, retaining only the practice of the Pillars of Religion in a community increasingly stripped of its Islamic cultural forms.

In the West, the neoscholasticism of Christian thinkers in recent times represents an awareness that modern systems of philosophy cannot replace the towering intellectual structure created by such medieval scholastics as Saint Thomas Aquinas (d. 1274). His teaching, or Thomism, is definitive for the Western Christian world. Likewise, in the Islamic world, the perennial philosophy embodied in the works of an Ibn al-'Arabī and other Muslim sages is an intellectual patrimony that remains to this day a source of inspiration for countless Muslims who are capable of understanding it and using it in the midst of the spiritual chaos that reigns in the East and the West.

The influence of such an intellectual legacy on the theological thinking of Islam should not be forgotten. In earlier times, theology was given a kind of rational underpinning by the influence of Islamic philosophical dialectic. Nowadays, theological doctrine is in need of much the same type of help. It is only in this fashion that the intrusions of modernist thinking can be effectively countered and refuted. Infiltrations of Western ideological systems inimical to the traditional outlook, such as existentialism, evolutionism in all its forms, socialism, Marxism, relativism, and the host of other theories exported by the West to the East, have already had devastating effects on Islam. Their presence in the world of Islam stems from the incredible forgetfulness (*ghaflah*) of the traditional intellectual perspective that has afflicted a significant number of cultural leaders. Even many religious leaders have succumbed to the allurements of these imported systems of thought. Their combinations of Islam and technologism, Islam and progressivism, Islam and republicanism, Islam and communism, Islam and revolutionism, and so on and so on, reveal just how widespread the spiritual *glaflah* within the community has become and how this had led to the appearance of small armies of religious chiefs acting out their roles as the blind leading the blind.

Under such circumstances, a vigorous reaffirmation of the Islamic intellectual tradition is now of the utmost importance.[9] It is necessary not only to combat the numerous antitraditional systems of thought that have arisen within *dār al-islām* in recent times but also for the sake of those who can appreciate its contents and applications. The Islamic version of the perennial philosophy has much in common with the Jewish and Christian philosophical traditions. They share a similar corpus of metaphysical principles that cannot but contribute to the indispensable task of interfaith understanding. In the intellectual formulations of an al-Kindī, an al-Fārābī, an al-Ghazālī, an Ibn Sīnā, or an Ibn al-'Arabī, the Islamic tradition has all the light it needs to defend itself against its exterior and interior enemies while at the same time upholding the universality of revelation. The latter principle, found in the Qur'ān and occasionally expounded by Ṣūfī sages in medieval times, is one of the most important teachings in comparative religion that Islam has to offer the world. For this reason, the Muslim metaphysician of the present day has a role to play in the intellectual exposition of the spiritual unity underlying the world religions whose original revelations stem from the same Divine Source that gave rise to Islam.

VII
The Arts of Islam

The Principles of Sacred Art

The revelations that created the different religions of mankind, such as Hinduism, Buddhism, Christianity, or Islam, have also had an aesthetic message which would emerge as their sacred arts in due time. So integrated are those arts into the perspective of the revealed message that one has to speak of an otherworldly presence operating within them, while allowing ethnic or regional variations to express themselves too. Although there are aesthetic elements in all scriptural texts, even if only the literary beauty and the radiance of the truth be taken into account, these are germinal in nature. They do not provide a complete teaching on the arts, nor does the initial period of a religion give rise to all the variety and richness of artistic development that one will see later in its history as a result of contacts with foreign cultures and their arts and the subsequent experimentation or trial and error necessary before the classic forms of a traditional art or architecture appear.

Earlier on, mention was made of the three principles of religion, or its three states or conditions, *īmān* ("faith"), *islām* ("submission", i.e. to the Divine Will), and *iḥsān* ("virtue"), that were defined in a famous *ḥadīth* involving Gabriel and the Prophet. The first one, faith, has to do with the doctrine of a religion; the second one, submission, has to do with the ritual observances; and the third, virtue, has to do with the moral code that must be followed or, more deeply, with virtue and the spiritual life. In Islam, if one were to situate the origins of sacred art in one of these three principles, it would probably have to be in the third, *iḥsān*, since it is connected with beauty (*ḥusn*), not only of the soul, but of all things. Yet, one should recall that all sacred art has relations with faith, since it is an expression of that faith to begin with. It has relations with the rituals of a religion, which the art is called upon to house with beauty in order to distinguish the liturgical life of the religion from ordinary existence. More to the point is the fact that the spiritual substance of a believer engaged in art, or in producing art, is reflected in the fruits of his hands. The more *iḥsān*, or beauty of soul, there is in the artisan, the greater will his art manifest the same Spirit that presides over the fortunes of his religion. It is not for nothing, therefore, that the contemplative Path of Islam stresses the third principle, *iḥsān*, as being the one that introduces a deepening tendency in the other two. Ṣūfism is the art of perfecting one's *iḥsān*, or one's spiritual life, through conformity to the indwelling Spirit, which engenders the beautification (*taḥsīn*) of the soul. This is a process that is no doubt subjective in nature, but the Spirit is also an objective reality which contains within itself the source of all beauty, and which cannot but radiate in the purified soul. That same radiance of the Spirit is to be found objectively in the sacred and traditional arts of Islam, for they are also expressions of an invisible presence. In other words, the Islamic revelation contains doctrine (*īmān*), methods of sanctification (*islām*), and a spiritual life (*iḥsān*) that is both subjective and human as well as objective and aesthetic, the latter being the sacred arts of Islam.

The necessity for all of these elements in a revelation — and they are common to all of the religions — lies in the integrality of human nature. Man has a thinking faculty, a will governing the ensemble of his tendencies, and a life or existential aspect, and these are all addressed respectively by *īmān*, *islām*, and *iḥsān*. We can understand that the doctrine of a revelation attempts to purify man's thinking about God and the world, that the rituals (including mental prayer) sanctify man's fallen will and regenerate him, and that the spiritual life permits man to remain within the directive influence of the Spirit. It is not immediately apparent, however, what the function of sacred art might be or why it is necessary in Islam and in all the other religions, or why it constitutes an essential feature alongside the doctrine (*īmān*), the method of realization (*islām*), and spirituality (*iḥsān*).

According to a *ḥadīth* of the Prophet, "God is Beautiful and He loves Beauty." We often associate revelations with the Divine Wisdom as being teachings that must be understood, or with the Divine Power or Will that seeks through a celestial message to redeem a particular humanity. But there is also the feminine nature of the Divinity, its attractive and expressive Beauty. This is often overlooked in evaluating the contents of the different revealed scriptures or the persons, like the Buddha or the Christ, who are, in their very humanity, the revelation itself ("the Word made flesh"). In

Islam, as we have already seen, the Ninety-Nine "Most-Beautiful Names" of *Allāh* relate either to the Divine Essence (the Names of Essence) or to the personal nature of God, the Names of Quality. These last are either Names of Majesty (*asmā 'al-jalāl*) or Names of Beauty (*asmā 'al-Jamāl*), according to case. From a certain perspective, the three categories of Names refer to the Divine Wisdom, the Divine Power, and the Divine Beauty, respectively. Since the Qur'ānic revelation is an unveiling of God's nature to man, it must include the Divine Beauty itself as one of the aspects of God divulged to man. This must be so not merely in a literary sense — the beauty of Qur'ānic Arabic is especially evident in the cantillation of its verses — but in numerous other ways. It is this celestial reality that makes the presence of sacred art a necessity in the revelation itself. It is an expression of the divine nature, of God's beauteous radiance, that cannot but manifest itself within the redemptive message. This holds true even for such a nontheistic religion as Buddhism, with its impersonal Nirvanic reality that is analogous to the impersonal Divine Essence (*adh-dhāt al-ilāhiyyah*) of Islam. In certain Mahayanic schools of Buddhism, especially Zen and Shingon, the Nirvanic Void is said to be infinitely beautiful. In its human manifestation, as the earthly Buddha, the marks of beauty have a saving quality for the Buddhist pondering the image of the Void (*Shunyamurti*). The Omnipotence of the Creator is not simply a blind force devoid of truth or beauty or consciousness. It is the expression of the artistic Divinity that "creates", like the artisan in this world, the entire Creation. Thus, the beauty one finds in the sacred arts of mankind is an expression of the Divine Beauty, "the radiance of the Truth", as beauty is sometimes defined.

While all sacred art has that quality of radiating aesthetically the truths contained in the scriptural revelation, and therefore of expressing them in its own way, it also has an attractive power. That power pulls the believer into his innermost being, there where his Spirit is to be found. This is a consolatory function that centers the restless nature of man's soul and nourishes it with infused graces. To the pedagogical character of all sacred art, which pertains to its expressive role, there is also to be added its healing or redemptive function, its power to dissolve the psychic complexes of fallen man. On the one hand, through its pedagogical role, it shows man what he must be like; on the other, through its graces and beatific radiance, it helps to redeem him.

The sacred arts of the different religions are not the same, no more than their respective doctrines are the same, even though the Truth is one. Just as the absolute Truth is possessed of numerous facets that can be accentuated in different ways, so likewise the infinite Beauty of the Divine Reality can be manifested in diverse sacred arts. That manifestation depends on the doctrinal perspective of the original revelation, to begin with, and on the ethnic qualities of the peoples affected by the religions that revelations established. There is here an important principle: The spiritual perspective of the religion, its doctrinal content, is what determines the flowering of the corresponding art. But while that principle is no doubt universal, the forms in which it manifests itself, the varieties of its styles, are largely subservient to ethnic, historical, or even regional considerations that seem to belie the interior unity of the art in question. The inspiring Idea in the art of a given religious civilization is what presides over its innumerable manifestations but those manifestations are subject to human or other circumstances. This is only a recapitulation, in sacred aesthetics, of the same law we observe in revelations themselves: Although their spiritual contents are universal, the external expressions, the forms, are governed partly by ethnic, geographical, and other factors that color the message.

The arts are not just either sacred or profane, for there are intermediate types, in Islam as in other religious worlds. A sacred art is a revealed art that has, like the message itself, a transcendent origin and functions as an artistic expression of that message. Not all the arts of Islam which have been transmitted from generation to generation are sacred, to be sure. But those traditional arts which have a central or absolute nature, as calligraphy, for example, which has to do immediately with the Qur'ānic "Word", and that therefore relate essentially to the revelation, are obviously sacred. Not all religions have the same sacred arts, though all of the traditional civilizations share more or less in the same arts. Some of these, like weaving and pottery, are to be found among the arts of the archaic traditional cultures, such as the Maori, the African, and the American Indian. It is therefore the centrality of the traditional art, its revelatory character as an indispensable element of the revelation, along with the doctrines, the rites, and the moral code, which make it sacred.

In principle, all the traditional arts, such as woodworking, painting, urban architecture, and music, were of nonhuman origins. That is why, in the old civilizations of the past, especially the archaic ones, each art was credited with having its celestial prototype. The same holds true for traditional teachings, or doctrines, like the cosmological disciplines, or even philosophy, in the Pythagorean sense. They were not of human invention, but descended from on high. Innumerable, then, are the arts of society in the ancient world that were attributed to divine roots. Nor can one make a catalogue of them without listing hundreds, and even thousands, of such arts, varying from culture to culture, and transmitted with greater or lesser accuracy of technique, greater or lesser depth of content or value.

The division of the arts into visual and auditive categories, for example, is due to the psychophysical structure of man's perception of things. One can see (visual), hear (auditive), smell (olfactory), touch (tactile), and taste (gustatory) the aesthetic aspects of the different arts because that is the way they present themselves initially to us through our sensorial nature which is in contact with the objects of knowledge around us. That the visual and auditive arts have a kind of priority is due, no doubt, to their essential roles in our own lives, whereas the other sensorial faculties are of lesser importance. We "see" the mosques, the mausoleums, the Ka'bah; we "hear" the chanting of the Qur'ān, the instruction in grammar, the theology of Ash'arism. But, in general, when speaking about Christian or Islamic, or even Shinto, arts we do not say that we "smell" or "taste" or "feel" Christian, Islamic, or Shinto arts, even though it is evident that all of these traditional cultures had olfactory, gustatory, and tactile arts. The various kinds of incense burned in Muslim homes, mosques, *khānaqāhs*, and elsewhere, permit us to "smell" the Islamic realities. Textiles, of gorgeous or severe patterns, reflecting the arabesques and geometric motifs found in mosques and on woodwork, are ways of "feeling" the Islamic religion. There are arts, admittedly, that combine one or more of the sensorial faculties. The truths imbedded in a particular religion come to its adherents, not only through its verbal doctrine, but also through their organs of sensation. These convey sensorial impressions to the aesthetic functions of the intelligence, so that the combination of different sensorial powers makes for a powerful artistic shock. It is the intelligence of man, of course, that discerns, through intuition, the truth radiating from an object of beauty. It is man's faculties of sensation that establish contact with the visual or auditive or tactile or gustatory or olfactory objects of art. Given that man has these powers, revelation, in its fullest extension of meaning, must embrace them likewise and integrate them into the message. Otherwise it would leave out of the salvific process a good deal of human experience. It is not simply through mental concepts that man is saved from the effects of the Fall: the revelation affects his entire being.

Islamic Nonrepresentational Art

Islamic art, like everything else in that tradition, is based essentially on *Tawḥīd* and *dhikr*. Its aesthetic theory, in other words, is fundamentally based on a metaphysical teaching about the Divine Unity.[1] That unity is impersonal and unconditioned, infinite and undifferentiated, when we are speaking about the ultimate Reality in itself. But the practice of art, its actual production, is really a form of *dhikr*. This is so not only for the artisan, but also for the beholder of the resulting beauty in the created object. It is a way of remembering God for the individual producer and for others who see or hear what he has created. Since the doctrine illuminates the contents of the art, and the form of the art illustrates the doctrine, it is evident that one must first understand the fundamental perspective of a given religion before one can grasp the moving spirit of its arts. In this case, *Tawḥīd*, which has been given metaphysical, theological, and spiritual explanations by the Muslim sages, is the eventual doctrinal foundation on which the arts repose, for it is the unique perspective of the Islamic revelation itself. Remembering God (*dhikr*) in one way or another is the whole purpose of *Tawḥīd*. The belief of Islam is that God is One; the practice of Islam is in essence to remember *Allāh*.

The nonrepresentational nature of Islamic art, which balks at the idea of representing living beings, comes partly from the ultimate, abstract character of the Divinity. It also comes from a certain tendency in Islamic thinking to conceive of the Omnipotence of God as removing all free will in man to create his own deeds. To represent living beings is somewhat like contesting the absoluteness of God's character as Creator by "recreating" them once again. If man's own actions are already subject to predestination, which abolishes all secondary creative powers, then the production of living beings in paintings or in some other artistic medium is a form of associationism (*shirk*). Even the partisans of free will in Islamic thinking are subject to the overriding influence of the threat of associationism, which can manifest itself in a thousand different ways, so to speak, and must not be thought of simply as mere polytheism.

One need not therefore look for historical connections with the aniconic tendencies in the contemporaneous Christian world of Byzantium or in the Zoroastrian tradition of the Persian Empire to discover the sources of Islamic nonrepresentational art. The metaphysical and spiritual perspectives of *Tawḥīd* and the consequences flowing from Muslims' preoccupation with the omnipotential creativity of God suffice in themselves to grasp why Islamic art is essentially disinclined to depict the Divinity itself and also to represent human beings, or living beings that "cast shadows".

It is easy to conclude that, in the overall history of religious thought in Islam, a kind of unwillingness to compare God with creatures or with created things, or Incomparability (*tanzīh*), is the general proclivity of the community. This is not to say that the other Qur'ānic teaching on Comparability (*tashbīh*) has no partisans, for it does. There are those sages who combine both. But a first reading of the Scripture gives to Incomparability a strong case. This is definitively established as a permanent dogma, theologically, by the religious thinkers' desire to remove all possibility of staining the transcendent Purity and Immutability of the Creator through identifying Him with impurer and mutable things in this world. Incomparability of the Creator implies that He cannot be given figurative form as a living entity of this world, and that one must not attempt to compete with Him in painting or depicting living creatures. Anthropomorphic representation of the Divinity is thereby excluded from the visual arts, as is all associationism that would permit man to create, in his own world, images that seem to have a life of their own.

One might be tempted to think that the relationship between an All-Powerful God and His powerful creatures, who have no wills of their own and therefore no creativity and no capacity to produce seemingly living things, might be an explanation for the proscriptions of human or living forms in Islamic art. But we must remember that the interdiction against representing God in anthropomorphic visual images does not hold true for anthropomorphic auditive images. We discern the latter in the numerous verses of the Qur'ān which speak of God's hands, feet, his sitting on the throne, and the like. We need not mention those Names of the Divinity that are clearly anthropomorphic in nature, like "the Seeing" or "the Hearing". Moreover, the imagery of powerless creatures who seem puppetlike in their fatalism does not take into account that a limited freedom of the will is preached in the Scripture and by some of the theologians and other teachers in the tradition. Finally, it is in the very nature of things that Incomparability (*tanzīh*), or the Transcendence of God, cannot account for the whole of the Qur'ānic teaching on the divine nature, and that Comparability (*tashbīh*), or the Immanence of God, must also have its say both in the doctrine of the faith and in its arts.

The Arab Arts

Whether the Arabs, as Semites, have an ethnic affinity with the auditive and not with the visual arts, and whether this also can account in part for the prohibition against images, is another question. Idolatrous practices among the pre-Islamic Arabs and the hideous descriptions of their idols that we find in the historical texts reveal that the Arabs of those days, "The Time of Ignorance" (*al-jāhiliyyah*), had a paganistic culture devoid of any aesthetic beauty in the representational arts. As a matter of fact, their representational arts were of unparalleled crudity among the peoples of the Mediterranean. The opposite is true for Arab auditive arts, such as poetry, prose, and oratory. These were orally transmitted and constituted an extraordinary legacy of perfection that Islam could only improve upon by introducing into it the idea of the transcendent One. Nor must one think that the Jewish prohibition of images — or "idols" — was without any connection with similar thinking in Islam. Jewish religious culture was to be found in Medina and outlying oases, and this could not but have some influence on the nascent faith, surrounded on all sides by an idolatrous world. The smashing of the scores of idols inside the Ka'bah by the Prophet Muḥammad after the conquest of Mecca in the year 630 was not, however, due to his Arab nomadic culture or to the influence that Jewish thinking might have had on his religious sensitivity. It was a prototypal action flowing from that Incomparability of God already mentioned and the nonassociationism that the Islamic religion engenders. The vindication of *tanzīh* at that very moment was accompanied by a tacit admission on his part that Comparability, or *tashbīh*, also has its rights: the icons of the Eastern Church found inside the Ka'bah were not destroyed, but were handed over to the Christians.

Mention was made, earlier on, that the Arabs were a people whose qualities were such that they were a fit vehicle for the Qur'ānic revelation. Their speech, their chivalric nomadic culture, their explosive and yet noble temperament, and many other human traits, were integrated into the message of Islam. Their negative qualities, such as their paganism, were rejected. Consequently, their idolatrous arts were among the discarded elements of their culture. But certainly the nomadic arts manifested in their garments, carpets, domestic utensils and wares were usable within the cultural framework of the newly-born faith. Those arts, because of their archaic nature, tended to be geometric, as we see among other tribal cultures elsewhere. Even the desert architecture of the small towns and oases, apart from Mecca and Medina, were not too far removed from the nomadic world in its timeless elements. Arab culture was not only prototypal for the scriptural nature of the revelation but also for the aesthetic dimensions as well, since these are part and parcel of the message.

The Qur'ān and Sunnah as Aesthetic Foundations

When seeking the origins of Islamic art we must not overlook the Qur'ān and the Sunnah as the aesthetic foundations of the faith. These two are obviously the determinants of the teachings and practices of both the *sharī'ah* and the *ṭarīqah*. But, as was said, no revelation is devoid of its aesthetic message, so to speak, and the same holds true for Islam. Therefore, it is in the Scripture and in the Norm of the Messenger that we must look for the spiritual origins of sacred art in Islam. This is so even though the arts of Islam derive a great deal of their technical perfection and some of their variant forms from contact with other traditional arts, Persian or Byzantine or Indian or Turkish, according to case.

The theologico-legalistic formulations of Islam were influenced, to a certain degree, by Talmudic, Greek, and other sources. Even the Ṣūfī Path has its Neoplatonic, Christian, Jewish, Hindu, Shamanistic, Buddhist, Zoroastrian, Chinese, and African influences, without for all that losing its essentially Islamic nature. There should be no surprise if Islamic art followed suit. This is all the more explicable in view of the essentially geometric and nonrepresentational character of that art. It can absorb regional and ethnic variations with considerable flexibility and yet remain within the aesthetic unity of *dār al-islām*. Let us remember that the doctrine of the Divine Unity itself is capable of application to the most diverse ethnic and racial populations precisely because it is so abstract and impersonal in its nonanthropomorphic essence. On the anthropomorphic plane it has universal appeal also because the human attributes of God are characteristic of humanity as a whole, and not of any one particular people.

The miraculous nature of the Qur'ān, which was the greatest miracle (*mu'jizah*) vouchsafed Muḥammad, stems from the Divine Presence in its letters and sounds, which in turn influences its grammatical and rhetorical excellence. It is in that supernatural beauty of the Qur'ān that we can discover the origin of sacred art in Islam. The "Word made book" meant that everything related to the visual and auditive characteristics of the Qur'ān must necessarily partake of a sacred art. The sacramentality of the Word in Islam is, to speak in comparative terms, analogous to the sacramentality of the Christ-Logos, perpetuated in the Eucharist. Just as the Christ-Logos accounts for the rise of the iconography and the ecclesiastical architecture of the Church, both of which enclose the Word in refulgent beauty, so likewise the Word in Islam, the Qur'ān, generated the sacred arts of calligraphy and mosque architecture. These, together with their ancillary arts, enshroud the message with the attractive and persuasive glow of transcendent beauty.

As noted already on several occasions, the Qur'ān by itself is really more like the theoretical formulation of *Tawḥīd* and therefore stands in need of the complementary practical application, the Sunnah of the Messenger, his living Norm. It is often forgotten that the Sunnah is not just simply a host of ritual observances or moral rules for the individual or society. The Sunnah is rather vast, indeed, and while the Five Pillars of Religion could be described as its salvific core, that is merely from a simplifying viewpoint. It embraces numerous other domains of social life, such as commerce, marriage, government, birth and death, education, medicine, etiquette, hygiene, posture, and gesticulation. It also describes the inner contemplative life of mental prayer, meditation, spiritual retreat, concentration, and virtue. The Sunnah contains the patterns on which the community will base its conduct and life. In his style of living, the Messenger was the "good Exemplar" of the message given to his community: "Ye have indeed, in the Messenger of God, a good Exemplar for whomsoever hopes in God and in the Last Day, and remembers God often" (Sūrah 33:21).

That being so, it is only natural that there should be an aesthetic Sunnah likewise which establishes the prototypal sacred arts of Islam. The imitation of the Prophet was not limited to conforming to his beliefs and ritual practices only. It included following his aesthetic Sunnah insofar as it applied to the visual and auditive arts. His home and the adjacent mosque, together with all the simple furnishings, such as floor mats, that went with them, were normative as well for the community. One has only to think of the rows of palm trunks of his mosque at Medina in colonnade form, reminiscent of an oasis enclosed within square or rectangular walls, to be reminded of the fundamental hypostyle mosques of later times, like the Great Mosques at Cordova, Qairawan, Damascus, or Isfahan, that are in really sophisticated elaborations on the Prophet's architectural Sunnah.

Even the square or rectangular form of mosque architecture, such as we see in the Prophet's day and afterwards, is an Islamic reconsecration of a fundamental geometric shape that indicates stability, immutability, static peacefulness, and even the telluric element itself, Earth, all of which can be intuited from the four-sided Ka'bah, the Sacred House, at Mecca. While all the other essential geometric forms, such as the cross, the triangle, the circle, the spiral, and the like, have their particular say within the artistic fruits of the Islamic faith, the square, or its variant, the rectangle, seems to have a special signification within the Islamic message. We see this in the four aspects of the Spirit, the Archangels Jibrā'īl, Mikā'īl, Isrā'īl, and Isrāfīl, that have cosmic roles; the four Orthodox Caliphs, the companions of the Prophet, Abū Bakr, 'Umar, 'Uthmān, and 'Alī, often pictured in relation to the Archangelic realities; the fact that Islam is the fourth of the Abrahamic traditions, and the final one; the four wives permitted the Muslim; the four seasons of the year; the four elements (Air, Fire, Water, and Earth); the four directions of space; and other quarternaries, which have been integrated into Islamic cosmology, for the tetradic principle is capable of considerable extension. Its application to the architectural Sunnah of the Prophet is the result of an aesthetic orientation intrinsic to the revelation itself. Even the concept of revelation as a "Book" implies a four-sided object.

Calligraphy and Architecture

The architectural Sunnah of the Prophet at Medina gave rise to the arts related to the mosque and the home. It was also prototypal for the allied edifices later on, such as the *madrasahs* ("religious colleges"), *khānaqāhs* and *zāwiyahs* ("Ṣūfī meeting-houses"). All of these have to do with the arts that house the liturgical or ritual practices of Islam. The proscription of images gave impetus to the cultivation of the arts immediately associated with the reading, writing, and cantillation of the Qur'ān. Alongside mosque architecture, the calligraphy of Islam is the other sacred art in the tradition having celestial backing. Although the Prophet himself was an illiterate, according to the tradition, as were practically all of the Arabs of his time, this does not mean that the writing of the Qur'ān was nonexistent or discouraged. The moment that the Qur'ān is a "Book", and that even its letters and sounds have supernatural resonance, the writing of it, the actual calligraphic art itself, was endowed with a unique property. This was true also for the cantillation of its verses, and indeed for all of the arts associated with the reading and writing and recitation of the Qur'ān. While the recitative Sunnah of the Prophet is the actual basis of the calligraphic art, the sound being the parent, as it were, to the letter of the text, the calligraphic art itself goes back to his companions who were literate: Ubayy ibn Ka'b, or Zayd ibn Thābit, or 'Alī ibn Abi Tiālib. They were among the amanuenses of the Prophet, who wrote down the Qur'ānic revelations with the Prophet's approval. It is possible that 'Alī himself, often called "the third of the three" (the Qur'ān, the Prophet, and 'Alī) in the perfection of his Arabic, might have received Prophetic sanction for the origination of Qur'ānic calligraphy. That the writing of the Qur'ān has Prophetic approval and is part of his Sunnah is seen, not only in his companions who kept written versions of the Book as it was revealed, but also in the Prophet's encouragement of the founding of elementary Qur'ānic schools for children (the *kuttāb* system of pre-Islamic origin that was revitalized by Islam). There the children would learn how to read and write the text, or memorize it, according to case, and this institution soon became widespread over the entire Islamic world, lasting down to our times.

The eventual fate of these prototypal arts of mosque architecture and Qur'ānic calligraphy established by the revealed message in the days of the Prophet is really the history of the intervention of ethnic and regional factors into their formal expression.[2] While the governing spiritual Idea is the same, the variations on the essential theme that we find in the arts of the Maghrib (Spain, Morocco, Algeria, and Tunisia), Egypt, the Fertile Crescent, Persia, the Ottoman and Mughal worlds, are proofs of the adaptability of the aesthetic contents in the Islamic revelation to the most diverse circumstances of race, people, region, and even epoch. The ethnic genius of the Arabs, architecturally speaking, reaches a kind of zenith and purity of expression in the serenity and rigor of form that one finds in the Maghrib. We can see this in the Great Mosque at Cordova, the Kutubiyyah Mosque in Marrakech, the Qairawan in Tunisia, the residential architecture of the Alhambra Palace in Granada, to say nothing of the extraordinary masterpieces of both mosque and residential architecture in such a city as Fez, in Morocco. The same Arab Spirit seems to have achieved a perfection of calligraphic style in the Mamūk illuminated and ornamented Qur'āns from the thirteenth to the sixteenth century. Similarly, with the other Muslim peoples, like the Turks, the Persians, and the Indian Muslims, we can discern peak moments in their artistic handling of the calligraphic and architectural arts of Islam. In all, both Arabs and non-Arabs, a certain decadence begins to intrude itself shortly before the coming of modern Western civilization in the nineteenth and twentieth centuries.

The Mosque

The mosque is the focal point of the ritual prayers of Islam, and especially of the Friday congregational prayers. While the variations in style can be quite wide, ranging from the large mosques with vast courts of Umayyad days to mosques with great halls (as in Persia) to the domed structures of the Ottoman Empire, the liturgical elements within the mosque remain the same from one end of the Islamic community to another. Although there is no particular central point in a mosque, the niche (*miḥrāb*), which serves to indicate the orientation toward Mecca, has an ornamental and ritual importance that has borne fruit in the magnificent *miḥrābs* of many great mosques, like the one at Cordova, for example. Near the prayer niche there is usually found a pulpit, or *minbar*, also going back to the Sunnah of the Prophet's small pulpit at Medina. This is reserved for the Friday sermon of the preacher. Both the *minbars* and the sermons preached from them have been accorded artistic expressions in various periods of the history of Islamic art, giving rise to exceptional woodwork and Arabic, Persian, or Turkish oratorical genres. The faithful line up within the mosque in rows facing the direction of prayer (*qiblah*) indicated by the *miḥrāb*. They stand on mats, carpets, or prayer rugs of infinite variation, with no furniture, such as pews in a church, anywhere in evidence. Thus, the inside of a mosque is very much like a reproduction, in highly stylized fashion, of the original nomadic surroundings of Islam. The oasis-like atmosphere within the mosque, with its arching or interconnected columns, call to mind the interlaced foliage of the palm trees. Indeed, the palm tree is the symbol of the Muslim, as the Prophet once said, no doubt because of the pliant nature it exhibits toward the buffetings of the winds, and is a symbol of the resignation of the Muslim to the decrees of Fate. Then there are the wooden Qur'ān stands, sometimes of rather ornate carving, the mosque lamps, and occasionally the great bronze candlesticks, all of which complete the interior elements of a mosque. On the outside, apart from the fountains for ablutions and the adjunct buildings that might be found, there is a minaret, square or otherwise, depending on the region, from which the call to prayer (*adhān*) is made five times a day.

Historically, mosques have been used not only as places for prayer but also for social and educational purposes. This is because they were the main centers where Muslims gathered frequently, or could be regularly found, during the course of the day. But their principal function is purely liturgical as the religious edifice that gathers together the faithful of a given quarter or area of a town, city, or countryside. The mosque exists as a manifestation of the social or communal aspects of the Islamic Law. The pedagogical functions of mosques, such as one finds in certain mosques where religious scholars instruct others in the Law, like the Azhar in Cairo, developed from very early times and gradually became institutionalized in the forms of the religious schools (*madrasahs*). These are really mosques with facilities for boarding students and their teachers.

The Sunnah of the Prophet allows the Muslim to pray anywhere when the time for prayer has come, thus turning the earth itself into a vast mosque, so to speak. The Muslim's home, in this respect, is traditionally in the same architectural style as one finds inside mosques. The same holds true for the ornamental fixtures in residential architecture. Often there is an actual room set aside for the daily prayers that is indistinguishable from a small mosque. This gives to the inside of the traditional Islamic home a prayerful ambiance, encouraged by the Sunnah of the Prophet. He did not want his followers to live in impious, tomb-like homes but, rather, to sacralize them as bastions of Islamic life. This accounts for the Islamic imprint one finds in palace architecture, fortresses, mausoleums, religious schools, and in the residential and urban architecture of the different periods and regions of the Muslim world. The lack of distinction between religion and secular life means that everything in Islam is to be integrated into the spiritual concept that the faith represents. This ''everything'' ranges from the Holy War (*jihād*) to commerce to eating and drinking to Qur'ānic reflection to the thousand and one things that go into the making of human existence. We find this mirrored in the Qur'ānic inscriptions carved in the walls and ceilings of homes or on the scimitars and helmets of warriors or on the mausoleums of great rulers. The fact that the Muslim's home is also a place of prayer means that his sacerdotal function is to be exercised there too. That is no doubt the reason why much of the residential art of Islam recalls that of the mosque.

The Zāwiyah

While we associate the mosque with its institutional form, we should be aware that the Arabic term for mosque is *masjid*, which means "The place where one prostrates". This is not confined to the classical building as such. It includes likewise every place where the Muslim can prostrate himself for his ritual prayers. Thus, a *masjid*, in that generic sense, can be his home, a fortress, a religious school, an open field, a tent, even a cave.

If this is true, then one of the ancillary forms of a *masjid* is the zāwiyah, or Ṣūfī meeting-house, known in Persian as *khānaqāh*. The *zāwiyah* can be any place where the Ṣūfī Shaykh presides over the meetings with his disciples. It can be a room in his home, a floor of a tower, a tent, a cave or, in the more specific sense, the building or complex of buildings that began to be associated with the Ṣūfīs from the eighth century on, historically speaking. But since a *zāwiyah* is really a *masjid* in an instructional sense, it actually originates with the *masjid* itself. The more contemplative Sunnah of the Prophet has him teaching in a "corner" (*zāwiyah*) of his home, or elsewhere, surrounded by circles of his companions, a pedagogical Sunnah observed to this day in the *zāwiyahs* of Ṣūfism and in the *madrasahs* and teaching mosques of the Muslim world. It is from these seances of the Prophet that the Ṣūfī derived the pattern for their own meetings. Even earlier, before his mission began, the contemplative life of the Prophet was apparent in his retreats in a cave on Mt. Ḥirā' (also called, significantly, Mt. Nūr, "Light"), where he would meditate. The symbolism of the cave as the "heart" of the mountain analogous to the innermost "heart" of man is clear enough in this practice. In many later *zāwihahs*, a number of meditational cells can be found for those contemplatives who enter them under the direction of their teacher for prolonged spiritual retreat, in conformity with the spiritual Sunnah established by the Messenger. It was in that cave on Mt. Ḥirā' that the first verses of the Qur'ān (1-5 of Sūrah 96, "The Clot") would be revealed to the Prophet on one of the last nights of the month of Ramaḍān ("The Night of Power" of Sūrah 97:2, "better than a thousand months"). These verses coincided with the beginning of his mission. Thus, the cave, as a spiritual retreat (*khalwah*), the *masjid*, where everyone meets for prayer, the instructional circles around the Prophet in a corner of his home, and the rest of the contemplative Sunnah of the Prophet, sooner or later gave rise to the *zāwiyah* in the classic sense of the term as a building exclusively for Ṣūfī meetings. Eventually even rulers would build *zāwiyahs* for the adherents of *taṣawwuf*, as they built *madrasahs* for the doctors of the Law to teach future religious scholars.

The Prophet's spiritual retreat into the cave on Mt. Ḥirā', where the Qur'ānic revelation began, is the pattern for the Muslim contemplative's withdrawal into a *khalwah* for the sake of illuminative and sanctifying knowledge, or *ma'rifah*, which is also a kind of "revelation". Therefore, the *zāwiyahs* of Islam partake of that central quality of sacredness associated with the architecture of the *masjids*. The mosques, to be sure, are for all the citizens of the community, and are primarily for the performance of ritual prayer (*ṣalāh*) in its collective form. The *zāwiyahs*, by contrast, are not for all the members of the community, but only for the minority interested in performing the Invocation (*dhikr*) of a Divine Name. As the Qur'ān says, showing the superiority of invocatory prayer over ritual prayer, "Verily, ritual prayer prevents transgression and grave sin, but the Invocation of God (*dhikru'llāh*) is greater" (Sūrah 29:45). In other words, exoteric Islam is manifested in the contemplative prayer of the mosques, whereas esoteric Islam is manifested in the contemplative prayer of the *zāwiyahs*. Both are institutionalized forms of the two dimensions of the Islamic revelation. Some of the *zāwiyahs* of the Muslim world, or even the Ṣūfī saints' tombs that are attached to them, are among the jewels of its architectural tradition. While it is true that the institutionalized forms of the *zāwiyahs* are not absolutely necessary for the contemplative life, it is also true that the mosques are not necessary either, in an absolute sense, for a life of prayer. One can pray easily enough outside of them. But, just as the Islamic tradition would suffer traumatically by the disappearance of its mosques, so would the case be if all of its Ṣūfī meeting-houses were somehow gotten rid of or closed down. That has happened in the name of secularistic nationalism in Turkey and has had tragic spiritual consequences for the Turks.

The Saints' Tombs

Alongside the mosque and the *zāwiyah* as the two fundamental architectural manifestations of the *masjid*, the Islamic tradition has seen allied forms arise, such as the saints' tombs. These are shrines which exist by the thousands in *dār al-islām*. Mausoleums for the great rulers or members of their families also exist like the Taj Mahal, built by Shah Jahan in the seventeenth century at Agra, India, for his favorite wife, Mumtaz Mahal (d. 1629), which is one of the architectural wonders of all time in its perfection. But the saints' tombs, like that of the shrine of the Prophet in Medina, are seen as centers for the pious to visit for the sake of seeking the spiritual intercession of the saint before God or for the graces present in his tomb. Some of these shrines have yearly pilgrimages connected with them at particular seasons. The pilgrimage to the tomb of the great Moroccan saint, 'Abd as-Salām ibn Mashīsh (d. 1228), "pole of the West" in northern Morocco, draws tens of thousands of the faithful from all walks of life. *Zāwiyahs* are sometimes built around the shrine of one or more Ṣūfī saints, and these can at times be works of rare beauty.

The religious scholars have not always been of one mind on the role of these tombs within the Islamic tradition. The more puritanical doctors of the Law have tended to see the cult of saints' tombs as an innovation (*bid'ah*) counter to the Sunnah of the Prophet. But others consider it as a good innovation(*bid'ah ḥasanah*) and in keeping with the tradition so long as there is no associationism between the saint's spirit and God in the mind of the pilgrim or the visitor to the shrine. The immense influence of these Ṣūfī saints' mausoleums in the spiritual life of the community is such that the mere cataloguing of the charismatic fruits (*karāmāt*) associated with one of the great shrines over the centuries would be an instructive lesson in the posthumous power of deceased Ṣūfīs. It would be inconceivable that these shrines would draw thousands of devotees, year after year for centuries, if they were utterly devoid of any spiritual influence. Some of them, like that of Rūmī (d. 1273), at Konya in southern Turkey, are shrines that combine the functions of mosque and *khānaqāh* (in this case, of the Mevlevi order, or the Mawlawiyyah), and are examples of the central architectural art of Islam. Let us not forget to mention the tomb of the Messenger of Islam in the very midst of his mosque in Medina. This is the unique shrine of the Islamic tradition. It has been associated with miraculous signs and phenomena for centuries on end. The same holds true for the tombs of his companions elsewhere in the Muslim world.

The whole question of saints' tombs in the Islamic tradition, both architecturally and spiritually, is something that seems not to have anything to do with the original forms of Islam. It is probably the result of a tendency in the collective psyche that could not but manifest itself with the passage of time. It could not have been present at the beginning of Islam without being confused with the idolatrous practices of the pre-Islamic Arabs. Only the gradual infusion of *Tawḥīd* throughout the general mentality of the community permitted the eruption of the cult of saints' tombs without the fear of associationism (*shirk*). However, as was said, this fear never quite died out in the minds of some of the religious authorities.

Islam has produced a variety of architectural arts, from the ones mentioned to the less central types, such as fortresses, palaces, towers and walls and gates, country homes, and walled-in gardens that reveal a profound sense of landscape architecture peculiar to the Islamic culture as such. It also produced an urban architecture, with its bridges, water systems, open squares, citadels, streets, residential quarters, caravanserais, markets, and religious schools. Such an extraordinary efflorescence of architectural art can be called Islamic because it incorporates the geometric motifs, the ornamental designs, the arabesques, the squinches, the arches, the stucco decoration, the stalactite niches, the floral design, the tilework, the woodwork, the Qur'ānic inscriptions, the square shapes, the domes, the columns, and everything else that we associate with the religious structures of Islam, or its mosque architecture. Other buildings might pertain to civil architecture, but very often they are distinguishable from the religious only in a few details and by functions. A *madrasah*, for example, like the 'Attārīn of Feẓ, is a *masjid* in its own right, for it has a prayer-hall. This overlapping of the religious function into apparently civil or secular domains is very characteristic of Islam as a religion, to say nothing of its arts in general.

Islamic Calligraphic Variety

The calligraphy of Islam also has the same universality or ubiquity of application as does its architecture. Indeed, the two are more often than not allied, especially in the Qur'ānic inscriptions carved into walls or on the domes of mosques and other buildings, or in their tilework and woodwork. The calligraphic arts of Islam have been carried to unmatched heights of perfection over the centuries in their different stylistic forms. To say that they have been allied with the architectural arts of Islam is only to describe part of their role. They have gone into practically all the so-called "minor arts", such as inlaid bronzes, arms and armor, faience ware, pottery, glass and rock crystal, bookbinding, miniature paintings, woodwork, engraved bronzes, enameled work, ivory work, stone and stucco work, and so on.

Because calligraphy is so essential to the Islamic revelation, its intrusion into the major and minor arts of Islam is like "the Word" projecting itself into profane and lifeless materials and reconsecrating them with a new life. This is an aesthetic principle that no doubt operates in all of the traditional civilizations subject to revealed messages of different perspectives. It shows how the arts participate in the regenerating force of the revelation. We must remember that, in Islam, the doctrine of *Tawḥīd* penetrated the social, political, economic, moral, and military life of the conquered peoples which came into Islam from Christian, Zoroastrian, Jewish, Hindu, and other traditions no longer believed in, giving to their collective life a fresh consecration to the Absolute. The same spiritual perspective that refashioned whole societies also reshaped the arts inherited by Islam from its Arab and non-Arab past, giving them a powerful reorientation.

Of all those arts, Arabic calligraphy was the one that would literally spread the Qur'ānic Word into all the objects of life made with art, leaving the "signature" of Islam on them. It promoted thereby, in both artist and patron, the "remembrance" (*dhikr*) of God. This was not only a penetration of the Word into all things with a halo of beauty; it was also their integration into the message of Islam, turning them into religious artifacts. The Qur'ān circulated in the psychic substance of the Muslim's soul, in his memory, thinking, and imagination. It imprinted them with its celestial verses. But it was also to be found in the visual calligraphic productions of Islamic art that were manifest in the thousand and one things made by the aesthetic spirit of the Muslims.

Islam did not invent calligraphic art, no more than it invented the arts of building and construction. In pre-Islamic times, among the Arabs, the perfect man was the one who could handle the pen and the spear, a combination signifying wholeness of character, chivalric virility and knowledge. While it is true that the Bedouin culture was largely oral and little prone to literacy, a certain number of the Arabs had mastered the art of reading and writing. There was a desert architecture among the Arabs that no doubt had a hand in forming the eventually sophisticated and elaborate structural forms of later times. There was also a calligraphic art of sorts that had been preserved among the tribes and small urban communities, such as Mecca and Yathrib (the Medina of later times), even though we know that oral literature was preferred.

Islam itself, once it came into the world, encouraged the art of writing through the numerous Qur'ānic references to "the Pen", "the Preserved Tablet", "the Book", "the Record", and all of these measures of the Law that require written testimony. The ancient Arabs of northern Arabia were primarily pastoral warriors of different tribes, but the oasis cultures and small towns harbored a merchant class which has left its mark on the imagery of the Qur'ān. It is among these traders, artisans, and small farmers that we find the art of writing especially cultivated, if only because accounts and records had to be kept.

Much more meaningful than commerce for the preservation of Arabic writing was the cult of the Quraysh style of speech, or classical Arabic, in its grammatical and rhetorical purity, by the best poets and orators. With the coming of the Qur'ān, all of this heritage had to be codified. 'Alī, the fourth Rightly-Guided Caliph, and Abu 'l-Aswad ad-Du'alī (d. 681), are credited with establishing the first moves in Islam to codify Arabic. 'Alī himself was a calligrapher of note, and it is of great importance to remember that numerous esoteric disciplines of Islam go back to him. He was either their originator or a transmitter from the Prophet, as we see in the "sciences of the letters", or numerology, that deals with the letters of the Qur'ān as numbers having mystical or divinatory significations.

Given the Islamic prohibition of the representation of living things, the Arab and non-Arab Muslims focused on Qur'ānic calligraphy as a powerful medium for the artistic expression of their faith. With architecture and calligraphy conjoined, and after an initial period of experimentation, when the arts of various peoples were called into the service of the new religion, the classic modes of the Islamic arts came into being with the early 'Abbāsid Dynasty of the eighth and ninth centuries.

The variety of calligraphic styles which soon developed all over the Muslim world was due in great part to the ethnic qualities that the different peoples of Islam contributed to its visual and auditive arts. Between the static, angular, and squarish Kūfic script and the cursive, dynamic, and roundish script, there are a number of styles that arose in the Islamic lands. Some of them are characteristic of entire regions, like the Maghribī ("Far Western") calligraphy of Spain and North Africa, which is still used in writing, or the Persian script, which also went into Central Asia, and is currently used. Some are in use everywhere, while others are confined, like Kūfic script, to purely ornamental purposes.

All of these styles that go into the writing of the Qur'ān as a book go also into the innumerable arts that employ the Arabic script along with arabesques and geometric motifs as part of the integral aesthetic composition. Knowledge of the calligraphic qualities of Arabic was required of all the artisans who used its script in, say tilework, ivory, pottery, woodwork, stucco stone, and glass. The calligraphic art embraces, accordingly, not only the Qur'ān copyists, who were no doubt the principal calligraphers, but also the numerous other artisans whose skills required a knowledge of the different elements of scriptorial Arabic. If Qur'ānic calligraphy be defined as one of the fundamental arts of Islam, then one has to include in this category the calligraphy of the tile setter, the woodworker, or the brazier.

The work that went into the written Qur'āns was not the product of one man, the scribe, but rather a complex coordination of different arts, such as vellum-making or paper-making, illumination, ink-making, leather-tooling, bookbinding, and other crafts. The scribe naturally had the principal role, and the names of some of the great ones in history, as well as of their patrons, are known. The copying of the Qur'ān, and even the commissioning of such work, were always considered pious deeds. In general, the scribe followed the traditional style of his particular region. If gifted, he might contribute, through inspiration, certain touches and original modifications to the script, but never to the degree of a radical departure from the accepted norm. In this fashion, gradual and cumulative differences can be detected in specific scripts over a long period of time. In recent times, when the Qur'ān began to be printed for mass distribution, it has been done in whatever style of script dominates in a region. Even so, a universal cursive form exists all over the Islamic world that is known as Naskhī, in which the Qur'ān and Arabic works in general have appeared in recent centuries.

Arabesques and Geometric Motifs

The intertwining of Qur'ānic script, arabesques, and geometric motifs in the illuminated Qur'āns and in all types of architectural and decorative visual arts is one of the outstanding characteristics of Islamic art. The geometric art is static and angular; the arabesque is dynamic and floral. Both are repeated endlessly, and each separate unit in a design grows out of a similar preceding one, so that an empty space is soon filled with the interlaced elements. This repetitive atomistic art, where the tiniest individual unit has an integrity of its own, the whole design being the sum total of these discrete parts, owes its origin to the Arab mind. Pre-Islamic Arabic poetry is a series of individual verses that are complete in themselves, the ode being simply the total of these distinct lines. The thought of the Arabs is repetitive and circular in its movement, like an arabesque, or the verses of the Qur'ān. They reveal the Arab nomadic culture, with its rhythmical, seasonal, and monotonous circle of existence, its alightings and departures, its comings and goings within the tribal lands. Arab thought is not a mosaic of different parts that make for a greater whole. It is a mosaic of complete individual units that reflect the unity of the whole, or rather, that go into a greater unity. This cultural trait was reflected in the particular integrity of the individual Arab, who was the smallest unit of the tribe, yet he represented the whole. If his honor was besmirched, the tribe was sullied; if he was praised, the tribe was praised.

The atomistic unity of Islamic art flows from the metaphysical principle of the Divine Unity that is reflected in the specific unities of this lower world. In Islamic art, which tends to be abstract, Divine unity is given nonrepresentational symbolism in the particular unity of each complete segment of an arabesque or geometric motif. This is Comparability (*tashbīh*), using the impersonal, nonanthropomorphic images derived from stylized floral or geometric forms, which cannot undergo idolatrous transformation. Their nonanthropomorphic nature in itself contributes to the notion of the Incomparability (*tanzīh*) of God as the pure Absolute beyond the personal Divinity. The unicity of geometric artistic forms, moreover, is something one finds in the natural world, as in crystalline shapes, or in snowflakes, so that the same Divine Unity that reflects itself in the intricate patterns of Islamic art reveals itself in the fundamental structures of Nature.

The static aspects of the geometric motifs are, like the Kūfic script of Arabic, angular and masculine, reflecting the Divine Rigor or Majesty (*al-jalāl*). The dynamic aspects of the arabesque floral designs, like the cursive and roundish Arabic script, are feminine, reflecting the Divine Mercifulness or Beauty (*al-jamāl*). These are the two aspects of *Allāh*, the one absolute and axial, the other infinite and spherical, to borrow a certain geometric symbolism, that reflect themselves in all the arts of Islam. We find them in the axial minarets and in the great domes of Safavid and Ottoman mosques, in the vertical and horizontal elements of Arabic script, not to mention the masculine and feminine human bodies, made in the "image" of their Creator.

The abstract properties of Islamic art, and its stylization of even such things as animals and human beings, as if to eliminate by anticipation any idolatrous movements of the mind in the onlooker, make it difficult to penetrate into its spiritual message. This is so if one has been previously conditioned by Western representational painting and sculpture. Yet the atomistic character of the art is not only analogous to what we find in the Qur'ān but also to what we find in Arab theological propositions that would have God renew the Creation with every passing moment. That is similar in the renewal of the same arabesque or geometric motif that the eye encounters as it passes from one element to another in an overall design. The daily life of the pious Muslim is likewise a renewal of the same Sunnah left behind by the Prophet, which is a behavioral and ritual arabesque that instills a certain geometric rigor into the amorphous passions and fallen substance of man. The repetitive nature of the Sunnah is an atomistic regeneration at every instant. Nothing in Islam is more analogous to this musical and rhythmical pattern of the arabesque and geometric designs of its arts than the practice of the Invocation of a Divine Name (*dhikr*). Each particular repetition is definitive, like the individual unity of an arabesque, the whole being a constant regeneration at every instant.

The Minor Arts

Persian, Mughal, and Ottoman miniatures seem to defy the usual rules against the representation of living beings. But they are highly stylized, generally speaking, even when, as in some Mughal paintings, a delicate facial realism is introduced. The Islamic spirit intrudes itself into these miniatures, and even into the other visual arts that make use of such images, as in the inlaid bronzes, the faience ware, the rock crystals, the ivory carvings, or the stucco friezes, by confining them to ornamentalized versions of living things. This delimits their naturalistic development, and curtails all attempts at realism. Very often the human beings, animals, birds, and plants so depicted are integrated into the surrounding geometric designs and arabesques or else, as in the miniatures, given a flat, two-dimensional treatment without perspective or shadowing. The miniature painting of Islam is a good example of how the universal spirit of faith has allowed the artistic talents of the different ethnic communities to express themselves freely. It was always held in check by the spontaneous awareness of the limits to this kind of art: it was kept within small proportions. Its themes were religious, mystical, literary, political, or even simply the joyous celebration of life. In technical perfection, some of the Persian miniatures are unrivaled, not only in the handling of lines but in the combination of colors. They are to be considered, accordingly, as among the glories of Islamic art, or of all art.

Miniature painting or other similar representational art secured legitimacy within *dār al-islām* by restricting itself to a flat surface and a nonrealistic approach. The case of sculpture, however, is different, especially that of busts and human figures: these were never admitted into the precincts of Islam at all. Their three-dimensional nature, their obvious connections with idolatry, and the implication that the sculptor, in creating a figure out of stone, was engaged in an evidently flagrant act of associationism with the creative act of God, made for the immediate rejection of sculpture as an artistic medium for the religion. Openwork carving in wood, ivory carving, and the like, were permitted because the figures were stylized within an ornamental background, and did not have the magical properties that a freestanding statue or portrait bust seemed to generate.

The Auditive Arts

The auditive arts of Islam, such as cantillation of the Qur'ān, music, singing, or those allied with visual elements such as dancing, have been developed to an extraordinary degree both in the religious and worldly spheres of life. The most important of these many arts are, of course, the ones that have a religious signification, in the widest sense of that word. Since the Qur'ān is the center of the faith, it was only natural that the recitation of the Book, by memory, or following one of the traditional methods of reading it, should develop into an art, that of cantillation. We should distinguish the ritual recitation of the Qur'ān, a kind of simple chanting with due regard for the rules established by the different schools, and the elaborate cantillation of the text by Qur'ānic reciters, some of whom, in the history of the religion, have reached great fame. There is said to be infinite grace in the letters and sounds of Arabic, due to the presence of the Uncreated Qur'ān in them. Calligraphic art communicates this grace in the letters visually. The chanting of the Qur'ān, in simple or elaborate fashion, communicates that grace through the sounds, so that seeing and hearing the Qur'ān conveys a celestial blessing (*barakah*).

For the simple ritual recitation of the Qur'ān, which must not be confused with the ritual of the daily prayer that is also a recitation, one can read the Scripture with the help of the different signs and indications that are included in the text. They show when to stop, when to prolong a certain sound, and other chanting rules. The cantillation of the Qur'ān, however, is much more elaborate. The entire text must be memorized from beginning to end, with all of its rules. This is an aesthetic, musical addition which Islam has permitted, as it has for the call to prayer (*adhān*). For the doctors of the Law with puritanical leanings, and even for some with broader outlook, these two types of musical art in Islam are as far as they are prepared to go in legitimizing the use of music. All other types of music, vocal or instrumental, are rejected by them as non-Islamic, or even irreligious. This opinion is based on a rigorous interpretation of the Sunnah, and is in any case an exoteric one.

As was to be expected, on the Ṣūfī plane of interpretation, things are less puritanical. We find singing, musical instruments, and dancing in the collective rituals of a number of Ṣūfī orders, such as the Mevlevi order or whirling dervishes founded by the Persian Ṣūfī Jalāl ad-Dīn Rūmī in the thirteenth century. Much of the singing as well as of the dancing is of an inspired nature, so we can speak here of an extension of sacred art. But this is purely on the Ṣūfī plane and therefore applicable to its adepts only, although popular expressions of these arts can be found in a number of Muslim countries. Nevertheless, the legitimacy of music and dancing has been questioned by some of the Ṣūfīs themselves on the score that they might provoke passional movements of the soul. These objections have generally been tangential and somewhat academic. It is true that the Sunnah of the Prophet does not generally depict him as integrating singing or dancing into Islam, much less using musical instruments. This does not mean that he was averse to these arts at all times and on all occasions, for we see him encouraging their use at weddings or at other propitious moments. From such origins, the Ṣūfīs derived their own use of singing and dancing as supports for the contemplative life, not as ends in themselves. None of these arts should be considered as essential features of the Ṣūfī Way. On the other hand, they have nothing in common with their counterparts of a worldly or secular nature. Their goal, really, is to make use of the natural rhythms of the psychophysical substance of man and to sublimate them, in a spiritual fashion, by turning them toward otherworldly realities. Much of this type of Ṣūfī music, singing, and dancing has spilled over into the popular arts of the Islamic world, giving to these folk expressions a qualitative depth they would not ordinarily have had, and showing, by their widespread diffusion, how the influence of Ṣūfism has penetrated into all the social classes.

Musical arts have been absorbed into the Islamic tradition as important elements of the religious life, but the case is different for theater. The very concept of a theater is counter to the general trend of Islam in disfavoring all individualistic solutions of free will that impugn the integrity and uniqueness of the Divine Will. Psychological elaborations of character, likewise, are rejected in advance by the fixed pattern of life given to the Prophets and Messengers in the Qur'ān. Their typology is that of the submissive believer, unquestioning in his acceptance of the manifestations of the celestial Will. There are no dramatic moments in a life lived according to the Sunnah. All problems arise from attempting to live outside of its blessed arabesques of conduct and prayerful attitudes, or at least that is the way the tradition might express itself. Accordingly, the psychological ramifications of character implied in dramatic art are excluded from the ideal of the Sunnah. Since everything has been foreseen in advance by the Divine Omniscience, so that "Not a leaf falleth but He knoweth it" (Sūrah 6:59), there can be no "dramatic" moments, nothing that can run counter to the omnipotent Will of God. Even so, the tradition has permitted mime and shadow-puppet plays, to say nothing of the special passion plays of the Shīʻī world (the *ta'ziyah*, "consolation"). The latter commemorate, during the first ten days of the month of Muḥarram, the martyrdom of 'Alī's descendants, such as Ḥusayn at Kerbela. But this kind of popular art is an outgrowth of the lamentational cult of the persecuted Imāms that would not be found in the Sunnī world at all. It bears a striking resemblance to the medieval Christian passion plays commemorating the sufferings of the Christ and is motivated by a similar desire to participate, if only indirectly, in the martyrdom of the hero. All of this is foreign to the Sunnī mental structure and, in any case, has no bearing on the overall Islamic tradition.

The Islamic Literatures

Equally important, alongside such traditional arts as music and singing, are the literatures of the Islamic peoples. These have been penetrated by the spirit of the religion and have functioned as the treasure houses of its doctrines and spiritual life. The principal Islamic tongues, Arabic, Persian, and Turkish, have arisen at various historical moments in the long life of the faith, in response to the ethnic needs and genius of these peoples. Other Islamic tongues, such as Urdu, could also be cited in this list of languages that have been influenced by the message of the religion. But Arabic and Persian, by virtue of the historical interplay of the two peoples in the early period of Islam, are certainly the key languages in which Islamic culture spread through the cultivated classes of society, not only in the Arab and Persian worlds, but in other regions.

Of all these languages, Arabic is the central one, in terms of its importance for the religion. The Qur'ān is of course not "literature" in the profane sense of the word, but the fact that it is written in classical Arabic, the language of the Quraysh, means that Arabic would play a formative role everywhere the Islamic faith spread. Apart from some exceptions, the body of literature preserved from pre-Islamic times is strangely impervious to any notions of a religious life that recognizes the transcendence of the Divinity. Composed mostly of poetry, it has been transmitted subsequently in the literary history of the Arabs as a model of poetical perfection, both in language and prosody, and this for centuries on end down to our times. Islam changed somewhat the content of the poetry, leaving the ancient forms intact. In this respect, the conservative forces embodied in the Arab nomadic culture, which preserved the purity of Arabic speech for so long a period of time, were reinforced by the immutability of the Qur'ān and the Sunnah. Tampering with the fixed structures of Bedouin poetry was tantamount to "innovation" in the received literary customs.

The prose of the Arabs, however, was different because exposure to non-Arab cultures gave to it a greater flexibility and precision. It became the *lingua franca* of Islamic culture for centuries. Even after the rise of Islamo-Persian literature in the tenth century as an independent vehicle for the expression of Persian values, it was still the language for the philosophical, theological, and scientific teachings of Islam. Its consonantal root system and the patterned modifications that it can make to the basic idea embodied in the fundamental consonants have made it an ideal language for the intellectual abstractions of metaphysical or philosophical ideas. With the introduction of Greek modes of argumentation, the scholastic style arose in all the disciplines after the tenth century, and it is in that literary vehicle we find the clearest expositions of the Islamic faith.

All of the traditional literature of the Arabs and non-Arab peoples was influenced by the literary protocol of the epistolary Sunnah of the Prophet. Even the most profane composition of medieval Islam began with the *basmalah* (the introductory consecrational formula of Islam, found at the beginning of all the Sūrahs of the Qur'ān, except the ninth) or an equivalent sacred formula. We find this illustrated in the letters written for the Prophet by his amanuenses, or in the correspondence of his companions. After the consecrational formula, there would be the blessings upon the Prophet (the *taṣliyah*), then a preamble (*dībājah*), followed by the body of the text, which would end with the *ḥamdalah* (the formula in praise of the Divinity that terminates a given necessary deed or action). Throughout the text, Qur'ānic verses would be interlaced with the composition, more or less like the arabesques on a mosque wall. Even *ḥadīths* would be introduced. The names of Prophets and messengers would be followed by special formulas asking for blessings upon them, and the names of deceased persons by still other sacred expressions drawn from the Qur'ān or the Sunnah. The use of these sacred sentences was of course the literary counterpart to the oral conformity to the Sunnah. Since this was an integral part of what is called *ādāb* ("religious etiquette"), which covered all kinds of human behavior, from sitting to drinking to eating to walking to greeting to writing, and to all types of actions that can be consecrated, it was an aspect of the Sunnah which was binding on all Muslims. For that reason we see the use of the same formulas in Persian or Turkish literature, often in Arabic, just as we notice the integration of Qur'ānic verses and *ḥadīths* into the actual text of a given work. This was but a literary equivalent of the geometric designs and arabesques found in the architecture and minor visual arts of Islam. It imparts to the unconsecrated matter of a work the qualities of a consecrated substance, a certain order and a repetitive grace. When one studies the influence of the Sunnah on the different order of life in Islam, the literary domain turns out to be of considerable importance, not only because it has transmitted these sacred formulas in all the genres of literature, but because in so doing a religious influence was imposed on the most peripheral and even worldly subject.

All of that literary protocol of a religious character has persisted down to our days. But one of the salient characteristics of modern literature, in the Islamic world, is the progressive elimination of these sacred formulas in the works of modernist Muslims. Secular literature in the past, like the *Thousand and One Nights* or the *Maqāmāt* of al-Ḥarīrī (d. 1122), in the medieval Arab world, or the Persian historians, was not really secular in the modern meaning of the world. It abounded with the sacred formulations of Islam, together with certain attitudes that characterize the traditional Islamic mentality for the last millennium and a half. Upon contact with the modern Western world in the last century, modernist Muslims gradually began divesting their literatures of these traditional elements, thus indirectly proving that such elements had a powerful influence in preserving these literatures within the pale of Islam.

While the different Islamic literatures all employ the traditional formulas, not only in the properly religious works but also in the secular works, that is only one way in which the spirit of the religion has penetrated into their formal structures. What constitutes a religious, as opposed to a secular, work is another question. The distinction between the two domains tends to be blurred, as we have already noted in discussing the visual arts, both major and minor, to say nothing of the sacerdotal role that Islam assigns to every believer, eliminating thereby the "layman" and a distinct sacerdotal class. Ṭabarī (d. 923), the great Muslim religious authority, was also an equally great historian; but it is clear that his approach to history, in his *Annals*, was determined by the realization that there are no purely secularist domains that escape religion. When one considers that Islam views even hygienic acts and warfare as religious deeds, then the literary distinctions between the religious and secular become difficult to trace in certain genres, to say the least. The spirit of Islam, in other words, its dominant Idea in the metaphysical or spiritual sense, has intruded itself into the different literatures. This is so not only through the traditional formulas just mentioned, but also with attitudes and a world view that reflect the Divine Unity in the unicity of the contents and forms of the multiple literary genres. They are the literary equivalents of the unicity we discern in the arabesques and geometric forms of the visual arts of Islam.

The Qur'ān is of course normative for Arabic and even non-Arabic literatures, as far as Islam is concerned. But one cannot speak of it as a genre of semipoetical prose, for its revealed character gives to it a uniqueness that is inimitable. It stands alone, without antecedent or sequel. It is normative by virtue of its celestial Origin, and for the Arabic language the Book has grammatical, syntactical, and rhetorical absoluteness, to be sure. But it is rather in the spiritual attitudes it imposes on its reflective readers that we see its influence on all traditional Arabic literature. Even the *ḥadīths* of the Prophet have exerted a similar directive force on the destiny of Arabic, but they cannot be classified as literary either, in spite of the fact that some of them are jewels of Arabic expression. It was only natural that the two foundations of Islam, the Qur'ān and the Sunnah (meaning here the literary structure of the *ḥadīths*), should have had an essential controlling influence on the future of Arabic, especially in its general spirit, given that they are of such crucial importance for the whole of Islam.

Reference has already been made to the atomistic nature of the poetry of the Arabs. The individual line is complete unto itself. Something of that atomistic character invaded practically all the forms of prose literature in the early centuries. The *ḥadīth*-transmitters passed on a particular *ḥadīth*, important or not, with a complete chain of authorities (*isnād*) taking the statement all the way back to the Prophet. In this fashion, tens of thousands of *ḥadīths* were in circulation, each one complete in itself, standing in no relation to any of the others. The *isnādic* device for handling bits of information or details or events or remarks was taken up by practically all the early genres of literary Arabic, from epistles to lexicography to history to other kinds of prose. The result is that the reader is overwhelmed by the apparently self-sufficient nature of every single thing transmitted. Historians make no summaries of their data, draw no conclusions: all of the facts, great or small, are placed at the reader's disposal to do with as he wishes. This atomistic approach, while patterned on the transmission of the *ḥadīths*, is nevertheless congenial to the Arab mind, as are the geometric patterns in the visual arts, or the arabesques. Just as the tiniest arabesque has a unity of its own, so the most insignificant fact or remark has its own value and must be transmitted, along with the more serious data, with the complete chain of authorities. It is only much later that the *isnādic* concept gradually fades from the scene.

The traditional literatures of the different peoples of Islam have developed a host of literary genres, as one might expect from a world civilization. We find poetry, history, essays, travel books, anthologies, treatises, scientific works, philosophy, grammar, theology, jurisprudence, ornate prose compositions, and others. All of these literatures share the same traditional view of God, the Universe, and Man, because the basic metaphysical, theological, and spiritual ideas of Islam infused all of their contents and brought everything more or less into line with the concept of *Tawḥīd*. But not everything in them is on the same level of depth: they go from the shallow to the deep, depending on the author. The most profound aspects of these literatures come from Ṣūfism, not so much in its doctrinal formulations — as the *Futūḥāt* of Ibn al-'Arabī (d. 1240) or the work on *al-Insān al-Kāmil* (*The Perfect Man*) by 'Abd al-Karīm al-Jīlī (d.c. 1417), which are confined to an intellectual minority — as in its more popular literary manifestations.

Early Ṣūfī literature is really made up of transmitted remarks, such as the *ḥadīths* of the Prophet, with the *isnādic* apparatus going back to a particular Ṣūfī. Sometimes these are startling in nature, designed to shock or to precipitate a meditational reaction in the listener, more or less like a Japanese Zen Buddhist *koan*, in the hopes that the resolution of its contents will bring about a deeper perception of the faith. Such ecstatic formulations, like the *Subḥānī* ("Glory be to me!") of Abū Yazīd al-Basṭāmī (d. 875), which sounds blasphemous but in reality is the Spirit glorifying itself through him, often got their authors into trouble, and were no doubt deliberately provocative. Later, Ṣūfism, in all the literatures, would espouse a variety of genres by way of reaching out to the mass of believers.

One can see the Ṣūfī penetration into all levels of society in the great *Mathnawī of Jalāl ad-D*īn Rūmī (d. 1273), a didactic poem in Persian that is immense in extent and unsurpassed in its presentation of mystical ideas in beautiful concrete images. Rūmī is himself a partisan of pure *Tawḥīd* along the lines of the metaphysical notions of *waḥdat al-wujūd* ("Oneness of Being") of Ibn al-'Arabī, whom he probably knew personally. It is possible that his *Mathnawī* has had such a great influence in Persian culture because the Persian poetical genres since the coming of Islam were much more supple than the rigid Arabic forms, and the collective awareness in Persia of the Immanence of the Divinity was much stronger than, say, in the Arab world. Whatever the reason, the *Mathnawī* stands as a kind of second Qur'ān in Persian. It is a stunning example of the inspirational influence of Ṣūfism on Persian literature and Islamic culture in the eastern part of the Muslim world.[3]

The Arab world of Islam has also had its Ṣūfīs whose poetic compositions had great diffusion: the original poetical genre called the *muwashshaḥah*, much more plastic than the ancient Arabic ode, was used by ash-Shushtarī (d. 1269) to create poems that are recited and sung to this day. Perhaps the greatest of the Arab Ṣūfī poets was Ibn al-Fāriḍ (d. 1235), an Egyptian whose *Dīwān* contains famous odes, like the *Khamriyyah (The Wine Poem*) or the *Naẓm as-Sulūk* (*The Poem on Mystical Wayfaring*), both of which are chanted in pious circles in our times. But a contemporary of his, another Egyptian, al-Būṣīrī (d. 1296), author of the famous *Burdah* (*The Mantle Poem*, after the Prophet's mantle), takes the palm in Arabic literature for composing a poem on the life of the Prophet that would have the greatest circulation of any Arabic ode. Every year, on the anniversary of the Prophet's birthday, the *Burdah* is recited in mosques, *zāwiyahs*, or large gatherings. From its inception, it has been enshrouded in an almost sacred role: it is said that its recitation, properly done, can have charismatic effects, heal the sick, overcome obstacles, and the like. A veritable liturgy has developed around its recitation, as if it were a rite of its own. Commentary after commentary has been written on it; it can be read, worn, or even eaten, almost like the Qur'ān. The fact that its author was a Ṣūfī and his poem had strands of Ṣūfism intertwined with the poetical accounts of the Prophet's life means that it had a pedagogical aim: it was not merely the poetical story of the Prophet's earthly life but also a mystical view of the Prophet as Logos.

The West and Islamic Art

The person conditioned to the fine arts of the West, from Greco-Roman times to the present, generally has problems with the traditional arts of Islam. Sculpture, painting, drawing, and architecture in the West not only go through different periods, but even through different conceptual frameworks. There is a civilizational hiatus between the Greco-Roman paganistic world and the Medieval Christian civilization in Western Europe and the Byzantine Empire. That Christian traditional civilization lasted for around a thousand years, from the fall of the Roman Empire in the West to the rise of the Modern World. The latter has its own secularist culture based on modern industrial civilization; and therefore it has its own fine arts, in amazing stylistic variety and profusion, to say nothing of its literary genres. The constant changing of art styles that has characterized the Western world after the loss of its traditional Christian civilization some time back, and the cult of individualism in the different arts, generate problems in understanding the stability of the Islamic aesthetic forms over the centuries of their existence and the absence of individualism as a cult in itself.

The long association that the Westerner has had with the various representational visual arts, from painting to sculpture to drawing, likewise makes for bepuzzlement over their absence in Islam. Even when the theory behind the prohibition of images of living beings that cast shadows is understood, there is still a psychological block in adapting to the impersonal, decorative character of Islamic arts. Great art, in the West, is commonly associated with representational images, like the sculpture of Praxiteles of Athens, the paintings of Rembrandt, or the architectural works that include wall paintings and sculptures as part of the general design. Psychological and aesthetic appreciations of such art are quite common in the West and stress individualistic reactions or states of mind. To turn from all of that to the nonrepresentational, nonindividualist art of Islam is to risk reducing it to a minor decorative art without depth or even content beyond the bare desire to fill empty space with arabesques and geometric patterns.

The depth of Islamic art, in reality, comes from the degree to which its architectural, literary, musical, and other arts reflect the different aspects of the Divine Unity, now its intelligibility, now its powerfulness, now its joyousness, or now combinations of them. Depth in the Islamic arts does not come, therefore, from any humanistic or representational arts as such. As is well known, sculpture and painting can be utterly devoid of depth. Moreover, all such arts tend to recapitulate the successive, downward steps of the Fall and to become, in the end, empty forms without spiritual substance.

While individual poets, architects, calligraphers, and miniaturists have risen to heights of fame within the history of Islam, the cult of the individuality as such has never been a feature of the art history of the religion, for the simple reason that the Sunnah of the Prophet tends to efface all individualism. Although Islam, like the Judeo-Christian tradition, agrees that man is made "in the image of God", this cannot give rise to the narcissistic tendencies that individualism seems to generate. It is not fallen human nature, but the primordial Edenic man, who is made in the image of his Creator. To the extent that the artist, whether architect or poet or glazier, rediscovers his original Edenic image by eliminating the veils or strata of forgetfulness (*ghaflah*), to that extent his art — and indeed, his whole being — reflects the qualities in the Divine Unity. The cult of individualism forgets that there is nothing in the individuality as such that can add a dimension or more to the natural qualities, or the outstanding qualities, that some persons are born with. Just as individualism can paralyze all spiritual life in the soul of a contemplative, so similarly, in the arts, the same individualism can stifle the flow of beauty or even truth in both the artist and his work.

Genius was not excluded from the exercise of the arts in Islam, but was manifested within the framework of the artistic tradition. Sinān (d. 1587), the Turkish architect of the Suleiman Mosque in Constantinople, and scores of other mosques and buildings, was an inspired artist who functioned within the rules of his art, while at the same time giving it a fresh vision. Similarly, Bihzād (d.c. 1514), the Persian miniaturist who imparted a new life into miniature painting, was himself the flower of a long-established artistic medium. Great Sūfi sages do not demolish the established patterns of their tradition; instead, they give them new orientations and life. In a similar way, the key artists of the Islamic civilization brought new vitality and perspective into their calligraphy, pottery, illuminated manuscripts, music, woodwork, architecture, poetry, singing, and the numerous other arts that went into the miraculous radiance of that bygone world of *dār al-islām*.

Sadly, that radiance is no longer in evidence anywhere in the Islamic world. Nevertheless, the loss of the traditional culture has not been uniform throughout Islam. Some lands have retained more of the arts and crafts than others. The general drift, however, is toward a passive acceptance of the modern Western forms of art and architecture. It is therefore encouraging to note that some Muslim governments actively promote the preservation of at least a handful of the traditional arts. Of course, in the old civilization of Islam, hundreds of such arts and crafts existed, and their practitioners were responsible for the creation of an aesthetic ambiance which corresponded to the teachings and practices of Islam. Much of that ambiance has now disappeared. Hence, any effort to preserve something of the art and architecture of Islam as a living force in the community cannot but have positive results on the religious culture.

True, we can find here and there the archeological remnants and the monuments testifying to the past grandeur of Islamic civilization. In themselves they are reminders of the spiritual contents of the religion. Yet Muslims cannot repose exclusively on the archeological debris of previous generations as supports for their religion while permitting the artistic chaos of the modern West to invade every single aspect of their lives. This would be cultural suicide.

In reality, there is a question of choice in this aesthetic sphere that must not be overlooked. If one builds a mosque that looks like a spaceship, it is because one has already made the choice not to build it in the traditional style. The same argument holds true for the ideological intrusions of the West into the mental structures of some Muslims. In other words, one chooses to be a Muslim Marxist, a Muslim existentialist, or the like, because one has already chosen not to accept, for one reason or another, the traditional teachings of the religion. Accordingly, those efforts now being made to preserve some of the artistic heritage of Islam represent an awareness that a choice is possible in both the intellectual as well as in the artisanal and architectural domains. When viewed against the appalling aesthetic decadence of the Islamic world, those efforts might seem modest enough, but they are nevertheless firm steps in the right direction.

VIII
The Contemporary Islamic World

Erosion of the Cultural Supports

The Islamic civilization that had been in existence for well over a thousand years before its demise in this century was a traditional world which reposed on a revelation. The Hindu, Chinese, Christian, Japanese, and even the archaic cultures of mankind, were likewise nourished by a celestial message and have also reached their terminal point in recent times. In a general way, it is no longer possible to speak of the existence, anywhere on the globe, of a traditional civilization in all its integrality.

In the nineteenth century, however, one could still say that some of those cultures, including the Islamic, were alive in certain ways. They were sick, but not equally so: the Shinto-Buddhist civilization of Japan, for example, seems to have been holding on to its way of life with some success, and the same could be said of the Tibetan and even of other somewhat isolated cultures. But that was prior to the coming of the West, which precipitated the downward movement of some of those cultures, already decadent before the arrival of the modern world. It also arrested the upward, spiritual revival of other cultures, like the efflorescence of Ṣūfism in North Africa in the first half of the nineteenth century, which French colonialism in Algeria and elsewhere succeeded in restraining, if not destroying.

By the time the First World War, that great watershed of modern history, came to an end, the last lights of Islamic civilization were flickering and beginning to go out all over the earth. Some went out more quickly in the Near East, some more slowly in, say, Morocco and Afghanistan. But at the end of the Second World War, which was yet another great watershed in the story of modern civilization, there was no longer any Islamic civilization left anywhere. Nor was there any other traditional civilization intact: they had all disappeared, as witness the Tibetan Buddhist culture being exterminated by the Chinese communists almost overnight.

As the twentieth century unfolded, and the effects of modern Western civilization on the Eastern cultures, including Islam, became obvious, it was thought by some that the different religions would gradually disappear from the scene, leaving one vast secularist civilization embracing the East and the West. The Westernization of society in Islam, for example, was held to be the prelude to the gradual extinction of the faith. But, while modern Western civilization has indeed trampled on the remaining traditional cultures and succeeded in creating a kind of international secularist world that is oblivious and even hostile to revelation, it has not eliminated the religions of the East, including Islam. The modern West has indeed stripped those religions of their civilizational supports in a thousand different ways, but it has not succeeded in stripping the populations of their religions. Islam as a civilization is no more; but Islam as a religion is still alive.

Whether those religions, like the Christianity of the past, can long exist without a civilizational framework and retain their traditional characteristics, is another question. Christian civilization disappeared gradually with the rise of the new, secularist, modern civilization, that destroyed the traditional institutions, like the monarchies of Europe, the crafts and guilds, and the social manifestations of Christianity, but it did not destroy Christianity itself as a religion. This is not to say that the modern secularist world, totalitarian in its presuppositions and methods, will not in the end gradually erode the form and even the inner content of the Christian religion, because it has already gone far in that direction.

This being so, the fact that the Islamic civilization has disappeared, but not the religion, should not lead to any optimistic views on the future of the faith itself. Quite the contrary, the dismantling of the cultural scaffolding of the religion has been similar to the disarming of a warrior: without his sword, he is defenseless. A religion without its traditional culture, intellectually, spiritually, artistically, and politically speaking, cannot long endure without gradually losing its very reason for existing as a religion: its salvific message. That, in essence, is what happened to the ancient traditions before they turned into paganisms: as time went by, the otherworldly qualities of these religious cultures gradually disappeared, leaving behind the paganistic cultural shells of the ancient Babylonians, Greeks, Romans, Egyptians, and others, whose remains we see strewn over the Mediterranean lands.

The Development of Islamic Civilization

In its origins, Islam had no civilizational underpinnings, nor could it have had, what with its nomadic culture and the harsh realities of the desert in northern Arabia. Further to the south, in the Yemen, there had been a kind of urban culture, a heterogeneous civilization that seemed to draw from the various paganisms of the Near East. But this was of no importance by the time the new faith came into the Bedouin world of the north, and in any case it was a settled way of life that was in direct contrast to the nomadic existence of the Arabs in the desert. Even after Islam exploded out of its Arabian homeland, its early Umayyad Caliphs kept themselves close to the desert and isolated their armies in encampments (*amṣār*) somewhat removed from non-Arab populations. But with the conquest of part or all of the Byzantine and Persian civilizations, the Islamo-Arab culture of the Bedouins soon began to absorb the civilizational elements of those ancient urban peoples. By the end of the Umayyad Dynasty, in the middle of the eighth century, we can already see the basic outlines of the future Islamic civilization emerging.[1]

Like all the other traditional civilizations of the past, Islamic culture was eclectic, drawing its elements from a host of different peoples and their ways of life. That eclecticism of Islam was governed by the fundamental notion of *Tawḥīd*, of course, and this is what prevented the borrowing and the assimilation of cultural elements from becoming a merely syncretistic patching together of disparate and ill-digested importations. Arab paganism had been syncretistic: the Arabs seem to have brought back from their desert wanderings the residues of the ancient religious paganisms utterly devoid of any spiritual content and saturated with magical powers, all of which Islam destroyed. The *Tawḥīd* of the new religion permitted it to absorb the different cultural elements without losing its basic spiritual perspective. On the contrary, it infused that perspective into all of those cultural importations, making them Islamic in the bargain. Initially, that process of assimilation would involve imperfect solutions. But, with time, more and more of the spirit of the religion would manifest itself. Thus, in the Great Mosque of Damascus, begun in 705 by the Caliph al-Walīd, and which was one of the first mosques with many of the classical architectural elements to be found later, there are mosaics of aniconic character that nevertheless depict trees and buildings and bodies of water in a naturalistic fashion. This was somewhat like the naturalistic floral decoration at the Dome of the Rock, begun by the Caliph 'Abd al-Malik in 687. The aniconic character of these mosaics already reflects the interdiction found in the *ḥadīths* against the representation of living beings, but the naturalistic decoration is not successful and would not be retained in the subsequent development of Islamic art.

After the formation of the traditional culture of Islam in the eighth century with the rise of the 'Abbāsid Dynasty, everything becomes crystallized. The teachings of the faith are given greater clarity in both an exoteric and esoteric way; the disciplines are codified, from the schools of jurisprudence to the *ḥadīths* of the Prophet; and the civilization of Islam becomes an immense world with its own arts and architecture, its own socio-political structures. This would last for well over a thousand years as a living tradition encompassing the lives of hundreds of millions of human beings. The civilization as a whole would have its ups and downs throughout those centuries. Its regional cultures, such as the Sāmānids of Transoxiana, the Almohads of North Africa and Spain, the Saljūqs of the Near East, would flare up in the arts and other domains and then gradually die out. Later on, in the fifteenth to the seventeenth centuries, the Ottoman Empire, the Safavid Dynasty of Persia, and the Mughals of India flowered out in extraordinary cultural manifestations that rank among the finest in the history of Islam, not only in the arts, but in the sciences and philosophy.

During all of that millennium, the *sharī'ah* of Islam was the unifying system. It had been given strong foundations in the *madhhabs* of the eighth and ninth centuries, and from then on the eminent doctors of the Law watched over its development, its application, its restoration after periods of decline, and the formation of its teachers and students. Perhaps at no one period in the history of the religion do we find a perfectly-implemented *sharī'ah*, since that was more of an ideal than an actual fact. Even in the days of the Prophet, concessions were made to the customary law (*'urf*) of the Arab tribes. And later, when Islam was everywhere triumphant, similar concessions would be made, for example, to the ancient Berber customary law, to say nothing of other legal systems. Even so, the *sharī'ah* reigned in spirit, if not always in legal fact. By this is meant that other legal systems were more or less rounded off to conform to the abiding attitudes of the religion. Great doctors of the Law, such as some of the chief muftis of Constantinople in the days of the Ottoman Empire, had considerable power over the Caliphal decisions and did not hesitate to use them. But the general rule was that while the Law governed everyone, from ruler to subject, the executive and judicial functions of the Islamic State should not be coalesced into one body. The rulers should have plenty of room within which to maneuver as rulers; the religious authorities should have their own functions in the public sphere. That had been the tacit agreement, so to speak, since Umayyad times. The earlier four Orthodox Caliphs were exceptional by virtue of their being the principal companions of the Prophet, having both executive and judicial functions in their own hands, as did the Prophet, who ruled under celestial mandate, so to speak.

Gradually, however, the formalism intrinsic to the Law, and even to the exoteric domain of Islam as a whole, began to take over the place. Excessive elaboration of the Law is matched in other forms in late Mamlūk Egypt. We find it in the rather overly-wrought mosques built in those days, in the conservative encyclopaedists like as-Suyūṭī (d. 1505), in the highly refined illuminated Qur'āns, and in the defensive and at times almost apologetic Ṣūfism of ash-Sha'rānī (d. 1565). Sclerosis of a spiritual kind had come over certain parts of the Islamic world.

Other parts would retain their spiritual vitality. But we can already discern, in the architectural constructions of Mawlay Ismā'īl (1672-1727), the most powerful of the early Moroccan 'Alawī Sultans, a kind of terminal development to the primordial quality of Maghribī art, a primordiality that was happily still evident in its *taṣawwuf.* In the eighteenth-century Ottoman arts, particularly in certain architectural features, we can detect the coming breakdown of the culture, even though it would be a long and slow process. As a general rule, from the eighteenth century on, the *sharī'ah*, in its public and collective facets, begins to disintegrate under the pressure of two forces. One, it succumbed to its own weight and opacity, leading to a kind of inner decomposition. Two, it was dealt a mortal blow by the intrusion of the foreign legal systems brought by Western imperialistic regimes, which also came with the destructive effects of modern secularist civilization. Whereas the first two centuries of Islam were formative for the establishment of the *sharī'ah*, which then held sway for around a thousand years, the last two centuries have been disintegrative, at least in regard to the collective life of the community. Disequilibrium was the result, and this in turn fostered the increasing decline of the traditional Islamic civilization. Without the backbone of its *sharī'ah*, it could not long survive the buffetings it received from the modern West.

The Coming of the West

Modern Western civilization came to the Islamic world as an imperialistic force acting in the name of the secularist ideologies which motivated it and which lay imbedded in the word "Civilization". That word spelled the end of the controlling influence of the Church over the destinies of men and women in Europe. True, the missionary activities of Christianity were given strong impetus by the colonialist systems of England, France, Holland, Russia, Spain, and Portugal. Previous to the formation of the modern West, the Christian powers of Europe had indeed set out to explore the world, from the fifteenth century on, and to claim it for this or that crown and for Christianity. That, however, was not the same as the much more effective and lethal brand of imperialism conveyed to the East by the modern West, no longer acting in the name of Christianity, but in the name of Civilization.

This was the Civilization that arose on the ruins of the old Christian culture of Europe still visible, more or less, on the eve of the French Revolution in the eighteenth century. That same century saw the first fruits, in the Industrial Revolution, of the philosophico-scientific premises of the Cartesianism of the previous century and the Age of Enlightenment. It was the new religion of Western man, if one might put things that way, and soon many Christians began to believe in it. Because of its immense material power, expressed in its industrial and military technologies, no Eastern culture could oppose it effectively. Those that attempted, like Japan, to stay the day of reckoning were soon brought to bay. It was everywhere triumphant, notwithstanding the dogged resistance that the conservative Eastern cultures put up to hold on to the precious heritage bequeathed to them by their ancestors.[5]

Decadence and Reform

When the West came to Egypt, Algeria, Central Asia, or to other parts of the Islamic community as a conquering, colonialist power, it more often than not encountered decadent cultures that had seen better days and were living on the cultural momentum of the past. They were like impoverished aristocrats living in the ruins of mansions long since gone to seed. This was not always the case, nor was the decline of a particular culture homogeneous in all respects. In certain areas, Islam was vigorous; in others, less so. To describe the entire traditional civilization of Islam in the nineteenth century, therefore, as decadent, would be to ignore those areas, here and there, where it was still alive and normal. But they are exceptions and as such they prove the rule that, all things considered, the Islamic world was not in good shape prior to the coming of the modern West.

That was not the first time that Islam had declined in one way or another. Numerous declines had occurred previously in this region or that province. They manifested themselves in either a stiff formalism that snuffed out the inner mystical life or else in a loose, immoral, and chaotic formlessness that dissipated all contemplative existence. But we are speaking now of spiritual decadence, not of economic, military, political, or legal decadence. Spiritual vitality can coincide with military vigor, as we see in the early conquests of Islam and in the expansive moments of the Ottoman Empire, or with economic vitality, as in the great emporia of Baghdad in the beginning of 'Abbāsid times — but the reverse is not true. Economic, military, political, or other types of civilizational vitality are not necessarily proofs of spiritual force. On the contrary, they might actually be proofs of spiritual degeneration, not only in the Muslim world, but outside. Acquisitive and possessive instincts for gain can also motivate entire cultures, at least for a while, just as they can be motivated by sheer expansionist passions. The upshot of all these remarks is that the spiritual life alone was the foundation of the traditional civilizations of the past: when it was ignored or forgotten, decadence set in; when it was appreciated and remembered, regeneration took place.

In the past, however, the declines of the Islamic tradition were regional. They did not involve the entire community from Morocco to Central Asia. Throughout the centuries of Islam, we see regeneration taking place in one area while decline was occurring elsewhere. In the seventeenth century, the spiritual force of the Ottoman Empire was evident in many facets of life in Constantinople and other cities in Turkey; but this was certainly not so in Cairo and other Egyptian cities. Not only that, but in centuries past, whenever there was a decadence, short-lived or long, the traditional forms of culture were not molested. They remained more or less intact, with only some exterior signs pointing to an inner loss of vigor. When the regeneration came about later, there was no need to start from scratch, for the artistic tradition had kept the external form of the religion from disappearing altogether. Enough of the culture remained, in other words, to furnish an immediate support for the regenerative efforts of the Spirit, when and if they were repressed. The retention of the cultural ambiance furnished by the Islamic arts is what permitted a certain continuity of mental receptivity in the population as a whole to future renovative surges of the Islamic message. This is one of the roles of the traditional artistic framework found in the old civilizations that must not be forgotten when wondering how saintly reformers, like the founders of the Ṣūfī orders in the thirteenth century, for example, as-Suhrawardī (d. 1234) of Baghdad, were able to affect the lives of so many people with immediate positive fruits. They did not have to create either a religion or its civilization. The two were already in symbiotic existence, and it sufficed to bring new life into the religion, which could not but affect the forms of the culture in many different ways.

The principle of reform in Islam, its renovation (*tajdīd*), is to be found in its spiritual Path, which is Ṣūfism. As the Spirit of the religion, it has always had the means of reviving Islam without disposing of the necessary traditional structures. On the contrary, Ṣūfism has always managed to infuse new life into them. Without Sūfism, Islam would be like a lifeless form. Nor would it last for very long without sooner or later deviating into a crude fundamentalism devoid of inner beauty, and even this would eventually disintegrate under the pressure of its own contradictions. Nevertheless, those spiritual renovations of the Islamic lands in the past covered great areas and their cultures because the traditional way of life was still followed by the people and their minds were also more or less fashioned by that tradition.

The spiritual life in Islam, as in other religions, has to do with the teachings and practices relating to the Divine Reality itself; it is these that the Path keeps alive from generation to generation. Ultimately, the spirituality of any tradition is manifested most directly by the presence of competent teachers of the Path and their saintly disciples in sufficient numbers to affect the other believers. Without these sages and saints, the spiritual life of Islam — to say nothing of Hinduism or Buddhism or any other tradition — gradually becomes extinct and the collective psyche of the believers begins to darken and to become unreceptive to things transcendent. While it is the saintly men and women of Islam who are the direct spiritual heirs of its revelation, they are not, of course, its only manifestations. They function as the interpreters of the doctrines and methods of the revelation. By their commitment to its principles — the *īmān*, *islām*, and *iḥsān* of the religion, according to the Prophet — they have a central role to play in keeping the integral tradition alive. But there is also the sacred art of the revelation, and this is likewise a manifestation of the spirituality of a tradition in a direct way, as well as being a criterion of that spirituality itself. When a tradition has few sages or saints, we are justified in concluding that the community has succumbed to the weight of forgetfulness. By the same token, when the sacred art of the tradition is no longer honored or manifested consciously by the hands of the believers, we are equally justified in making the same conclusion. Everything, therefore, that would tend to diminish the role of the Ṣūfī teachers and their followers in the Islamic world, or that would reduce the importance of the traditional arts for the collective life of the community as a whole, cannot but open the door to deviations that lead away from the transcendent Spirit.

All of this detour into the question of spirituality is of essential importance. Its traditional Islamic meaning, as understood by the exponents of the Path, must not be overlooked when trying to understand what happened to Islam when the modern West came that was different from what had happened to it in periods of previous decline. The moot point in all this is not so much that the coming of modern Western civilization gave the *coup de grace* to the sick Islamic culture as it is that the sickness of the civilization seemed so pervasive. While similar remarks could be made of Hinduism and the Chinese tradition of the eighteenth and nineteenth centuries, for example, we are still left with the question: why did these ancient cultures all show signs of general spiritual deterioration before the modern West came to deliver the mortal blow? It is as if they all became decadent simultaneously and by prior agreement.

The answer to this lies in the cyclical teachings of Islam, that agree with the general drift of similar doctrines in other religions: sooner or later, the whole process of *ghaflah* leads all mankind to the terminal stopping point of the Fall, and that is the Day of Judgment. The saintly reformers reach fewer and fewer numbers among the believers as the cycle of Islam wends its way through the historical life of the community. There comes a time when the actual spiritual substance of the community as a whole is no longer amenable to vast renovations. When that moment appears, one notices in the literature and in the visual arts that opacity of soul has become widespread throughout the community and that irremediable decadence has set in once and for all. Not that the still-living sages have no listeners or followers. They do, but now their numbers are very small in proportion to the great numbers of the faithful. From then on, with the increasing demolition of the traditional culture of the religion, the chances of spiritual reformation for everyone become less and less. That, in a nutshell, is the cyclical teaching behind the decadence one finds in the world religions. It is the same law of the Fall operating in all of them that accounts for the widespread weakness observable in them shortly before the West implanted itself in their midst. That law, plus the destruction inflicted by the West on the Eastern civilizations in the nineteenth and twentieth centuries, brought them all to their knees by the beginning of this century and finally destroyed them. The fragments of the traditional culture of Islam, which one sees here and there — apart from the archeological sites — are simply that — fragments. They probably will not linger much longer as modern Western industrial civilization takes over the scene more and more.

Nevertheless, before the West was able to triumph with its colonialist systems with *dār al-islām*, the Muslims fought, knowing full well that their backs were to the wall. It is a fact that many of the defensive efforts of the Muslim lands came from the Ṣūfī orders and their chiefs. ʻAbd al-Qādir al-Jazāʻirī (d. 1883), the Arab Ṣūfī leader of Algeria, united many tribes in the *jihād* against French colonialism. Another Ṣūfī, Shaykh Shāmil (d. 1871), led his people of Dagestan, in the Caucasus, in a long war for independence from Russian imperialism. The Sanūsiyyah order of Ṣūfism, founded by Muḥammad ʻAlī as-Sanūsī (d. 1859), spread out from Cyrenaica and sought to hold back French expansionism in the Sahara and, later, Italian colonialism in Libya. When the secularist Kemalists of Turkey sought to destroy the religious culture of that land, the Ṣūfī orders were among their most vigorous opponents.

Once inside *dār al-islām* as colonialist powers, the English, the French, the Russians, and the other countries of Europe with colonies, became the missionaries of modern civilization. All of the ideologies that began to appear with distressing frequency in the West were now transmitted to the colonies, and especially to the governing classes. Their children were educated in the West and became the paragons of the new hybrid culture, half Islamic and half Western, that sprouted in the Islamic world of the early part of the twentieth century. This hybridism affected everything and, as usual, the arts gave everything away: the clothing, the architecture, the crafts, the interior furnishings, the literature of the Muslims, revealed that the traditional civilization was dying. While such things might seem inconsequential at first glance, in reality they are of profound importance. The Sunnah of the Prophet has prescriptions for dress that have always been observed in the long history of Islam. The wearing of the turban and of garments that are prayerful in nature — sacerdotal, as it were — is a sign of religiosity. The doffing of the turban and of the traditional garments, which one finds in the Westernized Muslim governing classes of the first half of the twentieth century, is a sign of the times. This is true also for all of the other aesthetic compromises and capitulations made to Western culture by Muslims. For over a thousand years, it was precisely these very forms of the aesthetic tradition of Islam that surrounded the Muslims. They inculcated in them the Islamic values, protecting them in periods of decline from total subversion, and reminding them, through the reflective beauty of the arts, of the beauteous nature of the transcendent realities.

The disappearance of the traditional garments of Islam that one sees in the different parts of the East in the first half of the twentieth century could not but have long-range deleterious effects on the religion. This may not be well understood by the outsider, especially by the Westerner, who is not used to living in a world of traditional arts. But it was perfectly well understood by the modernized governing elite of Islam, who knew what they were doing when they sought to "modernize" Islam. When the Kemalists took over power in Turkey in the inter-war period, they went straight to the jugular vein of Islam and savagely forced Western clothing on the people. They compelled the population to use the Western alphabet, and to absorb Western institutions. Their aim was the destruction of as many of the traditional institutions of that land as they could get their hands on. It was not in the least necessary to prove to these secularist Turks, or to their imitators in other Islamic lands, that the traditional arts and institutions of Islam were powerful supports of the religion. They knew beforehand that, unless they eradicated as much of the Islamic heritage as they could, they could not impose successfully their Westernized ideologies on the mass of the Muslims.[3]

Ṣūfī Renovations

This is not to say that spiritual reforms were not possible in the Islamic lands after the coming of Western imperialistic regimes. The renovation of the spiritual life of the community that began in Morocco with the great Ṣūfī, Mawlay al-'Arabī ad-Darqāwī (d. 1823), would extend all the way to Constantinople and down into Africa as the nineteenth century wore on. It is an example of the efflorescence of the inner life of Islam at that time.

In the twentieth century, a number of Ṣūfī Shaykhs have also given a new vitality to the spiritual content of the Islamic message. Shaykh Aḥmad al-'Alawī (d. 1934), who is considered one of the renovators that the Prophet promised would appear in his community at the beginning of every century, actually taught tens of thousands of disciples in an Algeria that had been under French colonialist domination for almost a century.[4] He is considered by some to be one of the greatest Ṣūfīs in the entire history of Islam. The reformative efforts of such a saintly figure could affect tens of thousands of Muslims because the Algerian and the Islamic world of his day were by and large still within the traditional mold. The influence of the modernist governing elite had not yet seeped down into the mass of the believers, who continued to retain a certain receptivity to the deeper contents of the Islamic message. The case of the Ṣūfī teachers in the period after the Second World War has not been the same. Their followers have been much more restricted in numbers, the world around them has been in great part de-Islamicized by the modernists, and they have had to adapt their instruction to changed circumstances. The teaching career of Shaykh Muḥammad al-Hāshimī (d. 1961), of the Shādiliyyah-Darqāwiyyah order, was carried out in a Syria whose chiefs were socialists and whose culture was rapidly succumbing to the inroads of the modern world.

Apart from its reformative functions, Ṣūfism has also played a preservative role in the midst of the destructive nature of modern Western ideologies. It has struggled against violently antireligious ideologies, such as communism, when they have been inflicted upon the Muslim populations. In Central Asia, where Russian communist imperialism has been responsible for the death of a great number of believers, for the closing down of thousands of mosques, and for the systematic attempts of atheistic propaganda for over half a century to demolish the Islamic faith, the underground activities of the Ṣūfī orders have been largely responsible for keeping Islam alive among the millions of the faithful. These are rear-guard actions, so to speak, and represent attempts to prevent the spiritual devastation of modern Western civilization, whether communist or capitalist, from utterly overwhelming the saving message of the faith. In Kemalist Turkey, where the Ṣūfī orders had to go underground, a similar preservative function devolved upon Ṣūfism as a result of the anti-Islamic measures of the State.

Ṣūfism under Attack

It has not been simply the modernist Muslims, with their diverse and conflicting ideologies imported from the West or learned there during university training, who have sought to solve the problems of the old Islamic culture by destroying as many of the Ṣūfī institutions of the past as they could. The fundamentalist movements within the Muslim world have also been anti-Ṣūfī, but for different reasons. Their own reduction of the Islamic message to its literal signification and their puritanical tendencies have combined to give their view of Islam an extraordinarily limited perspective. We see this reformist spirit in the late nineteenth-century Salafiyyah movement in Egypt, which called for a return to the way of the pious Ancestors (*as-salaf*) of the early centuries by eliminating the numerous innovations that seemed to have encrusted themselves on the body of the Sunnah. The Salafi leaders — such as Muḥammad 'Abduh (d. 1905) — rejected the interpretations of Islam by Ṣūfī orders as being degenerative and anti-Islamic.[5] What is ironic, in the case of Muḥammad 'Abduh, is that he had at some youthful period undergone Ṣūfī influence. The same can be said of other figures in the modern reformist (or so-called reformist) movement of the late nineteenth and early twentieth century, such as Jamāl ad-Dīn al-Afghānī (d. 1897), the Persian Pan-Islamist and political activist in Egypt, Turkey, and Persia; Ziya Gök Alp (d. 1924), the founder of the Turkish nationalist movement and the theoretician of Ataturk's party; Muḥammad Iqbāl (d. 1938), the Indian Muslim philosopher and poet; and a host of others. All of these saw the reformation of Islam, or simply of their countries, through different eyes, of course; but they were more or less in agreement that the old state of affairs could not continue, and proffered their own solutions, which did not include the Ṣūfī orders.

In the past, the most severe criticisms of Ṣūfī circles, when they were degenerate, or of the Ṣūfī frauds and mountebanks, came from the Ṣūfīs themselves. Al-Ghazālī, in his *Iḥyā'*, has some rather harsh attacks on these poseurs. But other eminent Ṣūfīs of earlier times had also taken swipes at the charlatans who infested the ranks of the sincere mystics. In every period after al-Ghazālī's day, we find saintly teachers, like Ibn al-'Arabī, describing for us the portraits of the fakers, the quacks, the degenerates, and the dishonest who posed as Ṣūfī adherents or even as teachers of the Path. Some of the *zāwiyahs* became dens of vice and drug addiction; some were involved in worldly activities of the most diverse kinds; some were simply hostels for the slothful; and some were preoccupied with the various kinds of magical practices that one finds in all the traditional cultures of the past. These were all condemned and derided by the real authorities of the Path, who saw their errors and dangers for the unknowing. But we do not find authentic Ṣūfī teachers saying that, because some of the Ṣūfī orders are somnolent or sick or even moribund, we must do away with all of the Ṣūfī orders, including those that are alive and spiritually healthy. Moreover, the Shaykhs of *taṣawwuf* were receptive enough to notice what others can notice also, if they wish to, and that is the following simple point: If some of the Ṣūfī orders are in such bad shape, what must be the case for some of the *'ulamā'*, or some of the believers, or even some of the would-be reformers of Islam? In other words, there is an enormous chasm between the great Ṣūfī teachers who criticize all decadence in the institutional life of Ṣūfism and the modernist reformers of the Muslim world, as well as the fundamentalist puritans, who would like to abolish all of the orders, if possible.

The Process of Westernization

Things would have been completely different for the Muslim world had it preserved its teachings and practices and its traditional institutions, including its arts, while absorbing the military skill and equipment necessary to protect itself from the depradations of Western imperialism. The overwhelming military and industrial power of the West in the last century or so gave little chance to the Islamic lands to defend themselves from Russian, English, French, and other Western nations' efforts to carve out empires for themselves at the expense of the Muslim world. Even so, there were defensive military efforts made by the Muslims. But these were to no avail, and soon country after country fell to the imperialistic power of Europe. Once installed in *dār al-islām*, modern Western civilization, with its diverse ideologies, its industrial system, its indifference to the ways of life of non-Westerners, could not but destroy from within what was left of the traditional Islamic civilization.

It is at that point that the Muslims should have made every effort possible to regain their independence and to preserve their Islamic traditional culture, while learning all the military skills necessary to defend themselves once the Western imperialist regimes could be ejected from their lands. This, unfortunately, was not done. Instead, the governing classes took to Western culture and its attractions with enthusiasm. They were the ones whose sons were educated in Western schools and who set the cultural pace for everyone else in society. The Western-educated minority became the partisans of Westernization: they began to dress like Westerners, to talk with Western ideas, to yearn for Western ways of life. The intoxicating effects of modern Western civilization now began working on the minds of the Westernized minority in the Islamic world. They clamored for the demolition of the Islamic civilization in the name of progress, which was identified with Western civilization. For the great mass of Muslims, in the interwar period when the Western imperialist systems were expanded over the Islamic lands, the traditional Islamic culture was still very strong. Moreover, most of the masses were illiterate, and this saved them from the unbalancing effects that a modern Western education generally had on the Muslims trained in the West.

The creation of a whole class of Westernized Muslims by the Europeans — like their counterparts in India, China, and elsewhere — spelled trouble both for the Islamic world and for the Europeans themselves. For the Islamic world, the trouble came from having a kind of Trojan horse inside the community that would sooner or later empty its well-trained troops inside the walls of *dār al-islām* and rush to open the gates to Western culture. For the Europeans, the trouble came from an unforeseen direction. Since the French Revolution, that began the dismantling of the traditional monarchical systems in Europe, democracy and republicanism were increasingly associated with modern civilization as important elements of the ideology behind it. These were promptly absorbed by the Westernized minority, who began applying their concepts against the old monarchical culture of the East and also against the imperialistic regimes, who were not being very democratic in ignoring the wishes of the native populations. An additional concept, nationalism, likewise of Western origin, was added to the previous ones to create a powerful surge against Western imperialist regimes in Islamic lands.

After the Second World War, the Islamic lands began to regain their independence, leaving the Soviet Union as the unique imperialistic power controlling tens of millions of Muslims in Central Asia. With the departure of the West and the restoration of governing authority to Muslims themselves, again one would have thought that the first task they had to confront was the preservation of the fragments of Islamic culture that had survived the days of Western colonialism. But, once again, this was not done either. Instead, we witness among practically all of the newly-independent countries in the East prodigious efforts to catch up with the West, not only in military armaments, but also in cultural life. A few attempts in Pakistan to keep some semblance of Islamic legislation are not the same thing as a genuine effort to preserve all aspects of Islamic culture. Precious little of that millennial way of life was left to squander away with impunity, but the Islamic countries found ways to get rid of that heritage in their headlong haste to imitate the Western world.

Modernists and Conservatists

Within the Islamic world, the battle was between the modernists, or progressivists, who were of westernized formation, and the conservatists, who generally were educated in the East. The former were of all persuasions, as one would expect, given their Western education or outlook. But they tended to have a violently antitraditional mentality, which was applied to every domain from the political to the economic to the social, and took Western models as their ideals. With some, the total imitation of the West, lock, stock, and barrel, was the distant goal. Islam was seen as a kind of obstacle that would have to transform itself or be transformed before progress, as interpreted by the different Western viewpoints, could make much headway.

The conservative movements of the contemporary Islamic world, caught off guard by the powerful materialistic ideas and forces that have invaded the community and eradicated so much of its inherited past, have never been able to respond except with defensive and apologetic gestures. These have succeeded only in delaying, not in stopping, the gradual decomposition of the religious structures of Islam. The reason for this is not too hard to understand: conservatism in Islam, as in other religions, also believes in progress. The imperative categories of that notion have infiltrated conservatives' minds too, and not just simply the thinking of the progressivists. That being so, very often the disputes between them and the liberals or progressivists or modernists are just really over the degree of rapidity with which a given regional culture is to be overthrown by Western civilization. The *jamāʻat-i islāmī* (''Society of Islam'') of Pakistan, or *al-ikhwān al-muslimūn* (''Muslim Brotherhood'') of Egypt and elsewhere, or Khomeini's movement in Persia, all want progress too, as do the modernists. It is simply that their fundamentalist versions of Islam prevent them from proceeding with the same abandon in their capitulation to the Modern World as the so-called progressivists.

Both camps, in other words, are deviations from the traditional teachings of the Islamic faith. The aberrations of spirit found in the modernist wing of the contemporary Islamic world are so obviously anti-Islamic that no one needs much proof to know that the religion in their hands becomes a travesty of the real faith. A Marxist Muslim, for example, like the Marxist Christian, Hindu, Buddhist, or Confucianist, is not only a contradiction in terms; he is also an image of subversion, and this is easily grasped. Other modernists might have varieties of Western ideologies that would stamp them as ''rightists'' or ''leftists'', according to case. But their opposition to the traditional doctrines and ways of life is nonetheless clear enough for all to see. Now, the same holds true for the so-called conservative Muslims of all kinds. They would like to hold on to something of the Sunnah of the Prophet. But their rejection of the traditional intellectual, theological, and spiritual doctrines of Islam, including Ṣūfism, and their incredible passivity toward many of the worldly features of modern industrial civilization, especially in the arts, mean that the fundamentalist version of Islam that they have is in reality opposed to the Islamic tradition too. The latter camp, admittedly, still clings to the ritual observances of the religion. However, since their minds no longer are infused with the traditional teachings, their interpretation of Islam is colored by the prevailing ideas of the day. These come from the West, whatever might be the fundamentalists' attitude toward that West.

Evolutionism in the West and in Islam

To understand how the thinking of both the progressivist and the conservative Muslims ended up by being counter to the Islamic tradition, one has to examine, first, how a similar thinking arose previously in the West and, second, how it was exported to the East. In the West, to begin with, modern civilization began its career on the philsophico-scientific foundations of the sixteenth and seventeenth centuries. Since then, it has moved through different phases, culminating in the effective eradication of revelation as the guiding principle of society. This was explosively manifested in the eighteenth-century French Revolution and its aftermath in Europe. Into the vacuum of an increasingly secularized world, there came the dominant ideas of modern times, the ones that would play their respective roles in the abolition of Christianity from the government, education, law, morality, and society in general. As a result, the Christian faith was reduced to a shadow of its former self in the countries of Europe as the nineteenth and twentieth centuries unfolded.

With the passage of time, modern Western civilization came to be identified with purely quantitative and secularistic values. A thousand different ideas arose to capture the minds of the restless societies of the West, from republicanism to scientism to socialism to industrialism to communism to others equally divorced from the revealed message of Christianity. Even Christianity itself slowly succumbed to the corrosive influences of the modern world, abandoning a good deal of its traditional teachings and practices in an effort to keep up with the secularist thought that was calling the tunes more and more for all the West. The creation of the first atheistic State in the history of mankind, that of the Russian communists at the end of the First World War, signaled the beginning of a new phase in the development of the modern world since its origins several centuries before. The Russian communists destroyed the traditional Christian institutions of Sacred Russia and proceeded to de-Christianize society with unsurpassed brutalism. Atheistic Russia represented the convergence of all the secularizing strands of the modern world into one totalitarian system that incorporated the scientific, materialistic, republicanist, collectivist, secularist, economic determinist, and other tendencies in our times. The other side of the modern world, the capitalist, because it did not persecute religion and seemed more tolerant of different opinions, gave the impression that Christianity was safer. In reality, the same secularistic tendencies which operated in Russian were at work elsewhere, but without the atheistic totalitarianism and at a slower pace.

Underlying the capitalist and communist systems of modern Western civilization is the dogma of evolutionism in all of its diverse applications.

That is the fundamental ideology of modern times. This is not just simply the transformist biological evolutionism of Darwinism, although it was the first on the scene. It is the much more general idea that everything evolves, so that evolutionism affects political systems, economic laws, literature, the historical process, the cultures of mankind, morality, religion, the entire physical universe, and even the Divinity. The wedding of the notions of evolutionism and progress, which took place in the latter half of the nineteenth century, added an ameliorative direction to the evolutionistic teachings that could not but point to the West as the culmination of evolutionism, from the biological to the cultural. Hence, there arose the missionary task of the white man to civilize the natives ("the white man's burden") under his heel in the colonies. Likewise, since his culture had evolved to the highest degree, he was the perfect embodiment of the "Civilization" he took with him to the Islamic countries, and to the East in general, equally looking down upon all of them as inferior or backwards in the evolutionary scale.

The West exported all of these novel types of thinking to the East through its educational and cultural institutions in the Islamic world and elsewhere, to say nothing of its very presence in the midst of *dār al-islām*. That presence had an implacable military, political, cultural, and industrial power behind it that belied the greatness of Islam or of any other culture that stood in the way of its massive self-assurance. It was all the more persuasive to the Muslims in that Islam and the other religions of the East were in somnolent decline when the civilization of the modern West came, like an irresistible, omnipotent steamroller. While the imperialistic regimes eventually had to leave the Muslim world, as well as other cultures of the East, this was merely a politico-military departure. In fact, the aforementioned governing classes and the Westernized minority in general made sure that the principal notions of the modern West were kept alive and even expanded in the Muslim community. They were the first ones to be infected by the evolutionistic virus, and it is through them that, since the Second World War, an increasing number of Muslims have come to believe that everything evolves, including, of course, their own revealed message.

Lurking in the minds of all modernist Muslims, and forming as it were the invisible bond between them, is that evolutionistic dogma from the West that no one questions. In the West, evolutionistic thinking has produced, as one can well imagine, disbelief and irreligion on a vast scale. But it has also given rise to totalitarian ideologies — Hitlerianism and communism come to mind immediately — that aim at nothing less than competing with revelation for the control of men's minds. Evolutionism is in some respects the "religion" of modern man, since it accounts for everything by evolutionistic causality, from the origins of the species to God Himself. Thus it obviates the need for creationism, scriptural authority, and religion, to say nothing of the universally-held teaching on the Fall of man and his sinful will which can only be regenerated by revelation and faith. As the East, including the Islamic world, has surrendered to the revolutionistic way of looking at things, it has become a disbelieving East. But even when, among the believers, Darwinism might be rejected in favor of Islamic creationism, there is still the acceptance of evolutionism in its other Hydra-headed facets, with all that this implies culturally in the willing acceptance of things Western at the expense of things Islamic.

Evolutionistic ideology has entered all aspects of Islamic thinking, modernist or conservative, even if it be simply the belief in *taqaddum* (''Progress'') that a diehard fundamentalist Arab Muslim might have. The imitation of the Western world by the East in clothing, arts and architecture, morality, political systems, industrialism, literature, and nationalism is not because this has been foisted upon it by the West, although in the colonialist days deliberate destruction of Eastern culture was rampant. It is because the collective evolutionistic psychosis that formerly characterized only the West has now become part and parcel of the Eastern mentality, apart of course from the minds of those who follow the traditional teachings. Under the pressure of such Western notions, the cultural remains of the old Islamic tradition are no longer seen as worth retaining. By the time efforts are made to save this or that old Islamic building or craft or folk dance, the rest of the culture has gone to wrack and ruin.

If that is so for the arts and architecture, then it needs no great imagination to understand why the other traditional institutions of Islam, such as the monarchical systems, the artisanal societies, or the agrarian culture, have generally gone by the board as the Muslim world capitulated to Western values. Take, for example, the traditional monarchical institutions of Islam, from the Caliphate to the Sultanate. It was thought by the modernists, in imitation of their Western counterparts of the French Revolution and later, that if the monarchies were eliminated and replaced by republican systems, nothing but good would result. This was because progress decreed that monarchies represented earlier evolutionistic developments that must give rise, sooner or later, to republican forms of government. The Caliphate was abolished by the Kemalists of Turkey in the name of their secularist ideology borrowed from the West and used by them to destroy ruthlessly the Islamic institutions of that country. Similar imitations of Western revolutions against the various European monarchies of the nineteenth and twentieth centuries were carried out elsewhere in the Muslim world by the modernists with great success. Like their counterparts in the modern Western world, the Muslim republicanists knew instinctively that the traditional culture would be given a deadly blow by the elimination of the millennial monarchic systems. All of the traditional hierarchies of Islam that made for the stratification of society around the monarch, and all of the qualitative distinctions between the classes that were harmonized by Islam, would be done away with by the elimination of the sultan or the king or the amir, as the case might be. This would turn society into a proletariat mass that could be manipulated with a certain ease by the democratic demagogues. But, more importantly, it would destroy the hierarchic relationship between God and His creatures; for if being a king or a monarch in this world is intrinsically wrong or even against progress, then a new relationship must be established between creatures and *Allāh*, who is *al-malik al-qahhār* ("the Almighty King").

In the past, the traditional monarchic system of Islam had its good, mediocre, and bad rulers, as one finds elsewhere. If tyrants or bad rulers happened to occupy the throne, this did not incriminate the institution itself, and no society made efforts to destroy it. The evolutionistic imperatives of modern man were then nowhere in evidence. From Constantine the Great (311-337) to the last Byzantine Emperor over a thousand years later, Constantine XI (1448-1453), the Eastern Christian civilization saw scores of good and bad rulers. But the monarchic institution itself was considered sacred and untouchable, whatever might be its evil fruits from time to time. Similar thoughts emerged from Muslim political thinkers over the centuries in regard to the Caliphate, which existed in its Arab and Turkish guises in the Muslim world from the days of the Caliph Abu Bakr to the last Ottoman Caliph in the early 1920s. However, as soon as the newly-minted Western notion on progress arrived in the Muslim world, the republicanists went straight for the jugular vein of the religio-political system of Islam and overthrew the Caliphate, the monarchies, and the other similar traditional forms of government in Islam, claiming that they were degenerate and consequently had to be gotten rid of in favor of republicanism. Nor did it matter, really, whether one was a secularist thinker, like Ataturk in the interwar period, or a so-called Muslim fundamentalist, like the Shīʿī demagogue, Khomeini of Persia. The former had no use for Islam and, accordingly, brought down the Caliphate; the latter used Islam for his own religious dictatorship and brought down the Shah of Persia.

Fundamentalism in Islam

This leads to the question of fundamentalism in Islam, sometimes thought of as expressing the orthodox tradition. While fundamentalism is properly speaking a Protestant phenomenon of the twentieth century, which holds to the inerrancy of the Bible, creationism, and a kind of literalism that is opposed to the modernist interpretations of Christianity, there is an Islamic fundamentalism too that is likewise literalist. There has always been this kind of literalist or fundamentalist view of Scripture since the early period of Islam. We see it especially in the Ḥanbalī dogmatic theologians, who refuse to interpret the anthropomorphic imagery of the Qur'ān. They prefer instead to suspend all speculative functions of the mind and to accept such passages without asking any questions, such as, "How does God sit on His throne?" or "How does He hear and see?" Since it is not possible for the intelligence to accept for very long such adamant refusals to interpret Scripture, Ḥanbalism has recourse to constant voluntaristic suppressions of the speculative mind by resorting to affirmations of faith at every turn and by refuting on every occasion anyone who does use his mind to understand such scriptural passages. This seems to go against the entire Islamic tradition that is based on the intelligent understanding of the articles of faith. But, in reality, it stresses the saving virtue of faith itself: one must rely on faith, not reason, to be saved. That the two are not mutually contradictory is evident from some of the Ash'arī interpretations of a speculative kind that go against certain Ḥanbalī positions. Ḥanbalī fundamentalism, however, was never the whole of the Islamic faith, nor for that matter was Ash'arism. Beyond both of them was Ṣūfī *ma'rifah* and spirituality in general, to say nothing of its speculative esoteric doctrines. As al-Ghazālī said, theology was good for refuting heresies of various sorts, but it never led to the inner vision of Truth, which Ṣūfism alone could do. Thus, fundamentalist thinking at best is a kind of nonspeculative dogmatism that accepts the literal meaning of the revealed Scripture. At worse, it is a totalitarian system that is inimical to the exercise of intelligence.

Orthodox Islam, in its purest, most intelligible, and most universal doctrinal manifestation is to be found in the eminent Ṣūfī gnostic sages, such as al-Ḥakim at-Tirmidhi (d. 898), al-Junayd (d. 911), an-Niffari (d. 965), al-Ghazāli (d. 1111), 'Abd al-Qādir al-Jilāni (d. 1166), Ibn al-'Arabi (d. 1240), Abu 'l-Ḥasan ash-Shādhili (d. 1258), and Mawlay al-'Arabi ad-Darqāwi (d. 1823), to mention only a few. Shaykh Abu 'l-Ḥasan ash-Shādhili, for example, was not an orthodox Muslim merely because of his conforming to the Māliki *madhhab*, or having learned in his youth an Ash'ari creedal presentation of the articles of belief. These have to do only with exoteric Islam, and that is simply the external form of the faith, its dogmatic aspect. He was a traditional orthodox Muslim, first of all, because of the universal truths contained in the esoteric doctrine of the Islamic revelation as found in Ṣūfi gnosis. The spiritual universality of this perspective makes all the other views on Islam seem circumscribed, to say the least. In the second place, and on a lower doctrinal scale, so to speak, he was an orthodox Muslim because of his Ash'ari creed, which permitted him to explain the simple dogmas of Islam with a rational exposition for each article of belief. In the third place, and on the lowest scale of conformity, he was an orthodox Muslim because he was of the Māliki school of jurisprudence, one of the four great *madhhabs* which comprise the orthodox jurisprudential tradition of Sunni Islam.

Those three aspects pertain to doctrinal formulations of orthodoxy that can be grasped intellectually by anyone wishing to assess the Shaykh's standing in regard to the Truth or its manifestations in thought. To a certain extent, that must have been what his contemporaries did in evaluating him. But things are different with respect to his spiritual realization of the Absolute, or *Allāh*. Unlike doctrine, spiritual realization cannot be communicated to someone else by the Ṣūfī sage. Nevertheless, he can guide others toward their own realization of the Divine Reality, for the tradition attributes a celestial permission behind the guidance of an authentic Shaykh of the Path. That guidance with a view to spiritual realization is the whole point of the Path. Now, by his spirituality the real Shaykh proves the orthodoxy of his teachings, for the false teacher has no spirituality. "By their fruits ye shall know them," says the Gospel. This applies to the spiritual qualities of the Ṣūfī Shaykh, like ash-Shādhilī, and is a criterion or sign of the authenticity of his instruction. Thus, while it is true that doctrinal formulations suffice to reveal the orthodoxy, or the lack of it, of a teacher, his spiritual nature is an important supplementary clue.

The Muslim doctors of the Law, the *'ulamā'* as such, cannot claim for exoteric Islam the limitless truth of the spiritual Path nor for themselves the fruits of the spiritual realization of God. These two restrictions, immensely significant, condemn them at the outset to speak only about the Law and theological dogmas. As al-Ghazālī and others have said, the exoteric authorities have nothing to say about the Path because that is beyond their capacity. The fact of the matter is that the spiritual orthodoxy of Islam contains the exoteric tradition the way the limitless ocean contains an ice floe. The ice is also made of water, but frozen and crystallized, analogous to the dogmatic formulations of Islam in relation to the universal contents of revelation. The opposite, however, is not true: the ice floe does not contain the limitless ocean, no more than dogmatic Islam can express the boundless dimensions of the revealed message, even though it is a crystallized form of the Truth. If that is so, then it is not the doctors of the Law who are going to pass judgment on Ṣūfī esoterism, but the other way around, for the lesser cannot judge the greater.

Present-day fundamentalism, however, is a deviation from orthodox Islam and an altogether different species from the Ḥanbalī variety of traditional Islam. The latter is orthodox, while the former is not. Fundamentalism today tends to reject the traditional theological propositions of the faith and the entire contemplative esoterism of revelation. Not even an Ibn Taymiyyah (d. 1328), the Ḥanbalī jurist who inveighed against all innovations and certain Ṣūfīs, could reject Ṣūfism as an orthodox expression of the Islamic faith, and thus he spoke admiringly of the Ḥanbalī Ṣūfī 'Abd al-Qādir al-Jīlānī (d. 1166). In his day, the Islamic tradition could afford to have puritans and fundamentalists because it was saturated with the intellectual and spiritual lights of the great Ṣūfīs, theologians, and philosophers, and with the beauty of the aesthetic forms everywhere. That is not the case for the fundamentalists of the present: their traditional Islamic cultural framework has largely disappeared, and their own understanding of Islam has been shot through by Western ideologies.

The Muslim fundamentalists of our times have recapitulated what happened previously to their Western counterparts. In the West, the invasion of Christian thinking by evolutionistic concepts began in the nineteenth century and eventually triumphed in the twentieth-century theologians who incorporated into their teachings various forms of evolutionism, from Darwinism to Marxism, without bothering to ask themselves whether all this was in agreement with traditional Christian doctrine because, in their view, even doctrine evolved. Apart from the evangelical Protestant fundamentalists who accepted the inerrancy and infallibility of the Bible and who were creationists, the general trend among the modernist or liberal theologians was towards an evolutionistic interpretation of Christianity.

That was true even among many of the creationists who, while rejecting in advance all Darwinism, accepted nevertheless evolutionism in its political, economic, social, and historical forms, often without even thinking about consequentiality in their attitudes. Protestant or Catholic, the religion seemed anxious to show its pertinency to the times by frankly espousing the varieties of thinking that were characteristic of the different phases of the modern secularist world, with its innumerable theories and speculations that have changed like each year's fashions.

This has likewise happened in the Islamic world, not so much by deliberate analysis and choice, as by sheer imitation of the Western patterns of thought, even when that West was looked upon with disfavor or jaundiced eyes. Fundamentalism may give the impression of being orthodox, but that is simply because its believers observe the ritual laws of Islam, not because they adhere to authentic traditional teachings. More often than not, their fundamentalism is a mixture of correct ritual observance with some brand of Western thinking. It is a syncretistic Islam that leads to a kind of cultural hybridism. Selective and puritanical in its own view of the religion, fundamentalism is in direct contrast with the Islamic tradition, esoteric or exoteric. The tradition was at least consistent and coherent, while contemporary fundamentalism is not.

The Reaffirmation of Traditional Islam

It is only through a knowledge of the traditional doctrines, rituals, morality, and arts that one can perceive what constitutes authentic Islam. The supernatural or transcendent element of any traditional teaching or practice must not be lost sight of, for we tend to reduce the concept of tradition to its purely historical association as a transmission of ideas and external forms from generation to generation. Yet, without the transcendent realities imbedded in its historical structures, tradition would quickly lose its salvific content. But it is true, nevertheless, that the historical manifestation of the Islamic tradition, like that of others, is subject to a law of increasing elaboration or complexity of forms, as was previously observed. This law cannot but operate within the collective psyche of the Islamic civilization as it becomes worldlier or more dense, obeying the intensified pull of *ghaflah*, and necessitating greater and greater detail in doctrinal explanations. At what point all of these compensatory efforts no longer have any effect on the increasingly opaque nature of Islamic civilization, allowing the downward impetus of the Fall to exert a dangerous force, is difficult to say. Symptomatic signs of the increasing density of the collective soul of the community can be discerned in its different visible arts, its literatures, its religious formalism, and in the numerous concessions made by the Ṣūfī authorities to the doctors of the Law simply to keep the life of contemplation intact within Islam.

By the eighteenth century, the transcendent spiritual reality that should operate in all traditional life could hardly shine through the hardened strata of the Islamic religion. Maximum crystalline formulations of the traditional teachings had been reached, similar to the arabesques and geometric ornamentations covering an entire wall, leaving no room for further development. Soon afterwards came the dismantling of the tradition from the outside through Western imperialism, and from within through modernist or Westernized Muslims.

The introduction of modern Western civilization into the very midst of *dār al-islām* has produced the efforts to reinterpret the fundamental principles of the Islamic faith, *īmān*, *islām*, and *iḥsān* (''faith'', ''submission'', and ''virtue'', respectively), in conformity with the diverse and conflicting ideologies of the West. The efforts to reinterpret Islam in keeping with non-Islamic norms are what distinguish the modernists from the reformers of the past, who never looked outside the tradition for their inspiration. If we bear in mind that it is these principles that constitute the essence of Islam and define the conditions of being a Muslim, we can easily perceive that all misinterpretation of their meaning can lead to disastrous spiritual consequences. The opposite is also true: the restoration of their traditional meanings leads to regenerative spiritual results, as we see in the former periods of renovation in Islam.

Consider the principle of *īmām* (''faith''): in place of the traditional gnostic, philosophical, theological, and spiritual doctrines of the religion, we now find systems of thought borrowed from the West, such as pragmatism, utilitarianism, dialectic materialism, and the like. Even the Muslim sages of the past have been disinterred in order to label them with modernist slogans. Thus, the great Ṣūfī sage, Rūmī (d. 1273), for example, has been made to sound like a kind of early Darwinist. Because he speaks of the stratification of being in the mineral, plant, and animal kingdoms, as do others in his time, with the Spirit revealing itself more and more in the higher strata, this has been reinterpreted as a kind of evolutionistic teaching. In fact, the thesis that being is more manifest in the higher forms of life, with man occupying the summit, is a traditional doctrine known to the Ancients. It has nothing to do with the transformist Darwinism that attempts to make the higher levels of consciousness evolve from the lower and, eventually, from unconscious matter.

Consider the principle of *iḥsān* ("virtue"): in place of the profound traditional teachings on the spiritual and moral life, we now have Western interpretations on the nature of human conduct. Islamic psychology, the phenomenology of the mind as seen in the traditional cosmologies, and the psychotherapeutic science of virtue and vices taught in the initiatic Path have been relegated to the category of old-fashioned beliefs. Western versions of conduct, borrowed from Freudian or other sources, are the definitive standards for many Muslims. It is as if the moral code flowing from the *sharī'ah* and the *ṭarīqah* had been tossed into the lion's den of modern Western thinking. But that is not all, for the principle of *iḥsān* also contains the germinal notion of sacred art: interior beauty of soul generates exterior beauty of forms. The loss of the former produces the loss of the latter. For that reason, the decline in *iḥsān* in the collective substance of the community has produced a corresponding deterioration in the arts of Islam. Art, whether Islamic or otherwise, always reflects what is happening in the soul of a people. Thus, the absence of a traditional cultural ambiance in the Western world is reflected in the constantly-changing styles of art and architecture that reflect the restlessness of the Westerner's soul. In architecture alone, the Westerner has witnessed a bewildering variety of styles in the past century alone, from Neo-Gothic to Greco-Roman Revival to Functionalism, and so on. All of that has been dumped into the Islamic world with predictable consequences on the aesthetic ambiance of the Islamic culture and on the souls of the Muslims.
latter. For that reason, the decline in *iḥsān* in the collective substance of the community has produced a corresponding deterioration in the arts of Islam. Art, whether Islamic or otherwise, always reflects what is happening in the soul of a people. Thus, the absence of a traditional cultural ambiance in the Western world is reflected in the constantly-changing styles of art and architecture that reflect the restlessness of the Westerner's soul. In architecture alone, the Westerner has witnessed a bewildering variety of styles in the past century alone, from Neo-Gothic to Greco-Roman Revival to Functionalism, and so on. All of that has been dumped into the Islamic world with predictable consequences on the aesthetic ambiance of the Islamic culture and on the souls of the Muslims.

Only through the reaffirmation of the traditional intellectual and spiritual teachings and practices can Islam be revived. For the traditional Muslim of the past or the present, this reliance on the inherited principles of reform has always been self-evident. We see those principles operating for the first time in the mission of the Prophet. When he began preaching *Tawḥīd*, he was confronted by an immense population of Arab pagans. Those who rallied to his religion formed a tiny community in the midst of the surrounding paganism, which seemed indestructible. But he had the conviction that Heaven would always side with the faithful minority, then and later, and that Heaven would have the final word. For that reason, it is well to reflect on the Prophet's words, often quoted in periods of decline throughout the history of the religion: "Islam began as an exile, and it will become once again an exile as it was in the beginning. Blessed are those in exile!"

NOTES

CHAPTER I

The Cycles of Revelation

1. For a presentation of Islam by a contemporary Muslim intellectual, see Seyyed Hossein Nasr's book, *Ideals and Realities of Islam* (Boston, 1972), which deals with the many facets of the traditional faith. A more recent work, *Islam and the Destiny of man* (Albany, 1985), written by Charles Le Gai Eaton, is an account of the beliefs and practices of Islam with many historical observations. A fine summary of the religion can also be found in Frederick Mathewson Denny's *An Introduction to Islam* (New York, 1985). An anthology of different translations on the religion and its civilization up to the eleventh century, chosen with skill and taste, is to be found in Eric Schroder's book, *Muhammad's People* (Portland, Maine, 1955).

2. A great deal of information on the pre-Islamic Arabs is summed up in Part I of Philip K. Hitti's well-known *History of the Arabs* (New York, 1970), which also covers the classical period of Islamic history. For an overall view of Islamic history, see *The Cambridge History of Islam*(2 vols.; Cambridge, 1970), edited by P. M. Holt, Ann K. S. Lambton, and Bernard Lewis. A work that is not easy reading, but full of many insights, is Marshall G. S. Hodgson's *The Venture of Islam* (3 vols.; Chicago, 1974).

3. Frithjof Schuon analyzes the interrelationships and the contributions of each of the three monotheistic faiths to the Abrahamic tradition in chap. 6 of his *The Transcendent Unity of Religions* (New York, 1975).

4. For a study of the profound spiritual and other implications of the Fall, see Frithjof Schuon, *Light on the Ancient Worlds* (London, 1965), chap. 2, "In the Wake of the Fall."

5. In our epoch, the great Algerian Ṣūfī Shaykh, Aḥmad al-'Alawī, who died in 1934, represents one of those reformers. See the book on his life and thought by Martin Lings, *A Ṣūfī Saint of the Twentieth Century* (Berkeley, 1973).

6. René Guénon sets forth in succinct fashion the cyclical doctrines of mankind, drawn mostly from Hindu concepts, in his book, *The Crisis of the Modern World* (London, 1962), written in 1927; and his later work, *The Reign of Quantity and the Signs of the Times* (Baltimore, 1972), covers the metaphysical and cosmological facets of the human cycle in the light of both Hindu and non-Hindu traditions.

7. On "The Outbreathing of the Compassionate," see chap. 10 of Titus Burckhardt's *An Introduction to Sufi Doctrine* (Wellingborough, Northamptonshire, 1976), to which should be added chap. 12 of R. W. J. Austin's *The Bezels of Wisdom* (New York, 1980), a translation of the famous *Fuṣūṣ al-Ḥikam* by the Andalusian Ṣūfī, Ibn al-'Arabī.

CHAPTER II

Muḥammad the Messenger

1. *In Mecca the Blessed, Madina the Radiant* (New York, 1963), Emil Esin has brought together, with numerous illustrations, a good deal of biographical information on the Prophet and the traditional lore on Mecca and Medina.

2. Perhaps the best English biography of the Prophet along traditional lines, written with great charm and simplicity, is that of Martin Lings, *Muhammad: His Life Based on the Earliest Sources* (New York, 1983). The life and times of the Prophet are reconstructed, with great detail, in the work of a contemporary Muslim scholar, M. Hamidullah, *Le Prophéte de l'Islam* (2 vols.; Paris, 1959). For centuries the best-known biography of the Prophet in the Muslim world has been the *Sīrah* of Ibn Isḥāq, translated by A. Guillaume, *The Life of Muhammad* (London, 1967).

3. On the perpetuation in Classical Arabic of ancient Semitic grammatical forms, see Édouard Dhorme, "L'arabe littéral et la langue de Hammourabi," in vol. 2 of *Mélanges Louis Massignon* (3 vols.; Damascus, 1957).

4. Annemarie Schimmel's book, *And Muhammad Is His Messenger* (Chapel Hill, 1985), is a mine of information on the veneration of the Prophet throughout the Islamic world. The Muḥammad who emerges from her book is the one recognized by Islam and contrasts sharply with the Prophet in W. Montgomery Watt's *Muhammad: Prophet and Statesman* (London, 1961), which is a socio-political version of the Prophet's life and times.

5. For the Prophet as seen from a spiritual perspective that allows the Western reader to situate him within the context of the Judeo-Christian world and its values, see chap. 3 of Frithjof Schuon's *Understanding Islam* (Baltimore, 1972). In his small but richly-rewarding work, *Symbolism of the Cross* (London, 1958), René Guénon examines the concept of "Universal Man", an Islamic esoteric expression that applies preeminently to the Prophet Muḥammad.

CHAPTER III

The Nature of the Qur'ān

1. A penetrating discussion of the different facets of the Qur'ān can be found in Frithjof Schuon's *Understanding Islam* (Baltimore, 1972), chap. 2.

2. In his book, *The Event of the Qur'ān* (London, 1971), Kenneth Cragg describes the historical setting of the Qur'ānic revelation; and in his later work, *The Mind of the Qur'ān* (London, 1973), he examines the reactions to it by the faithful. See also chap. 3 of H.A.R. Gibb's *Muhammadanism: An Historical Survey* (New York, 1962), for the part played by Scripture in the development of the social and legal features of Islam.

3. For a traditional account of the collection of the Qur'ān, see Labīb as-Sa'īd, *The Recited Koran: A History of the First Recorded Version* (Princeton, 1975).
4. Muhammad Abul Quasem has translated Book VIII of al-Ghazālī's *Iḥyā'* in his work, *The Recitation and Interpretation of the Qur'ān: Al-Ghazālī's Theory* (Kuala Lampur, 1979), which has many details on how to recite the Qur'ān, as does the book by as-Sa'īd, mentioned in the previous footnote.
5. See William A. Graham, *Divine Word and Prophetic Word in Early Islam* (The Hague, 1977), for a study of these holy statements.
6. Among the many studies on Qur'ānic commentaries, see Helmut Gätje, *The Qur'ān and Its Exegesis: Selected Texts with Classical and Modern Interpretations* (London, 1976); A.F.L. Beeston, *Baiḍāwī's Commentary on Sūrah 12 of the Qur'ān* (Oxford, 1963); and Muhammad Abul Quasem, *The Jewels of the Qur'ān: Al-Ghazālī's Theory* (Kuala Lampur, 1977), which is a translation of al-Ghazālī's work, *Kitāb Jawāhir al-Qur'ān*.
7. Some of the early mystical exegetes of the Qur'an are studied by Paul Nwyia in his *Exégèse coranique et langage mystique* (Bierut, 1970).
8. A.J. Arberry's *The Koran Interpreted* (2 vols.; New York, 1955) is the English translation that most approximates the actual literary characteristics of the Arabic text; and M.M. Pickthall's *The Meaning of the Glorious Koran* (New York, n.d.) is an accurate translation but much less poetical than the former.
9. See on this question Frithjof Schuon, *Dimensions of Islam* (London, 1970), chap. 1, "The Use of Hyperbole in Arab Rhetoric," and chap. 4, "Some Difficulties in the Qoran and Other Scriptures."
10. Modernist interpretations of different types can be studied in J.M.S. Baljon, *Modern Muslim Koran Interpretation* (Leiden, 1961), and in J.J.G. Jansen, *The Interpretation of the Koran in Modern Egypt* (Leiden, 1980).

CHAPTER IV

The Spiritual Path of Ṣūfism

1. Annemarie Schimmel's *Mystical Dimensions of Islam* (Chapel Hill, 1975) is a brilliant historical study of Ṣūfism. William Stoddart's little book, *Sufism: The Mystical Doctrines and Methods of Islam* (New York, 1976) is a brief and clear exposition of the Ṣūfī Way. For excellent translations from important Ṣūfī works, with explanatory remarks, see R. A. Nicholson's *Studies in Islamic Mysticism* (Cambridge, 1921).
2. The limitations of exoterism are treated in chap. 2 of Frithjof Schuon's *The Transcendent Unity of Religions* (New York, 1975), while chap. 3 deals with the universality of esoterism in the context of the monotheistic traditions.
3. Louis Massignon, in his *Essai sur les origines du lexique technique de la mystique musulmane* (Paris, 1968), shows how the Qur'ān contains the origins of Islamic mystical thought and examines exhaustively the development of Islamic spiritual life in the early centuries. For a simple and meditative view of Ṣūfī teachings in their Qur'ānic roots, see Martin Lings, *What is Sufism?* (Berkeley, 1977), and

for a view of Ṣūfism in its essential nature, see Frithjof Schuon, *Sufism: Veil and Quintessence* (Bloomington, Indiana, 1981), chap. 6.

4. On him, see the translation of Louis Massignon's famous work, *The Passion of al-Hallāj: Mystical Martyr of Islam* (4 vols.; Princeton, 1983), which is an immensely erudite study of this great Ṣūfī within the framework of Islam before and after his day. In *Words of Ecstasy in Sufism* (Albany, 1985), Carl W. Ernst examines the ecstatic expressions of the Ṣūfīs, including al-Ḥallāj.

5. For the critical role of this eminent Muslim sage, see W. Montgomery Watt, *Muslim Intellectual: A Study of al-Ghazālī* (Edinburgh, 1963).

6. J. S. Trimingham, in his *The Sufi Orders in Islam* (Oxford, 1971), deals at great length with the numerous Ṣūfī orders that have arisen in the Islamic world over the centuries.

7. This work, translated by Richard J. McCarthy, *Freedom and Fulfillment* (Boston, 1980), describes the contemplative life of Ṣūfism that at last set al-Ghazāulī's mind to rest after the turmoil of his spiritual crisis and is comparable, as an autobiography, to the *Confessions* of St. Augustine within the Christian tradition.

8. For an excellent summary of Ibn al-'Arabī's life and thought, see Seyyed Hossein Nasr's *Three Muslim Sages: Avicenna, Suhrawardi, and Ibn 'Arabī* (Cambridge, Massachusetts, 1964). In his *Creative Imagination in the Ṣūfism of Ibn 'Arabī* (Princeton, 1969), Henry Corbin presents the thinking of the Andalusian sage and situates it within that critical watershed for both the Christian and Islamic worlds that was the thirteenth century.

9. The latter work has been translated, with introduction and chapter analyses, by R. W. J. Austin, *Bezels of Wisdom* (New York, 1980).

10. A remarkable study in comparative mysticism has been made by Toshihiko Izutsu in *Sufism and Taoism: A Comparative Study of Key Philosophical Concepts* (Berkeley, 1984), which reveals the underlying unity of these spiritual traditions.

CHAPTER V

The Sacred Law of Islam

1. For the Law of Islam in general, see Louis Gardet's *La Cité musulmane, vie sociale et politique* (Paris, 1961), which furnishes an excellent account of Islamic institutions; H. A. R. Gibb, *Muhammadanism: An Historical Survey* (New York, 1962), chap. 6, which deals in a clear and concise way with the Law; and Majid Khadduri, *Islamic Jurisprudence: Shāfi'i's Risāla* (Baltimore, 1962), which is a translation of the famous treatise on the principles of Islamic jurisprudence by the Imām ash-Shāfi'i.

2. On the *ḥadīths*, see James Robson, *An Introduction to the Science of Tradition* (London, 1963), which is the translation of *al-Madkhal*, a famous work by al-Ḥakīm an-Nīsābūr; and Muhammad Zafrullah Khan's translation of the well-known compendium of *ḥadīths* by an-Nawawī, *Gardens of the Righteous: Riyadh as-Salihin of Imam Nawawi* (London, 1975).

3. For the Islamic State, see Thomas W. Arnold, *The Caliphate* (New York, 1966), an old but still authoritative work; E. I. J. Rosenthal, *Politi-Thought in Medieval Islam: An Introductory Outline* (Cambridge, 1958); M. Hamidullah, *The Muslim Conduct of State* (Lahore, 1956); and T. W. Arnold, *The Preaching of Islam* (Lahore, 1956), still a remarkable history of the Islamic expansion.
4. A good summary that reconciles Sunnism and Shī'sm can be found in Seyyed Hossein Nasr's *Ideals and Realities of Islam* (Boston, 1975).
6. Frithjof Schuon gives a deep explanation of the problems involved in the Sunnī-Shiī'ī dichotomy in Chap. 5, "Seeds of a Divergence," of his *Islam and the Perennial Philosophy* (n.p., 1976).
5. On warfare in Islam, see Majid Khadduri, *War and Peace in the Law of Islam* (Baltimore, 1955).
6. For the traditional Islamic viewpoint, see M. Ahmad, *Economics of Islam* (Lahore, 1947).

CHAPTER VI

The Islamic Intellectual Tradition

1. Although somewhat dated, Duncan Black MacDonald's *Development of Muslim Theology, Jurisprudence and Constitutional Theory* (New York, 1965) is still a useful manual on Islamic theological thought. See also Ignaz Goldziher, *Introduction to Islamic Theology and Law* (Princeton, 1981), and the rather thorough study of Islamic theological principles by Harry Austryn Wolfson, *The Philosophy of the Kalam* (Cambridge, Massachusetts, 1976).
2. On Mu'tazilī theological schools, see W. Montgomery Watt, *The Formative Period of Islamic Thought* (Edinburgh, 1973).
3. In *The Theology of al-Ash'arī* (Beirut, 1953), Richard J. McCarthy examines Ash'arism and provides the reader with basic texts from the hand of al-Ash'arī. Frithjof Schuon explores the basic problems within Ash'arī thinking in *Islam and the Perennial Philosophy* (n.p., 1976), chap. 5, "Dilemmas Within Ash'arite Theology."
4. See A. J. Wensinck, *The Muslim Creed: Its Genesis and Historical Development* (Cambridge, 1932), for a collection of the different creeds in Islam.
5. The creed of Ibn al-'Arabī was based largely on the tradition established by ash-Shāfi'ī and Aḥmad ibn Ḥanbal, two of Islam's great jurists, and by the great Ṣūfīs. For a detailed study of his creed, see Roger Deladrière, *La Profession de Foi* (Paris, 1978), which is a translation of Ibn al-'Arabī's creed.
6. For a general survey of Islamic philosophy, see Mian Mohammad Sharif, ed., *A History of Muslim Philosophy* (2 vols.; Wiesbaden, 1963); Seyyed Hossein Nasr, *Science and Civilization in Islam* (Cambridge, Massachusetts, 1968), *Islamic Science: An Illustrated Study* (n.p., 1976), *Islamic Life and Thought* (Albany, 1981), and *Three Muslim Sages: Avicenna, Suhrawardi, and Ibn 'Arabī* (Cambridge, Massachusetts, 1964), all four of these last works written in a fine, lucid style.

7. Richard J. McCarthy, trans., *Freedom and Fulfillment* (Boston, 1980).
8. On Mullā Ṣadra, see Seyyed Hossein Nasr, *Ṣadr al-Dīn Shīrāzī and His Transcendent Theosophy* (Boulder, 1979). James Winston Morris, in *The Wisdom of the Throne: An Introduction of the Philosophy of Mulla Sadra* (Princeton, 1981), provides the reader with a thorough study of the Persian sage and a translation of one of his many works, *al-Ḥikmah al-'Arshiyyah.*
9. See on this whole question *Islam and the Plight of Modern Man* (New York, 1975), by Seyyed Hossein Nasr, for a Muslim intellectual's interpretation of the general tendencies of the modern world.

CHAPTER VII

The Arts of Islam

1. Titus Burckhardt, in *Sacred Art East and West* (London, 1967), has intuitive reflections on sacred art in general and Islamic art in particular; and in his *Art of Islam: Language and Meaning* (n.p., 1976), which is superbly illustrated, he explains in greater detail the nature of the arts in Islam. See also the important works by Ernst Kühnel, *Islamic Art and Architecture* (London, 1966), and Oleg Grabar, *The Formation of Islamic Art* (New Haven, 1973), for historical observations on Islamic art.
2. For the architecture of the Muslim world, see George Mitchell, ed., *Architecture of the Islamic World: Its History and Social Meaning* (New York, 1978), a magnificently printed work with numerous illustrations and studies by a host of experts on the principal types of Islamic architecture; and for calligraphy, see Martin Lings, *The Quranic Art of Calligraphy and Illumination* (Boulder, 1978), and Annemarie Schimmel, *Calligraphy and Islamic Culture* (New York, 1984).
3. A complete account of Rūmī's teachings as found in numerous translations from his well-known literary works, especially the *Mathnawī*, is given by William Chittick, *The Sufi Path of Love: The Spiritual Teachings of Rumi* (Albany, 1983).

APPENDIX I
Selected Glossary of Islamic Terms

'abd (pl. *'ibād*): creature, servant, worshiper, slave. In Islam, the relationship between God and His servants or worshipers is never filial, as in Christianity, but is instead a relationship between the Lord (*ar-rabb*), who possesses perfect Lordliness (*rubūbiyyah*), and the servant, who must manifest his servanthood (*'ubūdiyyah*), which consists in giving God His proper due in all things.

ahl al-kitāb: "People of the Book", a Qur'ānic phrase designating those communities that have received a revelation, or a Book, such as the Jews and the Christians; later in history, Islam recognized still other peoples with Books, such as the Zoroastrians and the Hindus.

'aqīdah: a creedal formulation setting out the principal tenets of belief with regard to God, the Angels, the Messengers and Prophets, the Day of Judgment, and the like, which the Muslim is supposed to know, together with the supporting arguments, according to certain theologians.

'aql (*al-*): reason or intellect (or intelligence), depending on context; if it is the former, then it refers to rational or discursive thinking; if it is the latter, then it refers to supra-rational or intuitive intellection. It is sometimes identified with the Spirit (*ar-rūh*, q.v.)

'ārif (pl. *'ārifūn*): the gnostic in Ṣūfism, who has gnosis (*ma'rifah*, q.v.) of God.

asmā' (pl. of *ism*, "name"): *al- asmā' al-ḥusnā*, the Ninety-Nine "Most Beautiful Names" of God, divided into Names of Essence (*asmā' dhātiyyah*) and Names of Quality (*asmā' ṣifatiyyah*), the latter into Names of Majesty (*asmā' jalāliyyah*), which have to do with rigor, and Names of Beauty (*asmā' jamāliyyah*), which have to do with mercifulness.

awliyā' (pl. of *walī*, q.v.): the saints.

'ayn al-qalb: the eye of the heart, referring to the eye of the Spirit that sees the Real (*al-ḥaqq*, q.v.) when it is unveiled; otherwise, it is veiled and has no vision of God or of transcendent realities. The purification of the inner eye of the heart is the primary concern of Ṣūfism.

barakah (pl. *barakāt*): grace, blessing, benediction; beings or things can have *barakah*. There is *barakah* in saints, holy places, relics, pious deeds, rituals, and the like.

basmalah: the introductory phrase to all of the Sūrahs of the Qur'ān except one, the ninth; it is *bismi 'llāhi 'r-raḥmāni 'r-raḥīm* ("In the Name of God, the Compassionate, the Merciful"), and is the formula used to consecrate all deeds when one begins them, the *ḥamdalah* (q.v.) being the formula used when the action has been brought to an end.

bāṭin: inward, interior, inner; as *al- bāṭin* ("the Interior"), it is one of the Ninety-Nine Names of *Allāh*; the word *bāṭinī* means "esoteric", and *'ilm al-bāṭin* ("the science of the inward") is esoterism.

bay'ah: a pact; more specifically, the initiatic pact between the Shaykh and his disciple that implies rebirth and entry into the Path; it is said to confer the Muḥammadan grace and power that are actualized by the efforts of the disciple under his teacher's guidance.

bid'ah (pl. *bida'*): innovation; it has the meaning of deviating from the established norms, particularly the Sunnah of the Prophet and of the leaders of early Islam; and it has a strong pejorative sense of nonconformism. Since emulating the Sunnah of the Prophet is desirable, all innovation is undesirable, but not renovation (*tajdīd*), which has to do with reviving the Sunnah with a fresh spirit.

dār al-ḥarb: the House of Warfare, or the non-Islamic world, which must be fought against until Islam has the upper hand or else peace treaties have been drawn up; opposed to *dār al-islām* (q.v.).

dār al-islām: the House of Islam, or the Islamic world; the Islamic community, where submission to the Divine Will reigns; opposed to *dār al-ḥarb* (q.v.).

dhāt (*adh-*): the Essence; *adh-dhāt al- ilāhiyyah*, the Divine Essence, as undifferentiated reality, contrasted with the Divine Attributes, or differentiated reality, of the Lord (*ar-rabb*, q.v.); the Divine Essence is the impersonal unity of *Allāh*, the Infinite, the Absolute, and the Eternal as such, beyond His personal nature.

dhikr: recollection, remembrance; as *dhikru 'llāh*, it means the Invocation of God, by repeating one of the Ninety-Nine Names, such as *Allāh*; it is the opposite of *ghaflah* (q.v.); the saint is said to be the person whose *dhikru 'llāh* is not merely sporadic but permanent.

falsafah: philosophy; a synonym for it is *ḥikmah* (q.v.).

faqīr (pl. *fuqarā'*): a poor man, but technically, in Ṣūfism, it means the initiate, the one who has received initiation and is treading the Path. Those who belong to the Ṣūfī orders are called *fuqarā'* (or dervishes, in the East).

faqīh (pl. *fuqahaī'*): a jurisconsult, a specialist in Islamic jurisprudence (*fiqh*, q.v.).

faqr: poverty, in the spiritual sense; one of the cardinal virtues of Ṣūfism; hence, the designation of the person who follows the Path as a *faqīr* (q.v.), a poor man, which in reality means that he seeks to rid himself of all the multiplicity associated with the self.

fatwā (pl. *fatāwā*): a legal opinion issued by a *muftī* (q.v.) on some particular point of the Law, and which he draws up in the traditional form.

faylasūf falāsifah): a philosopher, or one who knows Greek wisdom.

fiqh: jurisprudence in Islam, based on the Qur'ān (q.v.), the Sunnah (q.v.), *ijmā'* (q.v.) and *qiyās* (q.v.), that are known as the *uṣūl al-fiqh* ("the principles of jurisprudence") in Sunnī Islam.

fiṭrah: the primordial nature of man, as he was created, wherewith he recognizes the Oneness of God and is therefore conscious of *tawḥīd* (q.v.), unless he is veiled through associationism (*shirk*, q.v.) or disbelief (*kufr*, q.v.).

fuqahā': see *faqīh*.

fuqarā': see *faqīr*.

ghaflah: forgetfulness, not merely as a memory lapse, but as a psychophysical veiling of the heart. *Ghaflah* feeds the momentum of the Fall (*al-hubūṭ*, q.v.) and is responsible for the dispersion of attention that prevents *dhikr* (q.v.), so that the two are in contrast, as are *shirk* (q.v.) and *tawḥīd* (q.v.).

ḥadīth (pl. *aḥādīth*): a statement of the Prophet transmitted through a chain of authorities (*isnād*, q.v.). There are two kinds: a *ḥadīth nabawī*, in which the Prophet speaks under his own authority; and a *ḥadīth qudsī*, in which God speaks through the mouth of the Prophet. The overwhelming mass of *ḥadīths* are of the first kind, whereas there are only several hundred or so of the second type. The *ḥadīths* form the basis of the Sunnah of the Prophet.

ḥajj: one of the Pillars of Religion: the pilgrimage to Mecca, performed during the month of pilgrimage (*dhu 'l- ḥijjah*).

ḥamdalah: the formula *al-ḥamdu lillāh* ("Praise be to God"), which is used when ending an activity or when one observes something worth praising; used in conjunction with the consecrational formula, the *basmalah* (q.v.).

ḥanīf (pl. *ḥunafā'*): the pure believer, an adherent to the Abrahamic-Ishmaelite monotheistic tradition; one of such persons in the days of the Prophet.

ḥaqīqah (*al-*): Reality, as in *al- ḥaqīqah al-ilāhiyyah* ("The Divine Reality") or *al-ḥaqīqah al-muḥammadiyyah* ("The Muḥammadan Reality"). The Ṣūfī triad, *al-ḥaqīqah*, *aṭ-ṭarīqah*, and *ash-sharī'ah*, refer respectively to the Divine Reality, the Path, and the Law, with the first one pictured as a point in the center of a circle, the second as a radium going from the center to the circle, and the third as the outer circle itself. To get to the Divine Reality, one must follow the radium going from the outer circle to the inner point.

ḥaqq (*al-*): the Real, the Truth, God; one of the Ninety-Nine Names of God.

ḥikmah: wisdom, either in a spiritual sense or else as philosophy. The person who has wisdom is a *ḥakīm*, and he can be either the mystic or the philosopher, according to case.

hijrah: the Emigration from Mecca to Medina by the Prophet and his small band of followers in the year 622, which is the year 1 of the Hijrah.

hubūṭ (*al-*): the Fall from the Garden of Eden, implying the loss of the primordial state through the veiling of the heart. The recovery of the Edenic state is through the inner purification of the heart, that allows the contemplative to see, once again, the transcendent realities perceived by Adam before the *hubūṭ*. In Islam, the Fall is immediately followed by the revelation given to Adam (the redeemed Adam), who is the first of the line of Messengers and Prophets culminating in Muḥammad. After each message, addressed to a particular community, another Fall takes place, for *ghaflah* (q.v.) reaffirms itself. The process of rising and falling goes on until the Day of Judgment, when the entire momentum of the *hubūṭ* is brought to a definite end.

'ibādah (pl. *'ibādāt*): the ritual observances of Islam, such as the five daily prayers, the fast of Ramaḍān, and so on, which the servant (*'abd*, q.v.) performs.

'īd: festival, such as the *'īd al-fiṭr* ("Festival of Breaking the Fast of Ramaḍān") or *'īd al-aḍḥā* ("Festival of Sacrifice"), the two principal religious holidays of the Islamic calendar, the first marking the end of Ramaḍān; the second, on the tenth of *dhu 'l-ḥijjah*, being the animal sacrifice at Mecca during the pilgrimage and throughout the Muslim world, in commemoration of the near sacrifice of Ishmael (or Isaac, according to certain accounts) by Abraham.

iḥsān: virtue, morality, spiritual life; the third of the principles or states of religion, the other two being *islām* (q.v.), and *īmān* (q.v.), as described by the Prophet to Gabriel in the *ḥadīth* having to do with the contents of religion. It is especially from this principle that the Ṣūfīs extract the Path because it brings into play all of the spiritual virtues.

ijmā': consensus of the doctors of the Law, or of the notables of Islam, particularly in the early generations, on a legal point; one of the principles of jurisprudence used by the *fuqahā'* (q.v.) to draw conclusions of a jurisprudential nature on any given problem (see *fiqh*).

ilhām (pl. *ilhāmāt*): inspiration, in contrast to revelation (*waḥy*, q.v.). The sages and saintly people after the days of the Prophet receive inspirations, but not revelations, for the latter are reserved for Prophets and Messengers only. Inspirations are of an indirect nature, whereas revelation is said to be directly from God. Nevertheless, in spite of this distinction, upheld by the Ṣūfīs, some of them have received inspirations that are practically indistinguishable from revelations, but have not called them such so as to preserve the singular nature of the Qur'ānic revelation.

imām: leader, chief; one of the descendants of the Prophet in the Shī'ī concept of the Imāmate. An *imām* in a mosque is the one who leads the others in prayer; an individual can also be an *imām* in other fields of human endeavor; but the Shī'ī Imām is the person generally associated with this term.

īmān: faith, either in the sense of simple belief in God, or else in the deeper meaning of the word. In the three states or principles of Islam, *īmān* is the first or the second to be mentioned, and means faith in God, His Angels, His Books, His Messengers, the Day of Judgment, and the Predestination of good and evil. (See the other two principles, *islām* and *iḥsān*).

insān al-kāmil (*al-*): the Perfect, or Universal, Man; this is a Ṣūfī term for the axial saints who are like pillars between Heaven and Earth; the Prophet is the first and greatest of the Perfect Men in Islam. It is an impersonal reality between God and man, and corresponds to the created Logos.

ishrāq: illumination, in a spiritual sense; the *Ishrāqiyyah*, or Illuminationism, was a brand of mystical philosophy preaching the illumination of the Spirit through ascetical practices.

islām: submission to the Divine Will; one of the three states or conditions or principles characterizing Islam as a religion (see *īmān* and *iḥsān* for the other two) and is either first or second. More concretely, it means the Pillars of Religion: *shahādah* (q.v.), *ṣalāh* (q.v.), *ṣawm Ramaḍān* (q.v.), *zakāh* (q.v.), and *ḥajj* (q.v.).

'iṣmah: impeccance, spiritual infallibility; the condition of sinlessness attributed to the Prophets and Messengers, and even to the saints of Ṣūfism; the Imams of the Shī'īs are said to have *'iṣmah* also.

isnād: chain of transmission for each *ḥadīth* (q.v.), containing the names of the authorities who transmitted that *ḥadīth* from the Prophet and ending with the collector or final person in the line.

isrā': the Night Voyage of the Prophet from Mecca to Jerusalem on al-Burāq, the fabulous riding-mount guided by Gabriel, which forms an integral part of the *mi'rāj* (q.v.).

jāhiliyyah (al-): the Period of Ignorance preceding the coming of Islam; the pre-Islamic days of paganism in Arabia.

jihād: Holy War, either *al-jihā al-aṣghar* ("the Lesser Holy War") of actual military warfare or *al-jihād al-akbar* ("the Greater Holy War") of spiritual warfare between the virtues and the vices in the soul. The Prophet is said to have remarked to his followers, who had returned from warfare, "You have returned from the Lesser Holy War to the Greater Holy War," by which he meant the inner *jihad*, within the soul.

kalām: theology, or *'ilm al-kalām*, scholastic theology.

khalīfah (pl. *khulafaī'*): representative, vicegerent, Caliph; in the Qur'ān, man is called the *khalīfah* of God, or the Vicegerent of God, His Representative on earth; the phrase *al-khulafā' ar- rāshidūn* refers to the Orthodox Caliphs of early Islam, Abū Bakr, 'Umar, 'Uthmān, and 'Alī, who were intimate companions of the Prophet.

khānaqah (pl. *khawāniq*): a Ṣūfī meeting-house (in Persia and in the East), equivalent to *zāwiyah* (q.v.), where the Shaykh or Pīr of an order meets regularly with his disciples for instruction and *dhikr* (q.v.).

khātam al-anbiyā': the Seal of the Prophets (also, *khātam an-nabiyyīn*), a title given to Muḥammad in the Qur'ān; it signifies that he seals the line of Prophets extending from Adam to himself, so that no Prophet will appear after his time until the Day of Judgment.

khātam al-wilāyah: the Seal of Sanctity, a title given to the Christ because he seals the line of sanctity at his Second Coming.

kitāb (pl. *kutub*): Book, or Scripture; it also means revelation. In Islam, revelation is a Scripture, not a Person, like the Christ in Christianity. For that reason, all communities are said to have "a Book", whereas what is really meant is that they have "a revelation". See *ahl al-kitāb*.

kufr: disbelief, the opposite of *shukr* ("gratitude"); the disbeliever is a *kāfir*, one who disbelieves in God and revelation, and who is therefore ungrateful.

madhhab (pl. *madhāhib*): school of jurisprudence, like the Mālikī *madhhab*, in the Sunnī world, or the Twelver *madhhab* in Shī'ism.

madrasah (pl. *madāris*): a religious college for the training of the *'ulamā'* (q.v.) in the disciplines relating to the *sharī'ah* of Islam. It is the exoteric equivalent of the *zāwiyah* (q.v.).

mahdī (al-): the Rightly-Guided, a descendant of the Prophet who appears before the end of time, when injustice and corruption reign within the Islamic community, and who heads a Holy State that engages in warfare and restores temporarily the ties between Heaven and Earth. In Shī'ism, he is Muḥammad al-Mahdī, the Twelfth Imam, who went into occultation in the year 940 and has since been the Hidden Imam (*al-imām al-mastūr*) of the Shī'īs who will return before the end of time as the visible Mahdī. He must not be confused with *al-Masīḥ* (q.v.), the Messiah, who is Jesus.

ma'rifah: gnosis or the direct knowledge of the Divine Reality that comes through the spiritual Path; it implies perfect sanctity and wisdom in the gnostic, or the *'ārif* (q.v.). One must distinguish between the experiential knowledge of *ma'rifah* and ordinary theoretical knowledge, which is purely mental. In both cases, the *'aql* is involved: in gnosis, it is the *'aql* as intellect, or pure intelligence, situated in the heart; in mental knowledge, it is the *'aql* as reason, situated in the brain; the former is intuitive, the latter is discursive.

masīḥ (al-): the Messiah, who comes at the end of time, closing the cycle of mankind, and ushering in the Day of Judgment; as in Christianity, the Messiah in Islam is Jesus. He is the one who destroys the Antichrist, putting an end to his totalitarian Government and false religion. In Islam, the Antichrist is known as *al-masīḥ ad-dajjāl* ("The False Messiah").

mi'rāj: the Ascension of the Prophet from Jerusalem through the Heavens to the Divine Presence. This took place during the night of the *isrā'* (q.v.), and it involved, first, his descent into the infernal regions and, second, his Ascension from the Rock now covered over by the Dome of the Rock to the Empyrean. After that, he returned to Jerusalem and went back to Mecca that very evening. It is because of the *mi'rāj* that Jerusalem is a Holy City for Islam, alongside Mecca and Medina, the Dome of the Rock there being one of the earliest Islamic monuments.

muftī: an expert in Islamic Law who gives his legal opinion in the form of a *fatwā* (q.v.) and in accordance with the rules of his particular *madhhab* (q.v.).

mu'jizah (pl. *mu'jizāt*): a miracle, and more especially the Qur'ān itself, which is the principal miracle of the Prophet. Only Prophets can produce a *mu'jizah*; later saints of Islam do not have that capacity but they do have the power to produce *karāmāt* (pl. of *karāmah*), which are charismatic gifts, sometimes indistinguishable from the *mu'jizāt* of the Prophets.

mujtahid: a religious authority who has the requisite qualifications to engage in individual effort (*ijtihād*) with a view to formulating conclusions on all aspects of the Law, using the principles of jurisprudence (*uṣūl al-fiqh*) in a definitive fashion. In Sunnism, the gate of absolute personal authority is said to have been closed in the ninth century, with only relative authority left for later *'ulamā'*; but in Twelver Shī'ism, a more comprehensive *ijtihād* is still available to the religious scholars.

nabī (pl. *anbiyā'*): a Prophet, one who renovates a prior Message brought by a *rasūl* (q.v.) and prophesies on the future; all Prophets are said to be chosen from all Eternity, so that no one can choose to be a Prophet. Muḥammad was both a Prophet (he prophesied regarding the end of the world) and a Messenger. There are more Prophets by far than there are Messengers.

Muḥammad is said to have remarked that there would be no Prophet after his time, so that he himself is the Seal of Prophets (*khạtam al-anbiyā'*, q.v.).

nafs (pl. *nufūs*): the soul, the psyche; also, the ego. The soul is that reality of man that is intermediate between the Spirit (*ar-rūḥ*, q.v.) and the body. It is the soul that is saved or damned at the hour of death through judgment, the body being left behind until the Day of Resurrection. It is also the ego insofar as it opposes the operations of the Spirit (or the Intellect) in man, hindering its radiance from shining through.

najāh: salvation, in the sense of entering Paradise among the blessed who enjoy the beatific vision of the Divinity. Salvation is ordinarily interpreted as being posthumous, following upon the judgment of the soul at death; but the term is vast enough to include the mystical interpretation of salvation as being here and now through contemplative union with God.

qāḍī (pl. *quḍāt*): religious judge; one of the different types of religious authorities of Islam, who occupies himself with adjudicating particular cases brought before him. In the past, there was a hierarchy of judges, beginning with the chief magistrate (*qāḍi 'l-quḍāt*), and going on down to local judges.

qalb: the heart, which is the subtle organ of knowledge or feelings, synonymous with the inner Spirit of Intellect; veiled by the effects of *ghaflah* (q.v.), it becomes the domain of passions and ignorance. The purification of the heart through interior *jihād* (q.v.) is part and parcel of the Path, and leads to the unveiling of the "eye of the heart" (*'ayn al-qalb*), q.v.) through the triumph of the Spirit over the negative tendencies of the soul (*nafs*, q.v.).

qiblah: the direction of prayer facing Mecca, indicated in a mosque by the niche (*miḥrāb*) in a wall, frequently a work of art. Mosques are oriented toward Mecca, as are all Muslims who pray outside of mosques, giving the image of concentric circles emanating from the square edifice of the Ka'bah.

qiyās: argument by analogy; one of the principles of jurisprudence, along with the Qur'ān (q.v.), Sunnah (q.v.), and *ijmā'* (q.v.), according to which one may proceed to legal conclusions on any given subject not covered by the other three engaging in analogous reasoning; thus, if wine is prohibited because it intoxicates, then all intoxicating substances are prohibited.

qur'ān: recitation; the Scripture of Islam, considered to be the revealed Word of God to the Islamic community. The Qur'ān is said to have been revealed to the Prophet in piecemeal fashion over a period of some twenty-three years. Revealed in the Arabic of the Quraysh, it is the foundation of the religious practices, since the prayers and other devotional practices are recited in the sacred Arabic of the Qur'ān.

rabb (*ar-*): the Lord, *Allāh* as the personal Divinity, in contrast to *Allāh* as the impersonal Deity. Referred to in the opening Sūrah of the Qur'ān as *rabb al-'ālamīn* (literally, "the Lord of the Worlds"), He is the ontological principle of the Creation. Among the Five Presences (*al-ḥaḍarāt al-khams*) of Ṣūfism, the Divine Essence is the *hāhūt* ("the Ipseity"), the Lord is the *lāhūt* ("the Divinity"); and then, within the Creation, there are the spiritual world of the Universal Spirit, the Archangels, the different

Paradises of the blessed, and this is the *jabarūt* ("the Realm of Sovereignty"); the subtle, invisible world of the Cosmic Soul, or the *malakūt* ("the Realm of Dominion"), containing the myriads of souls, the *jinns*, the evil spirits and devils, and the Hells; and the world of visible and material things, the *mulk* ("the Realm of Royalty"), or the *nāsūt* ("the Realm of Humanity"). These terms are sometimes used in different arrangements, depending on the author as well as on the esoteric school, so that the arrangement herein given is not the only one. It will be noted that the tripartite nature of man, within the Creation, operates on the three great planes, his Spirit in the *jabarūt*, his soul in the *malakūt*, and his body in the *mulk* or *nāsūt*. It is with his Spirit that he can reach the *lāhūt* (the *rabb*), and, with His permission, go on to the Divine Essence in the *hāhūt*, the Oneness in itself. In ordinary Islam, distinctions exist between God and the world, but the levels of reality, as taught in the contemplative Way, are nonexistent, and union with God through the Spirit is out of the question, to say nothing of the tendency of exoteric Islam to reject the Divine Immanence in the universe and in man in order to fix its attention on the Divine Transcendence.

rasūl (pl. *rusul*): a Messenger, who founds a religion; he is also a Prophet. Both the Messenger and Prophet are chosen by Heaven and are considered to be without sin. Only four Messengers are to be found in the Abrahamic traditions, Abraham, Moses, Jesus, and Muḥammad; but there are numerous Prophets. Muḥammad, like the Christ, was both a Messenger and a Prophet, and Islam says of him that he will be the last Messenger and Prophet before the coming of the Day of Judgment.

risālah (pl. *rasma'il*): a Divine message, or revelation, sent to a particular community; the word is synonymous with *waḥy* (q.v.), *tanzīl* (q.v.), and *kitāb* (q.v.). It contains both the doctrine on the Real as well as the methods of sanctification and sacred art. The fundamental metaphysical notion of revelation is *tawḥīd* (q.v.), with *dhikr* (q.v.), in the widest sense, being the means of sanctification. The object of the revelation is the salvation of the members of a particular community (*ummah*, q.v.) through the principles of faith (*īmān*, q.v.), ritual submission to the Divine Will (*islām*, q.v.), and the practice of the virtues (*iḥsān*, q.v.).

rūḥ (*ar-*) (pl. *arwā*): the Spirit, both in a particular sense, as the Spirit of man, as well as in a universal and divine sense. The Muḥammadan Spirit (*rūḥ muḥammadī*) is the Logos, which is to be distinguished from the particular Spirit in man and the uncreated Holy Spirit (*rūḥ al-quds*) of God. Likewise, there is a subtle, vital spirit in the psyche of man that is responsible for the life-giving properties of the body. The transcendent Spirit in man must be distinguished also from his soul as such (*nafs*, q.v.), and indeed, from his entire psychophysical nature, which veils the Spirit (or Intellect) in unregenerate man.

ṣalāh (pl. *ṣalawāt*): ritual prayer, performed five times during the course of the day, and known by the time of the day in which it is performed, such as the early-morning prayer, the noon prayer, and so forth. It is recited in Qur'ānic Arabic and is said to be a source of grace and purification for the believer.

ṣawn Ramaḍān: the fast of Ramaḍān, the ninth month of the lunar calendar, during which the faithful are enjoined to abstain from eating, drinking, and all carnal relations from early dawn to sunset.

shahādah: the Testimony of Faith, *Lā ilāha illa 'llāh, Muḥammadun rasūlu 'llāh* ("There is no divinity but God, Muḥammad is the Messenger of God"). Composed of two testimonies, one on the Divine as such, the other on the Messengership of Muḥammad, the *shahādah* is the sacred formula of *tawḥīd* (q.v.) in Islam, and is in itself a prayer, when recited as a form of *dhikr* (q.v.).

shaqq aṣ-ṣadr: the splitting of the chest, which refers to the purification of the heart of the Prophet, when he was a boy, by one or two angels, who seized him while he was playing in the desert, dropped him to the ground, extracted his heart and removed a dark substance, whereupon they returned it to his chest and healed him. This cleansing of Muḥammad's heart refers no doubt to the restoration of the primordial nature in him.

sharī'ah: the revealed or sacred Law of Islam, that establishes the commandments (*al-awāmir*, pl. of *amr*) and prohibitions (*an-nawāhī*, pl. of *nāhiyah*) of the religion. It is based, fundamentally, on the Qur'ān and the Sunnah of the Prophet, to which other principles such as consensus (*ijmā'*, q.v.) and argument by analogy (*qiyās*, q.v.) are added. Its goal is to furnish a certain equilibrium to the individual and the collectivity in view of salvation (*najāh*). The *sharī'ah* is interpreted by the *'ulamā'* in accordance with the rules of their particular *madhhab* (q.v.), and they explain the actions that are obligatory (*farḍ*), recommended (*mandūb*), permitted or tolerated (*mubāḥ*), reprehensible (*makrūh*), and prohibited (*ḥarām*). Since both the Qur'ān and the Sunnah are immutable in their natures, the *sharī'ah* is also. It has, nevertheless, a principle of adaptability to circumstances in the actual differences of the *'ulamā'* belonging to the four great *madhhabs* of Sunnī Islam. Thus, the *sharī'ah* cannot be changed, no more than one can change the Qur'ān or the Sunnah; but it can simply go unobserved, which is what happens during declines in the history of Islam.

shaykh (pl. *shuyūkh*): spiritual master of the Path, called a *pīr* in Persian. It is he who guides others through the teachings and practices of *taṣawwuf*. Ṣūfism recognizes the authentic Shaykh (*shaykh kāmil*, "the perfect master"), who has the authority to teach the Path, and the formalistic Shaykh, who is simply preserving the forms of the Ṣūfī tradition without any celestial permission to guide others in the Path. A distinction has to be made between the spiritual authority of the Shaykhs of Ṣūfism, which has to do with the domain of the Spirit, and the religious authority of the *'ulamā'*, that concerns itself only with the Law and that has nothing to say on the inner contemplative life.

shī'ah: the minority sect of Islam that owes allegiance to its Imāms, beginning with the Imam 'Alī, claiming that he should have been the successor to the Prophet at the latter's death and that the Imāms should have ruled the Islamic community. There is no homogeneity in Shī'ism, for a variety of sects have arisen within it, some of extremist views. The Twelvers (the *ithnā 'ashariyyah*) of Persia are the most moderate, along with the

Zaydīs of the Yemen, whereas the Seveners (the *ismā'īliyyah*) have historically been associated with extremist groups of all sorts. Among the Twelvers, in particular, the cult of the Twelve Imāms, from the Imān 'Alī (d. 661) to the Imaīm Muḥammad al-Mahdī (in occultation since the year 940), takes on an importance that practically effaces the centrality of the Prophet Muḥammad for his community.

shirk: associationism, polytheism. Associating one or more gods alongside *Allāh* is the cardinal sin of Islam; but associationism can be much more extensive in meaning than mere polytheism: it can mean giving an absolutism to created things that belongs only to the Divinity. *Shirk* is said to be unforgivable, if present in the mind of the believer at death. It is the opposite of *tawḥīd* (q.v.).

silsilah: the chain of masters in a Ṣūfī order connecting the latest one with the Prophet. It is a master-to-master lineage that is in unbroken succession from the Prophet. Generally, the sequence of names in a *silsilah* begins with *Allāh*, then goes to Gabriel, and then to Muḥammad, and so on down to the Shaykhs of the present day, the object being to show the divine origin of the Path by citing first the Name of the Divinity, followed by that of the Archangel of Revelation, Gabriel (*Jibrīl*, in Arabic). The *silsilah* has something in it of the notion of apostolic succession taught by the Church to validate its rituals and the ordination of priests, inasmuch as the Shaykhs confer the initiatic pact (*bay'ah*, q.v.), which is the rite transmitted from the days of the Prophet and confined to the Ṣūfī Path.

Ṣūfī: an adherent to Ṣūfism. The word Ṣūfī, within the tradition itself, is generally limited to the saint who has reached the end of the Path, everyone else being called by other names, such as *fuqarā'*, or dervishes. It derives from the wool (*ṣūf*) worn by the early ascetics of Islam who followed a mystical discipline.

sunnah: the Norm of the Prophet in his words and deeds as transmitted by the companions and followers to later generations, principally through the vehicle of the *ḥadīth*-collections. The Sunnah is complementary to the Qur'ān, and the two are interrelated in the sense that, while the Qur'ān has only general notions about the different acts of worship (*'ibmadah*, q.v.), the Sunnah gives the precise details. The Sunnah is multifaceted: it has ritual, moral, political, military, financial, matrimonial, mystical, and numerous other aspects. The mystical Sunnah of the Prophet, as might be expected, is at times in contradiction to the other aspects, with the result that an overly meticulous observance of the Sunnah, down to the tiniest details, can lead straight to the extinction of all spiritual life in the individual, for the simple reason that the actual multiplicity of forms contained in the Sunnah ends up by dispersing the mind, to say nothing of the formalism that arises from all that.

sunni: one who belongs to the mainstream of the community, or Sunnism, as opposed to a Shī'ī, who belongs to the Shī'ah, or Shī'ism. Within Shī'ism there are certain sects, like the Twelvers, who come fairly close to the Sunnī tradition, excluding, of course, their political ideas about the succession to the Prophet and the cult of the Imāms. The Sunnīs are called *ahl as-*

sunnah ("The People of the Sunnah"), not because they alone follow the Sunnah, for the Shī'īs do also, but because they uphold the norms of religio-political life as established by the early Caliphs of Islam, beginning with the first three Caliphs, who are rejected by the Shī'ī authorities.

tanzīh: the incomparability of God in relation to creatures; His transcendence. This is often contrasted with "comparability" (*tashbīh, q.v.).*

tanzīl: descent, the revelation. The Qur'ān pictures itself as being a message that "descended" into the heart of the Prophet on the Night of Power (*laylat al-qadr*), one of the nights at the end of the month of Ramaḍān.

ṭarīqah (pl. *ṭuruq*): the spiritual or contemplative Path of Islam, as opposed to the *sharī'ah*, which is concerned with the life of action. The term *ṭarīqah* is synonymous with the word Ṣūfism and its cognates. It is the Path that moves from the *sharī'ah* to the Divine Reality (*al-ḥaqīqah*, q.v.). In its general sense, it means the spiritual Path as such; but in its more restricted and specialized sense, it can mean a Ṣūfī order, such as the Shadhiliyyah, the Qādiriyyah, or the Suhrawardiyyah. The Path has as its goal the spiritual realization of *tawḥīd* through gnosis, which in turn implies the perfect plenitude of the virtues, such as detachment (*zuhd*), patience (*sabr*), contentment (*riḍa*), gratitude (*shukr*), love (*maḥabbah*), hope (*rajā'*), and fear (*khawf*). The *ṭarīqah* is based on the Qur'ān and the Sunnah, like the *sharī'ah*, but more especially on their esoteric contents, which have to do with the contemplative life.

taṣawwuf: Ṣūfism, or Islamic esoterism, as opposed to Islamic exoterism. This is derived from the primitive notion of putting on a woolen garment; but its technical meaning is "the act of adhering to Ṣūfism", or "esoterism".

tashbīh: the comparability of God with creatures; His immanence. This is the opposite of *tanzīh* (q.v.), and tends to be rejected by Muslim theologians, who prefer to keep the divine nature transcendent in relation to the created world. Even so, the Qur'ān has both teachings, *tanzīh* and *tashbīh*.

tawḥīd: the affirmation of the Divine Unity; the fundamental metaphysical, theological, and spiritual proposition of Islam, given verbal expression in the *shahādah* (q.v.). *Tawḥīd* can be purely verbal, as it is in the great majority of believers, or it can be much more inward and mental, and even spiritual, as we find among the Muslim contemplatives. *Tawḥīd* by itself alone has a salvific force to it; and for that reason, *shirk* (q.v.), its opposite, is the cardinal sin of Islam, since it is the rejection of the interior evidence of the intelligence and of the exterior evidence of the revealed Book that God is One.

'ulamā' (pl. of *'ālim*): the religious authorities of Islam, as contrasted with the Ṣūfī Shaykhs, who are the spiritual authorities of the tradition. The 'ulamaī' are of diverse types, according to their specialization: the *fuqahaī'* (q.v.), the *muftīs* (q.v.), and the *qāḍīs* (q.v.), although all of these functions can be found in one person. The doctors of the Law generally train for their positions in a religious institution *madrasah*, q.v.) for many years, emerging with diplomas entitling them to exercise their functions. There are thousands of them in the Islamic world, and they operate within their particular *madhhabs* (q.v.).

ummah (pl. *umam*): the Qur'ānic term for community, by which is meant a community, great or small, that has received a message. The communities mentioned in the Book are often decadent and subject to chastisements for having succumbed to forgetfulness and mistreating their Prophets or Messengers. In the larger sense, the word implies a people, and even a culture and civilization.

waḥdat al-wujūd: Oneness of Being, a phrase attributed to the Ṣūfī Ibn al-'Arabī (d. 1240), which implies that all being derives from the pure Being of God, and that is distinguished from His Being by the different degrees of reality. It is, metaphysically, the ultimate expression of *tawḥīd*, and hence is the definitive word on the Qur'ānic teachings about the Oneness of *Allaīh*. The phrase is Ibn al-'Arabī's, but the teaching is essentially Islamic and, more particularly, belongs to Islamic esoterism.

waḥy: revelation, like the Qur'ān. Only the founders of a religion or the Prophets can have *waḥy*; the saints, on the other hand, can have inspiration (*ilhām*, q.v.). It has the same meaning as *kitāb* (q.v.), *tanzīl* (q.v.), and *risālah* (q.v.).

walī (pl. *awliyā'*): a saint, defined as one who has an unbroken awareness of the Divine Presence. In Ṣūfism, the saint is thought of as the person who has permanent remembrance through the Invocation of God (*dhikru 'llāh*).

ẓāhir: outward, exterior; as *aẓ-ẓāhir* ("the Exterior"), one of the Ninety-Nine Names of God, contrasted with *al-bāṭin*)q.v.), the word *ẓāhirī* means "exoteric", and *'ilm az- ẓāhir* ("the science of the outward") is exoterism.

zakāh: legal alms, given once a year as a pruning of one's wealth; one of the pillars of the religion.

zāwiyah: literally, a corner, or an angle; by extension, it means a Ṣūfī meeting-place, where the Shaykh sits, surrounded by his disciples; it is the Arabic equivalent of *khānaqāh* (q.v.).

APPENDIX II
The Ninety-Nine Names

According to a *ḥadīth* attributed to the Prophet, "Verily, God has Ninety-Nine Names, one less than a hundred, for truly He is Odd and loves the odd number; and whosoever recites them, enters Paradise." Although the list of the Ninety-Nine Names has been generally fixed in the order we see below, other Names, also drawn from Qur'ānic texts, could be included.

These Names figure in all Islamic metaphysical, theological, cosmological, and spiritual doctrines, and in Ṣūfism they play a key role. A *ḥadīth* says, "Pattern yourselves on God's characteristics"; and another one explains this more fully by saying, "Verily, God has ninety-nine characteristics; whosoever patterns himself on one of them, enters Paradise." Thus, the Ninety-Nine Names are prototypal states of being, allowing the faithful to approach the Divinity through one or another of its aspects. In addition, the recitation of these Names is in itself considered to be a means of grace. The use of a rosary (*subḥah*) with ninety- nine beads, to keep track of the recitation, is common in the Muslim world.

The Names are often divided into Names of Essence (*asmā' dhātiyyah*) and Names of Quality or Attribute (*asmā' ṣifatiyyah*); the latter are further divided into Names of Majesty (*jalāl*) and Names of Beauty (*jamāl*). The Names of Essence pertain to the impersonal Divinity while the others belong to the personal Being of the Divinity. But we also find other arrangements which make room for the Names of Perfection (*kamāl*).

Allāh is a Name of Essence and is considered to be the Name that synthesizes in itself all of the other Names, more or less like a colorless light contains in undifferentiated manner the different colors. Other names of Essence are *al- Qaddūs* ("the Holy"), *al-Ḥaqq* ("the Truth"), *an-Nūr* ("the Light"), and *al-Qayyūm* ("the Self-Subsistent"). Examples of Names of Beauty are *ar-Raḥīm* ("the Merciful"), *al-Ghafūr* ("the Forgiving"), and *ar-Razzāq* ("the Provider"). Such Names as *al-Jabbār* ("the Repairer"), *al-Qābiḍ* ("the Contracter"), and *al-Mudhill* ("the Abaser") are Names of Majesty, while *al-Ḥakīm* ("the Wise"), *al-'Aẓīm* ("the Mighty"), and *al-'Adl* ("the Just") are Names of Perfection. But certain of these

Names are at times subsumed under more than one category because of the multiple significations contained in the Arabic words, which no translation can bring out in simple, one-word English terms. Different authors — particularly the Ṣūfīs — will therefore classify the Names in different manner, depending on which of the significations they have in mind.

1. Allāh	God
2. Ar-Raḥmān	The Compassionate
3. Ar-Raḥīm	The Merciful
4. Al-Malik	The King
5. Al-Quddūs	The Holy
6. As-Salām	The Peace
7. Al-Mu'min	The One with Faith
8. Al-Muhaymin	The Protector
9. Al-'Azīz	The Mighty
10. Al-Jabbār	The Repairer
11. Al-Mutakabbir	The Imperious
12. Al-Khāliq	The Creator
13. Al-Bāri'	The Maker
14. Al-Muṣawwir	The Fashioner
15. Al-Ghaffār	The Forgiver
16. Al-Qahhār	The Dominant
17. Al-Wahhāb	The Bestower
18. Ar-Razzāq	The Provider
19. Al-Fattāḥ	The Opener
20. Al-'Alīm	The Knower
21. Al-Qaībiḍ	The Contracter
22. Al-Basiṭ	The Expander
23. Al-Khāfid	The Humbler
24. Ar-Rāfi'	The Exalter
25. Al-Mu'izz	The Honorer
26. Al-Mudhill	The Abaser
27. As-Samī'	The Hearer
28. Al-Baṣīr	The Seer
29. Al-Ḥakam	The Judge
30. Al-'Adl	The Just
31. Al-Laṭif	The Subtle
32. Al-Khabīr	The Aware
33. Al-Ḥalīm	The Gentle
34. Al-'Azīm	The Mighty
35. Al-Ghafūr	The Forgiving
36. Ash-Shakūr	The Grateful
37. Al-'Alī	The Lofty
38. Al-Kabīr	The Great
39. Al-Hafīẓ	The Guardian
40. Al-Muqīt	The Nourisher
41. Al-Ḥasīb	The Reckoner

42. Al-Jalīl	The Majestic
43. Al-Karim	The Generous
44. Ar-Raqīb	The Watcher
45. Al-Mujīb	The Responder
46. Al-Wāsi'	The Englober
47. Al-Ḥakīm	The Wise
48. Al-Wadūd	The Loving
49. Al-Majīd	The Glorious
50. Al-Bā'ith	The Resurrector
51. Ash-Shahīd	The Witness
52. Al-Ḥaqq	The Truth
53. Al-Wakīl	The Trustee
54. Al-Qawī	The Strong
55. Al-Matīn	The Firm
56. Al-Walī	The Friend
57. Al-Ḥamīd	The Praiseworthy
58. Al-Muḥṣī	The Counter
59. Al-Mubdi'	The Originator
60. Al-Mu'īd	The Restorer
61. Al-Muḥyī	The Life-Giver
62. Al-Mumīt	The Death-Giver
63. Al-Ḥayy	The Living
64. Al-Qayyūm	The Self-Subsistent
65. Al-Wājid	The Finder
66. Al-Mājid	The Noble
67. Al-Aḥad	The One
68. Aṣ-Ṣamad	The Eternal
69. Al-Qādir	The Able
70. Al-Muqtadir	The Powerful
71. Al-Muqaddim	The Expediter
72. Al-Mu'akhkhir	The Deferrer
73. Al-Awwal	The First
74. Al-ākhir	The Last
75. Aẓ-Ẓāhir	The Manifest
76. Al-Bātin	The Hidden
77. Al-Wālī	The Governor
78. Al-Muta'ālī	The Exalted
79. Al-Barr	The Benefactor
80. At-Tawwāb	The Accepter of Repentance
81. Al-Muntaqim	The Avenger
82. Al-'Afuw	The Pardoner
83. Ar-Ra'ūf	The Pardoner
84. Mālik al-Mulk	The Ruler of the Kingdom
85. Dhu 'l-Jalāl wa 'l-Ikrām	Lord of Majesty and Generosity
86. Al-Muqsiṭ	The Equitable
87. Al-Jāmi'	The Gatherer
88. Al-Ghanī	The Self-Sufficient

89. Al-Mughnī	The Enricher
90. Al-Māni'	The Preventer
91. Aḍ-Ḍārr	The Distresser
92. An-Nāfi'	The Benefactor
93. An-Nūr	The Light
94. Al-Hādī	The Guide
95. Al-Badī'	The Incomparable
96. Al-Bāqī	The Enduring
97. Al-Wārith	The Inheritor
98. Ar-Rashīd	The Rightly Guided
99. As-Sabūr	The Patient

APPENDIX III
The Names of the Prophet Muḥammad

The recitation of the Prophet's Names is a pious deed in Islam, but the list of them, drawn from the Qur'ān and the *ḥadīths*, is not fixed, as is the case for the Ninety-Nine Names of *Allāh*. They are to be found in various traditional works compiled over the centuries and run into the hundreds of Names, many of which have entered into the popular lore of the Muslim world. The following Names represent a selection, meant to give only a general idea of his attributes as seen within the Muslim world; they refer both to the historical Muḥammad and the transhistorical, spiritual reality of the Prophet, which reaches its deepest development in the doctrines of the Muslim mystics on the universal nature of the Prophet as the Perfect Man (*al-insān al-kaīmil*), the Logos intermediate between man and God.

'Abd Allāh	The Servant of God
Ajmal Khalqi 'llāh	The Most Beautiful of God's Creation
'Alam al-Hudā	The Flag of Guidance
Al-Amīn	The Faithful
'Ayn an-Na īm	The Source of Blessings
Dalīl al-Khayrāt	The Guide to Good Deeds
Dhikru 'llāh	The Remembrance of God
Al-Ghawth	The Redeemer
Ḥabību 'llāh	The Beloved of God
Al-Ḥāshsir	The Gatherer on the Day of Judgment
Imām al-Muttaqīn	The Leader of the God-Fearing
Al-Kāmil	The Perfect
Al-Karīm	The Generous
Kāshif al-Karb	The Effacer of Grief
Khalīl ar-Raḥmān	The Friend of the Compassionate
Khātim al-Anbiyā'	The Seal of the Prophets
Al-Mahdī	The Rightly-Guided

Miftāḥ al-Jannah	The Key of Paradise
Miftāḥ ar-Raḥmah	The Key of Mercifulness
Al-Muḥyī	The Reviver
Al-Munīr	The Illuminator
Al-Muṣṭafā	The Chosen
Ni'matu 'llāh	The Blessing of God
An-Nūr	The Light
Rāfi' ar-Rutab	The Exalter of Ranks
Raḥmah li 'l-'ālamīn	Mercifulness of the Universe
Raḥmatu 'llāh	The Mercifulness of God
Rūḥ al-Haqq	The Spirit of God
Rūḥ al-Quddūs	The Holy Spirit
Aṣ-Ṣādiq	The Truthful
Ṣāḥib al-Mi'rāj	The Possessor of Ascension
Sayyid al-Kawnayn	The Master of the Two Worlds
Sayyid al-Mursalīn	The Master of the Messengers
Shāfi' al-Mudhnibīn	The Intercessor on Behalf of Sinners
Aṭ-Ṭāhir	The Pure
Al-Waḥīd	The Unique
Al-Walī	The Friend

APPENDIX IV
The Prophets and Messengers in the Qur'ān

The Qur'ān mentions some twenty-seven Prophets and Messengers, but its teaching on the universality of revelation clearly implies that the number is much greater, as we can discern in this verse addressed to the Prophet: "We have indeed sent Messengers before you: among them are those whose stories We have narrated to you, and among them are those whose stories We have not narrated to you" (Sūrah 40:78). When asked how many Prophets and Messengers there are altogether, the Prophet answered: "One hundred and twenty-four thousand among whom three hundred and fifteen Messengers all told." The Qur'ānic text and that *ḥadīth* leave the door open for the Prophets and Messengers outside the familiar Semitic world of the Qur'ān. Those mentioned in the Book are for the most part known to the Judeo-Christian tradition, which issues from the same ancient Abrahamic roots; but some of them pertain more especially to the pre-Christian Arab world, such as Shu'ayb, Hūd, and Ṣāliḥ, sent to communities called Madyan, 'Ad, and Thamūd, respectively. Luqmān is a legendary figure associated with southern Arabia. In this connection, we should not overlook the fact that Mary — the Virgin Mary in the eyes of the Muslims — is sometimes looked upon as a Prophetess in her own right, but not in relation to any legislative functions. She is at any rate mentioned with astonishing frequency in the Qur'ān, and this cannot be purely incidental. Moreover, a *ḥadīth* of the Prophet would have it that "No human being is born without the devil touching it, except Mary and her son," and this also is yet another sign of her preeminence in a spiritual sense.

1. ādam	Adam
2. Alyasa'	Elisha
3. Ayyūb	Job

4. Dā'ūd	David
5. Dhu 'l-Kifl	Exekiel
6. Dhu 'l-Qarnayn	Alexander the Great
7. Hārūn	Aaron
8. Hūd	——
9. Ibrāhm	Abraham
10. Idrīs	Henoch
11. Ilyās	Elijah
12. 'Īsā	Jesus
13. Isḥāq	Isaac
14. Ismā'īl	Ishmael
15. Luqmān	——
16. Lūṭ	Lot
17. Mūsā	Moses
18. Nūḥ	Noah
19. Ṣāliḥ	——
20. Shu'ayb	Jethro
21. Sulayman	Solomon
22. 'Uzayr	Ezra
23. Yaḥyā	John the Baptist
24. Ya'qūb	Jacob
25. Yūnus	Jonah
26. Yūsuf	Joseph
27. Zakariyyā	Zachariah

LIST OF REFERENCES

Abul Quasem, Muhammad. *Recitation and Interpretation of the Qur'an: Al-Ghazālī's Theory*. Trans. of Book VIII of the *Iḥyā' 'Ulūm ad-Dīn* of al-Ghazālī Kuala Lampur, 1979.

______________. *The Jewels of the Qur'ān: Al-Ghazālī's Theory*. Trans. of al-Ghazālī's *Kitāb Jawāhir al-Qur'ān*. Kuala Lampur, 1977.

Adam, Charles C. *Islam and Modernism in Egypt*. London, 1933.

Ahmad, M. *Economics of Islam*. Lahore, 1947.

Arberry, A. J. *The Koran Interpreted*. 2 vols.; New York, 1955.

Arnold, Thomas W. *The Caliphate*. New York, 1966.

______________. *The Preaching of Islam*. Lahore, 1956.

Austin, R. W. J. *Ibn al-'Arabī: The Bezels of Wisdom*. Trans. of the *Fuṣūṣ Ḥikam* of Ibn al-'Arabī. New York, 1980.

Baljon, J. M. S. *Modern Muslim Interpretation*. Leiden, 1961.

Beeston, A. F. L. *Baiḍāwī's Commentary Sūrah 12 of the Qur'an*. Oxford, 1963.

Burckhardt, Titus. *An Introduction to Sufi Doctrine*. Trans. by D. M. Matheson. Wellingborough, Northamptonshire, 1976.

______________. *Art of Islam: Language and Meaning*. N.p., 1976.

______________. *Sacred Art East and West*. Trans. by Lord Northbourne. London, 1967.

Chittick, William. *The Sufi Path of Love: The Spiritual Teachings of Rumi*. Albany, 1983.

Corbin, Henry. *Creative Imagination in the Ṣūfism of Ibn 'Arabī*. Trans. by Ralph Manheim. Princeton, 1969.

Cragg, Kenneth. *The Event of the Qur'an*. London, 1971.

______________. *The Mind of the Qur'an*. London, 1973.

Deladrière, Roger. *La Profession de Foi*. Trans. of Ibn al-'Arabī's *Tadhkirat al-Khawāṣṣ wa 'Aqīdat Ahl al-Ikhtiṣāṣ*. Paris, 1978.

Denny, Frederick M. *An Introduction to Islam*. New York, 1985.

Dhorme, Édouard. "L'arabe littéral et la langue de Hammourabi," in vol. 2 of *Mélanges Louis Massignon*. 3 vols.; Damascus, 1957.

Eaton, Charles Le Gai. *Islam and the Destiny of Man*. Albany, 1985.

Ernst, Carl W. *Words of Ecstasy in Sufism*. Albany, 1985.

Esin, Emil. *Mecca the Blessed, Medina the Radiant*. New York, 1963.

Gardet, Louis. *La Cité musulmane, vie sociale et politique*. Paris, 1961.

Gätje, Helmut. *The Qur'ān and its Exegesis: Selected Texts with Classical and Modern Interpretations*. Trans. by Alford T. Welch. London, 1976.

Gibb, H. A. R. *Modern Trends in Islam*. Chicago, 1947.
______________ . *Muhammadanism: An Historical Survey*. New York, 1962.
Goldziher, Ignaz. *Introduction to Islamic Theology and Law*. Trans. by Andras and Ruth Hamori. Princeton, 1981.
Grabar, Oleg. *The Formation of Islamic Art*. New Haven, 1973.
Graham, William A. *Divine Word and Prophetic Word in Early Islam*. The Hague, 1977.
Guénon, René. *Symbolism of the Cross*. Trans. by Angus MacNab. London, 1958.
______________ . *The Crisis of the Modern World*. Trans. by Marco Pallis and Richard Nicholson. London, 1962.
______________ . *The Reign of Quantity and the Signs of the Times*. Trans. by Lord Northbourne. Baltimore, 1972.
Guillaume, A. *The Life of Muhammad*. Trans. of Ibn Isḥāq's *Sīrah*. London, 1967.
Hamidullah, Muhammad. *Le Prophète de l'Islam*. 2 vols.; Paris, 1959.
______________ . *The Muslim Conduct of State*. Lahore, 1956.
Hitti, Philip K. *History of the Arabs*. 10th ed.; New York, 1970.
Hodgson, Marshall G. S. *The Venture of Islam*. 3 vols.; Chicago, 1974.
Hourani, Albert. *Arabic Thought in the Liberal Age, 1798-1939*. London, 1962.
Izutsu, Toshihiko. *Sufism and Taoism: Comparative Study of Key Philosophical Concepts*. Berkeley, 1984.
Jansen, J. J. G. *The Interpretation of the Koran in Modern Egypt*. Leiden, 1980.
Kerr, Malcolm. *Islamic Reform: The Political Thought and Legal Theories of Muhammad 'Abduh and Rashīd Riḍā*. Berkeley, 1966.
Khadduri, Majid. *Islamic Jurisprudence: Shāfi'ī's Risāla*. Baltimore, 1962.
______________ . *War and Peace in the Law of Islam*. Baltimore, 1955.
Khan, Muhammad Zafrullah. *Gardens of the Righteous: Riyadh as-Salihin of Nawawi*. London, 1975.
Kūhnel, Ernst. *Islamic Art and Architecture*. Trans. by Katherine Watson. London, 1966.
Levy, Reuben. *The Social Structures of Islam*. Cambridge, 1957.
Lewis, Bernard, and Ann K. S. Lambton and P. M. Holt, eds. *The Cambridge History of Islam*. 2 vols.; Cambridge, 1970.
Lewis, Bernard. *The Emergence of Modern Turkey*. London, 1968.
Lings, Martin. *A Sufi Saint of the Twentieth Century*. Berkeley, 1973.
______________ . *Muhammad: His Life Based on the Earliest Sources*. New York, 1983.
______________ . *The Quranic Art of Calligraphy and Illumination*. Boulder, 1978.

__________. *What Is Sufism?* Berkeley, 1977.

MacDonald, Duncan Black. *Development of Muslim Theology, Jurisprudence and Constitutional Theory*. New York, 1965.

Massignon, Louis. *Essai sur les origines du lexique technique de la mystique musulmane*. Paris, 1968.

__________. *The Passion of al-Hallāj: Mystical Martyr of Islam*. Trans. by Herbert Mason. 4 vols.; Princeton, 1983.

McCarthy, Richard J. *Freedom and Fulfillment*. Boston, 1980.

__________. *The Theology of al-Ash'arī*. Beirut, 1953.

Mitchell, George, ed. *Architecture of the Islamic World: Its History and Social Meaning*. New York, 1978.

Morris, James Winston. *The Wisdom of the Throne: An Introduction to the Philosophy of Mulla Sadra*. Princeton, 1981.

Nasr, Seyyed Hossein. *Ideals and Realities of Islam*. Boston, 1972.

__________. *Islam and the Plight of Modern Man*. New York, 1975.

__________. *Islamic Life and Thought*. Albany, 1981.

__________. *Islamic Science: An Illustrated Study*. N.p., 1976.

__________. *Ṣadr al-Dīn Shīrāzī* and His Transcendent Theosophy. Boulder, 1979.

__________. *Science and Civilization in Islam*. Cambridge, Massachusetts, 1968.

__________. *Three Muslim Sages: Avicenna, Suhrawardi, and Ibn 'Arabī*. Cambridge, Massachusetts, 1964.

Nicholson, R. A. *Studies in Islamic Mysticism*. Cambridge, 1921.

Nwyia, Paul. *Exégése coranique et langage mystique*. Beirut, 1970.

Pickthall, M. M. *The Meaning of the Glorious Koran*. New York, n.d.

Pullapilly, Cyriac K., ed. *Islam in the Contemporary World*. South Bend, 1980.

Robson, James. *An Introduction to the Science of Tradition*. Trans. of *al-Ḥakīm an-Nīsābūrī's al-Madkhal ilā Ma'rifat al-Iklīl*. London, 1953.

Rosenthal, E. I. J. *Political Thought in Medieval Islam: An Introductory Outline*. Cambridge, 1958.

Rosenthal, Franz. *The Muqaddimah: An Introduction to History*. Trans. of Ibn Khaldūn's *Muqaddimah*. 3 vols.; Princeton, 1967.

As-Sa'īd, Labīb. *The Recited Koran: A History of the First Recorded Version*. Trans. and adapted by Bernard Weiss, M. A. Rauf, and Morroe Berger. Princeton, 1975.

Schacht, Joseph, and C. E. Bosworth, eds. *The Legacy of Islam*. Oxford, 1974.

Schimmel, Annemarie. *And Muhammad Is His Messenger*. Chapel Hill, 1985.

__________. *Calligraphy and Islamic Culture*. New York, 1984.

______________ . *Mystical Dimensions of Islam*. Chapel Hill, 1975.
Schroeder, Eric. *Muhammad's People*. Portland, Maine, 1955.
Schuon, Frithjof. *Dimensions of Islam*. Trans. by Peter Townsend. London, 1970.
______________ . *Islam and the Perennial Philosophy*. Trans. by J. Peter Hobson. N.p., 1976.
______________ . *Light on the Ancient Worlds*. Trans. by Lord Northbourne. London, 1965.
______________ . *Sufism: Veil and Quintessence*. Trans. by William Stoddart. Bloomington, Indiana, 1981.
______________ . *The Transcendent Unity of Religions*. Trans. by Peter Townsend. New York, 1975.
______________ . *Understanding Islam*. Trans. by D. M. Matheson. Baltimore, 1972.
Sharif, Mian Mohammad, ed. *A History of Muslim Philosophy*. 2 vols.; Wiesbaden, 1963.
Shaw, S. J., and W. R. Polk, eds. *Studies on the Civilization of Islam*. Boston, 1962.
Smith, Wilfred Cantwell. *Islam in Modern History*. Princeton, 1957.
Stoddart, William. *Sufism: The Mystical Doctrines and Methods of Islam*. New York, 1976.
Trimingham, J. S. *The Sufi Orders in Islam*. Oxford, 1971.
Watt, W. Montgomery. *Muhammad: Prophet and Statesman*. London, 1961.
______________ . *Muslim Intellectual: A Study of al-Ghazālī*. Edinburgh, 1963.
______________ . *The Formative Period of Islamic Thought*. Edinburgh, 1973.
Wensinck, A. J. *The Muslim Creed: Its Genesis and Historical Development*. Cambridge, 1932.
Wolfson, Harry Austryn. *The Philosophy of the Kalam*. Cambridge, Massachusetts, 1976.